Mythology for Storytellers

Mythology for Storytellers: Themes and Tales from Around the World

Josepha Sherman

SHARPE REFERENCE

an imprint of M.E. Sharpe, Inc.

SHARPE REFERENCE

Sharpe Reference is an imprint of M.E. Sharpe, Inc.

M.E. Sharpe, Inc.
80 Business Park Drive
Armonk, NY 10504

Library of Congress Cataloging-in-Publication Data

Sherman, Josepha
  Mythology for storytellers : themes and tales from around the world / Josepha Sherman.
    p. cm.
  Includes bibliographical references and index.
  ISBN 0-7656-8056-4 (alk. paper)
  1. Mythology   I. Title.

BL312 .S54 2003
291.1'3—dc21

2002036575

Printed and bound in Hong Kong

The paper used in this publication meets the minimum requirements of American National Standard for Information Sciences—Permanence of Paper for Printed Library Materials, ANSI Z 39.48.1984.

B (c) 10 9 8 7 6 5 4 3 2 1

Publisher: Myron E. Sharpe
Vice President and Editorial Director: Patricia Kolb
Vice President and Production Director: Carmen Chetti
Executive Editor and Manager of Reference: Todd Hallman
Project Editor: Wendy E. Muto
Editorial Assistant: Cathleen Prisco

In memory of those who died in the World Trade Center tragedy, 9/11/01

CONTENTS

2. MYTHS OF DEATH AND REBIRTH   89

Myths of Death   92

AN INTRODUCTION TO MYTHOLOGY

What is mythology? In this hectic modern world, where even Andy Warhol's brusque promise of fifteen minutes of fame seems to have been reduced to as long as it takes for a Web site to load, people often casually throw the word *myth* about and interchange it freely with *legend* without being aware of any deeper meaning. Someone might lightly say, "Santa Claus is just a myth," or casually remark that a pop singer or sports figure "is a legend in his own time."

But that is the shallowest possible use anyone can make of words that are rich with ancient significance and come from deep within the human psyche.

Perhaps that sounds a little too melodramatic. However, even the most modern of people can still feel the awe that comes from viewing the night sky, not the light-polluted, seemingly empty one of the modern cities, but a velvet-black sky blazing with lights. It is easy to imagine earlier people looking up at that light-studded sky and wondering. What are they, these strange, small fires? Why do they move across the sky? And what of the moon? Why does it change its shape regularly in a cycle that seems to match the pattern of a woman's flow of blood? Indeed, what of that? What of her belly swelling with child? What miracle puts a new life into the world? Where does it come from? Who are humans, really? And where is humanity going?

Yes, people can claim to know the answers to at least some of the great questions, or at least to know the surface answers, but there is a level deep within everyone that still wonders, still hungers fiercely for more than a dry, cold scientific definition or the somehow frightening admission, "No one knows why."

It is mythology that feeds that hunger and quells those fears.

Mythology has existed in some form in every human society that has left records of any sort. Myths turn up in the writings of ancient Greece, on the wall reliefs of ancient Egypt, and on the clay tablets of Mesopotamian Sumer. Long before the invention of writing, people were already leaving what are clearly mythic symbols on cave walls. These include, in addition to those familiar, realistically rendered animals, voluptuous women holding cornucopias—priestesses or fertility goddesses?—and stag-headed men who may be either shamans or animal spirits. What they meant to the people who painted them, we don't know and probably will never know, but they do tell one fact: These human ancestors did indeed have a culture that included mythic belief.

But what exactly does that mean? Before anyone can propose to retell myths, those of our own culture or someone else's, the definitions must be sure.

The defining of terms is not as easy as it might seem. Mythologists and folklorists disagree about fact and theory as frequently as any other scholars. They have argued over the semantics of a word like *mythology* for over a hundred years. But it can be safely said at least that mythology is the study and interpretation of myth and the body of myths of a culture.

Since the variety of the world's mythology is so vast, it is difficult to make too many generalizations about it, though basic themes can be identified, and some are discussed below. But it can be stated without too much argument that the elements that define a genuine myth—as opposed to something as shallow as "painless injections are a myth"—are these:

A myth has a serious purpose, no matter how many humorous elements it may contain. It exists because humanity needed an explanation for one of the big questions, such as the creation of the world, how humanity and the animals came to be, or why there is death.

A myth also teaches the behavior proper to a culture and explains the meaning behind certain customs, such as the rituals to be found in every religion, as well as letting us see the adventures and interactions of gods and humans.

The last point is simply that a myth is usually of unknown origin.

Since humans are, regardless of their different cultures, members of the same species, with the same wants, needs, and wonderings, all myths are going to have certain themes in common. Categorizing with broad strokes, they fall into:

- *Cosmic or cosmological myths (also known as creation myths)*. The myths in this category tend to be the most important of all, since these are each culture's explanation of how and why the universe and world came to be.

- *Myths of birth and life*. Where do we come from? Who are we? Where are we going? Myths that fall into this category attempt to explain some of the greatest personal mysteries, those experiences that are common to all mortal beings, as well as trying to prove the greatest of human hopes, that this life is not the end.

- *Myths of sex and procreation.* Allied with the myths of the creation of living things are, understandably, myths concerning sex and procreation. Some of these, such as those featuring Coyote, the main trickster figure of the American Southwest, can be blatantly lewd, even downright obscene.

- *Myths of death.* We usually try to deny death in our society, but myths about both the creation of death and the need for death are also part of human existence. In some cultures, such as our own, death is looked on as something to be dreaded and denied for as long as possible. Other cultures, from Asia to the native cultures of North America, though equally reluctant to think about leaving the mortal world, are more accepting, or at least more understanding, about what cannot be avoided.

- *Myths of rebirth.* There is hope at the end of the final battle or the mortal death. After the ashes die, a new world and new gods will be born. This leads directly into the subject of resurrection myths.

- *Myths of the gods.* This category includes the myths that attempt to understand the divine, in whatever form or forms a culture finds right for so powerful a force, and try to explain seemingly unpredictable or unjust events.

- *Myths of the heroes.* The hero in mythology can often be better categorized as a culture hero, one who is important to a society as a codified image of that society's ideals. He or she is rarely powerful enough to be the creator of the world. But a culture hero may still possess great supernatural or even divine powers. Raven, the culture hero and trickster deity of the Pacific Northwest peoples, is the one who sets the sun and moon in the sky. Maui of the Polynesian myths pulls up islands from under the sea. And Cuchulain, the Ulster hero, transforms himself into an inhumanly fierce warrior in battle.

Legends, by contrast, are generally about historic figures or events and are on a much smaller scale than myths. They are, therefore, outside the scope of this book. Davy Crockett, for instance, though he can be seen as a culture hero, has a documented birth, life, and death. Most of the legend cycle centered about him may be larger than life, but it is hardly on the mythic scale.

By contrast, the traditional western hero, the stranger who rides into town on a white horse to save the people from evil, then rides away again into the sunset, is also an American culture hero. But, thanks to his standard appearance and actions, he is a mythic type.

Are myths *true*? It seems unlikely that many people nowadays would expect to meet a centaur, yet some people claim to have seen (and even photographed) Bigfoot or the yeti. It also seems improbable that anyone would expect to come in contact with the Greek god Zeus, yet when Vance Randolph was collecting folklore in the Appalachians, he met people who firmly believed that they might meet Jesus one day while walking in the mountains. While the idea that Elvis Presley still lives has become a joke with most people, some members of the Elvis cult do believe that he is not dead and that "the King will come again."

And do not all people secretly believe in a golden age back there somewhere in the past? So did the Greeks and the Assyrians. The latter even left us a written complaint to the effect that nothing in modern times was as good as it was in the good old days. Even without more than a mention by Plato, there are those who want to believe in Atlantis, that long-ago, forever lost land of wonder.

Again, are myths true? To the extent that they answer the unanswerable, comfort our fears, and give us hope, yes, they are very true, indeed.

Myths are sometimes also true in the historical or legal sense as well. They can help settle quarrels—or help keep old hatreds alive. In the name of peace, clans in New Guinea quarreling over territory have resorted to long recitations of mythic names to prove which side is right without having to resort to violence.

But in areas with centuries-old quarrels, religious or ethnic, those ancient hatreds sometimes take on the character of myth themselves. Ask a Serbian, for instance, what the current conflict over Kosovo is about, and the answer will involve either racial hatreds dating to the Middle Ages or a simple, "It has always been so." In Northern Ireland there is a by now infamous and quite mythic hatred between the Catholics and Protestants, and under that between the Irish and the English, that dates as well to the Middle Ages.

The effect of enmity on a truly mythic scale can be seen in cultures as large as nations or as small as tribal groups, or even in the sports rivalries of one team against another. It may seem facetious to compare baseball to political conflict, but the rivalry between, for instance, the New York Yankees and the Boston Red Sox has been in existence for nearly a century, long enough to have acquired its own mythic power.

Myths can also be used as political reinforcement. In ancient Babylon, for instance, yearly rituals linked the royal house with the deity Marduk and the rest of the pantheon. Rulers in Saxon England claimed descent from Woden and the other Teutonic gods. And Nazi Germany claimed their own warped versions of Teutonic nobility and "Aryan superiority," even though they failed to understand that Teutons had no genetic relationship to the Aryan peoples of northern India. But then, myth does not need to be accurate if it is true—in this case to what a political cause wished it to be.

Whatever arguments may occur over the sociological, ethnic, and psychological meaning of myth—and those arguments are many and vociferous—the fact remains that all human cultures have been influenced, and remain influenced, by mythology on several levels.

Because myths so often contain divine elements—sometimes, as mentioned above, even centering about a deity—mythology has been called the first cousin, if not indeed the actual sibling, of religion. This fact should raise a warning flag for storytellers. Mythology is not a dead subject, safely stored away behind the glass of some scholarly museum till the storyteller comes to take it from its case. What may seem like no more than a tale of wild fantasy to a storyteller from one culture might be at the heart of another storyteller's living religion. Since myths are a basic part of the human experience and are so deeply linked with religious expression, a storyteller who wishes to work with mythology needs empathy as well as good scholarship.

At this point, a storyteller reading this may well want to know what sort of scholarship he or she needs, and why it would be needed at all. After all, is not knowing the stories themselves enough?

The simple answer is that, at the very least, it is common courtesy to read a myth, not in someone's literary or commercial retelling, but in a more culturally legitimate form. By that is meant not something impossibly dense and scholarly, but merely a myth collected in the field or recorded from a reputable source. Of course the stories can be retold; they are retold in this book. But a retelling should stay true to the original and not be deliberately and radically altered to make it into a "better" story.

However, before doing any sort of retelling, a wise storyteller should also be willing to delve a little more deeply into the culture to which the myth belongs. The myths of the Inuit are logically going to reflect the harsh environment in which they live, and as a result may not be as easily accessible to other, less northern cultures. The Inuit myth of Sedna is a prime example of this. In it, the young woman, Sedna, who is drowning in the frigid Arctic sea, tries to climb back into her father's boat. Terrified that she will capsize the boat, her father cuts off her fingers. Unable to hold on, Sedna sinks into the sea and dies as a human. Her severed fingers then turn into seals, while Sedna becomes a being of the sea.

Since this is a highly important myth to the Inuit, it would be very bad taste for a storyteller to give only a cursory reading to the story of Sedna. To ignore the power of this myth, or to misunderstand it and retell such an important and—at least to us—dark a northern tale with a Polynesian slant or a Disneyesque happy ending, would be close to verbal vandalism.

Now that we have gathered the definitions, we have a chance to see what mythologists and folklorists have to say about mythology.

As with all scholarly studies of any subject, the standards for study and analysis have changed over the centuries. The actual study of mythology and folklore can be traced, at least in some form, back as far as third-millennium-B.C.E. Egypt, where the multitalented vizier-architect-scholar-priest Imhotep is said to have collected folk proverbs, and to the first-millennium-B.C.E. Near East, where Babylonian royal scholars made collections of earlier tales.

But in general, there does not seem to have been any formal study of mythology until the time of the Hellenistic Greeks, in about the fourth century B.C.E. Up to that era, myths seem to have been taken as fact by the majority of people to whom they belonged—although, of course, there are always skeptics to be found within any culture. Did, for instance, most of the pre-Hellenistic Greeks really believe in the details of their mythology, with its seemingly all-too-human deities? That is difficult to ascertain. Popular culture and folk belief can be very different from a formalized system of religion, and their details are not always recorded.

It was the Greek philosophers who first recognized a split between *mythos*, myth, and *logos*, reason. Plato and Aristotle, to name two of the most well-known today, raised the cause of reason above all else. They condemned myth as unable to portray reality, save in those rare instances of historical myth where *mythos* and *logos* chanced to overlap.

Greek scholars of antiquity were as willing as their modern counterparts to push facts and create histories to back up their theories. The Greek writer Palaiphatos, to take just one example, came up with his own interpretation of the myth of Zeus and Europa. In the myth, the maiden Europa—who gives us the name *Europe*—is carried off to Crete by the god Zeus, who has fallen for her and has taken the form of a bull to kidnap her. Palaiphatos claimed, unfortunately without any scholarly or physical evidence to back up his theory, that the myth must have been inspired by some historical abduction of a mainland woman, possibly by a Cretan named Tauros, or Bull.

Continuing into the Roman era, myths were no longer accepted as out-and-out fact, but rather as allegories to be studied for hidden meaning. This trend carried into the monotheistic Judeo-Christian cultures. The Christians in particular generally refused to accept polytheistic myths as portraying any truth at all, save when they were considered as allegories. The Greek concepts of *mythos* versus *logos* appear in the New

Testament, particularly in the prologue to the Gospel of John, in which Jesus is portrayed as the epitome of *logos*.

The argument over the roles of myth, reason, and history continued in Europe throughout the Middle Ages without any genuine study of mythology being added to the body of scholarship. By the time of the Age of Enlightenment, the period of the seventeenth and eighteenth centuries, the theory of mythology as allegory had fallen into disfavor. In fact, myths themselves had come to be looked upon as antique, even ridiculous, reminders of a savage age that had little possible bearing on the modern world.

The discovery of "primitive" peoples beyond "civilized" Europe did little to change this view. Now scholars looked to what they called the "childhood of man," the world of the "noble savage"—the idealized primitive—for the origins of mythology, though they still saw little application of myths to their own times. To those more romantic-minded scholars, myth was simply itself, an inevitable expression of the human mind and, as such, as valuable as rationality.

It was the German scholar Christian Gottlob Heyne, active during the eighteenth century, who actually first coined the word *mythology*, from the Greek word *mythos*, which translates as "myth," "story," or even "storytelling." By it he meant the formal study of the myths themselves.

By the nineteenth century, the view of mythology had changed again. Now the study of mythology had become a valid field of scholarship, even a science, at least in Europe and the United States. As more and more myths from around the world became available through fieldwork and translations, scholars began to realize just how complex and deep-rooted the elements of mythology were. They studied the most ancient mythic epics available to them, such as the Sanskrit B*hagavad Gita* of India, believing that these would reveal stronger indications of more archaic ways and beliefs. Scholars such as the German Karl Otfried Muller, taking for his example the Greek story of Persephone, tried to prove that the less complex the myth, the more likely it was to reflect a more primitive pastoral society as its origin, while the more complex myths must indicate a more urban, more modern origin. This theory hasn't proved universally true.

This was not the only course that mythologists of the day were taking. As the study of linguistics led to the discovery of a basic Indo-European root for many of the world's modern languages, so mythologists sought to find equally common roots for myths through linguistic hints; some believed that *all* myths could be traced back to prehistoric Indo-Europeans. There is no genuine evidence for or against this theory, either.

Charles Darwin's newly formed theory of evolution moved mythologists to hunt for evolution in myths as well. Sir James Frazier's most famous work is the multivolume study *The Golden Bough*, which, unlike much of his other work, is still very much in print—though usually only in an abridged one-volume edition. In it he attempts to trace, through exhaustive studies, the origins of many myths back to the ancient rituals of agricultural societies. There is, however, no real evidence to prove his theory that ritual came first, with myth invented to explain ritual. Folklorist Sir Andrew Lang, author of the multihued *Fairy Books* of popular fame, also attempted to trace myths back to their origins in his scholarly work *Myths, Ritual and Religion*.

The twentieth century—not surprisingly, given the rapidly changing views of the world in all aspects—brought with it yet another interpretation of mythology. Mythologists began paying more attention to the stories themselves, as well as to their content. An ever-strengthening link was postulated between myth and the human mind, particularly since the science of psychology and psychoanalysis was gaining importance, thanks to the work of Sigmund Freud and Carl Jung.

Jung, who was fascinated by mythology as an expression of human need and the human psyche, focused on the myths' worldwide similarities, which he believed sprang from what he called the "collective unconscious," a shared series of memories buried within all human psyches. Jung also formed a related theory of archetypes. Archetypes are basic elements that crop up within every culture's tales and myths and resonate in our minds, such as the wise old man or the trickster. Archetypes are truly international, and they really do seem to be hardwired into all of us.

Indeed, even children who have not yet been exposed to myths make use of mythic archetypes in their stories. This author saw the result of a creative-writing test in upstate New York, in which the members of a third-grade class were told to create their own fantasy short stories. None of the children was aware of the world of mythology or even of fairy tales, though they had, of course, seen mythic concepts in television shows and movies. Despite the lack of knowledge of myths, each child, with only one exception, invented a story in which the child protagonist is given a magical tool by a wise old man or woman and goes off on a true hero's quest.

Nor are adults exempt from this need to rely on archetypal themes. We fit modern characters and situations into ancient archetypes: A president such as Eisenhower or Reagan has been looked upon, though usually not consciously, as a father, while Kennedy has been quite blatantly associated with an idealized King Arthur and the White House under his administration with an equally idealized Camelot—perhaps Albert Tennyson's prettier image rather than the more historic and less civilized fourth-century version.

Whether or not Jung's concept of the collective consciousness is correct, world mythology certainly does have certain broader themes that transcend all national or cultural barriers. There is an amazing persistence to these ideas. One of the most popular themes, mentioned above, is that of the unrelated yet similar myths of catastrophic floods—sometimes but not always supported by geological evidence—that appear in North America, Europe, Asia, and of course the Bible. Another is the fact that almost every culture includes a myth of the origin of fire that involves not its discovery but its theft. The best-known version, perhaps, is the Greek story of Prometheus, a demigod who stole fire from the gods on Mount Olympus to give to humanity because he pitied mortals. But there are also myths in which the fire stealer is Coyote or even a human hero.

There are also clear parallels that can be drawn between myths from separate cultures. For instance, there are strong similarities between the main theme of a creation myth from the Kalahari in Namibia and one from the Philippines. In both cases, the sky is so close to the ground that people must walk about bent over. In both cases, a woman impatient with this condition hits the sky, causing it to flee up into the heavens. Was there ever any actual contact between these two cultures? Possibly, since the people of the Kalahari may have come from Malaysia or the Philippines. But is there also a relationship to the ancient Egyptian myth of Nut, the sky goddess, being forced up and away from the arms of Geb, the earth god? There is a story with a vaguely similar theme from the Zuni of North America. Connections? Or are we once again delving into the human psyche and Carl Jung's collective unconscious? Unfortunately, when dealing with pre- or nonliterate people, or with scantily written records from the past, there can never be an easy answer.

Similarities aside, a good case can be made for claiming that each culture selects only those mythic images it needs. The Greek myths do tend to humanize their deities, while the ancient Indian myths seem, to Westerners at least, to be more abstract. Sumerian mythology shares ties with older traditions, including the shamanistic rituals of death and rebirth that appear in the Inanna or Ishtar myths: Hunting her slain lover, Dumuzi, or Tammuz, the goddess—the ancestor of the Greek Adonis—descends into the underworld, abandoning layers of herself as she goes, from her clothing to her jewelry to, at the last, her life. In some versions of the myth, she does recover her lover; in all versions, the goddess is reborn. This parallels the shamanistic rituals of many cultures, including those of Siberia, in which a shaman must undergo stages of symbolic death and rebirth.

And, as mentioned above in the summary of the Inuit myth of Sedna, though the basic elements of mythology may remain the same, the myths themselves will be influenced by a culture's environment. A corollary of this comment states that a culture can be defined by its chosen myths.

In one example, a British ambassador to New Zealand in the late nineteenth century knew the Maori language. But that wasn't enough knowledge to let him initiate peaceful negotiations. He needed to learn the Maori mythology as well before he could hope to understand the people and the references they made.

For those who may doubt that a culture can really be defined in such a way, one needs only to look at a familiar society as an example: the United States.

Which myths do Americans revere today? The overworked theme of "family values" is still held up as near to sacred by many Americans, to the point of becoming almost a mantra. But certain other mythic themes are no longer part of the national belief system. People now joke about the "Puritan work ethic," refuse to believe in the Horatio Alger character, and think that the idea of "work hard and you will be rewarded" is naive and unrealistic. Though Americans do still call Abraham Lincoln "Honest Abe" and tell children about George Washington and that cherry tree, the tendency is now to attempt to debunk such concepts and stories.

But who do Americans select as their chosen mythic figures? As a people, many Americans have come to cherish the archetype of the trickster, whether in the persona of Bugs Bunny or Bart Simpson, High John (the slave who continually tricked his master), or the politician who everyone knows is corrupt yet who can charm his way into reelection. Part of this love of the trickster may be due to the feeling of powerlessness that many people in today's society seem to have. Most people love trickster stories in which the little man wins over the big. One of the latest incarnations of the little-man-as-hero archetype is surely the cartoon figure Dilbert. And the main enemy of humanity is no longer seen as any one individual or as a satanic antagonist, but as the corporation or the bureaucracy.

Yet an element of mythic awe does remain in the United States. This is still a nation in which the media trumpets miraculous appearances of the Virgin Mary, where we hear stories of UFOs in which people claim to have been carried off by aliens (in much the same way in which people in the Middle Ages claimed to have been carried off to Faerie), and where newspapers run daily horoscopes. Americans think nothing of "taking the Lord's name in vain," just as people in the Middle Ages swore "God's blood," and today angels are mentioned in ordinary speech the way people in the Middle Ages casually mentioned saints' names.

This brings up another national characteristic: Americans tend to downplay supernatural might and turn powerful creatures into harmless ones. Angels have been popularized to the point of triteness. A being originally of great religious power has been downgraded to a cute image on a pin meant to be worn on a lapel as a so-called guardian angel.

Before angels became such common figures in popular imagery, it was the unicorn that was chosen by the public mind to become the heavily popularized mythic being. The unicorn gradually lost all its power as a medieval symbol of peril or a Christian symbol of utter purity, becoming instead an almost cuddly horned horse, or was crossed with the mythic Greek winged horse, Pegasus, to become a weird hybrid. The worst perversion of the mythic image was surely the unicorn with butterfly wings.

But American myths are not utterly sweet. Americans also tend to believe in the reality of mythically powerful conspiracies such as those created by the mysterious and all-knowing Illuminati or in government cover-ups. When one of the American heroes is assassinated, be it Martin Luther King Jr. or John F. Kennedy, people weave conspiracy stories about the crime, as if they need to be assured that a true hero could not be slain by some lone madman, but only by the mythic strength of an evil cabal. Americans have converted the archetypal wizard, with his stereotypical pointed hat and star-studded robe, into the technogeek, the Bill Gates or Steve Jobs, who is to be feared and even hated for using his powers to take too much control.

People fit—and sometimes force—modern stories or news items into archetypal patterns as well. Americans lack a genuine Robin Hood character, one with that "rob the rich to give to the poor" form of trickster altruism. But there is clearly still a need for a noble thief image in the national mythology, since Americans have tried to force such unlikely heroes as the nineteenth-century gunslinger and psychopath Billy the Kid into that mold. He is given an additional level of mythic grandeur by folk ballads that claim the "saintly Billy" was murdered, shot in the back by a "dirty little coward," or those who claim he never did die. Jesse James and, in this century, gangsters like Al Capone have also been subjected to a similar mythmaking process. (This is not strictly an American process, by the way; Australia has comparable mythic criminals.)

Americans have secular mythological rituals, too. Anyone who has ever witnessed the fervor attached to the World Series or the Super Bowl can attest to that, as well as to the almost mythic passion surrounding many sporting events and sports heroes. This mythic aura extends to the animal world as well. When the great racehorse Man o' War died in Lexington, Kentucky, in 1947, he was given a full ritual burial. No less than the governor of Tennessee delivered the eulogy. When, decades later, Man o' War's coffin was moved to the Kentucky Horse Park, the "desecration" of the move was viewed by some people in Lexington with almost mythic horror. It may be noted that no one was horrified when the body of a jockey was moved at the same time.

Animals also feature in American entertainment and popular beliefs as mythic heroes. There is, for instance, Lassie, the wonder dog who never failed to bring help to her (his, actually) master, or the wonder horses, like Roy Rogers' Trigger or Xena's Argo (named after Jason's ship, Argo), that seem to understand human speech and think human thoughts. These mythic animal heroes turn up in books, movies, and television.

Nor are horses and dogs the only mythic animals. The dolphin has been attached to mythology since the early days of Greece, usually in the role of a rescuer of drowning humans; there may even be some truth to the stories. But the dolphin has recently had additional layers of myth added to it. Nowadays, people tend to see it not as the genuine cetacean, but as something both greater and other than the animal. Whether in the persona of the superintelligent Flipper or as a member of the New Age gentle and intelligent pod, the dolphin has begun to be subjected to the same trivializing process that was worked on the images of angels and unicorns.

Americans also have our secular archetypal figures of death and rebirth in the codified images of Father Time and Baby New Year, as well as an archetype of national identity in the equally codified image of Uncle Sam and sacred images in our flag and the bald eagle. Anyone who has followed the near hysteria about flag burning knows how strong a symbol the United States flag has become. The eagle has been a mythic symbol of honor and pride since the Romans first used its image on their standards. It is not at all surprising that Benjamin Franklin was voted down during the Continental Congress when he suggested that the American bird should be a turkey!

Yes, a nation clearly can be defined by its myths. And just as clearly, we in the United States still do need our myths and mythmaking, and will take whatever forms of mythology we can get.

In fact, whether people realize it or not, mythology is very much and very obviously around everyone. People take for granted the names used for the days of the week. At least in English-speaking countries, those names are derived from Teutonic deities, such as Wednesday for Woden's Day and Thursday for Thor's Day, or from objects of mythic significance, such as Sunday for Sun's Day and Monday for Moon's Day. The names of the months are a mix of Latin numbering and mythology. October's name means "eighth month," for instance, while May's name comes from Maia, a Roman goddess of springtime, and July honors the deified Julius Caesar.

The penchant for giving heavenly objects mythological names persists into the space age. For instance, the planets are mostly named for Roman deities: Mercury for the god of messengers (and thieves), Venus for the goddess of love, Mars for the god of war, Jupiter for the king of the gods, Saturn for the god of the underworld, Neptune for the god of the seas, Uranus for the god of the sky, and Pluto for another underworld divinity. Only Earth itself doesn't fit the Roman pattern. Instead, it is named (at least in English-speaking countries) after the Saxon goddess of the earth. With the use of the telescope in the seventeenth century, astronomers made new discoveries, such as the moons of Mars and Jupiter, and decided to continue the trend of naming them after mythological characters. Jupiter's moons include Ganymede, the god's cup-bearer, while Mars, fittingly enough, has moons named for the war god's companions, Phobos and Deimos, Panic and Fear. The discovery of other celestial objects, such as Saturn's moons, had to wait for more modern technology, but they, too, fit the mythological pattern of names: Saturn's largest moon is Titan, the name of an ancient giant.

Mythological themes are evident in the visual arts, too, far too evident to be listed in any detail here. They can be found in works as widely diverse as Botticelli's painting *The Birth of Aphrodite*, the imagery carved on cathedral walls, the ritual sand paintings of the Navajo, and the surrealist paintings of Salvador Dalí.

Many playwrights and musicians have used mythology in their works as well. The Greeks were probably the first, or at least the first for whom there is record, with playwrights such as Euripedes and Aeschylus retelling their myths in plays meant not as religious rituals but as entertainment. The Sun King, Louis XIV, frequently held grand performances and masquerades inspired by Greek and Roman mythology, often with himself costumed literally as the sun or the king of the gods. From the eighteenth through the twentieth centuries, composers frequently made use of mythology. The late-nineteenth-century Russian composer Nikolai Rimsky-Korsakov, to name one example, wrote nine operas with mythological themes, such as *Snegourichka*, which includes the pagan Russian celebration of spring's rebirth. The nineteenth-century German composer Richard Wagner wrote many of his operas about mythological themes, from the Holy Grail in *Parsifal* to his epic reworking of German mythology in his Ring cycle. Twentieth-century composer Richard Strauss reworked Greek mythology in his shattering opera *Elektra* and in his fantastic *Die Frau ohne Shatten* (The woman without a shadow).

Authors who have been influenced by mythological themes are far too numerous to name here. They range from mystic poet William Blake, with his *Songs of Innocence* and *Songs of Experience*, to stream-of-conscious writer James Joyce and his *Ulysses*, from poet W. B. Yeats and the Irish and British writers of the so-called Celtic Twilight to fantasy great J. R. R. Tolkien and his masterpiece trilogy, *The Lord of the Rings*, as well as the literally hundreds of fantasy and science fiction writers of the nineteenth and twentieth centuries. In the world of graphic novels, which are basically comic books for adults, Neil Gaiman has used a great deal of mythology in his Sandman series, from the Greek god of death, Thanatos, turned into the god of dreams by Gaiman, to a personified Death as a friendly young woman.

Popular mythologist Joseph Campbell has raised a good deal of controversy among mythologists and folklorists, who tend to either strongly agree or strongly disagree with his theories of connected world mythic themes—or, rather, with the way that he connected the themes. But though scholars may agree or disagree, no one can deny that he did succeed in introducing a whole new generation in the United States and Europe to the mythological underpinnings of mind and society that they already subconsciously knew were there but had never really examined.

One of Campbell's most famous students was filmmaker George Lucas. Lucas added a new layer to mythological themes with his *Star Wars* movies and his fantasy movie, *Willow*, all of which are heavily inspired by archetypes. And most recently, television shows such as *Xena* and *Hercules* deliberately played wild and loose with mythologies of all cultures and times.

Those shows, as well as the genre of science fiction and fantasy novels, raise a question often asked by modern audiences. Is this a new mythology? Can new myths really be created? Here is a subject that has been debated at length among folklorists and mythologists without anyone coming to any clear agreement. This folklorist believes that there are no such things as new myths, merely old myths in new clothing. Just as every culture picks the myths it requires, so every generation dresses the myths to suit its needs.

Here are some cases in point. The most blatant place to start when dealing with "modern" mythology is with the original *Star Wars* movie and its archetypes. The main figure of the first three movies is Luke Skywalker, the mythic hero raised in ignorance of his true worth. Although Luke lacks the "baby in the bulrushes" mythic motif of Moses and Sargon of Akkad, among others, he does share elements with them as well as with the comic book hero Superman. Luke also shares a mythic element with Sigurd/Siegfried of Teutonic myth and Aragorn of Tolkien's *The Lord of the Rings* in that he possesses but has to learn to use the sword of his father.

In this, Luke is guided by another archetypal figure, Obi-Wan Kenobi, the wise old man, who can also be a warrior when the occasion calls for it. Obi-Wan shares his characteristics as sage with many earlier mythic figures, including Merlin of Britain, Vainamoinen of Finnish lore, and the wizard Gandalf, again from *Lord of the Rings*. In the second movie, *The Empire Strikes Back*, Luke encounters another version of the wise old man archetype: Yoda, teacher of the Jedi.

Luke is helped on his quest—which is another mythic theme, of course, the quest of the hero—by Han Solo, who combines the archetypes of trickster and rogue in the spirit of Robin Hood, and Chewbacca the Wookie, who plays the part of the (secondary) hero's companion. Darth Vader, of course, is almost too easy to identify: He is literally the dark lord, the adversary, throughout the first *Star Wars* movie at least, with a tie-in to Lucifer, the fallen angel. George Lucas brings in many other blatant archetype images, such as that of son fighting father and of the sinner redeemed.

The archetypes are a little less obvious, at least at first sight, when another modern icon is considered: the science fiction television and movie series *Star Trek*. But the mythic types really are there. After all, the classic USS *Enterprise*, the ship from the original series, going off to explore "strange new worlds" and seeking out "strange new civilizations," is clearly a modern descendent of the ancient ships of mythic exploration, such as the Greek Jason's *Argo* or the nameless vessel of the Welsh Maedun, who wandered amid magical islands.

The *Enterprise*'s captain, James T. Kirk, definitely has his mythic qualities as well. In his willingness to solve a problem not by force or cold reason but by trickery, he is a composite of trickster and rogue, like Jason and Han Solo. He also has the trickster's lustiness. Mr. Spock, the half-human, half-Vulcan first officer, plays two mythic roles. He is both the hero ignorant of his true worth, man of two planets and two species that he is, and the hero's companion and sage. Dr. Leonard McCoy, the acerbic ship's surgeon, plays the mythic role of the wise old man in his own gadfly way. The *Enterprise*'s engineer, Montgomery "Scotty" Scott, who can work wonders with machines, is a modern counterpart of the earlier wonder-working smiths out of mythology, such as the English Weland Smith and the Greek Hephaestus. A deliberate use of Roman mythology went into the naming of the Vulcans and their separatist cousins the Romulans, the latter with their twin worlds of Romulus and Remus. And a case can be made for the Klingons, at least those in the original *Star Trek* series, being modern variants on mythic ogres.

There are certainly a good many other myths in modern dress. Bugs Bunny, mentioned before as a clear archetype trickster figure, is, though his creators didn't realize it, the direct descendent of Hare and Rabbit of West African peoples and native cultures of the Southeastern United States.

It should be evident by this point that none of these images, modern though they may seem, is part of any truly new myth. Even Darth Vader, for all his high-tech protective mask and flowing black robes, is, as already mentioned, merely an ancient archetype in new—if impressive—clothing. And by now, any storyteller must agree that mythology truly knows no boundaries of time or space. All people hold their myths as a link with the human past. What new clothing will mythology be wearing in the future? That depends on culture and how it changes. There will still be questions to be answered. And where science or reasoning fails, there is mythology to fill the gap.

The stories in this book are not restricted to any one region or any one era. How could they be? Mythology really does belong to everyone.

1

THE CREATION

There are as many versions of the story of creation as there are human cultures. Details of the creation vary, of course, according to what aspects each culture finds most important. In some accounts, the world is created from nothing by the will or word of a deity, as in our familiar biblical account, as well as in myths from Egypt, Greece, and Mesoamerica. After the creation, the deity (or deities) may remain the central figure of religious life, as in Judeo-Christian beliefs, or withdraw from humanity, as in the Greek myths.

A related category of cosmic myth is the creation by birth, the world-parent myth. Here two divine parents give birth to the world or to divine or semidivine offspring. Sometimes, as occurs in Greek and Babylonian mythology, the children are forced, for the sake of their own survival or the survival of the newly formed world, to turn against their parents, even to kill them. In a variant form, as in Egyptian and Polynesian myths, the children push their parents, who are sky and earth, apart to make space for humanity.

Another category of creation myth involves the potent mythic symbol: the cosmic ocean. This mythic type, particularly common to Asia and North America, involves a magical being, a bird or an animal, that helps the creator by diving into the ocean and bringing up earth from under the primal waters. In some cases the diver is seen as a subordinate rival to the creator, or even an evil being. In all examples, though, the earth that is recovered from under the waters then expands into the world.

Still another form of cosmic myth involves divine death or sacrifice. In Babylonian myth, for example, the slain Tiamat's body—she who is a quite literal example of a monster mother—becomes the earth.

Some creation myths reflect the environment surrounding a specific culture. Sumer, lying as it did between the Tigris and Euphrates rivers in what is now Iraq, depended on irrigation yet was in constant danger from flooding. Therefore, it is not unexpected to find that water and its control are major elements in Sumerian creation myths. It is the primal sea that is the source of gods and earth. There can be no surprise, then, that the earliest written version of the archetypal flood myth that survives comes from Sumer.

Every culture, not at all unexpectedly, has a myth concerning the creation of humans and animals—indeed, of all living things. The method of creation, though, varies widely. Sometimes, as in the familiar biblical story, humanity comes as much from the will or the word of a creator as from anything physical such as dust. Other myths, such as that of the Babylonians, do hold stronger elements of the physical, telling of humanity sculpted from clay, blood, or other such substances.

Another form of mythological birth is a symbolic one. In myths of this sort, they may tell of the emergence of humanity from a specific sacred tree or rock. Or humanity may emerge from under the earth or from the lower worlds, as in Navajo myths, literally and symbolically from a narrow opening in the earth.

So, for that matter, can gods emerge. The ruler of the Greek pantheon, Zeus, was hidden as a baby in a narrow cave, a cleft in the rocks, in Crete, to protect him from his murderous father, Cronos, who had already eaten his other children. Zeus' emergence from the cave was clearly a second, symbolic birth; the cave is still revered as a sacred site of fertility.

The rituals of some human cultures echo this symbolism. In Cornwall, until fairly recently, it was considered good fortune to crawl through a natural hole in a rock. And in various initiation customs in shamanistic societies, a budding shaman is ritually "buried" in a cave and must find his way, his "rebirth," out of that cave.

Eggs, too, can be symbolic of birth, as well as of fertility and even rebirth. African and Chinese myths tell that humanity emerged from the inner to the outer layers of the world egg.

A Polynesian variant shows how the basic template of a myth may be sculpted by local environment, since the world egg is, in this case, replaced by a coconut.

THE BEGINNING OF CREATION
A Myth from Ancient Babylon

Several familiar world themes appear in this myth. The concept of the primal sea is one of the most common, turning up in the myths of cultures as far apart as ancient Egypt, pre-Christian Finland, and the Pacific Northwest of North America. Since our planet is, after all, at least two-thirds covered by water, it's not difficult to see why so many cultures would have the primal sea concept.

The theme of a divine father wanting to kill his divine offspring also appears in early Greek mythology. See the Greek myth "Theogony" later in this chapter, which takes the theme much further. The fight against a deadly mother figure appears in Aztec mythology as well. The psychological underpinnings of these myths are intriguing, but beyond the scope of this book.

Kudurru of Babylonian king Melishishu II shows emblems of the gods Anu, Enlil, and Ea. Above them are the crescent of the moon god, the star of Ishtar, and the sun of Shamash. At the bottom are a snake and scorpion of the underworld. (*Erich Lessing/Art Resource, New York*)

This is the author's free rendering of various translations of what is customarily known by archaeologists as "the epic of creation" cycle. While the earliest relatively complete versions date to the Old Babylonian era, circa 1900-1800 B.C.E., there is incomplete evidence hinting that other versions may be even earlier.

When the sky above had no name, when the earth below had no name, there was Apsu the first, the begetter of all, and there was Tiamat, maker, bearer of all. They mixed their waters together in the primal sea.

There was not yet made pasture or reed, marsh or solid land. They had not yet let gods be manifest.

But gods were born within them. Lahmu and Lahamu they were, their names pronounced as they were fully formed. Then Anshar and Kishar were born as well, surpassing the eldest two. Anshar made his son, Anu, from himself, like himself. And Anu was greater than his begetter, greater than the eldest four.

So it was that more and more gods came into being, and played together in the primal sea. Their noise grew, and the waves that they made while playing disturbed the primal peace.

At last Apsu made complaint to Tiamat. "Their ways are grievous to me. By day I have no rest. By night I have no sleep. I shall destroy them so that we may know peace."

Tiamat was enraged. "Shall we end what we have formed? Their actions may be noisome, but we should bear it with goodwill. I will not strike against them."

Apsu was not content. He summoned forth his minister, Mummu, and plotted. "How can we best be rid of the noisy lot?"

Mummu counseled, "Put an end to this here and now. By day you should know rest, by night you should know sleep."

Apsu was delighted. They plotted evil, he and Mummu against the gods, Apsu's children.

He did not know that Ea, son of Anshar and cleverest of the young gods, Ea who knew everything, was listening to this deadly plot that Apsu brewed. Ea in his turn fashioned a plan to save the gods. He made an artful master spell, recited it, and brought it restfully upon the waters. Ea's spell drenched Apsu and Mummu with deepest sleep. Ea bound Mummu as his captive. Then Ea slew Apsu, slew his deadly grandsire.

Now Ea ruled supreme in Apsu's place, taking on the radiance of royalty. He and Damkina, his wife, dwelled together in quiet splendor. And together they begot a son and called him Marduk. Marduk was a splendid son from birth, a fine and fiery hero god in every way.

But all the while, Tiamat raged in her heart. The waves were troubled as she thought of Apsu's death, and heard from those children still loyal to her what Ea had done. He had slain her mate. He had taken on the radiance of royalty. She would not have dominion torn from her grasp!

So Tiamat gave birth not to gods but to monsters, an army born of hate. Among them were the horned serpent, the rabid dog, the seething dragon, the hate-filled demon, the raging being half bull and half man, and the loathsome being half man and half fish. Through the veins of each snake in that army ran venom, not blood, and in the eyes of each dragon flashed deadly fire.

"Whoever sees them shall collapse from fear," Tiamat proclaimed. "Wherever they attack, they shall not retreat."

Not satisfied yet, Tiamat then raised up one of her offspring, he who is known only as Qingu. Not one description of him is there. But Tiamat was pleased with her creation, so pleased that she took him as her new mate and gave him the army's leadership.

When news of this most terrible of armies reached Ea, he sat stunned in silence for a time. Then, knowing he must have counsel at once, he hurried to his father, Anshar. But Anshar, looking out at the terror threatening them all, cried out in anger, "It was you who slew Apsu, it is you who enraged Tiamat, and it is you who must declare war against her army!"

Ea defended himself against his father's wrath, using soothing speech, calming words. "O my father, remember in your heart that I made a wise plan. I slew Apsu before he could slay us all. But when I slew him, who could have foreseen what is happening now?"

Anshar's wrath was calmed. "Go forth against Tiamat. Subdue her by your magic spell."

So Ea set out against Tiamat. But soon he hurried back to Anshar.

"My father, her strength is too great. My spells cannot counter it. My army cannot stand against her monsters. My father, send another against her before she destroys us all."

Anshar, raging, called upon his firstborn, Anu. "Stalwart son, valiant son, take a stand before Tiamat. Soothe her. Calm her rage. Stop her hatred."

When he heard his father's words, Anu set off to confront Tiamat and soothe her rage. But soon he hurried back to Anshar.

"My father, I cannot counter her hatred. Her strength is greater now, terrifying in its force. There is no hope of soothing her, none of calming her rage. I pray you, send another after her, before she destroys us all."

Anshar called forth all the gods. But they all sat tight-lipped in silence. Anshar, seeing them all helpless with fear, cried out, "Is there none among you to come forward?"

"There is one," Ea said. He summoned forth his own mighty firstborn, his champion, his brave son, Marduk.

Marduk bowed to Anshar. "My grandfather, let me go, let me win your heart's desire."

Seeing the fierce young strength of Marduk, Anshar's heart was lightened. "Go forth, my grandson. Trample the neck of Tiamat. Bring her to rest with your sacred spells. Go, quickly, with your chariot of storm. Let it not veer from its course!"

Marduk straightened proudly. "My lord grandfather, if indeed I am to be your champion, if I am to stop Tiamat and save the lives of all here, then let me be supreme among the gods."

It was agreed. The gods set out for Marduk a royal dais, and he took his place on it as sovereign. The gods proclaimed, "You are our champion. We bestow on you kingship of all there is. May your truth be without flaw; may your weapon never miss its mark. Now go cut off the life of Tiamat and let the winds bear away her blood!"

So Marduk raised up Deluge, his spear, and mounted his chariot, terrible Storm Demon. The four steeds who drew that chariot were Slaughterer, Overwhelmer, Soaring, and Merciless, and their teeth were bared in battle fury. Marduk drove them forward. He drove them to where Tiamat loomed like a terrible wave over her army. She cast a spell of falsehood at him, saying, "The gods rise up against you. They claim to have raised you up, but they are not at your side when you have the greatest need of aid."

For a moment Marduk faltered, overwhelmed by the force of Tiamat's spell. Then he shouted at her, "Deceiver! You pretend to warn, while you plan attack. You mean to murder Anshar and all the gods. Come within range and let us duel!"

Tiamat shrieked her rage and charged. She and Marduk closed in single combat, casting spell after spell. Marduk hurled the storm wind at her, and she opened her mouth wide to swallow it and him—but the raging wind held her helpless. Marduk drew his bow and shot. The arrow tore through Tiamat's belly, through her heart, through her body. She fell dead, and Marduk took his stand on the carcass, scattering her forces on all sides. Qingu he took prisoner, binding him as a traitor to the gods.

The battle was over. Marduk tore Tiamat's body in two, letting the wind cast away her blood. He flung one-half of the body into the air, where it became the dome of heaven. The other half, left lying, became the earth with all its mounts and valleys. Now Marduk set places in the heaven for the gods, and set the stars in their places as well. He used the stars to mark off years and months, weeks and days.

But Marduk was not yet finished with his work. The foam from the primal sea became billowing clouds in the sky. The winds he raised condensed water from the clouds to rain down on the earth.

Now it was time to deal with Qingu the traitor. The gods slew him, and from his blood Marduk made humanity.

But the doings of humanity is another tale.

Sources

Dalley, Stephanie. *Myths from Mesopotamia*. Oxford: Oxford University Press, 1989.
Kramer, Samuel Noah. *Sumerian Mythology*. New York: Harper and Brothers, 1961.
McCall, Henrietta. *Mesopotamian Myths*. Austin: University of Texas Press, 1990.

ANCIENT CREATION
A Myth from Ancient Assyria

This is also the author's free rendering of translations of the Assyrian creation myth and is here to show a variation in a region. While the Assyrian version isn't as complete a "story" as in the Babylonian creation myth, mostly because of scanty textual material (i.e., clay tables break), there is the additional element of the creation being incomplete without humanity.

*I*t was the four gods of the elements who created the earth and the heavens. It was the Annunaki, the sky gods led by Anu, their head god; Enlil, of earth; Shamash, the god of the sun; and Ea, god of water. They created earth and heaven, yet when they looked over their new creation, there was surely something missing.

It was humanity that the new world lacked, humanity to till the fields and celebrate the festivals. So it was that the first humans were created. They were named Ulligarra, which means "abundance," and Zalgarra, which means "plenty." Aruru, "lady of the gods," kept their destinies safe. The humans lived and thrived. And the new world was now complete.

Sources

Dalley, Stephanie. *Myths from Mesopotamia*. Oxford: Oxford University Press, 1989.
Foster, Benjamin R. *From Distant Days: Myths, Tales and Poetry of Ancient Mesopotamia*. Bethesda: CDL, 1995.

ATUM THE CREATOR
A Myth from Ancient Egypt

This is the basic, primal Egyptian creation myth in which Atum is the father and mother of creation in one. In the hieroglyphic texts there is apparently some variance as to whether this is a case of creation by will or by literally sexual means.

*F*irst there was nothing but the primal chaos, the great bubbling, churning turmoil of water that was to be called Nun. It was out of this chaos that all that is came into being, but the creation did not arise unaided.

From time to time the roiling chaos of Nun receded ever so slightly, drawing back from the first hilltop. On this hilltop, out of Nun, came Atum, great self-created primal god of sun and life, Atum, whose name implies "all": all that was to be. Neither and both male and female, Atum was alone. Yet there were to be more gods, engendered from Atum by Atum. From this primal one came a male god, Shu, air, and a female god, Tefnut, water. To these two creations, these two children of one parent, Atum assigned the roles of establishing order out of chaos. Shu gave the world the principles of life, while Tefnut gave it the principles of order.

Atum, the primal god of sun and life, was not content to rule alone. He created the air god Shu, who is pictured here separating the sky from the earth to establish order and give the world the principles of life. Detail from coffin of Nespawershepi, chief scribe of the Temple of Amun, twenty-first dynasty, c. 984 B.C.E. (*Werner Forman/Art Resource, New York*)

Yet while they worked on these tasks, Shu and Tefnut were lost amid the seething, foggy chaos of Nun. Their parent sought them but found nothing. So Atum removed his single eye, the *udjat*, and sent it out to find his lost children. They were found, and returned with the *udjat*. Setting it back in his head, Atum wept the first tears ever known, tears of joy.

And where these tears of joy struck earth, humankind grew.

But there was no world yet for them. Shu and Tefnut became the parents of two children, Geb, a male god, the earth, and Nut, a female god, the sky. Geb and Nut, in turn, created Osiris and Isis, Hathor and Set, who were to rule over humanity and all the ways of the world. And now humanity had a place on which to live and thrive.

Atum's work was done. He retreated from the new creation, content.

Sources

Hart, George. *Egyptian Myths*. Austin: University of Texas Press, 1990.
Quirke, Stephen. *Ancient Egyptian Religion*. New York: Dover Publications, 1995.
Shafer, Byron E., ed. *Religion in Ancient Egypt: Gods, Myths, and Personal Practice*. Ithaca, NY: Cornell University Press, 1991.

PTAH CREATES THE WORLD
A Myth Variant from Memphis, Ancient Egypt

This myth was chosen to show how a basic myth can be altered to fit a local region's patron deity. The same process occurs in folklore, such as a Russian tale of a peasant outwitting a royal court. In its earliest forms there is a generic tsar; in the later versions the generic figure has been replaced by a specific ruler, Peter the Great. The same process occurs in modern urban folklore, in which a generic movie star in the original urban tale is replaced by a specific actor by later tellers.

The ancient Egyptians tended to be highly adaptable about conflicting religious beliefs. Each *nome*, or district, had its own patron deities, who were added into the Egyptian pantheon, merging elements with already existing deities. There would have been nothing unusual in Memphis, which was the capital of Egypt until about 1700 B.C.E., having its own version of the creation myth, featuring its own patron god.

*P*tah the great god came forth from the primal waters, seeking a place to rest his foot. He was no longer young, the primal one, and he wished that place to rest his foot. So the god brought land up from out of the water and came ashore at the place, which he named Memphis, meaning that this was land.

Now there was land and sea, but no order. Ptah willed there to be other deities, other gods beneath him, and the earliest of deities save Ptah himself came into being. This was what the god willed; this was what he created through his words. And so Ptah, content, withdrew to let the others do the work of creating plants and beasts and humans.

Sources

Hart, George. *Egyptian Myths*. Austin: University of Texas Press, 1990.
Quirke, Stephen. *Ancient Egyptian Religion*. New York: Dover Publications, 1995.
Shafer, Byron E., ed. *Religion in Ancient Egypt: Gods, Myths, and Personal Practice*. Ithaca, NY: Cornell University Press, 1991.

COLORED CLAYS
A Myth of the Shilluk of Sudan

The concept of humanity being molded out of clay is a common image in world mythology, turning up everywhere from Africa to the Near East to Asia and North America. See, for instance, the two Chinese tales of Nü Wa creating humanity, later in this chapter. The idea that the different races come from different colors of clay appears in other myths as well. See, for example, the "Two Creators" myth from New Guinea, later in this chapter.

We also have the concept of humanity being molded from clay or earth in our Western sayings, such as "Ashes to ashes, dust to dust."

Juok the creator wandered the earth, creating all humanity in the colors that seemed right. In the land of the north, he found a pure white clay that pleased him. Out of it he shaped the ancestors of all the white races.

Then Juok wandered south, to the land of Egypt. The deep red of the mud of the Nile pleased him. Out of it he shaped the ancestors of all the red races.

At last he came to the land of the Shilluks. There he found black earth that pleased him. Out of it he shaped the ancestors of all the black races.

Now, the way that Juok created life from clay was this:

As he held a lump of clay, Juok thought and then said, "I will make man out of this."

Then Juok thought and then said, "Man must be able to walk and run. So I will give him two long legs."

So two long legs were created.

Then Juok thought and then said, "Man must be able to grow his crops and harvest his millet seed. So I will give him two arms. One will grip his hoe. The other will tear up weeds."

So two arms were created.

Then Juok thought and then said, "Man must be able to see what he does. So I will give him two eyes."

So two eyes were created.

Then Juok thought and then said, "Man must be able to eat his millet. So I will give him a mouth."

So a mouth was created.

After that, Juok thought and then said, "Man must be able to speak and sing. So I will give him a tongue."

So a tongue was created.

Last, Juok thought and then said, "Man must be able to hear speech and song. So I will give him two ears."

So two ears were created.

And Juok sent man out into the world as a perfect being.

Sources

Frazer, Sir James G. *Folklore in the Old Testament*. London: Macmillan, 1918.

Gaster, Theodor H. *Myth, Legend, and Custom in the Old Testament*. New York: Harper and Row, 1969.

IN THE BEGINNING
A Myth of the Yoruba of Nigeria

Here is one of the common forms of world-creating myths: The world is created out of the sea from a handful of earth, in this case scratched out into a world by a hen. It's a variation of the primal sea theme. For two more versions, see the Hungarian "The Saga of Creation" and the Wyandot "The Origin of the World," later in this chapter.

It's true, by the way, that the earth really does have an iron core.

A sacred palm tree depicted in seventeenth-century Yorubian brasswork. The sacred palm is a source of oil and of nuts used in divination. According to the Yorubian creation myth, the god of the sky, Olodumare, summoned Obtala to create the earth using a snail shell filled with soil, scraps of iron, a rooster, a pigeon, and a five-toed hen. (*Werner Forman/Art Resource, New York*)

*I*n the beginning there was no earth, no mountains, no forest. There was nothing but water, still and empty, water with no place on it for life to walk about. Only the gods could play here. But gods grow lonely with no humankind to worship them.

So one day the greatest, Olodumare, said to the great, Obtala, "There must be an earth. It is for you to create it."

"With what?" Obtala asked.

Olodumare gave him these things: a snail shell filled with soil, some pieces of iron, a rooster, a pigeon, and a five-toed hen.

"So be it," Obtala said.

He swung down over the water on a spiderweb bridge and threw down the pieces of iron to brace what would be the new world. Then he cast the soil over the iron, and there was the earth, a little island in the middle of all the water.

Now Obtala cast down the rooster, the pigeon, and the five-toed hen. They began to scratch about as their kind will do. Scratch, scratch, scratch went their claws, that rooster, that pigeon, and that five-toed hen.

And with every scratch, the earth was spread a little further, out and out over the water till a solid world was formed.

So it was, and so it is. And if you ask the men of science today, they will agree: There is a core of iron to our world, just as it was in the beginning.

Sources

Abrahams, Roger D. *African Folktales*. New York: Random House, 1983.

Courlander, Harold. *Tales of Yoruba Gods and Heroes*. Greenwich, CT: Fawcett Publications, 1973.

Gbadamosi, Bakare A. *Not Even God Is Ripe Enough: Yoruba Stories*. London: Heinemann, 1968.

BRINGING UP THE WORLD
A Myth of the Boshongo People of Zaire

This is a more unusual and unique view of creation: The world and its inhabitants as something that a deity with an upset stomach must vomit up. It's difficult to feel arrogant when faced with the thought of such humble beginnings!

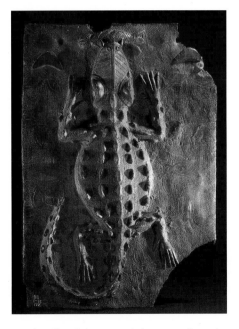

The Boshongo creation myth tells of the primal deity Bumba, who vomited up the moon, stars, and nine living creations: the tortoise, the leopard, the eagle, the crocodile, the fish, the heron, the beetle, the goat, and Tsetse the lightning. Bumba then vomited up all of humanity. (*Werner Forman/Art Resource, New York*)

The theme of lightning being a dangerous nuisance to be separated from the world turns up in other myths as well. See, for instance the Nigerian myth "Why Thunder and Lightning Live in the Sky," and the Wyandot myth "Henqn the Thunder," both in Chapter 4.

*I*n the beginning there was nothing. Then there was nothing and darkness, nothing and water.

Then, alone in the darkness and the water and the nothingness, there was the primal deity, Bumba.

Once it was that Bumba was seized with a terrible pain deep within. He strained and struggled, and at last vomited up the sun.

There was utter darkness no longer. Now there was day as well as night. The heat of the sun dried up much of the water, letting dry land be seen. But that was all there was.

Then Bumba's pain began again. He vomited up the moon and stars. Now there was proper light for the night as well.

But Bumba's pain had not yet ended. He vomited up nine living creatures, the tortoise, the leopard, the eagle, the crocodile, the fish, the heron, the beetle, the goat, and Tsetse the lightning. And last of all, Bumba vomited up humanity.

It was the creatures who then created all the beasts and birds, fish and insects.

Only Tsetse the lightning was no creator. She was a troublesome sort, striking here and there without warning. At last Bumba seized her and hurled her up into the sky. And there she stays, though now and again she still does strike at the earth.

But it was Bumba who is to be remembered, Bumba who created the very beginning of it all.

Sources

Abrahams, Roger D. *African Folktales*. New York: Random House, 1983.
Courlander, Harold. A *Treasure of African Folklore*. New York: Marlowe, 1996.
Feldmann, Susan. *African Myths and Tales*. New York: Dell Publishing, 1963.

TWO CREATORS
A Myth from the Kono of Sierra Leone and Guinea

Several familiar elements appear in this myth. First is the concept of there being not one or many but two creators, which appears in many myths, including some from Siberia and the New World. But this myth also includes an element more common in folklore than mythology: the master and apprentice motif. There is also the familiar folkloric motif of the apprentice falling for the master's daughter.

A third element in this myth is the "how and why" theme explaining why there are different races. See also "Colored Clays," earlier in this chapter.

*I*n the beginning, there was no sky, no land, only above and below. There were two beings, two great creators who lived back then. One was Alatanga, whose domain was the emptiness above the primal swampy waters. The other was Sa, who had a wife and daughter, and whose domain was under the primal swampy waters.

Now, Alatanga decided to begin creation. He started by drawing up solid land out of the swampy waters and adding decorations of trees and plants. Sa was delighted with what Alatanga had done, and offered him hospitality while he worked.

Now that there was a world and vegetation on it, Alatanga decided it was time for there to be light as well. But how could this be arranged? Sa had a rooster. He taught it a special song and told it to sing at a specific time.

Sure enough, when the rooster began to crow, the sun rose for the first time, and the first day began.

It was in Sa's dwelling that Alatanga met Sa's daughter, who was a beautiful young woman. Alatanga fell in love with her, and she with him. But Sa didn't want to lose his only child. When Alatanga told Sa that he wished to marry her, Sa refused.

So Alatanga and Sa's daughter fled to a far corner of the new lands. There they wed and raised a family of fourteen children. Half of these children were white and half were black. As they grew up they all spoke different languages, and their parents couldn't understand what they said. At last Alatanga was forced to return to Sa to ask him what had happened.

What had happened, Sa proclaimed, was a punishment on Alatanga for stealing Sa's only child. But Sa agreed to give the children what they would need to survive. The black children were given hoes, axes, and knives. The white children were given paper, pens, and ink. The white children left for what would become Europe; the black children stayed in what would become Africa. All of them had many children of their own, and those children and their children's children spread out over the world.

Sources

Leeming, David Adams, and Margaret Adams Leeming. A *Dictionary of Creation Myths*. New York and Oxford: Oxford University Press, 1995.

Parrinder, Geoffrey. *African Mythology*. New York: Peter Bedrick Books, 1982.

MOVING THE SKY
A Myth of the San of Namibia

This is a nice human version of a myth: A cosmic problem solved by an overwhelmed woman just trying to get dinner ready for her family. Variants turn up around the world: There's a very similar version, including that frustrated housewife, from the Philippines.

One important West African myth describes a woman who was unable to cook dinner for her family because the sky hung too low. With one stab of her stirring stick, the woman made the sky retreat to the heavens. A variation of the myth is depicted in this Ashanti brass weight, which shows a woman using a pestle to pound cereal. In actuality, the weight would have been used to measure gold. (© *The British Museum*)

The concept of the sky being too close to the earth is a common theme in world mythology. More often than not, earth and sky are seen as lovers who must be wrenched apart if the world is to thrive. See, for instance, the Maori myth "Rangi and Papa," later in this chapter.

*I*n the long-ago days soon after the beginning, the sky had separated only partially from the earth. It hovered low over the land, and the people who were there had to walk bent over nearly double. But what could be done? It was the way things were.

One day, a woman was trying to cook dinner for her family. But there wasn't room for her to put the stirring stick into the pot, let alone to stir the food. The woman gave a great cry of anger. She was tired, her family was hungry, and now she couldn't even stir the food to keep it from burning as it cooked!

She stabbed the sky with her stirring stick. The sky gave a yelp of surprise. And it leaped up into the heavens, where it is today.

So we can thank a woman with a hungry family for us not having to walk around bent over. We can thank her for the sky being up where it belongs!

Sources

Abrahams, Roger D. *African Folktales*. New York: Random House, 1983.
Biesele, Megan. *Women Like Meat*. Bloomington: Indiana University Press, 1993.
Eugenio, Damiana L. *Philippine Folk Literature: The Myths*. Diliman, Quezon City: University of the Philippines Press, 1993.

THEOGONY
A Myth from Ancient Greece

This myth has been debated by mythologists and psychologists alike. How ancient is it? Although the written versions date to classical Greece, the themes within it are clearly much older and very primal.

First, as in the Babylonian myth of creation (see above), is the theme of the monstrous father and the mother who turns her children against him. But in this myth the theme is carried out to its ultimate conclusion: the castration-death of the father by the son.

That Aphrodite, goddess of love (and lust), should have been born from the result seems wonderfully ironic.

The prophecy that Cronus receives, that one of his sons will overthrow him, turns up in world myths and folktales. See, for instance, the myth of Perseus in Chapter 5.

The earth mother goddess, Gaea, emerges from below as Athena (center) fights Gaea's sons. According to the Greek myth, Gaea's love with the sky produced the ocean and the earliest of gods. Relief from the Pergamon Altar, c. 180 B.C.E. (*Erich Lessing/Art Resource, New York*)

Then the cycle of father-son hatred continues with Cronus attempting to destroy his offspring by swallowing them and his being slain by Zeus. This can be seen in the modern sense of the never-ending cycle of child abuse, but it can also be seen as the triumph of Zeus, who represents the new order. Zeus has a symbolic rebirth by coming forth from the sheltering cave—which might also represent an attempt to make Zeus more "native," since many mythologists believe the deity was originally a northern god, not Greek at all. He might have been brought into Greece by the Doric invaders.

The final theme contained in this myth is that of the ages of man, and the belief that the "good old days" were finer than the current times. This is a very human belief; an Assyrian clay tablet, for instance, holds a complaint about "modern children who lack respect for their elders" and how things were better in the old days.

At first nothingness, the great void itself, came into being. Or, being all and nothingness in one, maybe it always was. From it, though, came broad-bosomed Gaea, Earth, lovely home of all that lives, and with her birth, Eros, Desire, without which there can be no wish for new life.

Out of the void next came Darkness and Night. And out of that pair's mating came, in turn, Light and Day. Now Earth produced star-spangled Sky to cover her. Then she created tall mountains and the wide and raging sea. Her love with Sky produced Ocean, deep and calming water, then the other earliest of gods, Coeus, Crius, Hyperion, Iapetus, Thea and Rhea, Themis, who is law, and Mnemosyne, who is memory, Phoebe and Thethys. Last of this lot came Cronus, youngest and boldest, he who came to hate his sire.

Earth also gave birth to monsters, the one-eyed Cyclopes and a brood of many-headed giants.

Sky hated all of them and would not let them be born, forcing them back within Earth. She, groaning with strain, found a new metal within herself and created a gray sickle of shining iron. "My children," she said, "you have a brutal father. Listen to me, and we shall have vengeance on him."

But the children of Earth were too frightened to speak—all save cunning Cronus, who snapped, "I have no love for our brutal father. I will carry out your plan."

Earth hid him in ambush, the sickle in his hands. As Sky came to Earth, Cronus leaped from hiding and severed his father's organs with one quick sweep of his blade. Drops of blood fell on Earth, and she birthed the terrible Erinyes, the spirits of vengeance, and the giants with their deadly spears. But what fell into the sea birthed a finer being: Aphrodite, who was love, rose from the sea froth.

Meanwhile, Sky named his children the Titans, which was a dark play on words in the ancient language, meaning that they had tightened the noose about their own necks for what had been done to him. And they, he vowed, would pay in days to come. Cronus, he added, had this destiny: He would be overthrown by one of his own sons.

Cronus remembered. He took Rhea to wife, and she bore him children, Hestia of the hearth, Demeter of the fields, Hera of marriage, Hades of the underworld, Poseidon of the oceans, and last, Zeus, lord of wisdom. And as each of these children was born, Cronus swallowed them. He would not let the dark destiny overtake him!

But just before she was to give birth to he who would be Zeus, Rhea managed to escape her husband and run to Earth for aid. Earth sent her to the Cretan town of Lyetus. There Zeus was born, and there Earth raised him, safe in an inaccessible cave deep in the holy ground, hidden in the woods of Mount Aegeum. Then Rhea wrapped a stone in a baby's blanket, and Cronus, never suspecting, swallowed it.

The young prince, hidden in safety, grew quickly in strength and wit. At last he was grown. Earth tricked Cronus, convincing him to vomit up the children he had swallowed. First he vomited up the stone, then the gods. And chief among the gods when all were freed was Zeus. It was he who led the gods against the Titans and banished the Titans forever from the heavens.

But what of mortals in all this? There were created in all five races of humans. The first, created by the Titans, was the golden race, those who lived in perfect peace and happiness and became, at death, guardians of humankind. The second race was the silver race, created by the gods but removed by Zeus himself because these arrogant new beings would not honor their creators. These beings then became underworld spirits. The third race was the bronze race, created by Zeus, but its people proved so warlike that they fought until they had destroyed themselves. The fourth race, which alone has no metal attributed to it, was the next created by Zeus, and it was that of the great heroes and demigods. And the fifth race still exists. It is the iron race, our world, the race that has been born to trouble and hard work. But it is the race that has the good mixed in with the bad, and hope forever mixed in with sorrow.

Source

Hesiod. *Theogony*. Indianapolis: Library of Liberal Arts, 1953.

YMIR AND THE CREATION
A Myth from the Norse

A people's myths reflect their environment. It's not surprising, then, to find that this myth from the ancient Norse involves creation out of ice and cold. As with the Greek myth of creation, in which Zeus replaces the older god, Cronos, so does Odin, or more correctly, Odhinn, represent a new order replacing the old. Does this mean a new invasion of humans replacing the ways of the old? Possibly. It may also symbolize new ways taking over within a culture.

One of the other main themes in this myth is the building of a world from a dead body of a giant or monster. Sometimes the body comes from a willing sacrifice, such as occurs in the Indian myth, "The Cosmic Egg," later in this chapter.

*T*here were, at the beginning, and perhaps even now, many realms, layers, planes of existence. The southernmost of those realms was Muspell, forever seething and blazing with flame. The northernmost was

Niflheim, forever covered with planes of snow and hills of ice. Between them lay Ginnungagap, chaos, vast emptiness. Here the slaggy lava rivers of Muspell met the icy rivers of Niflheim, and from that meeting were eternal clouds of mist and frost.

But in the very middle of Ginnungagap was a balance between heat and cold, and here the ice began to thaw. It dripped down. And each drop engendered life, until the drops had congealed into the form of a giant, Ymir.

Ymir was the first of the family to be known later as Frost Giants, cold and cruel.

Meanwhile, more of the life-engendering drops fell, congealing this time into the form of a cow, Audumla. Ymir fed off her milk, while Audumla fed off the ice, licking and licking at it.

The more Audumla licked, the more the ice took shape. By the end of the first day of her licking, a man's head had emerged, and by the end of the third day, the whole man was revealed.

The name of this first man was Buri. His son, begotten no one knows how, was Bor. Bor married Beatla, the daughter of the Frost Giant Bolthor, and had three children with her: Odin, Vili, and Ve.

There was strong hatred between the sons of Bor and the Frost Giants, particularly against Ymir. At last Odin, Vili, and Ve fought and slew Ymir. The torrents of blood from the corpse drowned all the Frost Giants save one giant and his wife, and from them the race continued.

Odin, Vili, and Ve made the world from Ymir's body. His flesh was the fields, his bones the mountains. His teeth were the rocks and boulders, and his blood the world-encircling seas. The three brothers raised his skull to form the dome of the sky, its four corners at the far ends of the world. Four dwarves sat at those corners, and their names were East, North, West, and South. Ymir's brain became the world's clouds.

But the new world was dark. Odin, Vili, and Ve took two great embers from Muspell and cast them up to be the sun and moon. Smaller embers became the stars.

And so the world and the heavens were created.

Sources

Crossley-Holland, Kevin. *The Norse Myths*. New York: Pantheon Books, 1980.
Sturluson, Snorri. *The Prose Edda*. Translated by Jean I. Young. Berkeley: University of California Press, 1954.

VAINAMOINEN AND THE CREATION
A Myth from Finland

Vainamoinen is one of the prime heroes of the *Kalevala*, which has been called the Finnish national epic. Rather than being one continuous tale like the Greek *Iliad*, though, it is a compilation of ancient mythic ballads assembled into coherent order by Finnish scholar Elias Lonnrot in the late nineteenth century. The subjects of these ballads range from the creation of humanity to the adventures of the heroes as they seek to win wives or slay monsters. See, for an example of the latter, "The Death and Rebirth of Lemminkainen."

Although this myth begins with a primal sea and a female being who is not a human, the central creator and main protagonist turns out to be nothing less than an archetype figure. An archetype is a basic symbolic figure found in every human psyche regardless of culture, and Vainamoinen definitely represents the archetype of the wise old man. The wise old man is the same role that Merlin plays in the Arthurian cycle, Gandalf fills in J. R. R. Tolkien's epic fantasy *The Lord of the Rings*, and Obi-Wan Kenobi plays in the motion picture *Star Wars*. Vainamoinen is even born old and wise, having stayed so long in his mother's womb.

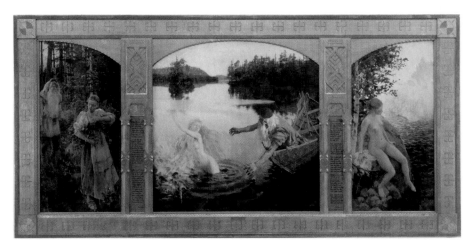

Akseli Gallen-Kallela's 1891 painting *Aino Myth*, which depicts a passage from the *Kalevala*, a compilation of old Finnish ballads and poems. (*Ateneum Art Museum/Antell Collection. Central Art Archives/Hannu Aaltonen*)

*O*nce there was nothing but the air and the ocean. That, and one virgin of the air. Lonely, she wandered in the empty mansions of the air, then left her realm, descending, and sank upon the mighty ocean, on that wide expanse of water.

Then a tempest tore the ocean and drove the maiden over waves, here and there, till she conceived and in the ocean grew great with child. Now she was the Water-Mother, floating on the endless seas. But never could she lose her burden, never could she give birth. For seven centuries, alone and weeping, she floated there upon the waves.

But at last a bird came flying, a lovely teal who lacked a land, lacked a tree, lacked all place to build her nest. The Water-Mother pitied her and bent up a knee, and the teal built her nest upon it. She laid seven eggs within the nest, six of gold, the seventh of iron.

For three days the teal brooded on her nest while the nest grew warmer and warmer still. On the fourth day the nest burned like fire, like molten flame, and the Water-Mother straightened her leg with a surge of pain. The eggs fell into the sea and shattered.

And that was the beginning of the world. One eggshell made the earth itself. Another eggshell made the dome of heaven. Its yolk was the sun, its white the moon, while its specklings became the stars and clouds.

Another nine years she lay rocking in the waves, the Water-Mother. On the dawning of the tenth she raised a hand and began creation, began the ordering of the world. At her gesture, headlands grew, and her feet dug caves for fish. Diving, she set depths to oceans; rising, she set rivers to flow, rocks to rise, all the fine forms of creation.

Still unborn remained her child, grown old and named Vainamoinen. Calling on the gods and forces, he sought his freedom but found none till at last he forced and battered his way out into the world.

And he was a hero born, mage and bard, the first of births—but that is for another story.

Sources

Lonnrot, Elias. *The Kalevala*. Translated by Francis Peabody Magoun Jr. Cambridge: Harvard University Press, 1963.

———. *The Kalevala*. Translated by W. F. Kirby. London: Athlone, 1983.

WITH THE HELP OF A MOLE
A Myth from Romania

This myth can be seen as more earthy, more literally down to earth, than the others. The idea of a Judeo-Christian deity taking advice from a mole may seem startling to some—but the story is probably a great deal older than it might seem. Deities creating the world with the help of lowly animals turn up in mythologies from around the world, and one can speculate that this tale may either represent the triumph of the "little guy" or reflect an ancient tradition of shamanistic animal helpers.

*I*t was God who made heaven. Then, after God had measured the space underneath heaven by using a ball of thread, the creator began forming the earth. A mole poked its head up and asked to help.

So God gave the mole the thread to hold while the creator wove the patterns of the earth. But the mole wasn't sure of its job. Sometimes it would let out too much thread. At last the earth had grown too large for the space under heaven.

The mole was so unhappy about what had happened that it burrowed into the earth. That is why moles live underground today.

God sent a bee to look for the missing mole with the message that the creator wasn't angry. God just wanted the mole's advice on how to correct the mistake.

Sure enough, the bee found the mole. But when the mole heard the bee's message, it just laughed. What, a humble mole help the creator?

The bee, however, wasn't going to give up, not just yet. It hid in a flower and waited. Aha, here was the mole. It was muttering to itself about what it would do if it was the creator.

"I would squeeze the earth," it said, "yes, squeeze it and make it smaller. Then there would be mountains, of course, and valleys, too. But that smaller earth would fit underneath heaven."

When the mole had finished, the bee flew straight to God and told the creator what had been said. God did what the mole had said, and sure enough, everything fit fine.

Sources

Bartlett, Sarah. *The World of Myths and Mythology: A Source Book*. London: Blanford, 1998.

Leeming, David Adams, and Margaret Adams Leeming. *A Dictionary of Creation Myths*. New York and Oxford: Oxford University Press, 1995.

THE SAGA OF CREATION
A Myth from Magyar Hungary

This myth begins with the basic primal sea theme seen in so many other myths, including the Babylonian creation myth that opens this chapter. Then the strong image of a male deity seems to lead to Christian elements—but is promptly placed back into the pagan era by the equally strong appearance of the female deity. The deities are now clearly identified as Eternity and the Heavenly Mother. Their golden son, Magyar, is just as clearly the culture hero, the hero who is the inspiration for a people, and in this case the one from whom the Magyar people claim descent. And finally there is the motif of a world created out of earth brought up by a successful diver.

The endless sea's waves roll and wave, roll and wave. No earth is there yet, no solid land.

But high in the heavens, above all the sea, sits the greatest of all, the Heavenly Father on his golden throne, the white-haired god of eternity, dressed in robes of black that bear a thousand shining stars. Beside him is his wife, the Heavenly Mother, dressed in robes of white that bear a thousand shining stars. They have existed for all of time and will exist for all of time to come.

In front of the eternal two stands their son, the beautiful golden-haired sun god, Magyar. He asks, "When shall we create the human world, my father?"

"My son, let us now create their own world for the humans now, so that they, your sons, shall have a home."

"How shall it be done, my father?"

"In the depths of the endless sea are the sleeping seeds, the dreaming eyes. They must be brought up from the depths so that a world can be created from them."

"I shall do it," cries the son.

He shakes himself and turns into a shining golden bird, a golden diving duck. Down he flies to the endless sea, and swims a while on the ocean waves. Then down he dives into the endless sea, hunting for the bottom. But he cannot reach it. Breathless, the golden one resurfaces.

He swims for a time, gathering his strength, regaining his breath. Then down he dives into the ocean depths, diving deeper, down to darkness. And this time his duck's bill strikes the bottom, strikes the sand. He catches some of it in his bill and shoots up for the surface like a golden arrow. He has brought up the sleeping seeds, the dreaming eyes.

The sand becomes the living world. And the dreaming eyes open and change and become the living beings. Human now, they thrive upon the world.

Sources

Degh, Linda. *Folktales of Hungary*. Chicago: University of Chicago Press, 1965.

Zampleni, Arpid. *Turanian Songs: Legendary and Historical Hero-Songs*. Translated by Gregory A. Page. Budapest and New York: Franklin Society, 1916.

THE COSMIC EGG
A Myth from Ancient India

Some myths are more metaphysical than others. Here is a creation of something from nothing—which also has echoes in modern scientific studies of quantum physics. The creator who appears in this myth is a willing sacrifice, splitting himself into the world and its inhabitants out of loneliness. Other myths create the world from the body of a slain deity or monster, such as occurs in the myth of Ymir, earlier in this chapter.

*A*t first there was nothing but the primordial ocean and the endless darkness of chaos. Then a golden egg floated in the ocean. For a billion years and more of mortal time did it float untouched, unaltered amid nothing.

There within the golden egg was something. It was Purusha, alone and growing ever more lonely. The fire of need, of longing for a world, heated the waters, heated the egg, and at last the egg cracked open.

Purusha rose from the broken shell with a thousand heads, a thousand eyes, a thousand hands, all and one at once. To ease his loneliness, he split himself apart. A quarter of him became the world, as well as the creator of Viraj, the female force of being. The remaining three-quarters Purusha dismembered to bring about the universe. Purusha's mouth became Brahma, the force of the universe; his mind and eyes became the moon and sun; his navel, the air; his breath, the wind; and his feet, the earth of the world. He became all of existence, everything and in everything.

But should Purusha ever reassemble himself, then everything would be ended.

Sources

Danielou, Alain. *The Myths and Gods of India*. Rutland, VT: Inner Traditions International, 1991.

Elwin, Verrier. *Myths of Middle India*. Oxford: Oxford University Press, 1949.

HOW THE WORLD WAS CREATED AND RE-CREATED
A Myth from India

A country made up of as many cultures and beliefs as is India is likely to have several versions of a creation myth. This one includes the concept of the cyclical state of being, in this case the cycle of floods that regularly cleanses the world.

There is also the "something from nothing" element, the lotus from which Brahma is born. Here the myth differs from the Greek and the Norse versions in that there is no slaying of the father or the older deity. Instead, most of the deadly creations reform, while the few who remain deadly ones become *rakshasas*, demons who prey on humanity.

The myth also has the theme of a subordinate creator, in this case Rudra.

*I*n the long-ago time before now, the earth was shaped not like an orb but like a wheel. In the center of the world was the heaven. It was called Mount Meru, and it stood higher than any mortal mountain ever stood. Encircling Mount Meru was the river Ganges, and along the banks of that river stood the cities of Indra and the other gods. The foothills of Mount Meru were the home of the *gandharvas*, the good spirits. Deep in the valleys lurked the demons. The entire world rested on the open hood of the mightiest of serpents, Shesha.

Whenever a flood covered the universe, and there were many floods in the beginning of days, mighty Shesha coiled up on the back of a tortoise. But at the end of each deluge, Shesha uncoiled again as the world was born anew.

Then after ages of this pattern, a difference arose. Even as water covered the world, a golden cosmic egg came floating over the flood. For a thousand years it floated, and for a thousand years the lord of the universe brooded over it.

At last a blazing bright lotus flower grew from the lord's navel. The brilliant lotus grew and spread to enfold the entire world.

Then the great Brahma sprang from the lotus with the powers of the lord of the universe. He created the world we know from the parts of his body.

Not all went smoothly. Brahma created ignorance but then discarded it. But ignorance survived and turned into Night. From Night were born the Beings of Darkness, who set out to destroy Brahma.

"How can you eat your own father?" Brahma asked them. That made some of the Beings of Darkness ashamed. They turned aside.

In Hindu mythology, Brahma is the creator of the universe and the top member of the triad of gods that includes Vishnu and Shiva. Cambodian sandstone sculpture, second quarter, C.E. 10. (*Réunion des Musées Nationaux/Art Resource, New York*)

But others of the Beings of Darkness refused to be turned aside. They remained fixed on their desire to destroy Brahma. They became the *rakshasas*, who are the demon-kind, the enemies of men.

Brahma now brought to life four immortal and heavenly beings, sages who could finish his work. But the sages quickly lost interest in the creation. This angered Brahma, and from his anger, the being Rudra rose up. It was Rudra who finished the work.

Sources

Danielou, Alain. *The Myths and Gods of India*. Rutland, VT: Inner Traditions International, 1991.
Elwin, Verrier. *Myths of Middle India*. Oxford, UK: Oxford University Press, 1949.

CREATION FROM CHAOS: THE TAO
A Myth from China

This myth focuses primarily on the theme of order out of chaos and the need for balance in the universe as well as in human existence. It includes a symbol that is well known (if not always truly understood) in the West as well as in the East: the circle of yin and yang, the balanced opposites.

*B*efore all that is became what it is, all was empty and vast, one and nothing, not light, not darkness, rest without resting.

From out of this everything and nothing came the Tao, creating the eternal oneness, the cosmic breath. From this, pure light arose, and was yang, hot and dry. From this, too, pure darkness descended and was yin, cool and moist. The light formed the sky, the dark, the earth. And from the endless swirlings of yang and yin come their rise and fall, now Yang ascendant, now Yin. From this come the day and night, as well as the ever-changing seasons. Summer is the highest point of yang, winter the highest point of yin. But the eternal balance is always kept.

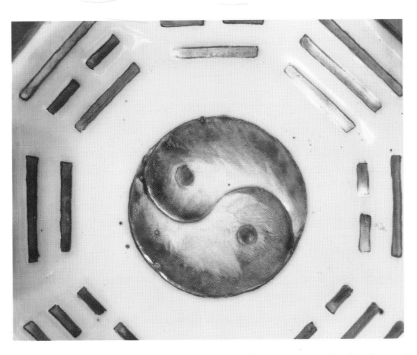

The yin and yang symbol, pictured here on a nineteenth-century ceramic plate from a Taoist temple, represents the balance of the universe. (*Werner Forman/Art Resource, New York*)

Sources

Birrell, Anne. *Chinese Mythology: An Introduction*. Baltimore: Johns Hopkins University Press, 1993.

Christie, Anthony. *Chinese Mythology*. New York: Barnes and Noble Books, 1983.

P'AN KU
A Myth from China

As in India, there are hundreds of cultures within China, and hundreds of versions of the story of creation. This myth begins with the theme of the world egg, or cosmic egg, that in which all that is to be is contained.

P'an Ku is a creator god in the literal sense, working so hard on his creation that at last, intentionally or not, he sacrifices himself and dies, his body becoming the final touches of the new earth. And just so that humanity doesn't get too haughty, note that humans come from the vermin on his body!

*A*t first there was nothing, nothing save this one thing: the great cosmic egg. And within the egg was all of chaos. Floating within the egg, within the all and nothingness of chaos, was P'an Ku, whose very name means "the divine undeveloped," "the divine embryo."

At last, fully grown, P'an Ku burst free of the egg. He was now four times the size of any human man, with two huge horns sprouting from his head, the horns that marked him as supernatural. His jaw was tusked, and all of him was covered with thick hair. But he was not monstrous, not cruel. He was a creator who sought to build order out of chaos.

From the instant of his breaking free of the cosmic egg, P'an Ku held a hammer and chisel—some say an adze—in his hand. With these tools, he began to build the world. It was he who used his hammer and chisel to break the sky free from the earth. It was he who hammered down the valleys and chiseled courses for the rivers, and he who hammered up the mountains and chiseled them into shape.

Now P'an Ku went to work once more, placing the sun, moon, and stars up in the heavens where they belong. He carved out the great bowls in the world for where the four seas would go.

By now, P'an Ku was deathly weary from his labors and from his great age. As P'an Ku collapsed and died, his sighs became the winds and the last cry of his dying voice became the thunder. His flesh became the rich soil of the earth, and his blood became the rivers, lakes, and seas. His hair became the plants and forests, and his teeth and bones the rich ores of the earth.

And last, from the vermin on P'an Ku's body came human beings.

Sources

Birrell, Anne. *Chinese Mythology: An Introduction*. Baltimore: Johns Hopkins University Press, 1993.

Christie, Anthony. *Chinese Mythology*. New York: Barnes and Noble Books, 1983.

NÜ WA CREATES HUMANITY
A Myth from China

Here is another myth of humanity being molded from clay. What makes this one different is that the newly made humans are not distinguished by color, but by status.

Another myth about this gentle young goddess can be found in Chapter 2, wherein she mends a hole in the sky and restores order.

*I*n the ancient, ancient days, it is said, that when sky and earth were separated into two things, there were plants and animals, birds and insects. One thing only there was not, and that was humankind.

Nü Wa was the youngest daughter of the emperor of heaven, Yandi. She went down to the new earth to see it all. It was truly a lovely place, fragrant with flowers in the fields and on the trees. The forests were full of birds and animals, the lakes full of fish. All there was that was right.

But one thing alone there was not. And as she walked amid all the newness, the loveliness, Nü Wa suddenly felt terribly lonely. There was something here that was not right after all. There was no one on this beautiful new earth who could talk, or laugh, or sing.

So Nü Wa decided to change that. She bent and picked up a handful of earth. Mixing it with water from a nearby pond, she began sculpting a figure in her likeness. As Nü Wa finished it, the small clay figure suddenly sparked into life.

This was the first human being.

But Nü Wa didn't want the first human to be alone. So she went right on making other human beings, women and men both, and watching them spark into life. They were happy to be alive. They laughed and sang. They danced happily about.

And Nü Wa was lonely no longer.

An illustration of the Chinese goddess Nü Wa from the first century C.E. Half woman, half dragon, Nü Wa created the first humans by shaping clay in her likeness. (*Mary Evans Picture Library*)

But one story adds to this. It says that Nü Wa did mold humans out of yellow clay. But, it says, she was very young, and the clay was heavy. So she dipped a rope into the clay and lifted it that way. Some clay clung to the rope, while other bits dripped off.

But all the clay became human beings. The clay that had stuck to the rope, the finely molded yellow clay, became rich and noble men and women, the type who are afraid to let go of their importance. Those that had dripped from the rope also became men and women. They were poor and low. But they were free. Which is better?

Sources

Birrell, Anne. *Chinese Mythology: An Introduction*. Baltimore: Johns Hopkins University Press, 1993.

Christie, Anthony. *Chinese Mythology*. New York: Barnes and Noble Books, 1983.

THE TWO SONS OF HEAVEN
A Myth of the Mongol People

Here is another myth involving two creators—but this is one of the "evil twin" myths of a good brother, Ulgen Tenger, and his less appealing brother, Erleg Khan. See also the Micmac myth, "Glooscap and His People," later in this chapter, for another case of good and evil twins.

This myth also includes the "earth diver" theme in its more complete form as a competition of birds or animals. See also "The Saga of Creation," the Magyar myth. Furthermore, the myth adds a "how and why" element, in this case involving the dog, his coat, and the reason for his doggy smell.

*I*n the long-ago days, there was Father Heaven, and there were his two sons, Ulgen Tenger and Erleg Khan. Ulgen Tenger was given the lordship of the upper world, while Erleg Khan was given the lordship of the lower world.

Now, in those long-ago days, the earth was covered with water. There was as yet no land at all. Ulgen Tenger thought that something surely must lie under all the water. So he asked the loon to bring up whatever lay below the water.

But the loon could not dive so deeply.

Next, the golden-eyed duck was asked to bring up whatever lay below the water. The duck dove deep enough. It brought up mud, which Ulgen Tenger spread out over the water. It became a small island. Ulgen Tenger lay down on the new land, smiled, and fell asleep.

Erleg Khan saw the island and was jealous. Since Ulgen Tenger was asleep, Erleg Khan stole silently up and tried to steal the new land out from under his brother. But what happened, much to his surprise, was that the land simply stretched out in all directions as he pulled, and became the world.

Ulgen Tenger woke. He molded animals and humans out of mud, then spread them out to dry. But what if his brother stole them? Ulgen Tenger brought the dog to life so that it could guard the new figures while he was away. It had no fur, this new dog, but it could speak. And it promised to keep watch faithfully.

Erleg Khan saw what his brother had done, and was jealous. He stole forward, wanting to see the new beings. The dog bared its teeth and would not let him come close. But the day was cold, and snow had begun to fall. The furless dog shivered.

Erleg Khan tempted him. If the dog would allow him to merely see the new bodies, why, he would give the dog a beautiful, beautiful fur coat.

The shivering dog agreed. He wanted that coat! He accepted that beautiful, beautiful fur coat and let Erleg Khan near the bodies. Erleg Khan laughed, then spat on the bodies. Now the race of humans would not be immortal. They would have diseases and die.

Ulgen Tenger returned. He saw that the dog had fur, and knew who had done that. Racing to the humans, he saw that they had been damaged, and knew who had done that—yes, and that the dog had betrayed his trust. Furious, Ulgen Tenger took away the dog's voice, made that beautiful coat foul-smelling, and commanded that from now on, all dogs would follow humans and obey them.

And so it was.

Sources

Heissig, Walther. *The Religions of Mongolia*. London: Routledge and Kegan Paul, 1980.
Metternich, Hilary Roe. *Mongolian Folktales*. Boulder, CO: Avery, 1996.

THE BEGINNING: IZANAGI AND IZANAMI
A Myth from Japan

Most versions of this myth are vague at their beginning, as befits the subject: the primal chaos. Whether or not a cosmic egg is involved depends on the version cited. It is also unusual in that the thing that

The "Wedded Rocks" at Futamugaura in Ise Bay. It is believed that the rocks sheltered the god Izanagi and the goddess Izanami, the legendary creators of Japan. (*Werner Forman/Art Resource, New York*)

holds creation gives birth to reeds, which then in turn give birth to the gods.

In addition, it is one of the few myths in which the two creators, Izanagi and Izanami, are clearly both brother and sister and husband and wife. Does that reflect an ancient custom, such as was typical of the Egyptian royal families, or is it strictly a mythic element? There's now no way to be certain. The myth definitely does reflect a cultural bias, though, showing a good male of the daylight and an evil female of the darkness. Or could it just be portraying the tragedy of a good marriage turned bad?

*I*n the beginning, there was chaos, roiling and formless as a sea of oil. Or perhaps there was a cosmic egg, formless yet life-bearing. Which it was, no one knows for certain.

But from the confusion arose a thing. What was it? It grew like a reed shoot and was the primal force of formed life. Immediately after it began to grow, other deities sprang into being, a confusion of existences, seven generations in all, equally balanced male and female, though there was nothing certain yet.

But out of the seventh generation of these deities arose one male god, Izanagi, and one female god, Izanami. Brother and sister, they went forth over the floating bridge of heaven, the arch of the sky, and plunged a glittering spear into the chaos foaming and roiling below them. They stirred it as a cook stirs a boiling soup. And the chaos began to congeal and thicken into land and sea. As the spear was withdrawn, a few drops fell from it and congealed into an island, Onogoro "island," that congeals on its own.

This was to be the center of the new earth. Izanagi and Izanami went down to it. Curious about themselves and their newly made forms, they studied each other, male and female, and knew that they were meant to be together.

Their marriage created god after god, deities of sea and mountain, forest and island, the eight islands of Japan. But when Izanami gave birth to the deity of fire, she was burned so badly that she died.

Grieving and raging, Izanagi beheaded the fire deity, and the flaming drops brought forth yet more deities.

But Izanagi ignored that. He followed Izanami to the land of darkness, where she now dwelled in a castle. There he begged her to return with him, saying that their work of creation was not yet complete. But she could not return; she had already tasted the food of the land of darkness. Telling him to leave, Izanami retreated into the castle. But Izanagi followed her—and saw her as a rotting corpse. Horrified, he recoiled. And Izanami, furious that he had seen her in such a state, sent demons of the land of darkness after him.

Izanami fled. The demons raced after him. He hurled his headdress behind him, and it turned to grapes.

The demons stopped to devour the grapes. But they soon raced after him. Izanami hurled the right-hand comb from his hair behind him, and it turned into a thicket of bamboo shoots.

The demons stopped to devour the shoots. But they soon raced after him. At last, at the door between the lands of light and darkness, Izanami fought off the demons with his sword, then hurled three peaches at them. Stunned by these signs from the living world, the demons retreated. Izanami blocked the passage between the two lands with a huge rock.

From the land of darkness, Izanami shrieked a curse: She would slay a thousand lives in the land of light every day.

Izanagi shouted back that a thousand new lives would be born every day. There must be a balance, and there would be a balance!

At last there was a reluctant peace. Izanagi and Izanami made the final break and pronounced themselves forever divorced.

Sources

Kawai, Hayao. *The Japanese Psyche: Major Motifs in the Fairy Tales of Japan*. Dallas: Spring Publications, 1988.

New Larousse Encyclopedia of Mythology. Translated by Richard Aldington and Delano Ames. London, New York: Hamlyn, 1968.

THE CREATION STORY
A Myth of the Tagalog of the Philippines

Here is another "primal sea" myth, but with odd protagonists: sky, kite, and bamboo. The myth doesn't explain where or how the primal humans originated, but simply continues on with them having too many children. From there it becomes the myth of how the human races began—and how the class structures and slavery began as well.

*W*hen the world began, there was no land, only endless sea, endless sky. Between those two, sea and sky, soared a hawk, the type known as a kite. Now, this bird, this kite, had been soaring and soaring for longer than time itself. And by now the kite was weary of this endless flying. But there was no place for her to alight.

Angry and tired, the kite began beating its wings so hard that the waters of the endless sea were stirred up. The great waves surged up and were thrown against the sky. The sky was angry, too. It began throwing down islands at the sea, small ones at first, then larger ones, so many islands that at last the sea was weighted down and could do nothing more than run back and forth. It does so to this day.

Now the sky ordered the kite, "Land on one of the islands. Build yourself a nest. And leave both sea and sky in peace!"

At this time there was the land breeze and the sea breeze. They met and mingled, and their child was a bamboo floating about on the waters. One day while the kite was on the beach of her island, the bamboo, riding the waves, came in toward land and struck the kite on her feet. What was this? Angry that she'd been struck, the kite pecked the bamboo as hard as she could.

The bamboo split open. From one section came a man, and from the other came a woman.

What was to be done with these two strange beings? All the birds and fish, the winds, and even the earthquake met and talked it over. At last it was decided: The man and woman should wed.

So they married. And from that marriage came children, many children. Too many children, surely! These were the ancestors of all the races on the earth.

By now, the first parents were growing very weary of having so many noisy, idle children around. They wished to be rid of them. But where could the children be sent? Every day there seemed to be more of them. At last their father grabbed up a stick and began beating them all.

The children fled in all directions. Some hid in the walls of the house. Some found hidden rooms in which to shelter. Some of the children ran outside. And some fled to the sea.

It came to pass that those who hid in the walls became the ancestors of slaves. Those who found hidden rooms became chiefs of the islands. Those who ran outside were free people. And those who had fled to the sea—when their children came sailing back years later—they were the first white people.

Sources

Cole, Mabel Cook. *Philippine Folk Tales*. Chicago: A. C. McClurg, 1916.
Eugenio, Damiana L. *Philippine Folk Literature: The Myths*. Diliman, Quezon City: University of the Philippines Press, 1993.

SOMETHING FROM NOTHING
A Myth from Melanesia

This is one of the few myths that begin not with a primal ocean but with a primal desert, and a creator, Qat, and his eleven brothers, who are born when a rock splits open. It contains the variation of carving humanity from wood rather than modeling humanity from clay, as well as a symbolic death and rebirth. And it contains the "twin brothers" theme. Even though Marawa isn't a twin, he is definitely inept, though not truly evil, and his meddlings do bring about death for humanity.

There is another origin theme in this myth: the origin of darkness, which in this case has to be imported from other lands.

There was the world, and nothing else. It was a desert, empty, sterile, caught in endless light. There was no summer, no winter, no oceans with their tides. Utterly stagnant was it all, until the coming of Qat.

Where did Qat come from? He was born, it is said, on Banks Island of Vanna Lava, the very center of the world. A rock split suddenly and Qat emerged—his mother the rock Qatgoro, his father no one—along with his eleven brothers. Qatgoro, it is said, can still be seen near the village of Alo Sepere.

What was Qat? No one knows for sure. A powerful spirit, certainly. For it was Qat who decided it was time for there to be life. He began to make up things, plants, trees, animals, and as soon as he'd made them up, they came to life.

Now Qat decided to make up something new. He carved human figures from the wood of the dracaena tree, giving them arms and legs and all the right joints. Qat hid them away for three days in the shade the trees cast. Then he stood the figures in a row and danced. They began to move. Qat played upon his drum. The figures began to move, then to dance. Soon they were able to run about by themselves. Qat divided them up, male and female, so that each man had a woman and each woman a man, then let them go off to be free.

Now, of those eleven brothers, one was an envious sort, Marawa. He wanted to make up life, too. But Marawa was not the cleverest of the brothers. He made his figures from the wood of a different tree, which was the first mistake. He danced before them correctly, though. But when the figures began to move, instead of hiding them in the shade, Marawa hid them in a hole in the ground and covered up the hole. Since Qat had left his figures for three days, Marawa left his for seven, just to be sure. But when he dug up the figures—oh, they were rotten! They stank!

It is Marawa's fault that death came into the world.

Meanwhile, Qat decided to have pigs stand on two legs like humans. But they looked so silly that his other brothers began to laugh and mock the pigs. Qat felt sorry for the pigs, so he made their legs shorter so that they could walk properly on all fours.

Now his brothers found something else they didn't like. They were tired of light, everlasting, never-dimming light!

Qat didn't know what to do about this. He didn't know how one made up the opposite of light. So he began hunting about. Qat heard that there was said to be something called "night" over in the Torres Islands. Off he sailed, with a gift of pigs. That, they say, is how pigs got to the Torres Islands.

At last Qat returned to Vanna Lava. He showed his brothers how to make sleeping mats. But no sooner had they lain down on the mats than they sprang up again in alarm.

The sun was disappearing below the western horizon! Qat shook out the night over the world, and that was the beginning of the first darkness.

Now the brothers were really afraid. What if the darkness never ended?

It would end, Qat assured them.

The brothers lay back down on the mats. What was this? Their eyes were closing! Were they dying?

It was only sleep.

Only birds know when the night should be over. Qat listened for the birds to start chirping and singing. With his knife, he cut a hole in the darkness. The light had returned, and it was the first day.

So it has gone ever since, day, night, and day again, and so, thanks to Qat, it will keep on going.

Sources

Andersen, Johannes C. *Myths and Legends of the Polynesians*. Rutland, VT: Charles E. Tuttle, 1969.

Codrington, R. H. *Melanesians: Studies in Their Anthropology and Folk-lore*. Oxford: Oxford University Press, 1891.

Poignant, Roslyn. *Oceanic Mythology*. London: Hamlyn, 1967.

THREE CREATIONS
A Myth of the Dusuns of Borneo

Here's a myth showing a creator experimenting with the proper materials for building humanity, and ending by modeling humans out of clay. There's a charming ending to the story, in which the creations aren't considered perfect until they can laugh.

*O*nce there was only one, Towadakon, alone in all the world. Towadakon decided that there must be more than this aloneness. There must be other beings who could speak and dance and laugh.

"I will make people," he said.

But of what should people be made? Towadakon cut down a tree and smoothed the bark off the trunk. He carved a man from the trunk.

"Speak," he commanded the man of wood.

But it stood as still as its parent tree.

"I don't want this thing," Towadakon said. "It can do nothing."

So he threw the wooden figure away and looked for something else out of which to make people. Towadakon found a large, smooth stone and carved a man from it.

"Dance," he commanded the man of stone.

But it stood as still as its parent stone.

"I don't want this thing," Towadakon said. "It can do nothing."

So he threw the stone figure away and looked for something else out of which to make people. But there was nothing . . . except earth. Towadakon molded a man out of earth.

When he said to it, "Speak," it said nothing.

When he said to it, "Dance," it did nothing.

But when Towadakon said to it, "Laugh," the figure of earth began to laugh. And as it laughed, it became human.

And it was with laughter that the human race began.

Sources

Furness, William H. *Folk-lore in Borneo: A Sketch.* Wallingford, PA: n.p., 1899.
Poignant, Roslyn. *Oceanic Mythology.* London: Hamlyn, 1967.

RANGI AND PAPA
A Myth from the Maori

This is a myth of the separation of earth and sky, who are portrayed here as lovers who don't wish to be separated. They are creators who would never allow their creations to live if their love were permitted to continue. When they are torn apart and the world expands, the myth adds an explanation for hurricanes. The ancient Egyptians also had a myth of how sky, Nut, and earth, Geb, who were lovers, had to be separated for the good of humanity. For a different view of the same theme, see the San myth "Moving the Sky."

*I*n the dawn of time, Rangi and Papa lay entwined, as they had lain as lovers since before time began. Rangi was Father Sky and Papa was Mother Earth. And over the endless ages, divine children were born to them. Indeed, from their endless loving, all that was to be was created.

But so tightly entwined were they that there was no room for what must be. The divine children were cramped and crowded, unhappy and unhappier yet with each new birth. They met—how could they not in those crowded conditions?—and whispered plots on how their lot could be bettered.

It was Tu, he who would be known as Father of Humanity, who spoke first. "We must kill Rangi and Papa!"

The others overruled this with cries of horror. Over their noise, Tane-mahuta, he who would be known as Father of Forests, spoke up. "Let us separate Rangi and Papa. If we do, then Rangi will truly be Father Sky over us, guarding us, and Papa will truly be Mother Earth, nurturing us."

The others agreed with cries of gladness. Only Tawhiri, he who would be Father of the Winds, was silent. He was saddened and angered by the thought that Rangi and Papa should be separated after so long an embrace.

A woodcarving depicts the Maori gods Rangi, the sky father, and Papa, the earth mother. In the Maori myth, the divine lovers are separated from their embrace by Tane-mahuta, father of the forests. (*Werner Forman/Art Resource, New York*)

Now all the deities took turns trying to push and pry their parents apart from each other. The gods of fields and ocean tried and failed. They could not budge the two at all. The others tried and failed as well. Rangi and Papa continued to cling to each other.

But now Tane-mahuta tried. The Father of Forests slid roots between Rangi and Papa, then forced leafy branches into the small gap. He sent the force of all the trees into the gap, branches growing upward, roots growing downward. The gap grew, and grew again. Slowly Rangi and Papa were parted; slowly light and space swept in between them. All that was created spread out over Mother Earth, below Father Sky.

But Rangi and Papa raged. "How could you do such a thing to us?" Papa cried. "How could you work so terrible a crime against your parents?"

Tawhiri, Father of Winds, heard and heeded. He whirled up into the realm of Father Sky and fought with Tu, Father of Humanity. To this day, those two fight. And when Tawhiri is at his utter rage, then humanity is plagued with hurricanes. Each storm he sends is a memory of Rangi and Papa, divine lovers forever separated.

Sources

Alpers, Antony. *Maori Myths and Tribal Legends*. London: John Murray, 1964.
Reed, A. W. *Myths and Legends of Maoriland*. Sydney: Angus and Robertson, 1950.

TA'AROA
A Myth from Tahiti

This begins as another cosmic egg myth. But there is a difference: Ta'aroa does create everything from his body, but he remains alive, part of everything. He also calls upon a helper to aid him in creating humanity. See as well the Chinese myth "P'an Ku" and the Indian myth "How the World was Created and Re-Created" in this chapter.

First there was nothing but the cosmic egg. Then within the egg was Ta'aroa. He lived alone in the boundaries of the egg's shell for time outside of time, but at last he knew he must learn what lay outside his shelter.

So Ta'aroa hatched free of the egg. He found himself alone again, this time in endless, directionless chaos. Ta'aroa called for up or down, for light or dark or shape, but there was nothing.

Since he could not retreat back into the broken-open eggshell, Ta'aroa built a new shell for himself, much smaller than the old, and retreated within that instead, mulling over what should be done next.

At last he decided a world must be built. The new shell would be its round surface, and the old shell would be the arch of sky over it. Ta'aroa decided that he would be a deity of four aspects: sky, earth, foundation, and underworld. He also cast himself into the aspect of sea.

But the new world needed finishing. Ta'aroa's own body became the new world's art. His arms and legs were its strength, his bones were its mountains. His organs were the clouds in its sky, his intestines the fish of the sea. His blood was the rainbow. Now Ta'aroa was all of everything and part of it all.

Ta'aroa, though, kept his head for himself. He knew he needed an assistant, so he called upon Tu, a marvelous craftsman deity. Tu helped Ta'aroa design humanity.

So Ta'aroa's work was at last complete.

Sources

Andersen, Johannes C. *Myths and Legends of the Polynesians*. Rutland, VT: Charles E. Tuttle, 1969.
Knappert, Jan. *Pacific Mythology*. London: Aquarian Press, 1992.

CREATION OF EARTH AND LIFE
A Myth from Samoa

This is an example of how highly detailed a creation myth can be, with
divisions and subdivisions of every branch of nature, from sky to rock.
It is included not so much for its storytelling use but as an indication
of how much detail a professional storyteller in some cultures was
expected to memorize and recite without mistake. See also "Creating
Gods and Life" in Chapter 4.

In the time before time, there was no sky, no land, no sea, no living
things. There was only one alone in all of that great expanse, and that
was the god Tagaloa. His full name is Tagaloa-fa'atutupu-nu'u, which is to
say, Tagaloa the creator of all. Nothing else was there, although all things
were about to be created. Nothing else was there save where he stood.
Under his feet sprang up the primal rock.

Then Tagaloa said to the rock, "You shall split up." The rock split. From it
came Papa-ta'oto, the rock that lies upon the ground, then Papa-sosolo, the
rock that creeps in heat. From it came Papa-lau-a'au, the rock of the reef,
and Papa-tu, the rock that stands up. From it came Papa-'ano-'ano, the rock
that cannot be cut, and Papa-'ele, the rock that is clay. From it came Papa-
'amu-'amu, the rock that is coral, and his children.

Tagaloa was not yet done. He stood facing the west, spoke words we know
not, and struck the rock with his right hand. It split open toward the right
side, and the earth and sea came forth.

Then Tagaloa turned to face the east and spoke again to the rock. The fresh
water of the earth poured out. Then Tagaloa spoke again to the rock, and
the sky soared up, and with it, Ilu, immensity, Mamao, space, and Niuao,
the clouds. Many other creations did Tagaloa draw from the rock. And last
of them came man and spirit, heart and will and thought.

Then Tagaloa said to the rock:

"Let the spirit and the heart and will and thought join together inside the
man."

They joined together there, and man at once became intelligent. Joined to
the earth, there were now a couple, Fatu, the first man, and 'Ele-'ele, the
first woman.

Sources

Grey, Sir George. *Polynesian Mythology*. London: Whitcombe and Tombs, 1956.
Mead, Margaret. *Coming of Age in Samoa: A Psychological Study of Primitive Youth for
    Western Civilization*. New York: William Morrow, 1961.

Sproul, Barbara C. *Primal Myths: Creating the World*. New York and San Francisco: Harper and Row, 1979.

THE CREATION OF MAN
A Thompson Indian Myth

There are two sections to this myth. The first deals with the quarrel between Sun and Earth, and its resolution. The second section concerns the Old One, the creator, who turns Earth into the earth and creates humanity and intelligence for humans.

In the long-ago days before the world was formed, Sun and Earth, Moon and Stars were beings who lived together. Earth and Sun were wife and husband, but Earth was never satisfied with him. She was forever nagging that he was ugly, or mean, or too hot.

At last Sun could take no more of her scolding. He left her, taking Moon and Stars with him.

Now Earth was very lonely and very sad.

But the Old One had been watching and knew changes must be made. He assigned Sun, Moon, and Stars to the sky, and ordered them to never again desert Earth. Then the Old One turned Earth into solid land. Her long green hair became trees and grass, her bones the rocks, and her blood the life-giving springs.

The Old One told Earth, "You will be a mother to all that live. For from you will spring their bodies, and to you they will return. You will feed them and shelter them, and they will love you."

Soon after, Earth gave birth to the first humans. But they were empty of thought or emotion. They neither ate nor drank, but merely . . . were.

The Old One would not let this mindlessness remain. He moved among the people, giving them thoughts and appetites, needs and wants. He created birds, animals, and fish, and gave them their ways of life.

Then Old One taught women how to make lodges and mats, how to find roots and berries and store them. He taught men how to make fire and to hunt and fish. He taught couples how to have children.

Now that he had finished teaching the people all that they must know, the Old One told them, "I must leave. But if you need me again, I will return. Remember that Sun is your father, Earth your mother."

The people remembered. And they still remember.

Sources

Teit, James A. *Mythology of the Thompson Indians*. New York: Brill and Stechert, 1912.

Thompson, Stith. *Tales of the North American Indians*. Bloomington: Indiana University Press, 1966.

THE ORIGIN OF THE APACHES
A Myth of the Jicarilla Apache

Several cultures in North America, including the Apache and the Hopi, have origin myths that feature the emergence from an underworld to the earth. But in the case of the Apache and the closely related Dine (more commonly but less accurately called Navajo), archaeological and linguistic evidence shows that they both belong to the Athabascan linguistic group and in the distant past migrated down from Alaska. Could they, once they'd arrived in the Southwest, have adapted local mythology to their own needs?

Included in the Apache myth is the origin of rabbits, here transformed from disobedient girls. Other tales from around the world also feature transformation as punishment, including stories about many of the British standing stones, which are said to have been sinful girls or women.

The concept of animals or birds sent out to see if the floodwaters had receded is another world theme, perhaps most familiar to Western readers from the story of Noah's Ark. For more on the great flood, see the stories of the flood in Chapter 2.

There in the realm that was under the earth, the place called Un-gó-ya-yên-ni, there was no sun, no moon, no stars. There was only the faint light that issued from the eagle feathers that the people who lived there carried. But so faint was that light that no one was content. The leaders of the people met to find a plan that would light Un-gó-ya-yên-ni more brightly.

"Let us make a sun and a moon," suggested one chief.

So the people designed a great golden disk and placed it in the sky of Un-gó-ya-yên-ni. The new sun made one complete pass across the sky. But it was too small to give enough light, so the people took it down and made it larger.

They put the sun back in the sky. But it was still too small.

Again they took it down and made it larger. But the sun was still too small.

The people repeated this four times until the sun was finally large enough and bright enough. Then they made a silver moon and placed that in the sky as well. And all the people rejoiced at the bright golden day and the silver night.

Only two did not rejoice. These two were workers of dark magic who were angry that the darkness should be replaced by light. They tried to destroy the sun and the moon so many times that the sun and the moon fled from Un-gó-ya-yên-ni and escaped into the sky of this world, where they were left alone, and where they continue to shine even to this day.

But Un-gó-ya-yên-ni was dark once more.

The people gathered in the gloom. What could they do now? They talked and danced, sang and made medicine. The sun might be gone, but the people decided to go in search of it. Their shamans caused four mountains to rise up, mountains that grew each night and rested each day. For four nights the mountains grew, until they nearly touched the sky of Un-gó-ya-yên-ni.

And there they stopped. What had gone wrong? Four boys, lightweight enough to scramble up and out, were chosen to find out why the mountains had failed to grow all the way up to the opening in the sky. In the outside world, the boys found the tracks of two girls. The girls had sneaked out in the night, and because they had done so before the mountains had finished growing, they had broken the magic. The two girls were hiding deep in a burrow in the ground. When the shamans learned who had spoiled the magic for the people, they transformed the two girls into rabbits. That was the creation of rabbits, and it was a good one for the people. The rabbit has provided food for humans down to the present.

But how were the people to get out now? They built a ladder and set it on the top of the tallest mountain. It reached the opening in the sky of Un-gó-ya-yên-ni. They sent the badger out to explore. But soon the badger returned and warned that there was water, nothing but water, everywhere but right around the opening in the sky. The badger's legs were so covered with mud that they were nearly black. And so badgers' legs remain dark to this day.

"We must wait for the water to subside," the people said.

In four days they sent the turkey up to explore. But the turkey returned to warn that there was yet no land at all to be seen. The turkey's feathers were so covered with drops of water that they shone with iridescent light. And so turkey feathers shine with iridescence to this day.

At last the wind swirled about the people and told them, "If you ask me to help you, I will drive back the water."

So the first prayers ever were made to the wind. The wind remains a powerful deity to this day.

The force of the wind drove back the waters to where the oceans lie today. The people were free to climb up and out.

Unfortunately, the wind had performed his work too well. He had dried up so much of the water that there was none left for the people to drink. But the wind answered the people's prayers, and springs and rivers sprang up.

All the people were then Apaches. But as they traveled out over the earth, groups separated from the others. They began to take different clan names and different languages.

And so the earth was populated.

Only the Jicarilla people stayed by the hole. Three times they circled it. At last they were asked, "Where do you wish to stop?"

The Jicarilla people answered, "In the middle of things."

So they were led to a place near what is now Taos. There they stopped, and there they stay, in the center of things.

Source

Mooney, James. "The Jicarilla Genesis." *American Anthropologist* 11 (1898).

FOUR CREATIONS
A Myth of the Hopi of Arizona

In this neatly ordered myth, the primal creator does what is right, then produces a nephew creator, who in turn does what he can, then creates Spider Woman to deal with the creation of plants, animals, and human beings. Spider Woman is an important figure throughout the Southwest's mythology, a powerful being who is generally beneficial to humans in need of her aid.

Almost all cultures have some version of a myth of the destruction of sinful worlds and the rebirth of cleansed ones, whether it be the biblical story of Lot or this one, in which successive worlds are swept aside and rebuilt. The ant is often seen as industrious in mythology and folklore, as well as in Aesop's fable "The Grasshopper and the Ant."

Incidentally, tree-ring dating indicates that the Hopi have lived in Oraibi since at least c.e. 1150.

At the start of things, there was no time, no place, no life, only endlessness, in which existed only the primal creator, Taiowa. It was Taiowa who created a finite being, Sotuknang, named as Taiowa's nephew.

Sotuknang's first order was to create universes, nine in all, and to establish nine solid worlds. This he did. His second order was to give these

A towering spire of sandstone in Arizona's Canyon de Chelly, known as Spider Rock, is named after Spider Woman. A powerful figure throughout the Southwest's mythology, Spider Woman is believed to be the creator of plants, animals, and humanity. (*Werner Forman/Art Resource, New York*)

worlds lands and seas. This he did. His third order was to give these worlds air and wind. This he did. His fourth order was to create life on these worlds.

How was this to be done? Sotuknang went to the first world that was to have life, and created Spider Woman. He gave her the power to create life.

Spider Woman mixed earth and saliva and modeled the first two beings. She sang the creation song over them, and they sprang to life as Poquanghoya and Palongawhoya. Ponquanghoya's job was to properly solidify the world. Palongawhoya's job was to properly resonate sound throughout the world. And both beings were sent to the poles to be sure that the world rotated as it should.

Spider Woman now made all the plants, the insects, the birds, and the animals, all from earth and saliva, and sang the creation song over all. Last of all, she made human beings, red, white, yellow, and black, four men and four women, and sang them to life. They had no speech, so Sotuknang gave them four languages and told them to always respect their creator.

The people spread out over the earth. They and the animals could speak with each other and were peaceful—at first. But as they multiplied, they began separating from each other, each one aware of the other's differences. At last only a few people from each language group remembered their creator.

Reluctantly, Sotuknang said that he must destroy this world. Only the people who still respected the creator were saved. They were given refuge with the ants in their mounds. There the people learned charity. The ants shared their food, even when they had little.

Meanwhile Sotuknang had cleansed the world with fire and begun anew. The people returned to it and promised to respect their creator. They could no longer speak with the animals, though, and feared them. The people built walls to protect themselves. And soon there were walls between people, too. Wars began. And only a few people still respected their creator.

Once again Sotuknang was forced to destroy the world. Once again, the people who remembered their creator were given shelter with the ants. This time, the world was destroyed when Palongawhoya and Poquanghoya were ordered to stop the world from turning. This sent the world out of control, tearing up mountains and churning seas.

The world was created anew again. The people crept out of the ant mounds and began multiplying once more. But they had not yet learned. Once again they began warring with each other, trying to destroy each other. Only a few still respected their creator.

Sotuknang knew that for the fourth time, he must destroy the world. This time the destruction would be a great flood. Spider Woman saved the people who still respected the creator by hiding them within a giant reed. The floodwaters swept away land and forest and sank the mountains. But the people floated safely in their giant reed. Soon, they knew, a fourth world would be ready for them.

Spider Woman warned them. This time things would be far more difficult for the people. They must keep their hearts and minds open to the place of emergence. And if they truly sought it, they would find it.

The people sailed on, crossing vast oceans, finding land but knowing each time it was not the place of emergence.

At last they came to a large island. They walked across it—only to come to another sea. They built new rafts and sailed across it. After many days of sailing, the people came to a new, vast land. The cliffs of its shore towered over them. Only by opening their minds did they find the place of emergence.

Sotuknang waited. He warned them that this fourth world would not be as beautiful or as safe as the first three. There would be heat and cold, rain and snow and drought. But if they respected their creator, all would still be well.

The people spread out over the fourth world. The Hopi settled in the arid lands that lie between the Colorado River and the Rio Grande. This hard place would never let them forget their respect for, and link with, the creator.

Sources

Waters, Frank. *Book of the Hopi*. New York: Ballantine Books, 1963.

THE ORIGIN OF THE WORLD
A Myth of the Wyandot People

Another place of origin for some cultures is a land in or above the sky. In this myth, it is a hole that has been accidentally—or possibly deliberately—dug all the way through the sky and lets the first human woman fall down to the primal sea below.

This is a very powerful myth for many of the related tribal groups of northeastern North America, including the Oneida and Iroquois. And it is a living tradition for many people in those tribes. Within it can be found several mythic elements, including the two swans who hold the young woman up; Great Turtle, who is a mythic figure of power in himself; and the "earth diver" scene, in which the world is brought up from under the primal sea. Swans are magical figures in almost every culture in which those birds are common. They often appear in world mythology and folklore as shape-shifting swan maidens. Great Turtle is a main figure in northeastern mythology as far west as the Winnebago people of Wisconsin.

Once the sun and moon are created, a new theme enters: the quarrel between them, and the explanation of why the moon shrinks and recovers every month.

Small Turtle is an interesting being, not as wise as Great Turtle, but powerful in her own way. It is she who rescues wounded Moon, and she who gets to live in the sky.

The rainbow is seen in different ways by different peoples. Those of the Judeo-Christian traditions see it as a covenant with the divine. The Kalahari peoples see it as ominous. And the Wyandot and the ancient Norse saw the rainbow as a bridge.

Now the myth shifts to the story of the good twin, Tsensta', and the evil twin, Taweskare, one a creator, the other a destroyer, and the inevitable fratricide that follows their fights.

*I*n the days before the world had humans on it, the people, the Wyandot, lived in a land above the sky.

Then one day the chief's only daughter fell ill. All the medicine men tried and failed to heal her. So the chief sent his swiftest runner to find and bring back an ancient shaman who lived apart from the others.

The ancient shaman took one look at the sick girl and told the people, "You must dig at once under the roots of the great apple tree that stands near the chief's lodge. The remedy," he stated, "lies under there."

So they hastily dug a hole under the roots and placed the sick girl in it. Was it deep enough? No! The people continued to dig, deepening and widening the hole.

With a terrible roar, the tree fell through the hole they had dug and vanished, dragging the girl down with it.

The horrified people looked down through the hole and saw a world that was nothing but endless water.

On that water swam a pair of large white swans. They saw the tree fall and hit the water with a mighty splash. But as they fought the waves the tree had caused, they also saw the girl fall, and quickly swam under her to catch her. She landed on their soft white backs, and there she rested.

"What a lovely creature we have caught!" the swans said. "But what is she? And what are we to do with her? We can't just go on swimming and holding her up forever!"

Off the two swans swam to find Great Turtle, the wisest of the wise, and brought the strange creature to where he sat. Great Turtle sent a runner to call all the animals to council so that they could decide what to do with her.

The animals gathered, bird and beast alike, and stared at the girl in amazement. "What is she?" they wondered. "What should we do with her?"

Great Turtle ruled, "One thing alone you must not do: You must not throw her into the water to die. Since she has been sent to us in so strange a fashion, there is powerful meaning to her coming. We must find a proper place for her to rest."

The swans told them all about the great tree that had fallen into the waters. Great Turtle said, "Let us return to where the tree fell. Then someone can dive down to its roots and bring up some of the earth that must still be tangled in them. That earth will make an island on which the creature can live. And I shall gladly hold the island on my back."

So off they swam to where the tree had fallen. Great Turtle ordered, "Otter, you are a fine diver. Dive down to the roots of the tree and bring up some earth."

Otter dove down and down, and was soon out of sight. Time passed, and more time. Just when the other animals were sure he would never return,

Otter came struggling back up through the water to the surface, so exhausted that he fell down dead. He had not reached the roots.

Next, Muskrat dove down and down. But he, too, failed, and he, too, died.

Beaver tried next. But he, too, failed, and he, too, died.

Diver after diver tried to reach the roots. Diver after diver failed and died. At last Great Turtle refused to order anyone else to dive. "Too many have already lost their lives! Only a volunteer will be allowed to dive."

No one spoke for a long time. Then small, ugly old Toad said, "I will try."

The animals all burst into laughter. What, ugly old Toad succeed where so many better divers had failed?

Toad merely shrugged, took a deep breath, and down she went.

The animals waited. They waited and waited, seeing nothing down there in the water. Just when they were sure Toad must have drowned, she came struggling back to the surface. Opening her mouth, she spat out a few grains of earth onto Great Turtle's shell, then fell down dead.

Small Turtle started spreading the grains of earth out over Great Turtle's shell. The earth began to grow and stretch out into an island. Soon it was large enough to make a home for the girl. The swans swam up to it, and the girl stepped off into the island. It continued to grow until it had become our island, the world we know.

But it was dark on the island. So Great Turtle called another council of the animals. A great light, they decided, must be placed in the sky.

Small Turtle spoke up. "If I could climb into the sky, I could use some of the lightning to make a light."

"Try," Great Turtle said.

Now, Small Turtle might have been small, but she had some great powers. She called, and a vast cloud loomed up. In it the animals saw rocks and broken trees being tossed about.

But Small Turtle never hesitated. She climbed up into the cloud, and it rose up into the sky. Once she was there Small Turtle busily gathered as much as she could of the lightning. She made Sun out of it. Then, so that Sun could have a mate, she made Moon, which was much brighter than it is today.

Now the animals dug a hole through the earth so that Sun and Moon could get to where they must be to begin their cycles.

The proper order of this trip was for Sun to go first, but Moon slipped through instead. So angry was Sun that he fought with her and nearly killed her.

When Moon did not appear, Small Turtle went in search of her and found her, weak and sad, in the underground world. Small Turtle brought her out, but Moon never shone as brightly again. What's more, Sun and Moon never made up after their quarrel. Every month Moon thinks that all will be well, and grows and shines brightly. But then she loses hope and shrinks away again, sliver by sliver, until she starts to hope again when the next month comes.

From then on, Small Turtle was known as Keeper of the Sky, and forever after made the sky her home. Whenever she needed to be at a council of the animals, she would ride down on the cloud that had first taken her up into the sky.

But Deer grew envious. He wanted to live up in the sky, too. So he went to Rainbow. "Let me climb up into the sky."

At first Rainbow refused. "What business do you have in the sky?"

Deer had no answer.

Rainbow also asked, "Who is sending you up there?"

Again Deer had no answer. But he kept asking, "Let me climb up into the sky."

And at last Rainbow gave in. He spread out into a brightly colored path that joined the earth to the sky. Deer hurried up into the sky.

Now, when the next council of animals was called, Deer did not appear. Great Turtle grew angry and called for Small Turtle. Down she rode on her dark storm cloud.

Great Turtle asked her, "Where is Deer?"

Small Turtle replied, "He's living in the sky. I have seen him there many times. Rainbow let him climb up there."

She showed the animals Rainbow's colorful path, stretching from the earth into the sky.

"Since Deer has shown us the way," Great Turtle said, "we will all follow him."

So all the animals climbed up into the heavens over Rainbow. They are the spirit animals, and they lived up in the sky forevermore.

Now, the girl who had fallen to earth was now a woman living with her "grandmother." This was an old woman she had found on the island.

Strangely, strangely, the woman who had fallen to earth was suddenly with child. She was bearing twin boys. One said to the other, "I will not be born in the manner of other children. Instead, I shall tear my way out through her side!"

"No!" the other twin cried. "That would kill our mother!"

"It makes no difference to me. I shall do as I wish."

So it was that the good twin was born in the manner of other children. But the evil twin tore his way out and slew his mother. And the "grandmother" knew instantly that one twin was good and the other evil. She took charge of them both, seeking to raise them properly, hoping that she could change the evil in the twin to good.

What work they were trained in was making the island ready for the coming of humanity. But no matter what the "grandmother" did, the good twin, Tsensta', remained kind, while the evil twin, Taweskare, remained cruel and disrespectful.

As they grew to be adults, Tsensta' designed the island so well that if he had no twin, hunger, work, and pain would have been unknown. But no matter what Tsensta' did, Taweskare would always find a way to twist it, claiming that what he did was keep things fair, so that people wouldn't find life too easy. But as Taweskare's evil strength grew, it was clear that he worked from sheer wickedness. Tsensta' would design gently rolling plains and lovely forests, with no rough ground. Taweskare would twist the earth into hills and mountains. He would make mounds of rough rocks and sharp stones, and block the forests with thorns and swamps. If Tsensta' designed rich fruits and berries, Taweskare would spoil them so that the fruit grew small and the berries hid amid thorns.

Finally the twins could no longer tolerate each other's work. Tsensta' knew that his brother bore a secret doom, that he would die on the antlers of a stag—but it was no secret to Tsensta'. He gathered piles of antlers and spread them along a trail, then chased Taweskare down that trail. Taweskare ran straight into the antlers, stumbled, and was stabbed to death.

After Taweskare's death, Tsensta' returned to his work, doing what he could to erase the evils his brother had created. But he could not rebuild the paradise he'd had in mind. People would have to suffer and work hard for a living. But they would still have joy.

And at last, when all was done that could be done, Tsensta' made the people.

Sources

Barbeau, Marius. *Huron and Wyandot Mythology*. Ottawa: Government Printing Bureau, 1915.

Thompson, Stith. *Tales of the North American Indians*. Bloomington: Indiana University Press, 1966.

THE TWIN CREATIONS
A Myth of the Wyandot People

For comparison, here is a second version of the myth, with a girl falling to the primal sea through her brothers' anger, and with the fight between the twin brothers toned down so that all that happens when the lesser twin tries to create life is that he ends up with monkeys. Since monkeys are hardly native to the realm of the Wyandot, this version shows what happens when a myth takes on outside influences.

*I*n the days before the world, a family of brothers and sisters lived together in the land above the sky. Life was not always easy for them. Their only meal each day was made from the corn they could gather from their corn patch.

Tired of having to gather corn for every meal, one of the young women decided, "Maybe the easiest way to do this is to just cut down the stalks. Then I can gather all the ears of corn once and for all."

So she cut down the corn stalks and gathered them all. Her brothers cried out, "You have ruined everything! You have destroyed our corn patch!"

And they dropped her through a hole in the sky, down to the world ocean far below.

Wild geese swam on that ocean. They saw the woman falling, and gathered together so that she could land gently on their backs.

But they soon got tired of carrying her, and looked for someone to take their place.

Turtle rose up out of the water and took their place. The woman who had fallen from above now rested on Turtle's back.

Then Toad dove to the bottom of the waters and came back up with a mouthful of earth. Giving it to the woman, Toad told her to sprinkle it all about her.

The woman did just that. The land grew around her, and became the world. Toad gave her seeds of corn, beans, and all the plants that could be eaten.

But after she had lived on the land for a time, the woman grew lonely. She said, "I wish I had a child."

Sure enough, soon after, she found twin boys lying alone, with no sign of any parents to care for them, and took them as her own. But while the older twin was good and kind, the younger twin was not good. He wanted only to spoil whatever his older brother made.

The elder brother created all the living beings and also the people.

His younger brother then came forward and said, "I, too, will make some people."

But he had neither the skill nor the power of the elder brother. And what he created weren't people, but monkeys. That may have shamed him. He never tried creating people again.

Sources

Barbeau, Marius. *Huron and Wyandot Mythology*. Ottawa: Government Printing Bureau, 1915.

Thompson, Stith. *Tales of the North American Indians*. Bloomington: Indiana University Press, 1966.

CREATION OF EARTH AND HUMANITY
A Myth of the Arapaho People

Here is a myth that combines creation by thought with the "earth diver" theme. It also contains the molding of animals and humans out of clay, and the assignment of different people to different regions.

*A*t the beginning, there was only one thing: water. And on that water floated the creator, Flat Pipe. It was lonely being the only one amid all the empty ocean, so he decided that there must be a change. But before he acted, he called to Man Above, the Unknowable, for advice.

"You must call upon helpers," Man Above told him. "With their aid, a world can be created."

Flat Pipe took that advice. Since there was water all around him, he thought of water people. He thought of ducks, and ducks came into being.

"Why are we here?" they asked Flat Pipe. "What are we to do?"

"You must dive to the bottom of the waters," Flat Pipe told them. "Bring me whatever is down there."

The ducks fidgeted uneasily. "How deep are the waters?" they asked.

"There is no way to know that from the surface," Flat Pipe said. "They may be very deep or quite shallow."

"We'll send the smallest first," the ducks decided.

So the tiny teal dove first. Down he swam, and down, till the others could no longer see him.

But soon the teal struggled back to the surface of the waters, gasping for air. "I . . . couldn't . . . reach the . . . bottom," he panted. "The . . . water is too . . . deep for me."

So the middle-sized mallard dove next. Down he swam, and down, till the others could no longer see him.

But after some time the mallard struggled back to the surface of the waters, and he, too, was gasping for air. "I . . . couldn't . . . reach the . . . bottom, either," he panted. "The . . . water is . . . too deep for me, too."

"Thank you for your efforts," Flat Pipe said. "But you just do not have the strength. I must think of stronger water birds."

He thought of geese, and geese came into being.

"Why are we here?" they asked Flat Pipe. "What are we to do?"

"You must dive to the bottom of the waters," Flat Pipe told them. "The ducks have already tried, but they do not have the strength. You must bring me whatever is down there."

"We are stronger," the geese agreed.

So the great geese dove next. Down they swam, and down, till the others could no longer see them.

But after a long time the geese struggled back to the surface of the waters, and they, too, were gasping for air. "We . . . couldn't . . . reach the . . . bottom, either," they panted. "The . . . water is . . . too deep for us, too."

Flat Pipe sighed. He thought about yet another water bird, the swan. And swans came into being.

"Why are we here?" they asked Flat Pipe. "What are we to do?"

"You must dive to the bottom of the waters," Flat Pipe told them. "The ducks and the geese have already tried, but they do not have the strength. You must bring me whatever is down there."

"We are stronger than ducks or geese," the swans agreed.

So the strong swans dove next. Down they swam, and down, till the others could no longer see them.

But after a long time the swans struggled back to the surface of the waters, and they, too, were gasping for air. "We . . . couldn't . . . reach the . . . bottom, either," they panted.

"I send you a warning," Man Above said to Flat Pipe. "You have created three water peoples in a row. You can create no more of them."

"What else can there be?" Flat Pipe wondered.

"Perhaps there can be something that lives on land and water both," Man Above suggested.

"What is land?" Flat Pipe wondered.

And he began to think about what it might be: Something unlike the water, yes, maybe something solid. Something on which people could walk, not swim, and not need wings.

An idea came to him, and he thought of a being that could walk and swim and need no wings. He thought of a turtle. And a turtle came into being.

"Why am I here?" she asked Flat Pipe. "What am I to do?"

"You must dive to the bottom of the waters," Flat Pipe told her. "The ducks, the geese, and the swans have already tried, but they do not have the strength. You must bring me whatever is down there."

"I will try," the turtle said, and dove.

She was gone a long time. She was gone a very long time.

"She will not return," the ducks said.

"She has drowned," the geese said.

"We will not see her again," the swans said.

"Wait," Man Above said. "If Flat Pipe has done things right, the turtle will return."

Sure enough, here came the turtle, swimming up and up through the water. She spat out a mouthful of earth.

"Well done!" Flat Pipe cried. "Now the world shall be made."

That small bit of earth began to grow and spread, spread and grow till it reached from horizon to horizon. The birds landed on it, and the turtle crawled around on it.

But this was not enough. Flat Pipe took some of the earth and molded a man and woman from it. He molded the buffalo. Then Flat Pipe molded all the other creatures, all that walk or creep, fly or swim.

"These are many living things," Flat Pipe said.

"These are too many for one piece of land," Man Above warned.

So Flat Pipe divided the earth up into land and sea. He placed animals and people in the different lands. Some of the people were lighter-skinned, others were darker-skinned.

"Now, stay where I've put you," Flat Pipe said.

But of course we know that they didn't stay put. All kinds of people can be found all over the world nowadays, even in places they don't belong.

Sources

Erdoes, Richard, and Alfonso Ortiz. *American Indian Myths and Legends.* New York: Pantheon Books, 1984.

Marriott, Alice, and Carol K. Rachlin. *Plains Indian Mythology.* New York: New American Library, 1975.

CREATION BY THOUGHT
A Myth of the Winnebago People of Wisconsin

This myth features Earthmaker's delight in the realization that he can think creation into being. As in the Borneo myth "Three Creations," it also features the need for a human body to contain a soul.

No one knows what it was that Earthmaker lay upon when first he came to consciousness. He moved, right leg, left leg, right arm, left arm, then lay still for a moment more, thinking of what should be done next.

As Earthmaker thought, he suddenly began to weep. Tears flowed from his eyes and fell in torrents. At last he stopped and looked below him. Something bright sparkled there. His tears had formed the seas and lakes, streams and rivers.

Earthmaker thought: "It is so. If I wish, my wish will become what I would, even as my tears became the seas."

So Earthmaker wished, "Let there be light."

And it became light.

"It is so," Earthmaker said. "The thing for which I wished came into being."

Now he wished for the earth.

And the earth came into existence.

Earthmaker looked at the earth. He liked it, but it had not yet settled down. It rocked and groaned. He wished it to be quiet, and the earth became quiet.

"Since what I wish becomes so, I shall now make a being that is like myself."

So Earthmaker took up some earth and modeled it into a likeness of himself. But when he spoke to the figure he had just created, it did not answer. Earthmaker realized that it had no mind, no thoughts.

So he willed a mind and thoughts into it.

But the figure still did not answer when he spoke to it. Earthmaker realized that it had no tongue.

So he willed a tongue into its mouth.

But the figure still did not answer when he spoke to it. Earthmaker realized that the figure had no soul.

So he willed a soul into it. He breathed into its mouth.

And this time, when Earthmaker spoke to it, the first human answered.

Sources

Radin, Paul. "The Winnebago Indians," *The Thirty-Seventh Annual Report of the Bureau of American Ethnology*, Washington, DC, 1923, pp. 212–213.

GLOOSCAP AND HIS PEOPLE
A Myth of the Micmac People of Canada

Glooscap is a very popular creator figure who is an adventurer as well; he undertakes a series of quests in the mortal world. But this myth shows him as creator as well as combatant in the epic battle with his evil brother.

The myth also shows the creation of Lox, a darkly mischievous figure who has elements in common with amoral, unpredictable trickster figures like Puck of England and Coyote of the American Southwest.

In the earliest days, there was the world, but it was just a place of empty forest, empty sea. As yet, there were no people and no animals.

Then Glooscap arrived, come down from the sky with his twin brother, Malsum.

The great chief Glooscap looked like an ordinary, if handsome, man—if an ordinary man was twice as tall and twice as strong as any other—and he possessed great magic, which he used always for good. Although he lived, too, like an ordinary man, Glooscap never fell ill, never grew old, and never died.

Malsum, too, was tall and strong, but unlike Glooscap, he hardly looked human: His head was that of a wolf. Malsum knew great magic, too, but never used it for good.

Glooscap tethered his canoe on a rocky island he had called into being and named Uktamkoo—the land we now call Newfoundland—and set to work. From the rocks, he made the Megumoowesoos, the Little People, who are small hairy beings who are magical musicians. One of the Megumoowesoos, Marten, caught Glooscap's eye, and he made Marten his servant, although the being came to be more like his younger brother.

Next, Glooscap made humans. He shot arrows into the trunks of ash trees, and out of those trees came men and women. These were the first of the Wabanaki people, "those who live where the day breaks." Pleased with what he'd created, Glooscap gave a great shout of joy that shook the trees.

Now he served as teacher to the people. As their great chief, he taught them all they would need to know about living in their world. He showed them how to build birch bark wigwams in which to live and canoes in which they could travel easily. He showed them how to make weirs for catching fish, and how to identify plants for food or medicine. He taught them the names of all the stars, who were living beings in themselves.

From among the humans, he chose an elderly woman, calling her, respectfully, Noogumee, or Grandmother. Noogumee became the great chief's housekeeper.

The great chief Glooscap works his magic as a woman and child look on. Possessing enormous powers, Glooscap created the first people by shooting arrows into the trunks of ash trees. (*Mary Evans Picture Library*)

Now it was time to add the animals. Glooscap made them out of clay and rock, giving each its name as it sprang into existence. There was Miko the squirrel and Team the moose, there were more and more with every second.

Meanwhile, Glooscap's brother, Malsum, was growing more and more envious with each new being. He, too, wished to be a creator—but he lacked that power. The envy grew and burned within him, and at last could resist it no longer. Malsum gathered up a handful of clay and whispered an evil spell over it.

The clay twisted out of his grip and landed on the ground in the form of a strange animal. It was not a beaver or badger or wolverine, but something that was all of them and none of them. And it was able to change its shape, taking any form it chose.

"His name is Lox!" Malsum exclaimed, proud of his creation.

"So be it," Glooscap said. "Lox may live among us in peace."

Now, Glooscap had made all the animals very large and strong. Lox, the newly made troublemaker, saw his first chance to make some mischief.

Putting on his wolverine body, Lox said to Team the moose, "My, what splendid antlers you have! Why, they are taller than any tree! You could toss a man on your horns to the top of the world."

Team was not the wisest of the animals. He said to Glooscap, "Please give me a man so I can toss him on my horns to the top of the world!"

"That is not a good thing!" Glooscap exclaimed. "Grow smaller."

And with that, the moose was the size it is today.

Meanwhile, Lox put on his badger form and said to Miko the squirrel, "What a magnificent tail you have! With it, I imagine you could smash every lodge in a village."

"I imagine so, too," Miko said.

But before he could do just that, he was caught by Glooscap.

"Grow smaller," Glooscap said. And the squirrel shrank to the size it is today. "From this day forth," Glooscap said, "you will live in the trees—and keep your tail where it belongs."

And that is why the squirrel carries its tail curled up over its back.

Meanwhile, Lox put on his beaver shape and said to Mooin the bear, "My, what a wonderfully large mouth you have. If you met a man, you could eat him in a gulp. Yes, you could swallow him whole!"

But Glooscap overheard this. "Grow smaller," he said, and the bear shrank to the size it is today, with the mouth it has today. "From this day forth," Glooscap said, "you may swallow only small creatures."

And that is why the bear eats only small animals, fish, and wild berries.

By now, the great chief was growing angry at the way his animals were behaving. In fact, he was beginning to wonder if he should have made them at all. So he warned the lot of them:

"You are made as man's equal, yet you wish to be his master. Be careful, or he will become yours!"

Lox didn't like threats. He knew how jealous Malsum was of Glooscap. And he also knew that since they were both magic beings, each of them could only be slain in one certain way. What that way might be, Lox didn't know, since the brothers guarded their secrets carefully.

But the sly Lox knew that both brothers also talked to the people of the sky, and trusted them with secrets. So he spied on both.

"Little does Malsum know," Lox heard Glooscap say to the stars, "that I can never be killed except by a blow from a flowering rush."

"Little does Glooscap know," Lox heard Malsum say to the stars, "that I can never be killed except by a blow from the roots of a flowering fern."

Now Lox had both secrets. He said to Malsum, "What will you give me if I tell you Glooscap's secret?"

"Anything you wish!" cried Malsum.

So Lox whispered, "Nothing can hurt Glooscap save a flowering rush. Now give me a pair of wings so I can fly."

Malsum only laughed. "What need has a beaver of wings?"

Off he sped to find a flowering rush. The angry Lox hurried to find Glooscap. "Malsum knows your secret and is about to kill you. If you would save yourself, know that only a fern root can destroy him!"

Glooscap snatched up the nearest fern, root and all, just in time—for his evil brother was upon him, shouting his war cry. All the animals, angry at Glooscap for reducing their size and power, cheered Malsum. All the humans cheered Glooscap.

The fight was short—and deadly. Malsum lunged, and Glooscap threw the fern. The fern root stabbed Malsum in the heart, and he fell dead.

The humans cheered. The animals slunk angrily away.

Lox trotted up to Glooscap. "I'll take my reward now," he said, "a nice pair of wings."

"Traitor! I made no such bargain!"

Glooscap hurled stones after the fleeing Lox. Wherever the stones landed, they turned to islands, and are there to this day.

Lox remains, too, lurking on the edges of things and just waiting to cause more trouble.

Glooscap called his people to him. "I made the animals to be your equals, but they have shown nothing but selfishness. From now on, they will be your servants."

Then he showed the men how to make and use bows and arrows and stone-tipped spears, and showed the women how to scrape hides and turn them into clothing.

"Now you will have power over even the largest wild creatures. But if you kill more animals than you need, or kill for the joy of it, you will meet a terrible giant named Famine, and die from his touch."

When the humans had promised to obey him, Glooscap set out in his canoe for other lands.

"I must leave you," he called back, "so that you will learn to live on your own. But you may seek me out in time of trouble, and you will find me."

So he left, and had many other adventures in the world. But Glooscap never forgot the promise he had made to his people.

Sources

Partridge, Emelyn Newcomb. *Glooscap the Great Chief and Other Stories*. New York: Sturgis and Walton, 1913.

Spicer, Stanley T. *Glooscap Legends*. Hantsport, Nova Scotia: Lancelot, 1997.

HURAKAN CREATES THE WORLD
A Myth of the Mayan People

Hurakan—who gives his name to the word *hurricane*—is a hot-tempered creator, the god of wind and storm. The myth included here begins with the theme of the primal sea, then continues to the theme of the molded human who needs a soul. But in other myths, it is Hurakan who, when the first humans anger the gods, brings a flood to destroy them.

*O*nce there was nothing save water, a calm, endless, motionless expanse of water, the primal place wherein no life yet existed. No mortal life, that was, for at the bottom of the primal sea lived two fiery deities, of sun-like flame that could not be extinguished by mere water. These two were named Tepeu and Gecumartz.

Since there were only the two beings, they spoke often with each other, not liking the idea of solitude. And they both realized that there must be a start to change, and that start must be the dawn. And with the dawn must come true creation.

Tepeu and Gecumartz planned dawn and heaven, and in that heaven was Hurakan, its heart, the lord of storm and rain. It was Hurakan's role, now, to begin creation. He looked down and saw mist above the primal water, nothing else. So Hurakan cried out commandingly, "Let emptiness be filled! Earth, be there!"

And the waters receded, and the earth was revealed.

Now the plants were created, then the birds and insects and animals. But none could speak to praise the gods. This was not as Hurakan wished, so he created humanity.

But this was not an easy task. Of what should humanity be made? Hurakan tried earth and mud. But this first attempt met with failure. The people so made could barely move. Their brains were muddy, without sense. And they melted away as soon as the sun's rays struck them.

Hurakan made new people out of wood. They could walk and talk—but they had neither minds nor souls. They had no blood, no hearts, and no memory of who they were or of the gods. Since they had no souls, they were mindlessly cruel to each other and the birds and animals.

So Hurakan sent a great flood to wash them into sodden masses. They were pecked and bitten by the birds and animals. Only a few survived and ran off into the forests. Their offspring became monkeys.

Now Hurakan tried one more time. He used sacred cornmeal dough—and this time the people he built lived and thrived. They became the ancestors of the Queche Maya. And the gods were satisfied.

Sources

Portilla, Miguel Leon. *Pre-Columbian Literatures of Mexico*. Norman: University of Oklahoma Press, 1969.
Taube, Karl. *Aztec and Maya Myths*. Austin: University of Texas Press, 1994.
Tedlock, Dennis, trans. *Popol Vuh*. New York: Simon and Schuster, 1985.

THE FIFTH SUN
A Myth of the Aztecs of Mexico

Two themes are clear in this myth. The first is the need for sacrifice that is so strong in Aztec religion: The world would end, it was believed, unless the gods were fed on human blood. The Aztecs also felt that they must continue the ritual of sacrifice if the sun was to keep moving. They killed war captives and offered the hearts and blood to Nanahuatl. Because the Aztecs felt that they kept the sun going for themselves and others, they called themselves the People of the Sun.

The second theme in this myth is a more familiar one in the world's mythology and folklore: The ugly brother, the one looked down upon by the others, will turn out to be the hero, or in this case, the dominant god.

*O*meteuctli was the supreme creator. He it was who created the four gods of the four early suns. After that work, Ometeuctli created over a thousand other gods. Each of these became a star in the heavens.

But before all could work properly, there must be a fifth sun. The four gods of the four suns knew the painful truth: The fifth sun could be created only through the sacrifice of one of them.

Reluctantly, the four gods of the four suns built an enormous bonfire. But which of them would be the sacrifice? None of them could agree to be the one.

But there were two other gods, Nanahuatl and Teucciztecatl, who might serve as willing sacrifice. Yet surely Nanahuatl could not be the one! He was poor and ugly, his body covered with sores. The sacrifice must be Teucciztecatl.

Teucciztecatl ran boldly toward the fire pit—then hastily backed away. He tried again—and again backed away. He tried four times to jump into the fire pit but could not find the courage. He could not sacrifice himself.

Just then Nanahuatl raced forward and bravely hurled himself into the fire pit. He was instantly reborn as the fifth sun. This sacrifice gave Teucciztecatl the courage to follow him into the fire. And Teucciztecatl became the moon.

But none of the gods could see the new sun. Nanahuatl refused to rise unless he was given the hearts and blood of the other gods. One of the most terrible of the gods was Morning Star. Furious, he challenged Nanahuatl to a duel. But Nanahuatl defeated Morning Star and cast him down to be the lord of the underworld. After that, the remaining gods agreed that it was wiser to make sacrifices of themselves. From then on, the sun, Nanahuatl, rose in proper fashion in the east every day.

Sources

MacKenzie, Donald A. *Myths of Pre-Columbian America*. Mineola: Dover Publications, 1996.

Taube, Karl. *Aztec and Maya Myths*. Austin: University of Texas Press, 1994.

QUETZALCOATL
A Myth from the Aztecs of Mexico

Quetzalcoatl is a deity often seen as a savior figure who brings agriculture and wisdom to the people. But in this earlier myth of the primal sea, he is seen as a young hero god who slays a water monster in the way European heroes might slay dragons.

Another myth states that with the help of Tezcatlipoca, both deities in the form of giant snakes, Quetzalcoatl tore the dangerous earth goddess, Coatlicue, into two pieces so that the earth and sky could be formed. Still another claims that he was the son of the sun god and of Coatlicue.

As the importance of the cult of Quetzalcoatl grew, the myth's conclusion, when he sails off into the east, spelled the downfall of the Aztec kingdom. When the Spaniards arrived from the east, the Aztec

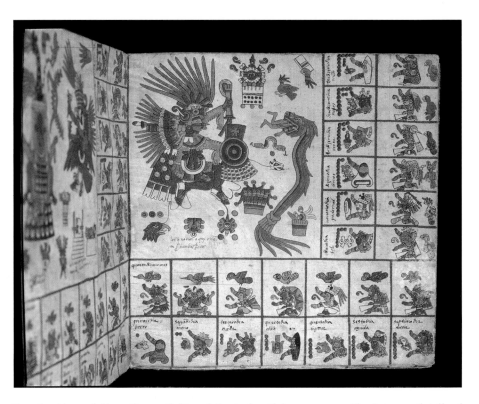

Together the gods Tezcatlipoca (left) and Quetzalcoatl devour a man. The Aztec myth tells of how the two created the fifth world by slaying the giant sea monster. (*Giraudon/Art Resource, New York*)

people at first mistook Cortés for Quetzalcoatl returned—and corrected their mistake far too late.

$\mathcal{Q}$uetzalcoatl, he whose name means "plumed serpent," was the god of earth, water, and vegetation. But some say that he was also the god of creation. And this is the tale they tell.

After the creation of the fifth sun, the gods saw that the world was covered with nothing but endless ocean. Only one being lived down there in all that restless water, and that was a monstrous female creature. So huge was she that if she splashed on one side of the watery world, she created tidal waves on the other. There would never be land, or life, on the new world as long as she existed to block all change. But none of the gods wanted to act. They didn't wish to fight the monster.

Quetzalcoatl refused to wait idly while nothing proper happened to the new world. He would be the one to act. But he could not slay so mighty a monster by himself. He asked his friend and fellow god Tezcatlipoca to help him. Down the two deities dove into the endless sea. With defiant cries, they attacked the sea monster. Tezcatlipoca lunged at her, and she whirled to him. But before she could strike, Quetzalcoatl's sharp sword of gleaming black obsidian sliced open the monster and slew her.

Now the world could begin. Tezcatlipoca and Quetzalcoatl cut apart that huge corpse. They formed the land from her body, the grass from her hair. They formed the lakes from her eyes and the caves from her mouth, ears, and nostrils. So it was that the fifth world, our world, was formed.

Sources

MacKenzie, Donald A. *Myths of Pre-Columbian America*. Mineola: Dover Publications, 1996.

Taube, Karl. *Aztec and Maya Myths*. Austin: University of Texas Press, 1994.

CREATION FROM ILLUSION
A Myth of the Uitoto People of Colombia

This must surely be the most existential of myths, with a god who is himself only appearance willing the entire world to exist out of illusion.

$\mathcal{I}$n the beginning there was nothing but illusion, nothing that really, solidly existed. Then there was Nainema, "he who is only appearance." Nainema touched illusion in his dream, pressed it against himself, and lost himself in deepest thought.

There was nothing yet to support the illusion, not a tree, not a rock. Only through his breathing did Nainema keep illusion attached to his dream. He hunted through his thought, trying to find what was at the heart of illusion. But he found nothing.

"I hold that which does not exist," Nainema said.

He hunted through the nothingness and caught emptiness. Nainema tied emptiness to the thread of his dream and pressed it together. Now he held the illusion like a fluffy bit of raw cotton.

"I have attached that which did not exist," Nainema said.

He seized the illusion and stamped on it again and yet again, forming it into earth. At last the illusion was his, firm earth. And Nainema finally allowed himself to stand on this new, firm earth of which he had dreamed. He spat again and again, and the forests arose, fresh and new. Last of all, Nainema lay on the new earth and drew out of it the blue, cloud-speckled heavens and set that lovely covering over it.

His work was done. Illusion had been made real.

Sources

Bierhorst, John. *The Mythology of South America*. New York: William Morrow, 1988.
New Larousse Encyclopedia of Mythology. Translated by Richard Aldington and Delano Ames. London, New York: Hamlyn, 1968.

AMANA
A Myth of the Calina People of South America

Here is a female creator who makes the world out of the primal sea. She is a hero as well, saving her creation from the fires of the sun and burying the fire serpents—which is also an explanation of the volcanic fire that now and again breaks free. The myth ends with a clever balance of light and darkness, and a satisfied Amana.

There was darkness and emptiness at the beginning. Then there was Amana, the first being in all the primal chaos of the cosmic sea. Her home was the Milky Way, and she swam through the primordial waters with whales and fish. The turtle, upon whose back she would ride, was her ally and friend.

At last Amana grew weary of eternal darkness. She created the sun. Now that there was light, she decided to create worlds as well, making them beautiful by adding mountains and forests, rivers and fields.

But her first creation, the sun, was revealed as her enemy. It hated the life she was building, and burned up whatever plants and animals it could find. It sent fire serpents to eat the moon and scorch the earth.

Amana caught the fire serpents and buried them deep underground. From time to time, they still do break free, and those escapes are what we call volcanic eruptions.

As for the sun, Amana took its power away. She created two new forces, Tamusi, light, and Tamulu, darkness. These two opposites hated each other. But they could not escape each other. There can be no light without darkness, no shadow without light. So they agreed to a truce. Tamusi would rule over the day, and Tamulu would rule over the night. Both hated the fire serpents. Tamusi struck them down with his lightning. Tamulu smothered them with his black cloak.

Now Amana set a new command on them. Tamusi created all the beings that live by day. Tamulu created all the beings that live by night.

Amana was content.

Sources

Bierhorst, John. *The Mythology of South America*. New York: William Morrow, 1988.

New Larousse Encyclopedia of Mythology. Translated by Richard Aldington and Delano Ames. London, New York: Hamlyn, 1968.

THE BIRTH OF HUMANITY
A Myth of the Yupa of South America

This myth begins with the eerie motif of the bleeding tree (used to effect by Dante in *The Inferno*) and continues with the carving of humanity from wood rather than from clay. As in the Melanesian myth "Something from Nothing," earlier in this chapter, there is a symbolic burial of the wooden carvings and a symbolic rebirth as the box is opened.

*I*n the beginning of things, there was only the creator walking the new world. One day the creator went into the forest, felling trees, hunting, always hunting. At last he found the one tree that would do, the one that spurted blood when the axe struck it.

The creator quickly felled this tree and from it carved two small figures. Satisfied with this work, the creator cut down a second tree and carved a box from its wood. Satisfied with this work, too, the creator placed the two small figures into the box.

"Come," the creator commanded a woodpecker. "Sit upon these figures as though they were two eggs."

With that, the creator closed the box and left it in the forest for several days.

Several days later, indeed, the creator's companion went into the forest. She found the wooden box. What was this? She heard voices and laughter from within. The creator's companion opened the box, and the woodpecker flew out. Within the box, there were two happy, healthy human children. Taking them from the box, the creator's companion brought them home and raised them till they were old enough to be husband and wife. From that first human pair came children, and from their children came children, until all the world was populated.

Now the creator came to the humans and told them how they had all come from wood, from one tree, and were therefore all kin. After this, no brother married sister. The woodpecker that had helped in the creation was honored by them all.

The people held a great feast for the creator. But they were mortal and must stay on earth. Still, they could take joy in knowing this: When their mortal lives were done, they would go to the creator and live forever in that distant land.

Sources

Bierhorst, John. *The Mythology of South America*. New York: William Morrow, 1988.
Wilbert, Johannes. *Yupa Folktales*. Los Angeles: University of California, 1974.

2

MYTHS OF
DEATH AND REBIRTH

Death is an ambiguous force at best. Some people may imagine Death as a frightening figure, a skeleton in a moldy cloak, but the personification may also be that of a gentle mother or a somber but not terrible angel. There are even myths about a reluctant Death. In a myth from India, a female Death, anguished over having to take lives, attempts to flee from her destiny until she realizes that she is essential to the unfolding of the divine plan.

Sometimes a myth may tell how death was brought into the world through a misunderstanding or a messenger's failure. In a Zulu myth typical of this type, it is a chameleon who is the messenger sent by the creator to tell humanity that they can choose if they wish to be immortal. But the chameleon (or the dog, or some other animal messenger) does not deliver the divine message on time, and because the creator receives no answer, humanity becomes mortal.

Death may be created by a divinity in a myth type that involves the first man and woman. This primal couple is faced with a painful choice: They may live forever but alone, or have children and become mortal. Not wanting to be forever alone, the couple chooses mortality, as in myths from the Malagasy Republic and other parts of Africa.

Some myths go a step further, acknowledging a practical need for death. As a Coyote myth from the American Southwest warns, if no one dies but people go right on being born, the world will soon become impossibly overcrowded.

There are also myths of death on a larger scale, centering on the death of the world or even of the entire universe. A Pawnee myth states that there will, in time, come an end to everything living and a return to the heavens. Norse mythology describes Ragnarok, the Twilight of the Gods, the final battle in which even the gods will die. A Christian story tells of Armageddon, the ultimate conflict between good and evil. The story of Armageddon was inspired by an actual battle fought between the Egyptians and the Hittites in the first millennium B.C.E. at Megiddo, in Palestine, but that historical background does not take away from the story's mythic significance.

The idea of a predetermined final battle has links with other myths of destiny, of fate or predestination resolved or overthrown. The Greek hero (or antihero), Jason, was fated to overthrow his father's usurper. Arthur of Britain was predestined to be the one who pulled the sword from the stone and became king. Odin defied the Norns, the three Norse Fates, to build Valhalla—and eventually lead Valhalla and the human realm to Ragnarok.

The most common resurrection myth deals with the desperate human need to know that mortal life is not the end. Variants of this type teach that there is both an immortal soul and an afterlife. Most myths, from the Egyptian to the biblical, state that there is a heaven of some form, a happy afterworld, for the worthy. Some add that there is also a place of punishment for those who have done evil, whether it is the fiery hell of the Judeo-Christian tradition or the icy realms of the Norse myths. The Egyptians postulated the complete destruction, body and soul, of their evildoers.

There are numerous forms of the resurrection myth from around the world that relate to the agricultural cycle. These range from the Tammuz story of the ancient Near East to the English ballad of John Barleycorn, which was collected in this century but is apparently the last vestige of an ancient English myth.

In such myths, the main figure is almost certainly an agricultural deity who is harvested like the crops in the autumn and returns to the earth with the new seedlings every spring. That Tammuz and, after him, the Greek Adonis should be slain by a boar's horn to the groin adds another, and very obvious, symbolic element to this idea.

In other resurrection myths, the protagonist is shown as a symbol of eternal life, either the murdered victim who returns to life, such as the Egyptian Osiris, or the willing sacrifice who dies so that others may be redeemed.

There is another, related archetype, the human protagonist of a death and rebirth myth: the hero who will return. In this type of myth, the hero has not truly died, but instead has gone into a magical sleep under a hill or in a tree, like Merlin, or been carried off to another plane of existence, like Arthur to the magical Isle of Avalon. In all the myths of this type, it is understood that the hero will come again when his people are most in need, either as a rescuer of those people or as the herald of a better age—whether that hero is King Arthur or "King" Elvis. A variant on this theme can be found in Hindu myth, in which a god may be reborn as a human avatar, or incarnation, such as the hero Rama, protagonist of the epic *Ramayana*, who was the avatar of the god Vishnu.

Flood myths belong in the death and rebirth category, as well, since they feature nothing less than the death and rebirth of the world itself. The world flood is a common theme throughout the world's mythology, probably because so many regions in the world are prone to catastrophic flooding, although there is no geologic evidence to support a flood in human experience that covered the entire world.

Besides the well-known flood of the Old Testament, there are at least twenty other great floods described in the world's mythology, from Asia to North America. Most of these seem to be linked, as in the biblical account, with human sinfulness and the rebirth of the human race. Almost all the flood stories feature two innocent humans as protagonists, a man and a woman or, quite often, a boy and a girl, as well as a sacred vessel of salvation, such as Noah's ark of the Old Testament, the vessel in the earlier Sumerian epic of Gilgamesh, or the giant turtle that rescues two children in a myth from the Pacific Northwest.

MYTHS OF DEATH

DEATH COMES TO HUMANITY
A Myth of the Khoikhoin People

There are several myths from different peoples in sub-Saharan Africa that involve the coming of death to humanity through a mistaken message and a faulty messenger. See, for instance, the Nigerian myth that follows, "The Messenger Fails."

In this Khoikhoin myth, it is the moon itself that wishes to save humanity from death. The chameleon, which does move with a deliberately slow pace (especially when hunting), is the original messenger. And the hare, who is as much a show-off here as the one in Aesop's famous fable "The Hare and the Tortoise," who is the faulty messenger.

The hare, not too coincidentally, is often seen as a trickster in both African and Native American folklore—as well as in our modern Bugs Bunny cartoons. Here he suffers the punishment of a cleft nose and lip, and the moon in turn gets the scratches that, in this myth at least, explain the marks we see on it today.

The Khoikhoin people despise the hare and refuse to eat it. The San of the nearby Kalahari Desert share a similar story, but in their case they distrust the chameleon. It's a custom to place twigs over a dead chameleon in a symbolic burial to avoid misfortune.

How did humanity learn of death? The moon forever wanes and waxes, waxes and wanes. And it was the moon who sent a chameleon, that slow-legged lizard, to humanity with an urgent message: "I die, but in dying live. So you shall also die, but in dying live."

Off went the chameleon with the message. But no matter how hard he tried, he just could not move very swiftly. Soon a hare overtook him and asked mockingly, "Where do you go in such a hurry?"

"I carry an urgent message from the moon," the chameleon said, and he repeated what the moon had told him.

The hare thought, "Well now, let me just carry this message myself. It is so important a one that when people hear it and realize that I am the messenger, it will bring me fame!"

The chameleon, pictured here at the top of a wooden dance mask from Cameroon, appears frequently in African mythology—often playing a role in the tortoise-and-hare motif. In the Khoikhoin story, the fame-seeking hare plays a crucial role in bringing death to humanity. (*Werner Forman/Art Resource, New York*)

He leaped away, leaving the chameleon in his dust. But, alas, the hare was known for his foolishness. Afraid that he would forget the message, he repeated it to himself over and over as he raced along. Unfortunately, each time that he repeated the message, the hare made a new mistake, mixing the message up even more.

By the time that the hare reached the humans, the hopeful message from the moon had become something else entirely. The hare proclaimed, "As I die and in dying perish, so you shall also die and perish."

When the moon heard what had happened, she was furious. She struck the hare so hard that she left a cleft in his nose and lip that his children bear to this day. The frightened hare struck back, scratching the moon's face, leaving marks that can be seen even to this day.

But no matter what the moon or the hare did, it was too late for humanity. The rule had been set, and from that day on, humans had to die.

Sources

Biesele, Megan. *Women Like Meat*. Bloomington: Indiana University Press, 1993.
Partridge, A. C., ed. *Folklore of Southern Africa*. Vol. 2 of ELISA Series. Cape Town, South Africa: Purnell, 1973.

THE MESSENGER FAILS
A Myth from Nigeria

Here is another example of a mistaken message concerning avoidance of death and, in this myth, two erratic messengers. In this myth it is the supreme deity, not the moon, who sends the message. There's also the theme of symbolic burial under ashes and proposed rebirth from under the ashes.

In the days after humankind came to live upon the earth, the supreme deity, Chuku, thought over the matters of life and death. Something must be done for humanity.

At last Chuku sent a dog to humanity with a vital message: Should anyone die, they must be laid on the earth and strewn with ashes; they would then return to life.

But the dog was tired and stopped to rest. Chuku sent a sheep with the same message, but the sheep forgot it completely. When asked for the message, the sheep simply told humanity, "Go bury your dead."

By the time the dog arrived with the correct message, it was too late. Death was there to stay.

Sources

Walker, Barbara K., and S. Warren Walker, eds., as told by Olawale Idewu and Omotayo Adu. *Nigerian Folk Tales*. New Brunswick: Rutgers University Press, 1961.
Wyndham, John. *Myths of Ife*. London: Erskin MacDonald, 1921.

HEISEB AND DEATH
A Myth of the San of the Kalahari

Heiseb is an ambiguous figure in San mythology, a trickster who thinks nothing of pulling deadly or at least painful pranks on his acquaintances. But here he is seen as a tragic figure who can do nothing to save his own son.

In the Kalahari, strict rules concerning food are necessary if all are to survive, and so the boy gorging himself on the berries would be seen as a truly serious breach of propriety.

Here the ambiguity of Heiseb's character appears. Does he really think that his son is dead? Or is the appeal of a trick too powerful for him to resist, even at the expense of his son's life? Being outside the culture, we can't know the answer. Or perhaps there is none . . . .

*O*nce in the long-past days, it happened that there was a terrible drought, bad even for the desert world. Heiseb, he who is both man and much more than man, trickster and magician, was wandering the barren land with his wife and their young son, hunting for food. But there was nothing to be found, and by now, for all of Heiseb's strange powers, they were very hungry indeed.

Then on the horizon they sighted a tree. As they neared the tree, they saw to their delight that its branches were laden down with berries of a rich, luscious red. So ripe were the berries that they were falling to the ground.

Heedless of his parents, their boy ran to pick them up. Hungry though he was, this greed still was not proper behavior. So his father scolded him.

"These berries are for adults, not for greedy children."

His son cried out, "I am dying of hunger."

With that, the boy fell to the ground and pretended to be dead. But he was, after all, the son of one who was more than human, and his pretense was far too realistic. Who can say? Heiseb may have believed it genuine. Then again, not even Heiseb could always predict what he might do.

"There is nothing for the dead but burial," Heiseb proclaimed.

And he buried the boy.

But of course his son wasn't really dead. The boy secretly dug his way out of the grave. When his mother saw the empty grave, she knew her son still lived. As soon as she saw him, she took him home with her.

But when Heiseb saw the boy, he said, "I thought my son dead. I buried him. The dead must remain dead."

His words had terrible power. As soon as he had spoken them, his son fell down dead. And since that day humans have died and known that there is no return from the grave to the world of the living.

Sources

Biesele, Megan. *Women Like Meat*. Bloomington: Indiana University Press, 1993.
Courlander, Harold. A *Treasure of African Folklore*. New York: Marlowe, 1996.

THE ORIGIN OF DEATH
A Myth of the Maasai People

This myth is another variant on the theme of the mistaken messenger and the mixed-up message—but in this case there is a personal touch to it, and a tragic twist in that it's the messenger's own son who dies because of the messenger's mistake.

*I*n the beginning of the world there was no death. Nor was death intended for humanity. It was Leeyio's job to see that it stayed that way. He was the first man put on earth by Naiteru-kop. And it was Naiteru-kop who said to him, "Whenever a man or woman dies and you are confronted with the corpse, always remember to say this: 'Man die, woman die, and come back again; moon die, and remain away.' Can you do this thing?"

Leeyio assured the deity that he could, indeed, do just that.

But as it happened, no one died for many a month. Everyone stayed healthy and hearty. More time passed, and more again.

Then at last someone did die, a neighbor's child, and Leeyio was summoned. But by this time he'd nearly forgotten what he was supposed to say. So what came out was not the right thing: "Moon die, and come back again; man die, woman die, and remain away."

The child did not return to life.

More months passed. And this time it was Leeyio's own child who died. This time Leeyio remembered the right words and hastily said, "Man die, woman die, and come back again; moon die, and remain away."

But the child did not return to life. When Leeyio ran to Naiteru-kop in despair, Naiteru-kop told him, "You are too late for this. Through your own mistake and carelessness, death was born when your neighbor's child died."

Sadly Leeyio bowed his head. Yes, it had been his fault.

So that is how death came to be, and that is why up to this day when men or women die, they do not return, but when the moon dies, it always comes back again.

Source

Kipury, Naomi. *Oral Literature of the Maasai.* Nairobi: East African Educational, 1983.

WHY PEOPLE DIE
A Myth from Madagascar (Malagasy Republic)

Here is a myth involving a form of population explosion and control. There's a charming concept of the choice being left up to the man and woman, who decide they'd rather have children than live a lonely, endless life. For another myth on the subject of the necessity of death, see "How Coyote Kept Death for the People," later in this chapter.

*I*t happened back in the long-ago days soon after the creation of First Man and First Woman. The creator of all things looked down to see how everything was going with them.

What the creator found was that First Man and First Woman had had children. Their children had had children. And since there was no death, everyone was going right on living and having more children.

This could not be, the creator thought sadly. If things went on as they were, soon the world would run out of food for all those people. Soon the world would run out of room for them!

So the creator spoke to First Man and First Woman. "I offer you a choice. You may have the gift of eternal life—but no children. Or you may have the gift of children, but at the end of a span of time, you will die."

First Man and First Woman looked at each other. "It would be wondrous to have eternal life," they said. "But life without children would be terribly lonely."

They made their choice. And so from then on, people did die, but they knew the happiness of children.

Sources

Abrahams, Roger D. *African Folktales*. New York: Random House, 1983.
Courlander, Harold. A *Treasure of African Folklore*. New York: Marlowe, 1996.

THE SLAYING OF HUMANITY
A Myth of Ancient Egypt

The theme of an angered deity or deities destroying sinful humanity is a worldwide one, to be found in the Old Testament, North American mythology, and here in the mythology of ancient Egypt.

A sculpture of the lioness-goddess Sekhmet from the tomb of Tutankhamen. Sekhmet was sent to spy on the people by the sun god, Ra, whose reputation as a great god had grown tarnished by human arrogance and blasphemy. However, Ra was forced to intervene when Sekhmet nearly succeeded in destroying the entire human race. (*Borromeo/Art Resource, New York*)

But here, instead of a destructive flood, the vessel of the gods' vengeance is the lion-headed goddess, Sekhmet, who is not an evil being, but a fierce one. She does have her gentler side: Sekhmet was the patron of the Egyptian physicians' bonesetters guild.

The theme of the battle-maddened warrior who can only be stopped by a trick turns up in ancient Ireland as well, in the story of the hero Cuchulain, who has to be shocked out of his battle madness by the unexpected sight of a row of bare-breasted maidens. In Norse belief, the berserker (literally "bearskin") was a warrior who was thought to become a bear either symbolically or literally and could be stopped only by exhaustion.

In the ancient days, Ra, the sun god, was king of the gods and humanity. For many years humanity thrived under his reign and gave thanks and proper respect to the deity. But even gods may age, and as Ra began to grow old, humanity turned from respect to mockery.

When Ra saw and heard this blasphemy against him, he raged and called the other gods to him. He told them the story of humanity's arrogance.

Then Ra turned to his father, Nu, and said, "You are the firstborn of the gods, and I, your son, seek your counsel. Humanity speaks evil of me and angers me greatly. But I will not destroy them before I have heard your advice."

Nun replied, "I am older, but you are a greater god than I. If you turn your eye upon those who blaspheme you, they shall perish."

Following his father's advice, Ra turned his terrible gaze upon the blasphemers, but they ran to hide in the shadows, where the eye of Ra could not harm them.

So Ra sent his eye down among humanity so that they could not hide. He sent his eye in the form of Sekhmet, goddess and lioness in one. She stormed into the hiding places and rent the blasphemers. Much of humanity was slain in that bloody time.

And Sekhmet roared, "I have been mighty among humanity. It is most pleasing to me."

But having tasted human blood, Sekhmet would not be so easily appeased. And now Ra was afraid that in her lion rage she would destroy the human race completely. After all, he wished to rule mankind, not see it destroyed.

There was only one way to stop Sekhmet. He must trick her. Ra ordered his servants to brew seven thousand jars of beer and stain it red as blood, then take the beer to where Sekhmet meant to slaughter what remained of humanity. Ra's servants poured the beer out onto the fields, flooding them.

When Sekhmet came to where the beer flooded the fields, she thought it was a field of blood. Delighted, she drank deeply of it. Soon the beer went to her head. She fell asleep and forgot all about her hunt.

So it was that Ra saved the humanity that he had so nearly destroyed.

Sources

Quirke, Stephen. *Ancient Egyptian Religion*. New York: Dover Publications, 1995.

Simpson, William Kelly, ed. *The Literature of Ancient Egypt*. New Haven: Yale University Press, 1972.

ORPHEUS AND EURYDICE
A Myth from Ancient Greece

This myth is likely to be familiar to many readers, as it has been told and retold in many forms, from straight translation from the Greek to movies such as *Black Orpheus*. It also was the inspiration for a medieval fairy tale in which Orpheus becomes a king who rescues his wife not from death but from Faerie.

The taboo, the sacred or magical prohibition against doing a certain deed, is common to every culture. Sometimes it turns up as a mere folk rhyme, such as the children's "Step on a crack, break your mother's back," but it can be much more serious, such as the Gaelic *geas* or taboo placed upon Cuchulain that meant death to him if he broke it. Here the breaking of the taboo results in high tragedy for Orpheus, destroying not his life but his reason for living.

For a similar myth that ends more happily for the protagonists, see the Kikuyu myth "Sacrificed by Her Kin," later in this chapter.

*O*rpheus was the son of Apollo, god of music, and the muse Calliope. With so noble a heritage, he was born with amazing talent. His father presented him with a lyre and taught the boy to play it. Soon Orpheus was such a wondrous musician that men and women wept to hear him, and even the wildest of beasts grew tame hearing him play.

Lovely young Eurydice and he met, and loved, and became joyous husband and wife. But not long after their marriage, a shepherd made advances to Eurydice. She ran from him—and in her haste stepped on a snake lying hidden in the grass. It bit her, and poor Eurydice died.

Orpheus released his grief in song, expressing bitter sorrow in music to gods and men alike. But no one could aid him. And at last, his grief unchecked, Orpheus vowed to snatch Eurydice back from the realm of the dead.

So Orpheus traveled down to the underworld. His song moved all who heard it, and even Cerberus, the terrible three-headed dog who guarded the river Styx, whined and crouched down to let Orpheus pass. At last Orpheus sang before Hades, the king of the underworld, and Persephone, Hades' wife. Persephone wept to hear his sorrow, and even Hades bowed his proud head.

"You may take Eurydice away with you. But there is one condition. You must lead her, and you must not so much as glance back at her until you both have reached the upper air and the land of the living."

"I shall do it," Orpheus swore.

He led Eurydice up the dark, rocky, steep passages. Utter silence surrounded them, wearing down on Orpheus' nerves. What if Eurydice wasn't following him? What if Hades had tricked him?

Detail from a Greek vase shows Orpheus playing the lyre before Hades, king of the underworld, and his wife, Persephone. Orpheus was so grief-stricken by the loss of his young wife, Eurydice, that he traveled to the underworld in an attempt to bring her back from the regions of the dead. (*Erich Lessing/Art Resource, New York*)

No! He would not look back.

They climbed further up in the darkness and heavy silence. What if it wasn't Eurydice following him? What if it was some demon of the underworld?

No! He would not look back!

They were almost at the entrance to the upper world, the world of the living. Was Eurydice still following? Was it Eurydice? Was she—

Orpheus glanced behind him. Instantly Eurydice was swept away from him, back to the underworld. Orpheus was left alone once more.

Sources

New Larousse Encyclopedia of Mythology. Translated by Richard Aldington and Delano Ames. London, New York: Hamlyn, 1968.
Ovid. The Metamorphoses. Translated by Horace Gregory. New York: Viking Press, 1958.

THE WOMAN WHO WAS DEATH
A Myth from India

This is a singularly compassionate myth of a reluctant Death who grudgingly comes to realize just how necessary she is to the scheme of things.

A female Death is relatively uncommon in the world's mythology. More common is a male figure or skeleton image, or the angel of death, who in Jewish tradition is male. Neil Gaiman's mythology-inspired graphic novels of the Sandman do, incidentally, feature a compassionate female Death.

On the day of the beginning, Lord Brahma created the earth and all that lived upon it: plant, animal, human.

One thing only did Brahma not create, and that was death. And so the created ones lived and thrived and multiplied till all the lands and seas were crowded. Famine came, and illness, yet there was no escape from pain. And the earth itself groaned beneath the weight upon it.

When Lord Brahma saw this suffering, he cried out in sorrow, and created from himself a woman, skin and hair and eyes dark and beautiful as night, and said to her:

"Your name is Death. And your task shall be to destroy life."

When the woman who was Death heard these words, she wept in horror. Not waiting to hear what else Lord Brahma might say, she fled from him.

But there was no escaping Lord Brahma. "You are Death," he told her. "The taking of life is your destiny."

Again she fled, weeping at these bitter words. Again Lord Brahma found her where she hid.

"I created you to be the destroyer of life," he told her. "It is as it must be."

A third time the woman who was Death fled, till she reached the very ends of creation. But there again, on that very edge of emptiness, Lord Brahma overtook her. And this time there was no place left to which Death could flee.

"O my lord, spare me!" she pleaded. "Why should I do this cruel thing? Why should I harm those who have done me no harm? I beg you, let me not be Death!"

"Daughter," Lord Brahma said gently, his great, wise eyes warm with pity, "you have not heard me out. If there is life, there must be an end to life."

"But how cruel to—"

"Hush, daughter. Listen. Death shall not be evil, or cruel, or without virtue. Without death, there can be no peace, no rest for the suffering, the aged. Without death, there can be no rebirth. Daughter, death shall not be the destroyer of the world, but its protector."

When Death heard these words, she pondered. She dried her tears. And at last the woman called Death smiled a tender little smile, a mother's smile. She bowed low before Lord Brahma and went forth to do his bidding.

And so all things came in time to die, and to be reborn. Order was restored to the earth.

Sources

Danielou, Alain. *The Myths and Gods of India*. Rutland, VT: Inner Traditions International, 1991.

Van Over, Raymond. *Sun Songs: Creation Myths from Around the World*. New York: New American Library, 1980.

CHOOSING DEATH
A Myth of the Poso People of Indonesia

Here's a highly ironic myth, a case of a wrong choice made—and made out of human impatience.

The theme of benefits being lowered from heaven turns up in Chapter 3 as well, in "The Origin of Cattle."

*I*n the beginning of days, the sky was close enough to the earth for the creator to let down some of his gifts to humanity in a basket tied to a rope. He would not explain his gifts when they were first given, wanting humans to puzzle things out for themselves.

One day the creator lowered a stone. The first humans studied the stone, expecting some hidden mystery. But there was none; this was simply a stone, just like any other. So they put it back in the basket and called up to the creator, "We don't want this stone. Give us something else."

So the creator pulled the stone in the basket up and up again.

Then the basket was lowered again. This time the first humans found a banana in it. They rushed to the basket to take the fruit and gobble it down.

"So you have chosen," the creator said. "Because you have picked the banana, your life shall be like its life. When the banana tree bears fruit, the stem withers and dies. So shall you die, and your children shall take your place. But had you chosen the stone, your life would have been like its life— immortal and untouched."

The first humans mourned, but what was done could not be undone. And so, through the choosing of a banana over a stone, death came to the world.

Sources

Cavendish, Richard, ed. *Legends of the World: A Cyclopedia of the Enduring Myths, Legends and Sagas of Mankind.* New York: Schocken Books, 1982.

Frazer, Sir James G. *The Belief in Immortality and the Worship of the Dead.* London: Macmillan, 1913–1924.

THE BIRD THAT BROUGHT DEATH
A Myth of the Aranda of Australia

This is the first of two myths dealing with the origin of death through malice. Why the magpie should be so jealous and angry of the humans is not explained, but not all elements in a myth are always clear to outsiders.

The idea of a people climbing up into this world through a hole turns up in Native American mythology as well. See, for instance, "The Origin of the Apaches," in Chapter 1. People may also reach this world by climbing down from a land in the sky. See the Wyandot myth "The Origin of the World," also in Chapter 1.

The first people climbed up into this world through a hole in the ground. But the other men were angry at the man who had first climbed up, because he had crowded the women on the way. So they ruled that he must die.

But death was not a permanent matter in those long-ago days.

The first man lit a blazing fire, then lay down beside it. The others pointed a magic bone at him. The man lay where he was for two nights, then died, and the others buried him.

The women began a women's dance, moving in a circle to the rhythmic shouts of the men: "Bau! Bau! Bau! Bau!"

Now the dead man began returning to life. He started digging his way up out of the soil.

Urbura the magpie saw what was happening, and it outraged him. Why? No one knows. Perhaps he didn't like humans, or didn't like the idea that death wasn't a permanent thing for them. So while the dead man climbed back into life and the dancing women encircled him, Urbura hurled a heavy spear at the man, thrusting it deep into his neck, then dove down to stamp him back into the ground with magical force.

"Remain!" Urbura shrieked. "Remain rooted for all time! Do not try to rise again. Stay in the grave forever!"

With that, the first humans rushed off, wailing and weeping with grief. Urbura flew off to his own home, where he remained.

But his harm remained. If the dead man had been able to return to life, all who died would return to life. From that day on, though, no one has been able to return from the grave.

Sources

Smith, William Ramsay. *Aborigine Myths and Legends*. London: Senate Books, 1996.
Streblow, T. G. H. *Aranda Tradition*. Melbourne: Melbourne University Press, 1947.

THE MOON AND DEATH
A Myth of the Wotjobaluk People of Australia

In this myth, it is a bitter old man who brings death to the people. As in the previous myth, no reason is given for his malice; we just have to accept it was there.

Here again it is the moon that is seen as the granter of immortality, as in the Khoikhoin myth earlier in this chapter.

*I*n the ancient days when animals were people and people were animals, whenever one died, the moon would look down and say to the dead one, "You—get up again." Then the dead one would return to life.

But there was one old man who was a bitter old man. He didn't want this endless up and about, dead and alive. And before the moon could say, "You—get up again" to a dead man, the old man cried, "Let them remain dead!"

That curse was a powerful one. And it worked far, far too well. From that day on, thanks to one bitter old man, none but the moon itself ever came to life again.

Sources

Howitt, A. W. *The Native Tribes of South-East Australia*. London and New York: Macmillan, 1904.
Smith, William Ramsay. *Aborigine Myths and Legends*. London: Senate Books, 1996.

HOW COYOTE KEPT DEATH FOR THE PEOPLE
A Myth of the Caddo

The main theme of this myth is, of course, that death is necessary if there are to be births, or else there will be no room on earth for everyone. For another myth with this theme, see the Malagasy myth "Why People Die," earlier in this chapter.

Coyote is one of the most famous tricksters in mythology, perhaps the only one recognized by people who don't know anything else about myth. Since a trickster is an ambiguous figure at best, neither good nor evil, some versions of this tale have Coyote acting from logic, while others have him acting as a deliberate troublemaker. There is no "right" version.

*I*n the early days, when the rules of the world were still being set up, the people of power held a council meeting. At that meeting was Coyote the trickster.

"Why should there be death?" the people wondered. "Let us do away with it!"

"Death is already a law," Coyote reminded them. "You cannot do away with it so easily."

"We shall change the law!" the people cried. "Folk will still die, but they shall not stay dead forever. We shall build a great lodge, a place of power. Into it the spirits of the newly dead shall fly. Out of it they shall walk, living folk once more."

"How very nice it sounds," Coyote said. "But you forget one thing, O wise people: If folk keep right on being born, yet no one stays dead, the world shall be a crowded place very soon! How are you going to feed all those people, O wise ones? Where are you going to put them?"

No, no, the people would not listen to Coyote. They drove him away with cries of "Cruel one! Heartless one!"

Coyote watched from a secret place while the people spoke their spells and chanted their chants. "They won't listen to sense. It's up to me to do something about this."

So Coyote added his own quiet, sly spell to what the people had set on their lodge of power, and waited to see what would come next.

It was not long before a human man died. The people played their flutes of bone, and the dead man's spirit whirled on the wind toward the lodge, drawn by their magic. In another moment it would enter, then exit as a living man.

But Coyote leaped out from hiding in a blur of wild gray fur and slammed shut the lodge door.

"No!" the people cried.

But they were too late. The spirit could not enter, and the power of the bone flutes was broken. The spirit whirled off on its proper path away from the land of the living, and Coyote laughed in triumph.

"Your spell is shattered!" he called to the people. "Thanks to me, the lodge is now a hut of useless grass!"

That was all Coyote had time to say, for in the next moment, all the raging people of power were chasing him.

Of course he escaped. But from that day to this, all coyotes still run looking back over their shoulders, just in case the people of power might be catching up to them.

Sources

Dorsey, George A., ed. *Traditions of the Caddo.* Washington: Carnegie Institute, 1905.
Erdoes, Richard, and Alfonso Ortiz. *American Indian Myths and Legends.* New York: Pantheon Books, 1984.

THE HUSBAND'S QUEST
A Myth of the Tachi Yakut

Here is a myth that shows how universal mythology can be. Like the tragic tale of Orpheus and Eurydice, earlier in this chapter, the protagonist is a newly bereaved husband who refuses to give up his wife to death. The difference here is the ending, in which that *deus ex machina* snake sends the man off to the afterlife to join his wife. Whether or not this is a happy ending and whether or not she, already dead, remembers him, is open to interpretation.

Once there were a happy husband and wife. But alas, the wife died. Her husband sat by her grave, not eating, not sleeping, for two nights.

After the two nights had nearly passed, he saw her rise from the grave, brush the earth off herself, and start for the Island of the Dead. He tried desperately to seize her, but she slipped away.

The husband followed. Every time he tried to seize her, she slipped away. But each time delayed her a little more.

Overtaken by daybreak, she stopped. He stopped, too, but he could no longer see her. He waited.

Sure enough, when it grew dark again, he could see his wife as she started forward once more. They traveled on through the night. At daybreak she stopped once more, and her husband could not see her. He did see a well-marked trail ahead of them, though, and on it footprints of his dead friends and relatives. In the evening his wife got up again and went on.

And so they traveled by night and stopped by day over and over again.

At last his wife stopped and for the first time spoke to him. "What do you think to do? I am nothing now. Do you think you are able to bring me back to the life I left?"

"I think so."

"I think not. I am traveling to a different kind of land now."

She started off once more. Nor did she speak to him again.

At last they came to the Island of the Dead. It was joined to the mainland by a bridge that constantly rose and fell like a wave over a swiftly flowing river.

Ahead, the husband could see the dead crossing over this bridge. When the dead were halfway to the Island of the Dead, a bird suddenly fluttered in their face. Some of them were frightened, lost their balance, and fell into the river. They became fish. The ones who were not afraid made it safely to the Island of the Dead.

Suddenly the chief of the dead said, "Somebody has come."

His people told him, "There are two. One is for us. The other stinks of life."

"Do not let him cross!" the chief of the dead commanded.

When the wife crossed the bridge and stepped onto the island, the chief of the dead asked her, "Who is that living man?"

"He was my husband."

Meanwhile, the chief's people asked the man, "Do you want to come to this land?"

"Yes. And I will."

He started across the bridge. It rose and fell, but he kept his balance. The bird flew up in his face, but he refused to fall, and crossed over onto the Island of the Dead.

"You should not have come here," said the chief of the dead. "Yes, we have your wife's soul, but not her body. That remains in the grave. She will be happy here. Go back to the world of the living."

But the man would not leave. After three days of waiting, the chief of the dead had the woman brought to him. "Is this still your husband?"

"He was."

"Do you want to go back to him?"

"I cannot. This is my place now."

"Do you see?" the chief of the dead said to the man. "Go back to the land of the living."

"Let me speak to her."

"So be it."

The man spent all that night talking to his wife, trying to convince her to come home with him. At last, exhausted, he fell asleep.

When the man woke he found himself alone, sleeping not beside his wife but beside a fallen tree.

The chief of the dead said, "You see that we cannot make your wife as she was. She is dead, and you are alive. Go back to the land of the living."

Sadly the man agreed. "I am going back. No one returns from the Island of the Dead."

He returned to his village. But maybe he no longer cared what he did or where he went, because he failed to see a rattlesnake in time. It bit him.

And he went to join his wife forever on the island of the dead. They are both there even now.

Source

Kroeber, A. L. *Indian Myths of South Central California*. Vol. IV of *American Archaeology and Ethnology*. Berkeley: University of California Press, 1907.

MYTHS OF THE GREAT FLOOD

THE FIRST GREAT FLOOD
A Myth from Ancient Mesopotamia

Anyone who has grown up in the Judeo-Christian tradition is surely in for a surprise upon reading this myth, since it predates the biblical story of the flood. Does this discredit the story of Noah? Not at all. As noted above, there certainly have been plenty of great floods in the geologic past. But the two tales have enough similarities that one certainly must have influenced the details of the other, from the idea of an ark to the releasing of the birds to find land, although here the bird is a raven, not a dove.

The protagonist of this myth, by the way, turns up as a wise old man archetype in "The Epic of Gilgamesh" (see Chapter 5). The Dilmun mentioned in the myth is an imaginary version of a real Bronze Age city, located in Saudi Arabia.

The gods, led by Enlil, looked down upon the earth and frowned. There were far too many people upon it, and far too many who refused to follow the proper laws the gods had set. They must, they all agreed, cleanse the earth of its overpopulation.

Only the god Ea, who kept an eye on humanity, thought otherwise. The human race, he mused, must not be erased. So he warned one honorable man in a dream. Utnapishtim was this man's name, and he and his craftsman friends built a huge ship. It had seven decks in all. And because they dared not hesitate, they finished it in a week.

Utnapishtim now loaded the huge ship with his family, the craftsmen and their families, and two of each kind of all living creatures.

No sooner had all safely boarded than the waters of the great abyss rose up. It stormed without rest for six days and night. Even the gods were shocked by the fury of the flood and wept for all the people who had been drowned.

At last the storm ceased. The flood's waters covered everything but the peak of Mount Nisur. Here Utnapishtim's boat landed.

But what could come of that? Was there yet any dry land on which they all could live? After seven days had passed, Utnapishtim released a dove to see if it could find dry land, but it soon returned, having found no place to land.

Utnapishtim waited another seven days, then released a sparrow. But it, too, returned.

Utnapishtim waited another seven days, then released a raven. It did not return. At last, Utnapishtim realized, the waters had receded, at least enough for everyone to disembark.

Grateful for the lives of himself and his people, Utnapishtim made a sacrifice to the gods. For his faithfulness, he and his wife were given immortality and lived together in Dilmun at the end of the earth.

Sources

Dalley, Stephanie. *Myths from Mesopotamia*. Oxford: Oxford University Press, 1989.
Gardner, John, and John Maier. *Gilgamesh*. New York: Alfred Knopf, 1984.
Kramer, Samuel Noah. *Sumerian Mythology*. New York: Harper and Brothers, 1961.

TELEPINU'S ANGER
A Myth of the Ancient Hittites

It's not unusual to see a story about a son having a fight with his father, or of a spoiled young man having a temper tantrum—but in this case the myth dates to the first millennium B.C.E. and involves the Hittite deities. Is this the record of a long-forgotten drought? Or is it a distant echo of the Greek myth of Demeter, whose hunt for her lost daughter, Persephone, also brought fertility to a standstill? The story of Demeter can be found later in this chapter.

The Hittites, for those who may not recognize the name, were a warrior people who lived in ancient Anatolia and are particularly noted as the people who discovered the use of iron. They also share with the Egyptians the distinction of having signed the first international peace treaty, during the reign of Ramses II (1304–1237 B.C.E.).

Once Telepinu, god of fertility, quarreled with his father, Tarhun, god of storms. No one knows what caused the quarrel, though it was not the first argument that sons have had with fathers, and it was certainly not the last. All that is known of this quarrel is that Telepinu became so angry he rushed away from Tarhun. And with him went the spirits of the gentle winds and the ripening grain. Telepinu carried with him all the lush green growth of fields and forests.

At last, worn out, he came to a meadow in the midst of wilderness. Here Telepinu lay down and fell into a deep, deep sleep.

Now the whole earth suffered. There were no winds to stir the grain, there was no grain for animals to eat, there were no babies born into the world.

Tarhun knew what was wrong, and said to all the other gods, "Go find my son, Telepinu. Beg him to return to me."

But the other gods could not find Telepinu.

Tarhun sought advice from his father, Telepinu's grandfather. The older god declared in an old man's rage that it was all Tarhun's fault. Tarhun was the one who had made Telepinu so angry, and if he did not find his son and get everything restored, the old god would kill Tarhun.

Tarhun then went to his mother, Nintu. She soothed her son and advised him to simply find Telepinu. Then she would see that everything was made right.

But Telepinu still could not be found, and again Tarhun sought out Nintu. She told him to stay calm and not worry. She would send a bee to find the missing god.

Sure enough, the bee found the missing god and woke him from his sleep with a sharp sting. This only angered Telepinu even more. Raging, he dried up streams and brought flooding to the coasts, drowning animals and humans.

The goddess of healing and magic, whose name we have not, chanted soothing charms, and a human was called up to pray to Telepinu for peace. Slowly the anger was removed from Telepinu's heart.

And all was as it had been before.

Sources

Gaster, Theodor H. *The Oldest Stories in the World*. Boston: Beacon, 1952.
Kramer, Samuel Noah, ed. *Mythologies of the Ancient World*. Garden City, NY: Anchor Books, 1961.

DEUCALION AND PYRRHA
A Myth from Ancient Greece

Here is yet another version of the great flood and two righteous survivors. Deucalion and Pyrrha, too, build a boat that comes to rest on a mountaintop, in this case Mount Parnassus in Greece. This story

According to ancient Greek mythology, Zeus spared only two—Deucalion and Pyrrha—when he destroyed all of humanity by flooding the world. Here, Deucalion and Pyrrha toss stones over their shoulders to create a new race of people. (*Scala/Art Resource, New York*)

almost certainly postdates the Mesopotamian and biblical versions, and lacks details such as the animals coming on board the ship or the birds sent out to find land.

*I*n the ancient days, Zeus, ruler of gods and men, grew angry with the wicked ways of the human race and vowed to destroy them all by a flood.

Only two would he spare. One was Deucalion, who was king of Phthia in Thessaly, and the other was Deucalion's wife, Pyrrha. They alone would survive because they alone had led good lives and remained faithful to the laws of the gods. So Zeus sent Prometheus, Deucalion's father, to warn him of the coming flood. Deucalion and Pyrrha built a boat, just in time. Zeus sent down torrents of rain for nine days and nine nights, but Deucalion and Pyrrha were out of harm's way in their boat, which carried them at last to a safe resting place atop Mount Parnassus.

But they were now alone. What could they do? They went to the Delphic oracle, which had been too powerful to be destroyed by the flood. The oracle ordered them to cast their mother's bones over their shoulders.

After much thought, Deucalion and Pyrrha realized that this must mean the stones of Mother Earth. So they threw stones over their shoulders, and up from the stones sprang a new race of people.

Sources

Dundes, Alan, ed. *The Flood Myth*. Berkeley: University of California Press, 1988.
Larousse World Mythology. Secaucus, NJ: Chartwell Books, 1977.

THE FLOOD GIANTS
A Myth from Ancient Lithuania

This is another version of a deity, angry at sinful humanity, sending a flood to destroy them. In this case, the agents are water and wind working together. The motif of the ark turns up, but in a folkloric version: the nutshell that magically becomes a boat. The image of the nutshell boat can even be found in Shakespeare's plays.

The motif of the comforting rainbow is almost certainly taken from the biblical version. The portion of the myth in which the old couple jump nine times over the "bones of the earth" is pagan and, like the idea of the nine couples springing up, is probably much older than the arrival of Christianity into the region in the first millennium C.E.

The great god Pramzimas looked out from his heavenly window and saw among humanity nothing but war and injustice. Angrily he sent two giants, Wandu and Wejas, water and wind, to destroy the earth.

After twenty days and nights of storm, little was left of the old world. Pramzimas looked out to see, and threw down a nutshell. It landed on the peak of the tallest mountain, where some people and animals had sought refuge. They all climbed into the nutshell boat and survived the flood.

Pramzimas' wrath faded. He ordered the wind and the water to abate. The people who had survived in the nutshell boat spread out over the drying earth, all except for one elderly couple who stayed where they had landed. Pramzimas sent a rainbow to comfort them, then told the couple to jump over the bones of the earth, the rocks, nine times.

They did so. And up sprang nine other couples. It is from these nine couples that the nine Lithuanian tribes descend.

Sources

Greimas, Algirdas J. *Of Gods and Men: Studies in Lithuanian Mythology*. Translated by Milda Newman. Bloomington: Indiana University Press, 1992.
Leeming, David Adams. *The World of Myth: An Anthology*. New York and Oxford: Oxford University Press, 1990.

ALEXANDER THE GREAT FLOODS THE WORLD
A Myth from Turkey

Alexander the Great may seem an unlikely protagonist of a flood myth—but a whole cycle of myths and folktales sprang up about him, turning him from a historical figure who died relatively young into a godlike figure who will never die.

This particular myth combines an odd mix of medieval elements— the conflict between Moslems and Christians—and geologic origin tales, such as the origin of the Strait of Gibraltar.

Alexander the Great, pictured here in an Austrian church's stained-glass window, conquered much of the world and quickly became a central figure in a wide range of mythological tales. In the myth from Turkey, Alexander the Great almost floods the world in an attempt to drown Katife, queen of Smyrna. (A. M. *Rosati/Art Resource, New York*)

*I*n the days of Iskender-Iulcarni, who is also known as Alexander the Great, when he had conquered much of the world, he demanded tribute from Katife, queen of Smyrna.

She refused. Worse, the queen threatened to drown him if he continued.

"This cannot be!" Iskender roared. "Queen Katife shall be punished!"

He would drown her in a great flood, Iskender determined, and hired both Moslems and infidels to make a strait, the Bosphorus.

He paid the infidel workers only one-fifth as much as he paid the Moslems. But when the work on the canal was nearly done, he paid the Moslem workers only one-fifth as much as he paid the infidels. The Moslem workers quit in disgust. Before the infidel workers could finish the canal, the Black Sea broke through the dikes and flooded the land. Not only did it drown Queen Katife and her country, it drowned many other lands. Indeed, the whole world would have been flooded, but people ran to Iskender-Iulcarni to plead with him. At last he was prevailed upon to open a new strait, the Strait of Gibraltar. The flood escaped out into the great ocean, and the world was saved.

Sources

Dundes, Alan, ed. *The Flood Myth.* Berkeley: University of California Press, 1988.
Hoppin, Frederick C. *Great Adventures in History and Legend.* Philadelphia: David McKay, 1940.

THE FLOOD OF GOOD AND EVIL
A Myth from Ancient Persia

In early Iran, before Islam gained a foothold, there was Ormuzd, a deity of supreme good. There was also a force of supreme evil, Ahriman. It was believed that good and evil were forever battling and that a balance must always be maintained.

In this myth, a series of floods are created to destroy the evil that is threatening to overwhelm the earth. In the process, the myth includes an explanation for the roar of thunder, the birth of rivers, and the salt in the oceans.

*I*n the earliest of times, good and evil were already enemies. In those times, the earth had many foul beings created by the most evil of beings, Ahriman.

Ormuzd, the supreme force of good, would not let evil control the world. He sent the angel Tistar, who is also known as the star Sirius, to the earth.

Tistar descended to the earth three times, the first time in the form of a man, the second in the form of a horse, and the third in the form of a bull. Each visit caused ten full days and nights of rain. And each raindrop was as large as a bowl. The water swiftly rose to the height of a tall man and covered the whole earth.

The first of the three floods drowned the evil creatures, but as they died, they fled into holes in the earth.

The second of the three floods began with Tistar, who had taken the form of a white horse, battling the demon Apaosha, who took the form of a black horse. Ormuzd saw the battle and blasted the demon with lightning. Humans can still hear the echo of the demon's cry in thunderstorms. Tistar won the battle and caused rivers to flow. The poison that washed from the land during the second flood turned the seas salty.

The third flood was the greatest of all. The waters were blown to the ends of the earth by a mighty wind and became the sea Vourukasha, the "wide-gulfed."

The balance of good and evil was restored. But the battle continues even to this day.

Sources

Cavendish, Richard, ed. *Legends of the World: A Cyclopedia of the Enduring Myths, Legends and Sagas of Mankind.* New York: Schocken Books, 1982.
Hinnells, John R. *Persian Mythology.* London: Paul Hamlyn, 1973.

THE JUST MAN AND THE FLOOD
A Myth from Ancient India

This myth begins with the cosmic egg and the birth of Brahma, then continues with the story of the just man, the sage named Manu, and the miraculous fish. This ever-growing fish has its analogues in folkloric creatures from around the world, from lowly lice to dragons, that grow from small to amazingly large. But the point of this myth is the unfailing kindness Manu shows to the fish. This gains him the warning of the great flood.

And now the motif of the great boat, the ark, turns up, together with a warning that Manu must include in it "the seeds of everything." In this space age, that sounds very much like the science-fiction idea of taking species into space as frozen embryos!

Then the myth takes a turn that seems odd to Western readers, when the offerings become a beautiful woman—who becomes Manu's daughter.

*I*n the days before time, floods often covered the new earth. But then, when yet another flood covered the world, the world spirit threw a seed into the waters. The seed grew inside an egg and at last became Brahma.

After one year of being, Brahma split his body into two parts. One half was male, and the other half was female.

Viraj, who was male, grew inside the female half. And it was Viraj who then went on to create Manu.

Manu was a sage, a *rishi*, who lived ten thousand years in the worship of Brahma.

Now, one day, while Manu was meditating by a stream, a fish raised its head out of the water and begged, "Please save me from the fish that chases me!"

Manu scooped up the fish and placed it in a pond. The fish thrived and grew. And after some time, it outgrew the pond.

"I have no room to swim," the fish said to Manu. "Please, put me in the river Ganges."

Manu picked up the fish and placed it into the river Ganges. The fish thrived and grew. And after some time, the fish grew too large for the river.

"Once again I have no room to swim," the fish said to Manu. "Please put me into the ocean."

Manu took the fish from the river and carefully put it into the ocean. There the fish said, "I am content."

And then Manu learned a startling truth: He had rescued Brahma himself. In return for Manu's unfailing kindness, Brahma warned Manu that the world would soon be destroyed by a great flood.

"You must build a great boat," Brahma warned, "and place within it the seven *rishis* and the seeds of everything."

Manu hastily did as Brahma stated. No sooner had he gotten all aboard the boat than the great deluge began. Once again everything in the world was covered by water. Manu's boat tossed about on the waves and at last came to rest on the tallest peak of the tallest mountain of the Himalayas. There Manu moored it to a tree.

After many years had passed, the floodwaters receded. Manu came down from the mountain into the valleys. There Manu performed the proper sac-rifices, offering up milk, clarified butter, curds, and whey to Brahma. He did this every day for a year. And at the end of the year his offerings had become a beautiful woman.

"I am your daughter," she said.

The two remained true in their devotion to Brahma, and Manu went on to father the human race.

Sources

Danielou, Alain. *The Myths and Gods of India*. Rutland, VT: Inner Traditions
International, 1991.
Dundes, Alan, ed. *The Flood Myth*. Berkeley: University of California Press, 1988.

MANU THE CREATOR
A Myth of the Hindu People

This is another version of the previous myth, wherein the fish returns Manu's kindness by dragging his ship safely through the floodwaters to a safe mooring, then turns into Parjapati Brahma, who tells Manu that he will be the creator of every living thing.

The great sage Manu, son of Vivasvat, practiced ascetic fervor. In his purity of will, he stood on one leg with one arm raised, looking down without blinking, for ten thousand years.

While he so stood on the banks of the Chirini, a fish swam up to him and asked to be saved from larger fish. Manu took the fish to a jar. As the fish grew, Manu took the fish to a pool. As the fish grew, Manu took the fish to the river Ganges. At last, as the fish grew, Manu took the fish to the ocean.

As soon as it was released into the ocean, the fish told Manu, "Soon all earthly things will be dissolved in the time of the purification."

It commanded Manu to build a strong ship with a sturdy cable attached and to embark with the seven *rishis* and certain seeds. Manu must then watch for the fish, since the flood could not be safely crossed without its help.

Manu did as he was ordered. The flood came, and his boat rode the waves. Manu stood at the rail, watching for the fish. The fish swam up and told Manu to fasten the ship's cable to it.

Manu did. The fish dragged the ship through the wild waters for many years, but at last brought it safely to the highest peak of Himavat, which is still known by some as Naubandhana, "the binding of the ship."

The fish then revealed itself as Parjapati Brahma and told Manu that he should be the one to create all living things and all things moving and fixed. And so it was that it was Manu who called things into existence.

Sources

Danielou, Alain. *The Myths and Gods of India*. Rutland, VT: Inner Traditions
International, 1991.
Dundes, Alan, ed. *The Flood Myth*. Berkeley: University of California Press, 1988.

THE ORPHANS AND THE FLOOD
A Myth from Yunnan Province, China

Here is a combination of motifs. One is the great flood. Another is that of the poor orphans whom no one wants to help who turn out to be winners—in this case, survivors. A third is that of the two virtuous people who are the only survivors of the flood. Then there is the motif of the multiple suns and moons that must be shot down for the sake of the world. For two other tales of multiple suns, see the Cambodian Hmong tale "Why There Is Day and Night," in Chapter 3, and the Chinese tale "Hou Yi and Chang'er," in Chapter 5.

*A*fter death came into the world, sky and earth alike began to lust for human souls and bones. That was the beginning of the great flood.

Now, in those ancient days, there lived two orphans, a boy and a girl. They were very poor, with barely enough to eat. No one in their village would help them.

A badge from a nineteenth-century Chinese court official's robe, embroidered with a dragon. As rulers of the four seas, dragon kings are approached to avoid droughts and to avert floods. In the story of the orphans and the flood, the young boy and girl use the dragon king's bow and arrows to shoot down all but the brightest sun and moon. (*Werner Forman/Art Resource, New York*)

One day two golden birds flew down to the orphans. "Beware! Beware! A huge wave is coming to flood the world."

"What can we do?" the boy asked.

"Where can we go?" the girl asked.

"You must take shelter in a gourd and not come out until you hear us sing again."

The two children hurried to warn their neighbors, but no one in the village would believe them.

"We cannot wait," the boy said to the girl.

They sawed off the top of a great gourd and crept inside, pulling the top back into place behind them.

For ninety-nine days there was neither wind nor rain. The earth grew parched and dry. Then the rain began, wild torrents of water that flooded the world and washed everything away.

The children huddled together in the gourd as it rode the waves. Would they never hear the birds again? Would they never walk on dry land again?

But then at last they heard birdsong. The boy and girl crept out of the gourd and found themselves on a mountaintop. Below them the floodwaters had receded.

But now—oh, strange and terrible, there were nine suns and seven moons in the sky, scorching the earth all day.

Then the two golden birds flew down to the children, bearing between them a golden hammer and a silver pair of tongs. "You must get the bow and arrows of the dragon king," they told the children, and explained to them how that could be done.

So the boy and girl went to the pond under which the dragon king lived, and started hitting the reef roof of the dragon king with the hammer. This made so much noise that the dragon king said to his fishy servants, "Go up there and find out who is making that racket."

As soon as the fish reached the surface, the children grabbed them with the tongs and threw them on the bank.

Below, the dragon king fumed and paced. At last he said, "I will go up there and check matters out for myself."

But as soon as he surfaced, the children caught him with the tongs. To free himself, the dragon king had to give them his bow and arrows. With these magical tools, the boy and girl shot down all but the brightest sun and moon.

Now they needed to find other people. They went north and south, east and west, but saw no one else. The golden birds appeared again and said that there were no other people.

So as soon as they were grown, the boy and girl married. They had six sons and six daughters, and these children, who set out in all directions, became the ancestors of all the races.

Sources

Walls, Jan, and Yvonne Walls. *Classical Chinese Myths*. Hong Kong: Joint Publishing, 1984.
Werner, E. T. C. *Myths and Legends of China*. Singapore: Singapore National Printers, 1922.

THE HUNTER'S WARNING
A Myth from Mongolia

This myth begins in folkloric fashion, with a hunter rescuing a snake from an attacker and being promised a reward in exchange. That the snake turns out to be the dragon king's daughter, the daughter of the king of the snakes, or another royal being is a common variation.

The gift of understanding the language of the animals is another common motif. Sometimes the gift is an actual gem or stone, as in this myth and several from sub-Saharan Africa. In other stories, the gift comes from tasting forbidden food, as in the Welsh story "Gwion's Rebirth," later in this chapter, or dragon's blood, as in the Teutonic story "Sigurd," in Chapter 5.

What makes this myth particularly poignant is the hopeless choice faced by the hunter: Warn the people and be turned to stone, or fail to warn them and see them all drown. At least his sacrifice is honored by the people he saved.

Once a kind and generous hunter named Hailibu heard a cry for help. Rushing through the forest, he found a small white snake being attacked by a crane, a large and hungry bird. It was the snake that had called for help, so Hailibu chased off the crane with shouts and waves.

"You have saved me," the grateful snake told Hailibu. "Soon I will help you."

On the next day Hailibu came upon the same white snake—but this time she had come with a retinue of other snakes.

"I am the dragon king's daughter," the snake told him. "My father wishes to reward you for saving me. But here is what you must do. No matter what he offers you, ask only for the gem that my father keeps in his mouth. With that gem," she added, "you will be able to understand the language of the animals. But I warn you: If ever you tell your secret to anyone, you will be turned to stone."

Hailibu went to the dragon king, turned down his many other treasures, and was given the stone.

Years later Hailibu heard some birds saying that the next day the mountains would erupt and flood the land. He went back home to warn his neighbors, but they didn't believe him. To convince them, he told them how he had learned of the coming flood, then told them the full story of the precious stone.

When he had finished his story, he turned to stone. The villagers, seeing this happen, fled. It rained all the next night, and the mountains belched forth a great flood of water.

When the people could finally return, after the floodwaters had receded, they found the stone into which Hailibu had turned and placed it at the top of the mountain. For generations after, their descendants have offered sacrifices to the stone in honor of Hailibu's sacrifice.

Sources

Leeming, David Adams. *The World of Myth: An Anthology*. New York and Oxford: Oxford University Press, 1990.

Metternich, Hilary Roe. *Mongolian Folktales*. Boulder, CO: Avery, 1996.

THE PERILOUS FISH
A Myth of the Valman People of New Guinea

This myth has in it the motif of the good man who will be spared from the flood. Here the flood comes not because of wholesale wickedness on the part of the people, but because they break a prohibition by eating the strange fish. But since the breaking of a taboo can lead to death, this isn't a small transgression at all. There is no ark in this story, but a refuge in a coconut tree.

There was once a very good man who kept all the rules of his people. One day his wife thought she saw a big fish in the lake. She called her husband, but he couldn't see any fish until he hid behind a banana tree and peeked through its leaves.

This was a warning. The fish that could be seen only in special circumstances was not to be eaten by mortals. The man was frightened and told his family that they must not catch and eat that fish.

But other people laughed at the man's warning. They caught the fish and, still laughing, ate it.

When the good man saw that, he hastily drove as many animals as he could up into trees and climbed into a coconut tree with his family.

Sure enough, as soon as those foolish others ate the fish, a wild flood of water burst from the ground and drowned everyone there.

The water rose as high as the treetops, but then it sank again just as rapidly. The good man and his family, and the animals he'd saved, climbed back down again. As soon as the land was dry enough, the good man and his family laid out a new farm, and all went well with them.

Sources

LeRoy, John, ed. *Kewa Tales*. Vancouver: University of British Columbia, 1985.
Poignant, Roslyn. *Oceanic Mythology*. London: Hamlyn, 1967.

THE FORBIDDEN NAMES
A Myth of the Skagit People

This myth focuses on the power of words, four special names that are too powerful for humanity to know. Words are indeed powerful, as the Judeo-Christian tradition states: "In the beginning was the word." And when the four words are misused, that causes the flood.

In this myth, there is the boat, in this case the giant canoe. There are five human survivors, rather than the more common two, though the myth does not specify whether they are particularly moral. But what is specific to this story is the birth to a survivor of Doquebuth, the new creator, and the re-creation of humanity from the bones of those who had lived before the flood. The myth then continues with the creation theme that explains the different languages of the world. And unlike the Judeo-Christian flood myth, this one states that someday there will be another flood.

When the creator made the world, he gave four special names for it—for the sun, the water, the earth, and the forests. He warned that only a few people, those with special learning about the weight of the knowledge, should know all four names, or there would be sudden changes in the world, far too sudden.

But humans are not as good as they should be about keeping secrets. After a while almost everyone had learned the four powerful names.

Mount Rainier, known as Takhomah to the Skagit people, was only one of two mountains that did not succumb to the terrifying flood. According to the Skagit story, the great flood was caused by humanity's inability to keep the forbidden names a secret. (*Mary Evans Picture Library*)

Sure enough, as soon as someone without the needed learning said one of the names, the world changed. The change came in the form of a terrifying flood.

Only five people were spared. They had hastily carved out a giant canoe, climbed into it, and filled it with males and females of all the plants and animals.

The floodwaters rose and covered all the world save the peaks of Kobah and Takhomah, the mountains now known as Baker and Rainier.

At last the canoe came to a rest on the prairie. Born to one of the couples who had survived was one of great power. He was Doquebuth, the new creator.

The Old Creator came to him in dreams. First he told Doquebuth that he must wave his blanket over the water and the forest and name the four powerful names of the earth. He did, and fertility returned to the world.

Next Doquebuth gathered the bones of the people who lived before the flood. He waved his blanket over them and named the four powerful names, and they became living people again. But because they had been remade, they were not as they had been. At first they couldn't even talk. Doquebuth had to make new brains for them from the soil. Then they could talk, but spoke many different languages. So Doquebuth blew them to places all over the world.

But someday another flood will come and change the world again.

Sources

Clark, Ella E. *Indian Legends of the Pacific Northwest*. Berkeley: University of California Press, 1953.

Norman, Howard. *Northern Tales, Traditional Stories of Eskimo and Indian Peoples*. New York: Pantheon Books, 1990.

THE LAST PEOPLE
A Myth from the Aztecs of Mexico

This is a flood myth with an unusual twist. The good family is warned by the Old One to build a great canoe. They survive the flood and land safely. But then they break a prohibition and cook fish when they have been warned not to build a fire. As a result, they are turned into monkeys and buzzards, and the myth ends with the Old One creating new and better people.

*I*n the long-ago days, the Old One grew sad and angry with humanity. They had not been honoring him, nor had they been keeping the Old One's rules.

"They must be destroyed," the Old One decided.

But one family were good, hard workers, forever tending their fields of maize, and the Old One thought that they alone would be spared.

So he said to them, "You must listen well to what I say. I will destroy all the people in the world except for you. You must find the biggest cedar tree in the forest. Cut down that tree and hollow a great canoe out of its trunk. You must then fill the canoe with enough food and water for many days. Soon I will make the rain fall, and it will fall harder and faster than ever it has rained before. If your boat is not ready, you shall surely drown."

The family hurried to do what the Old One had commanded. And after days of hard work, they were ready. They had cut down the tree and hollowed a great canoe out of its trunk. They had piled it high with food and drink.

The rain started. The family climbed into the boat and pulled their sleeping mats over its top to keep the water out of it.

They slept.

In the morning they woke when they felt the canoe lurch. The canoe was floating. The water rose all day and all night, and soon their canoe was floating above the tallest trees.

The day passed, and the water rose. When the family woke the next morning, they cried out in alarm.

"There's nothing but water!" they cried. "Nothing but water as far as we can see!"

They floated on for days. As the Old One had warned, they soon had eaten all their food and drunk all their water. Before they could begin to starve, however, the Old One ordered the waters of the earth to go down, back to the oceans, lakes, and rivers.

The hungry family found dead fish lying on the ground. They started to eat the fish raw.

"Wait, wait, we will build a fire and cook them. They will taste better that way."

But the Old One commanded, "Do not build a fire."

Why was this commanded? No one knows. But as soon as the Old One was gone, the family began to wail and cry. They were hungry, and they didn't want to eat raw fish.

Soon the aroma of cooking fish reached the Old One's nostrils. His orders had been disobeyed! Furious, he stormed down to the family and changed the father and mother into chattering monkeys and the children into buzzards.

That was the end of the last people. The Old One then created new and better people, and was content.

Sources

Portilla, Miguel Leon. *Pre-Columbian Literatures of Mexico.* Norman: University of Oklahoma Press, 1969.

Taube, Karl. *Aztec and Maya Myths.* Austin: University of Texas Press, 1994.

Tedlock, Dennis, trans. *Popol Vuh.* New York: Simon and Schuster, 1985.

THE MAN AND THE DOG
A Myth of the Huichol of Western Mexico

Here is another tale of a man warned of a coming flood, in this case warned by the earth goddess. Instead of a true boat, his boat is a large box, which the goddess seals up. When his box-boat comes to rest on a mountain, it is the parrots and macaws who change the land to drain it.

Now the myth takes a new twist, with the man's bitch secretly becoming a woman who takes care of his house. This is a common theme in the world's mythology. Sometimes, as in Japanese tales, the mysterious housekeeper is a fox spirit. Sometimes the mysterious housekeeper is human but hiding for reasons of her own or for no apparent reasons at all.

Baptism is an important ritual in many cultures, past and present. For instance, the ancient Welsh seem to have practiced a form of it, dipping a child in the sea. And Christianity also has a baptismal ceremony. The ritual baptism in *nixtamal* water in this myth is the power that keeps the dog-woman a woman.

A farmer clearing his fields one day stopped in surprise. The trees he had cut away had grown back! Maybe he had not cut them back enough. The farmer set out to work again.

But the trees grew back overnight.

On the fifth day of clearing and regrowth, the farmer went out to his fields to hear a voice that was never a human voice.

"I am Grandmother Nakawe, goddess of the earth," it told him. "I have made the trees grow back like this because I wish to talk to you."

"I am listening," the farmer said.

"You may cease your farming. You are working in vain because a flood will be here in five days. Listen to my words, and you will be safe."

The farmer was not a fool. He followed the goddess' instructions and carved out a large box from a fig tree. He climbed into it, taking with him five grains of corn, five beans of every color, a coal of fire with five squash stems to feed it, and a dog, his black bitch.

"Well done," said Grandmother Nakawe.

She closed him into the box, then caulked the cracks. The flood came as she had predicted, and the farmer floated in the waves for five years, sailing south, then north, then west, then east. At last the whole world went under the waves.

Finally the box came to rest on a mountain. The world was still under water, but at the will of the goddess, parrots and macaws pulled up mountains and created valleys to drain the water, and the land dried. The goddess, who had sat upon the box with a macaw during the flood, smiled, nodded, turned to wind, and disappeared.

The farmer climbed out of the box and found a home for himself and the bitch in a cave, and began clearing the land for a farm. But something strange happened. Every evening he returned home from work in the fields to find his meal prepared. Yet there was no other human but himself.

One day the farmer pretended to leave for the fields but hid instead, spying on the cave. He found that as soon as she thought he was gone, the bitch took off her skin and became a woman. The farmer rushed in and threw her dog's skin into the fire. She gave a whine like a frightened dog, but he bathed her in *nixtamal* water and she remained a woman. They married and repopulated the earth.

Sources

Bierhorst, John. *The Mythology of Mexico and Central America.* New York: William Morrow, 1990.

Davis, E. Adams. *Of the Night Wind's Telling: Legends from the Valley of Mexico.* Norman: University of Oklahoma Press, 1946.

THE SNAKE BROTHER
A Myth of the Jivaro People of Ecuador

In this myth, the theme of a broken prohibition appears again, and leads to another theme, transformation. The boy who has eaten the taboo food, the cooked snake, goes through a series of transformations before becoming a snake.

From that point on, the snake plays the role of divine messenger, warning his brother of the coming flood. The myth takes the standard course: The boy tries to warn the people, who refuse to heed him. The flood in this myth is clearly a local one, and at the end of it, there's the less common image of the boy and his snake brother walking off to find new lands.

Once two brothers went hunting in the forest, looking for food for their people. Their arrows brought down a fat, heavy capybara. It was too heavy for the boys to carry, so they hurried to find a pole on which they could carry it.

But when they hurried back, they found no capybara, nothing but empty ground. Who could have stolen it?

"We will pretend to leave," one boy whispered to the other. "But only you will leave. I will wait and see if the thief will return."

The other brother left. The first brother stood as still as the trees around him.

Aha! Here was the thief, a giant snake, creeping out of the hollow tree in which it had hidden.

"Brother! Come help me!"

His brother came running. Together they built a fire to drive the snake out of the hollow tree. With a hiss, the snake fell—and landed right in the fire, where it died.

"I am so hungry," the first brother said.

"No! Do not eat!"

But he wouldn't listen. He ate some of the snake's roasted flesh.

"I am so thirsty!" he cried.

He ran to the nearby lake and drank.

Suddenly he was a boy no longer. He was transformed first into a frog, then into a lizard, and finally into a snake, which grew rapidly.

His brother was frightened and tried to pull him out, but the lake began to overflow. The snake told his brother that the lake would continue to grow and all the people would perish unless they made their escape. The snake told him to take a calabash and flee to a palm tree on the highest mountain.

The brother told his people what was happening, but they didn't believe him. He gave up trying to convince them and fled to the top of a palm tree on the top of a mountain. Sure enough, the flood came roaring out over the land.

The boy returned to the ground many days later when the waters had subsided. Vultures were eating the dead people in the valley. Sadly the boy went to the lake.

"You were right," he told the snake.

He carried away his brother in a calabash, and they traveled off to find a new land together.

Sources

Bierhorst, John. *The Mythology of Mexico and Central America*. New York: William Morrow, 1990.

Dundes, Alan, ed. *The Flood Myth*. Berkeley: University of California Press, 1988.

SEVEN STONES
A Myth from the Ekoi of Nigeria

This myth begins with the first two humans, who come from the land above the sky. For another tale involving the descent of humanity from the sky, see the Wyandot myth "The Origin of the World."

Water, or rather, the means to create it, is a gift that must not be abused. But of course it is abused, by one of the first humans' lazy grandsons, and a flood ensues. As with "The Snake Brother," preceding this myth, the flood here is a local one, and in the end only the lazy man is punished.

*T*he first people to live on the earth were Etim 'Ne and his wife, Ejaw. They came there from the land above the sky.

At first there was no water on earth. Etim 'Ne looked up to the sky and asked the god Obassi Osaw for water. He was given a calabash with seven clear stones and was told what to do. When Etim 'Ne dug a small hole in the ground and placed a stone in it, water would well out to become a lake.

With water, the land prospered, and so did the first two people. Time passed, and children were born to them, seven sons and seven daughters.

More time passed, and the sons and daughters grew up. They married and had children of their own. Etim 'Ne gave each household a river or lake of its own. When three of his sons proved to be poor hunters who didn't share their meat in the proper fashion, he took away their rivers, but returned them when the sons agreed to try harder.

When his grandchildren had grown up and established their own homes, Etim 'Ne sent for them. He told them to each take seven stones from their parents' river and plant them at regular intervals to create new streams.

All the children did as they were told—except for one who was lazy. He gathered a whole basketful of stones, then dumped them out in a pile. Water poured up, flooding his farm. Nor did the water stop there. The flood threatened the whole earth.

All his children ran to Etim 'Ne. Etim 'Ne prayed to Obassi. The god stopped the flood. But a lake remained where the lazy son's farm had been.

Etim 'Ne was very old by now. He told his children and grandchildren to remember him as the bringer of water to the world. And then, peacefully, he died.

Sources

Abrahams, Roger D. *African Folktales*. New York: Random House, 1983.
Dundes, Alan, ed. *The Flood Myth*. Berkeley: University of California Press, 1988.

HOSPITALITY REPAID
A Myth of the Bakongo of Zaire

The moral of this myth is clear enough: Kindness to the unfortunate is not only a good deed, it's a deed that can have a powerful reward. Here the kindhearted people are saved from a flood.

The theme of an ugly beggar or worn old woman who is much more than the outer appearance turns up in myths and folktales from around the world. Sometimes the figure seeking charity is a fairy woman in disguise, sometimes a holy being, and sometimes an angelic one.

There really have been villages swamped by floods or a rising ocean, such as can be seen off the coast of some of the British Isles, but they also turn up in myth and folklore, including the Cornish tale of the lost city of Ys.

Once, long ago indeed, a woman came to a town called Sonanzenzi, nestled in a green valley. The woman was old and weary, covered with sores and dust.

When she asked for hospitality at the first home she reached, the people turned her away. "We don't like beggars here."

When she asked for hospitality at the second home she reached, those people turned her away, too. "We don't like beggars here."

In fact, all the people in the town turned her away, until she had reached the very last home in Sonanzenzi. There the people took one look at the weary old thing and said, "Poor thing, you look so weary! Come inside and rest."

The husband of the household brought her cool water to drink. The children brought her clean clothes. And the wife of the household brought her a meal.

At last the old woman was rested and fed and ready to leave. "You must pack up and leave with me," she said, and her voice wasn't that of a weary old woman at all. "This town is accursed and will be destroyed tonight."

The family heeded her warning. Packing up their belongings, they hurried away. Sure enough, that night the flooding rains came. They quickly turned the valley into a lake and drowned all the people of Sonanzenzi. They say that the houses can still be seen where they lie deep under the lake.

Sources

Courlander, Harold. A *Treasure of African Folklore*. New York: Marlowe, 1996.
Feldmann, Susan. *African Myths and Tales*. New York: Dell, 1963.

MYTHS OF REBIRTH

ISIS AND OSIRIS
A Myth from Ancient Egypt

As happened in ancient Greece, Egypt had overlays of new culture over old. But unlike what occurred in Greece, with invaders overturning the mythic system and installing their own pantheon on top of the old, Egypt tended to absorb local gods into its pantheon and mesh newer deities into the existing mythic system. See "The War of Horus and Set," in Chapter 4, for a council of new and old gods together. Isis, Osiris, and Set are some of the newer gods, which may be why a myth was needed to show Osiris not as king of the gods (that role was already filled by Ra) but as king of the underworld.

Isis was one of the most popular deities, both in Egypt and, later, in imperial Rome. She is a complex character, the mistress of magic, the devoted mother, the fierce competitor—see, for example, "Isis Gains Her Magic Powers," in Chapter 4. Among her other attributes, she is the goddess of married love, and her refusal to lose her husband to death is the strongest theme of this myth. Set, the envious brother of Osiris, is not a truly evil figure, or at least wasn't seen as such by the Egyptians. He is the god of the desert wastes, a chaotic and dangerous being. Set is also portrayed as being redheaded, and the Egyptians shunned redheads and even went so far, in some cases, as to avoid the color red altogether. In addition, the pig was said to be the animal of Set and was ruled unclean. In fact, it was said that a man meeting a pig on the shore of the Nile would jump into the river, risking crocodiles, rather than chance touching the unclean animal.

Was Osiris originally a god of the underworld, or of vegetation and rebirth? And rather than taking on the role, was it already his? Although there's no evidence, it's true that Osiris is usually portrayed with green skin, marking a clear link with the agricultural gods who die with the harvest and return with the spring.

*I*n the dawn of time, there was Osiris, who was lord of all the gods, and his wife, Isis, who was mistress of magic, and they loved each other truly. But there was also Set, brother to Osiris.

Isis (right), the mistress of magic, appears with her brother-husband Osiris (center), the lord of all gods, and Horus (left), the falcon-headed son of their union. According to Egyptian legend, Horus grows up to avenge his father's murder and succeed him as king. (*Réunion des Musées Nationaux/Art Resource, New York*)

Set, god of the desert wastes, was fiercely jealous of his brother. Why should Osiris and not he be lord of all the gods? The jealousy festered and brought Set to murder his brother, to cut him down, and then, so that Osiris might not return to life, to hack the body into pieces and cast them away.

When Isis found her husband so foully murdered, she grieved deeply. But, being mistress of magic, she did not give up hope or waste too much time in mourning. Instead, Isis set out over the world on the terrible task of gathering up all the pieces of her murdered husband's body. Many tales are told of the mysterious woman who would appear seemingly from nowhere, then vanish just as swiftly.

But at last the terrible task was done. Isis assembled all the pieces of her husband's body in proper order. Some tales say she had been already pregnant before Osiris was slain; other say she worked strong magic so that she and her dead husband could engender a child. Either way, Isis knew the child she carried would be his father's avenger.

Now she turned to the magic needed to bring Osiris back to life. Great and strange was the spell, but it worked. Osiris lived again, and Isis rejoiced. But since it was in the mortal realm that he had been slain, Osiris could walk in it no longer. From then on, he ruled from the underworld, his skin now green to show the mortals that every spring, like Osiris, the vegetation would live again.

Sources

Hart, George. *Egyptian Myths*. Austin: University of Texas Press, 1990.
Simpson, William Kelly, ed. *The Literature of Ancient Egypt*. New Haven: Yale University Press, 1972.

SACRIFICED BY HER KIN
A Myth from the Kikuyu of Kenya

An unwilling sacrifice in mythology is rarely a successful one. In this case, the rains do come, but it is possible for the sacrificed girl to be rescued from the underworld—primarily because the young man who loves her is clever and determined and, unlike Orpheus, makes no tragic mistakes.

*T*his was in the ancient days. There was a year without rain, then a second year without rain, and a third year without rain. The grass turned brown, the animals fled, and the crops of the people withered and died.

That third year, the people gathered together and told their shaman, "If there is no rain soon, we will all starve. What can we do to bring the rain?"

The shaman studied the omens over and over. At last he said, "There is a young woman among us, and her name is Wanjiru. Let each family bring a goat to her family that the village may pay her bride price. And then, if there is to be rain, she must be sacrificed."

The young woman cried out in horror. But her family said nothing to defend her. They accepted the goats and stood back as the villagers surrounded Wanjiru.

"I am lost!" Wanjiru cried.

Her feet sank into the earth. Then she sank up to her knees, then her waist.

"I am lost!" she cried again. "At least the rain will come."

She sank up to her neck.

And the rain came, pouring down in torrents. Now her family could have saved her, but they still stood back, afraid.

"My family has undone me!" Wanjiru cried, and vanished under the earth.

But the story does not end there. There was a young man who loved Wanjiru and had planned to wed her. He had been away from the village and did not know what had happened.

"Where is Wanjiru?" he asked when he returned.

When the people told him what had been done, the young man cried to her family in fury, "How could you do this to your own child?"

They hung their heads, ashamed.

The young man grabbed up his spear and shield. "Wherever she has gone, I will follow her!" he cried, and sank into the earth.

He found himself in a dark land, on a dirt road. The young man followed it until he came to where Wanjiru stood, looking lost and alone.

"Don't be afraid," the young man told her. "You were sacrificed to bring the rain. The rain has come, so I have come to take you back!"

He took her on his back as if she'd been a child, and climbed back up to the surface of the earth. "You shall not return to your family," he said. "They treated you so shamefully."

"I will return," Wanjiru said.

Together they confronted her family. They all rejoiced to see her returned. The young man sighed. This was, after all, Wanjiru's family. So he paid them the bride price in goats, and he and Wanjiru were married.

Sources

Abrahams, Roger D. *African Folktales*. New York: Random House, 1983.
Feldmann, Susan. *African Myths and Tales*. New York: Dell, 1963.

THE DEATH AND REBIRTH OF LEMMINKAINEN
A Myth from Finland

Lemminkainen is one of the main heroes of the *Kalevala*. For details on that collective epic, see the notes for the myth "Vainamoinen and the Creation," in Chapter 1.

Lemminkainen is portrayed throughout the *Kalevala* as a brash, handsome, almost arrogant young man, the sort who thinks nothing of taking and then abandoning woman after woman but doesn't mean any real harm. His mother's role is reminiscent of the determination of Isis, and like Isis, she must reassemble the body before Lemminkainen can be restored to life. The myth is as much about her as it is about the young hero, and it is she who gets the final word.

*I*n ancient days, there were heroes in the northern lands such as Lemminkainen, young and handsome, often kind but often reckless. Many loves he'd had, many loves he'd left behind. One such was the maiden Kyllikki, wooed and won, then left behind. Little did Lemminkainen, young and reckless, know a lowly cowherd had sworn vengeance against him. Nasshut, a blind and crippled cowherd, vowed that he would slay the hero.

Onward went the handsome hero. He had seen the home of Louhi, deep within that northern forest, seen her lovely daughters, too, and wished to wed one for himself. But Louhi would not give a daughter to a hero without testing. First he must hunt down and catch the moose of Hisi, then the fire-breathing stallion. Last of all, he must slay the swan that swam in the Tuonela River, the boundary between the living and the dead.

So, taking courage, Lemminkainen spoke these words in supplication:

"Ukko, O thou god above me,

O creator of the heavens,

See my snowshoes well in order,

Then endow them both with swiftness,

That I rapidly may journey

Over marshes, over snow fields,

Over lowlands, over highlands,

To the forest hills of Juutas."

And he called out to the woodlands:

"Greetings bring I to the mountains,

To the valleys and the highlands,

Greetings to the greenest fir trees,

Greetings to the white-barked aspen,

Greetings bring to he who greets you,

Fields, and streams, and woods of Lapland."

So he hunted for his quarry. He saw the moose of Hisi, threw his lasso, snared the antlers, and caught the great beast and brought it back to Louhi. But she insisted that he still must catch the fire-breathing stallion.

Undaunted, Lemminkainen headed outward for this second test of heroes. On the lowlands, in the forests, everywhere he sought the stallion, hunted for the fire-breather. Finally, on the third day of his hunting, Lemminkainen climbed a mountain. And at last he saw the stallion, breathing smoke from mouth and nostrils.

Then the daring Lemminkainen spoke a hero's supplication:

"Ukko, O thou god above me,

Thou who rule all the storm clouds,

Open thou the heaven's vault,

Let the icy rain come falling,

On the flaming horse of Hisi,

On the fire-breathing stallion."

Ukko, that benign creator, heard the prayer of Lemminkainen and sent the cold rain down in torrents on the fiery stallion. The fires were doused, and Lemminkainen, drawing nearer, gently slipped a bridle on the stallion's head. Tamed, the stallion followed him back to Louhi.

But Louhi would not give her daughter to him, not until he'd passed the third test. He must kill the swan that swam in the Tuonela River, the river with its death-dark water.

So the reckless Lemminkainen started out to hunt the wild swan. Never did he know he, too, was being hunted. Nasshut, blind and crippled, he who'd sworn to kill the hero, lay in ambush with a crossbow. Finally he heard the footsteps of Lemminkainen drawing nearer to the river and the swan.

Nasshut shot, and pierced the hero to the heart.

Nasshut cut the body into five parts and then tossed them in the river. "Swim thou in there, Lemminkainen. Hunt forever in those waters!"

But the story is not ended.

Lemminkainen's aged mother wondered where her son had wandered. She had powers more than human, but she could not answer this. Then she chanced to see his hairbrush—and saw blood drops oozing from it. And she knew her son was dead.

Quickly she threw on her long robe and fleetly set out on her journey, hunting for her Lemminkainen. Soon she'd reached the home of Louhi, and asked her, "What have you done with Lemminkainen?"

Louhi said, "For all I know, he's fallen prey to hungry wolves or angry bears."

Lemminkainen's mother answered, "You are only speaking falsehoods. Wolves cannot devour us, nor can bears do any harm. What have you done with Lemminkainen?"

Louhi said, "For all I know, he's drowned within a raging whirlpool."

Lemminkainen's mother answered, "Once more you are speaking falsely. What have you done with Lemminkainen? If you try to lie a third time, I shall send you sure destruction."

Louhi snarled at her, then told her the truth. "He has gone to hunt the swan in the Tuonela River. More than that I do not know."

Now the mother sought her lost one, sought a long time for her hero, sought and sought, but did not find him. She asked the trees if they had seen him.

But the trees said only, "We have care enough already, what with men and fire and axes."

So she asked the moon if it had seen him.

But the moon said only, "I have troubles of my own. All the night I have to wander."

So the mother sought the sun and asked the sun if it had seen him.

And the sun in pity told her of the hero's fate.

Lemminkainen's mother, weeping, rushed off to the forge of Ilmarinen, master smith. "Ilmarinen, metal artist, forge for me a rake of copper. Forge the teeth of strongest metal, teeth a hundred fathoms long."

Ilmarinen quick made the rake in full perfection. Lemminkainen's anxious mother hurried to the Tuonela River. With the rake of magic metal she raked the river and brought to land her son's sad fragments. But the mother shaped her son anew with all her magic. Flesh to flesh and bone to bone she bound his body back together, all the while reciting prayers:

"Where the skin is broken open,

Heal the injuries with magic;

Where the blood has left the body,

Make new blood flow in abundance;

Where the bones are rudely broken,

Mend the breaks in true perfection."

Thus she healed her murdered son and brought him suddenly back to life. With honey brought from heaven's height, she gave him back his mind and speech. "Wake," she told him, and he woke, blinking at her in surprise.

"I have been sleeping for a long while!"

"Longer still would you have slumbered were it not for me," she answered. "Forget the daughters of cold Louhi. They are not the ones for you."

And Lemminkainen, filled with wisdom now at last, agreed. With his loving, faithful mother, he set out for home and family.

Sources

Lonnrot, Elias. *The Kalevala*. Translated by Francis Peabody Magoun Jr. Cambridge: Harvard University Press, 1963.
————. *The Kalevala*. Translated by W. F. Kirby. London: Athlone, 1983.

DEMETER AND PERSEPHONE
A Myth of Ancient Greece

This is one of the more archetypal myths. Reduced to its most basic level, its characters are simply the earth mother, the spring maiden, and death, and its story is just as simply that there can be no fertility for the land unless the maiden is reborn each spring. It's possible, though not provable, that this myth, being so primal, predates the arrival of the Doric peoples into Greece, bringing with them Zeus and the other Olympians, and that when the new beliefs were merged with the older ones, Hades was made the brother of Zeus.

The pomegranate was seen as a fertility symbol in the ancient Near East and ancient Greece because of its hundreds of seeds. There is both irony and blatant symbolism in the idea that Persephone must stay in the underworld for half the year because she ate a single pomegranate seed. There is also a strong link to European folklore: Eating the food of Faerie or its analogs ties a human there forever.

*I*t all began with Persephone, daughter of the goddess Demeter— Demeter, without whom the crops cannot grow or the harvest be reaped. Persephone, young and beautiful, was playing in the summer fields when she was seen by Hades, god of the underworld. Hades not only saw her, he fell passionately in love with her, swept her into his chariot, and sped back to his realm with her.

Now, it must be understood that Hades was the brother of Zeus, and possibly not at all unattractive to Persephone. But that part of the story is unknown.

The goddesses Demeter (left), Triptolemus (center), and Persephone (right) are depicted on a votive relief from Eleusis, c. 440-430 B.C.E. Through a deal struck by Demeter and Hades, god of the underworld, Persephone spends half the year in the living world and half in the underworld. (*Nimatallah/Art Resource, New York*)

All that can be told for certain is Demeter's horror when she called for her daughter and no daughter answered. Demeter searched the world for Persephone, hunting and hunting, all in vain. Neither god nor mortal could give her any help. And in Demeter's grief, she forgot about the ripening grain, the fertile fields. The world lay sere and withered while she mourned.

But at last Helios, god of the sun, revealed that he had seen Hades carry off Persephone. Demeter, raging, insisted that Hades bring her back. But Hades pointed out to Demeter that Persephone had eaten food in the underworld: one pomegranate seed alone, it had been, but that was enough to bind her to the underworld.

This could not be. Persephone could not stay forever in the underworld on the weight of a single pomegranate seed. Demeter and Hades agreed that there must be a balance, a bargain struck.

So it was decided. For half a year Persephone would return to the living world. And that would give the world springtime and fertile summer. But for the second half of the year, Persephone would return to Hades in the underworld. And that would give the world harvest autumn and winter.

And so the balance remains to this day.

Sources

Cavendish, Richard, ed. *Legends of the World: A Cyclopedia of the Enduring Myths, Legends and Sagas of Mankind.* New York: Schocken Books, 1982.

Ovid. *The Metamorphoses.* Translated by Horace Gregory. New York: Viking Press, 1958.

INANNA'S DESCENT TO THE UNDERWORLD
A Myth from Ancient Sumer

This myth is over three thousand years old, the symbolic love story between Inanna, goddess of love and war in one, and Dumuzi, the mortal (also an agricultural figure) who dies and is reborn. It's a myth that has come down to us in many guises, including the Babylonian myth of Ishtar and Tammuz and the Roman myth of Venus and Adonis. Only in the later versions does the story become only that of Adonis' death and seasonal resurrection. And only in the later versions does the death of Adonis/Tammuz/Dumuzi become clear: In the most blatant symbolism, a boar gores him in the groin.

But it is in the earlier versions that the oldest elements appear, particularly in this tale of Inanna's descent, in which she loses layer after layer of what makes her herself. In some versions the goddess even gives up her life and is herself reborn. This entire quest does sound very similar to stories of the shaman's journey, such as come from Central Asia and Siberia, in which layers of being must be surrendered, down to life itself, before the shaman can gain his or her powers.

The rescue of the goddess is singularly clever. Ea, who is a wise, even cunning deity, knows that anyone going after Inanna to take her place will be lost. So it is that no living being goes after Inanna, but a mere illusion of one, Asushunamir.

While it isn't clearly spelled out in the myth, there is peripheral evidence that Inanna's return to the living world ensures that Dumuzi will periodically be reborn.

*T*here was the strongest of love between the goddess Inanna, who is love and lust together, and the mortal Dumuzi. But mortals die, and gods may sometimes mourn. And sometimes some of them determine to do more than mourn. They will not let their lovers go.

Kurnugi is the land from which no one returns. It is the dark house wherein dwells Erkalla's god, the house wherein those who enter never leave, where dust is their only food and darkness their only way.

To Kurnugi, that land from which no one returns, that place of the dead, was great Inanna determined to go. No other god could stop her or persuade her otherwise.

When she arrived at the gate of Kurnugi, Inanna commanded, "Gatekeeper, open your gate for me! Let me come in! If you do not open the gate for me to come in, I shall smash the door and shatter the bolt; I shall raise up the dead and they shall eat the living! The dead shall outnumber the living!"

The gatekeeper cried out, "Stop, lady, do not break it down! Let me go and report your words to Queen Ereshkigal."

The gatekeeper hurried to Queen Ereshkigal. "Inanna is here!"

When Ereshkigal heard this, her anger caused her face to turn as pale as a cut-down tamarisk, while her lips turned as dark as a bruised kuninu reed. "What drove her here to me? What impelled her spirit hither? I am as I should be! Should I drink water with the spirits of the dead? Should I eat clay for bread, drink muddy water for beer? Should I bemoan the men who left their wives behind? Should I bemoan the maidens wretched from their lovers' laps? Or should I bemoan the tender babe sent off before his time?

"Go, gatekeeper, open the gate for her," the queen concluded in a voice as cold as clay. "Let her enter. Treat her in accordance with the ancient rules."

The gatekeeper went and opened the gate to Inanna. "Enter, my lady. May the palace of Kurnugi be glad to see you."

He let her in through the first door, but stripped off and took away the great crown from her head.

"Gatekeeper, why have you taken away the great crown from my head?"

"Go in, my lady. Such are the rites of the mistress of the underworld."

He let her in through the second door, but stripped off and took away her earrings.

"Gatekeeper, why have you taken away my earrings?"

"Go in, my lady. Such are the rites of the mistress of the underworld."

He let her in through the third door, but stripped off and took away the beads from around her neck.

"Gatekeeper, why have you taken away the beads from around my neck?"

"Go in, my lady. Such are the rites of the mistress of the underworld."

He let her in through the fourth door, but stripped off and took away the ornaments from her breast.

"Gatekeeper, why have you taken away the ornaments from my breast?"

"Go in, my lady. Such are the rites of the mistress of the underworld."

He let her in through the fifth door, but stripped off and took away the girdle of birthstones from around her waist.

"Gatekeeper, why have you taken the girdle of birthstones from around my waist?"

"Go in, my lady. Such are the rites of the mistress of the underworld."

He let her in through the sixth door, but stripped off and took away the bangles from her wrists and ankles.

"Gatekeeper, why have you taken away the bangles from my wrists and ankles?"

"Go in my lady. Such are the rites of the mistress of the underworld."

He let her in through the seventh door, but stripped off and took away the robes from her body.

"Gatekeeper, why have you taken away the robes from my body?"

"Go in, my lady. Such are the rites of the mistress of the underworld."

Naked and unafraid, Inanna went down to Kurnugi. As soon as Inanna had descended to the land of no return, Ereshkigal saw her. Inanna, heedless of all but rage, flew at her, and the queen cried to her vizier:

"Go, Namtar, lock her up in my palace!

Release against her the sixty miseries:

Misery of the eyes against her eyes,

Misery of the sides against her sides,

Misery of the heart against her heart,

Misery of the feet against her feet,

Misery of the head against her head—

Against every part of her, against her whole body!"

Now, back in the mortal realm, sadness reigned, for there could be no love or lust with Inanna gone to the underworld. The bull ignored the cow, the boy and girl ignored each other, the man slept in one room and the woman in another.

Papsukkal, vizier of the great gods, hung his head. Dressed in mourning clothes, his hair unkempt, he went before the gods and wept.

"Inanna has gone down to the underworld and has not come up again."

The wise god Ea created a person, an image, Asushunamir, whose name means "good looks."

"Go, Asushunamir, set thy face to the gate of the land of no return. The seven gates of the land of no return shall be opened for thee. Ereshkigal shall see thee and rejoice. When her heart has calmed and her mood is happy, let her utter the oath of the great gods.

"Then ask her this: 'Pray, lady, let them give me the life-water bag so that I may drink from it.'"

So he went, and so it happened. As soon as Ereshkigal heard his request, she struck her thigh and bit her finger, restless with worry. "You have asked of me something that should not be asked. Asushunamir, I will curse thee with a mighty curse!

"The food of the city's gutters shall be thy food,

The sewers of the city shall be thy drink.

The threshold shall be thy habitation,

The besotted and the thirsty shall smite thy cheek!"

She knew that as soon as Asushunamir was hers, she must keep a balance by returning Inanna. She did not know that Asushunamir was a mere image, not reality.

So Ereshkigal told her vizier, Namtar, "Sprinkle Inanna with the water of life and take her from my sight!"

And Namtar sprinkled Inanna with the water of life and took her from the queen's presence.

When through the first gate he had made her go out, he returned to her the robes for her body.

When through the second gate he had made her go out, he returned to her the bangles for her hands and feet.

When through the third gate he had made her go out, he returned to her the girdle of birthstones for her waist.

When through the fourth gate he had made her go out, he returned to her the ornaments for her breast.

When through the fifth gate he had made her go out, he returned to her the beads for her neck.

When through the sixth gate he had made her go out, he returned to her the earrings for her ears.

When through the seventh gate he had made her go out, he returned to her the great crown for her head.

But Inanna knew her rebirth was not in vain. As she was reborn, so would Dumuzi return to her every spring. "You shall not rob me forever of my only love!"

And so indeed they did not.

Sources

Foster, Benjamin R. *From Distant Days: Myths, Tales and Poetry of Ancient Mesopotamia.* Bethesda, MD: CDL, 1995.

Jacobsen, Thorkild. *The Harps That Once . . . : Sumerian Poetry in Translation.* New Haven: Yale University Press, 1987.

Kramer, Samuel Noah. *Sumerian Mythology.* New York: Harper and Brothers, 1961.

THE STORY OF MARKANDEYA
A Hindu Myth from India

The idea of piety or charity being so powerful that death itself is cast aside is a strong theme in Hinduism, but it is not unique to that religion. In Jewish lore, for instance, there is a second-century tale of the rabbi Akiva, whose daughter was fated to die on her wedding day, and yet her act of charity on that day overturned that fate.

Neither is the idea of death being a sentient unique. There are European tales of death being trapped by a clever human or even serving as a human boy's mentor. Even in modern times, we continue the theme in such movies as *Death Takes a Holiday*, the living—and rather charming—figures of death in fantasy writer Terry Pratchett's Discworld novels, or fantasy and horror writer Neil Gaiman's Sandman graphic novels.

The myth of Shiva killing Yama is worshiped at the shrine of Tirukkadavur in India. There people come to celebrate *shashti abda*

The god of death, Yama, with a bull's head, as depicted in a nineteenth-century wood and copper sculpture. In Indian and Tibetan mythology, he is the guardian of the south (region of death). (*Réunion des Musées Nationaux/Art Resource, New York*)

poorthi, or sixtieth birthdays, praying that Shiva's blessings will prolong their lives.

In the ancient days there was a good man, Mrikandu Munivar, who worshiped the great god Shiva. He asked the god for the boon of a son. And his boon was granted. But he had to choose between a son who would be strongly gifted but short of life, or a son who would have long life but be an utterly untalented fool.

Mrikandu Munivar chose the former. So it was that he was, indeed, blessed with a son, whom he named Markandeya. Now, Markandeya was an ideal son, an excellent youngster of good heart and kind deeds, one who was a devotee of Shiva—but one who was fated to die when he reached the age of sixteen.

On the day of his destined death, Markandeya sent prayers of worship to Shiva. So devout were his prayers that when the messengers of Yama, the god of death, came for him, they were unable to take his life.

When Yama learned that his messengers had failed in their duty, he was outraged. Since they had failed, he came in person to take away the life of young Markandeya and hurled his noose, aiming for the boy's neck. But he missed! The noose landed instead around Shiva's shrine—and Shiva sprang out of it in full fury. One mighty blow slew Yama, killed death himself.

But if balance was to continue, death must not be slain. Shiva revived Yama but told him that this return to existence had one condition: Markandeya the devout would live forever.

And so it was vowed.

Sources

Danielou, Alain. *The Myths and Gods of India*. Rutland, VT: Inner Traditions International, 1991.

Nivedita, Sister, and Ananda K. Coomaraswamy. *Myths of the Hindus and Buddhists*. New York: Farrar and Rinehart, n.d.

THE REBIRTH OF THE BODHISATTA
A Buddhist Myth from India

While this is not a story in the truest sense of the word, this myth is included because it does give a good basic look at the Buddhist concepts of rebirth and self-purification, incarnation after incarnation.

Once there lived a very good and kindly king and queen. The queen gave birth to a beautiful baby, a son, and the king, rejoicing, chose a name for his son that would help him in life. The boy was named Prince Goodspeaker.

Now, this was not the baby prince's first life or his first birth. Ages past, he had been a loyal follower of an enlightened one, a teaching Buddha, and had longed to become such a wise one.

Through the long cycle of birth and rebirth, he had lived in many forms, sometimes as an animal, sometimes as a powerful being, sometimes as an ordinary human being. And in each life he sought to learn from his mistakes and strengthen his characters. He sought to eliminate the three causes of unwholesomeness from his mind. These are three poisons: the poison of craving or greed, the poison of anger, and the poison that is the delusion of a separate self. And he sought to replace those three poisons with the three purities: the purity of nonattachment, the purity of loving-kindness, and the purity of wisdom.

So it came about that the prince, who sought to at last experience complete truth, came to be called Bodhisatta, or Enlightened Being. It was through the adventure of the mind, not the body, through the endless puri-

Bodhisatta, or Enlightened Being, sought to experience complete truth through purification of the mind. Reincarnated many times, he eventually became the Buddha known by the world today. (SEF/*Art Resource, New York*)

fying of his mind, that after all the lives he lived, he at last became the Buddha who is known by the world today.

Sources

Cavendish, Richard, ed. *Legends of the World: A Cyclopedia of the Enduring Myths, Legends and Sagas of Mankind*. New York: Schocken Books, 1982.

Danielou, Alain. *The Myths and Gods of India*. Rutland, VT: Inner Traditions International, 1991.

NÜ WA MENDS THE SKY
A Myth from China

Nü Wa, the same goddess who was the protagonist in the myth "Nü Wa Creates Humanity" in Chapter 1, is listed in China's earliest dictionary, which dates to the first century C.E., as being "in charge of breeding of all living things," which implies that her powers extended into fertility.

She may also be the wife of Fu Xi, who taught humanity how to domesticate animals. There is an illustration of Nü Wa from the first century that shows her as a woman with a snake's tail.

*I*t was the goddess Nü Wa who had created human beings. She was happy to see them enjoying their lives.

But up in the heavens, things were not so peaceful. There was Gong Gong, the god of water, and there was Zhu Rong, the god of fire, and they were forever arguing. But this time, their quarrel grew beyond mere words into a terrible fight. It was a battle that took them all the way from the heavens to the mortal earth.

It was a battle that the god of fire won. Furious, the god of water struck his head against Buzhou Mountain with such force that the mountain collapsed. Down came the big pillar that held heaven from earth, and half of the sky fell in, leaving a gaping hole. The earth was cracked open, and floodwaters sprouted from beneath the earth. Many people died in the disaster.

Nü Wa was shocked. These were the people that she had created. They should not be undergoing so much suffering. She decided to mend the sky and end this horror.

She set up a kiln. In it, she melted together colored stones of all colors and used this mix to patch the sky. Next, Nu Wa killed a giant turtle. She turned its four legs into pillars to support the part of the sky that had caved in. Last, Nü Wa burned a huge pile of reeds and used the ashes to dam up the flood so it couldn't spread.

Nü Wa was satisfied. Now the people could live happily again. There was only one trace left: From then on, the sky slanted slightly to the west, and so ever since then, the sun and moon move to the west in their daily journeys.

Sources

Birrell, Anne. *Chinese Mythology: An Introduction*. Baltimore: Johns Hopkins University Press, 1993.

Christie, Anthony. *Chinese Mythology*. New York: Barnes and Noble Books, 1983.

THE LORD OF THE LAND
A Myth from Japan

This myth has a very human aspect: the older brothers hating their superior younger brother. There's a superficial resemblance to the biblical story of Joseph. But the brothers here take the ultimate step and actually kill Ohkuni-nushi. What might make it seem strange to

Westerners is that once he has returned to life, Okhuni-nushi doesn't try to avenge himself. Maybe it is enough that he has returned as the lord of the land, the lord of green and growing life.

*O*hkuni-nushi, whose name means "the lord of the land," was the highest god of the land in ancient Japan.

And since he was such, his brothers hated Ohkuni-nushi even when he was young, and plotted to kill him.

They said to him, "Let us go boar hunting. You can show us your talents, brother. We'll chase one of the big red boars down out of a mountain, and you can show us how you'll catch it at the bottom."

Ohkuni-nushi agreed, suspecting nothing. But instead of a wild boar, his brothers threw down on him a big, red-hot stone and burned him to death. Then, because they feared him and his powers even then, the brothers tore open a crack in a tree, pushed him inside it, and sealed it up again.

But they had reckoned without their mother and the force of a mother's grief. Through her entreaties to the other gods, Okhuni-nushi returned to life. He did not return to avenge himself, but went underground, where he found himself a wife. Who she was is not part of the story. What is important, at the very heart of things, is this:

Okhuni-nushi had been slain, gone underground, and then returned to life. He came back to the earth to become once more the lord of the land, the lord of green and growing life.

Sources

Kawai, Hayao. *The Japanese Psyche: Major Motifs in the Fairy Tales of Japan*. Dallas: Spring Publications, 1988.

New Larousse Encyclopedia of Mythology. Translated by Richard Aldington and Delano Ames. London, New York: Hamlyn, 1968.

PARE AND HUTO
A Myth from Polynesia

This myth begins with a folkloric motif: the princess in the glass tower, or in this case in the solitary hut, who is to be kept from meeting unsuitable men. Other isolated heroines appear in tales from, among others, Egypt, Greece, and Ireland. Sometimes it is a prince who is kept isolated, as in one of the earliest folktales from Egypt, "The Prince and His Three Fates," which is approximately three and a half millennia old. In all cases, though, the isolation fails.

Once Pare has met Hutu, a new motif appears: the star-crossed lovers. Most stories of this sort end in tragedy, and at first it seems as though this myth will turn tragic as well, when Pare hangs herself.

But then the myth becomes a variant on "Orpheus and Eurydice." As in the Kikuyu myth "Sacrificed by Her Kin," there is a happy ending as Hutu rescues Pare's spirit, restores her to life, and marries her.

*N*ow, Pare was a beautiful young woman of high lineage, and that was nearly her undoing. Because she was both lovely and highborn, it was ruled that she be kept separate from the others of her village, and she could not marry until a man of equally high lineage could be found.

So poor Pare lived alone with only a servant, seeing no one else, going nowhere. Her home was richly ornamented, and she wanted for nothing— save freedom and a man who loved her.

Then a young chief from another village came to compete in the local games. His name was Hutu, and he was both a master dart player and a fine singer. The sound of his voice reached Pare, and she longed to see him. She slipped out of the house to the farthest wall of the enclosure and saw Hutu. In that moment she loved him.

Just then, a breeze threw one of Hutu's darts almost at Pare's feet. She snatched it up, and when Hutu asked for its return, she invited him into her home.

Now, Hutu had also fallen in love with Pare as well. They both knew that his lineage was not as high as hers and that he was breaking the law by being alone with her. But neither could resist the other. At last Hutu fled, ashamed of his weakness.

Pare, overcome by grief, hanged herself, and her soul descended to Po, the underworld.

When Hutu learned of this, he cried out that he would find her again. He hunted till he'd found Te Ringa, threshold to the underworld. There sat great Hina, who guards the pathway down to Po and directs the souls of the dead down whichever road they must go.

She did not wish a living man to pass. But when Hutu refused to leave or be alarmed by all her threats, she tried to trick him into taking the pathway for the souls of dogs. Hutu was not fooled. He offered her his dagger of enchanted green stone, and at last Hina agreed to show him the right pathway into Po. She gave him a basket of food and drink and warned him not to taste any food offered to him in the underworld, for if he did, he would never return. And she also warned him that as he entered, a great wind would sweep him off the ground. He must be sure that when he landed, it was with both feet on the path.

Hutu entered. The great wind did sweep him off the ground, but he made sure that both feet landed on the path. Following it down into Po, he came to a village of the dead, one that seemed a mirror image of the village he'd left. Sure enough, where Pare's house would stand was a mirror-image house. And there he found Pare.

But she did not see him. She neither acknowledged him nor even turned her head to him. Hutu called to her, threw spears, spun tops, did everything he could to force her to notice him. But she was one of the dead.

Then an inspiration struck him. Hutu caught a long, slender tree and bent it down, then released it. Yes, it flew up in a perfect arc. He pulled the tree back down again, then grabbed Pare—and the moment he touched her, she knew and embraced him. Hutu jumped, and he and Pare were carried up by the tree, up and up to the roots of trees reaching down from the world above. They caught the roots, let go of the tree, and climbed back up to the land of the living.

Hutu carried Pare back to where her lifeless body lay, and her spirit dove back into it. Pare was alive once more! Now no one could deny that she should wed the man who had dared the world of the dead to bring her safely back. And so it was.

Sources

Cavendish, Richard, ed. *Legends of the World: A Cyclopedia of the Enduring Myths, Legends and Sagas of Mankind.* New York: Schocken Books, 1982.

Grey, Sir George. *Polynesian Mythology.* London: Whitcombe and Tombs, 1956.

GWION'S REBIRTH
A Myth from Ancient Wales

While the mythology of Wales wasn't written down until Christian times, a great deal of the ancient elements remain—including within this story of Gwion. By the time it was written down, the powerful, dangerous Cerridwen, who was probably originally a goddess, had been toned down in this story to being merely a witch, but echoes of her power remain.

The folk process, incidentally, turned the Roman poet Virgil (or Vergil) into the mighty magician of Toledo, mentioned in the myth; the magician has a cycle of tales about him.

The next motif in the myth is that of the forbidden food that will grant the taster great knowledge. In "Sigurd," in Chapter 5, Sigurd gains knowledge of what the birds are singing. Gwion gains astonishing wisdom.

Next is a theme found in mythology and folklore alike: the transformation flight, in which the quarry and the hunter both shape-shift. Once Cerridwen swallows the grain that is Gwion, the mythic element resurfaces. As in the Pacific Northwest tale of "Raven Steals the Sun," once Gwion is swallowed, Cerridwen finds herself pregnant. And when he is born, she can't bring herself to kill him. So, like Moses, Sargon of Akkad, and Superman, among others, Gwion is cast adrift upon the water. For another version of the motif, see "Perseus," in Chapter 5.

But Gwion is no longer himself. He grows to be Taliesin, who has been so surrounded in Arthurian lore that the real man, a fifth-century poet, has become almost entirely a figure of myth.

*I*n the ancient days of the land of Cymru, which the English name Wales, there lived a nobleman with his wife. Tegil Voel was his name, and Cerridwen was hers. And with them lived their two children. Their daughter, Creirwy, was the most beautiful girl in all the world. But their son, Afagddu, whose name means "darkness," was by far the ugliest boy in all the world. Alas for Afagddu, he had nothing much in the way of clever wits, either.

Now, some people say that Cerridwen was a witch, others that she was more than merely human, but all agree that she decided that if Afagddu could not shed his ugliness, he would at least have intelligence to rival that of the supernatural beings.

And some say that the recipe she used was from her own learning, but others claim she found it in the books of Vergil, the great magician of Toledo. However it was done, Cerridwen began boiling up a cauldron of both wit and wisdom. The recipe she used needed no less than a year and a day of simmering, with specific herbs to be picked and added at specific times. This meant that Cerridwen could not forever be stirring the cauldron for that entire year and a day. So she found herself a boy, Gwion, son of Gwreang, to do the stirring when she could not. Gwion, she knew, was no one, a nobody that the world would neither note nor miss.

Three things she warned Gwion: He must not let the fire go out, he must not stop the stirring, and he must never, never taste the brew within the cauldron.

Gwion was a nobody, but he was not a fool. He agreed to all three and meant to keep his word. But when the recipe was all but finished, three drops of the brew splattered up, scalding hot, and struck the boy's finger. With a yelp but without thinking, he put his finger in his mouth.

And in that instant, he was flooded with new wisdom, with the knowledge of past and present and future—and with the immediate knowledge that as soon as the potion was finished, Cerridwen meant to kill him!

Gwion fled, but Cerridwen pursued him. She was overtaking him, so Gwion, with the potion's wisdom, turned into a hare. But Cerridwen became a greyhound, overtaking him.

Gwion turned into a fish and dove into a river. But Cerridwen became an otter, overtaking him.

Gwion leaped up, growing wings, turning into a sparrow. But Cerridwen became a hawk, overtaking him.

Gwion turned into a grain of wheat and fell into a barn, one among a mound of wheat. But Cerridwen became a black hen and gobbled up the Gwion-wheat.

When Cerridwen went home in her own shape, she soon realized that she was pregnant, and realized, too, that it was Gwion who grew within her. But when he was born, Cerridwen found him so beautiful a baby that she could not kill him. Instead she tied him up in a leather bag and threw him into the sea for the sea to settle.

But the bag did not sink. The waves carried it to where Prince Elphin fished.

A strange fish the prince caught that day! Elphin named the child he'd found, the reborn child who had been Gwion, Taliesin, which means "fine value" or "gleaming brow."

Taliesin grew and thrived in his new self, and through rebirth and the taste of the potion of wisdom, he went on to become a wondrous bard, a musician, and a wise scholar, and one day became a teacher to King Arthur the Great.

Sources

Jordan, Michael. *Myths of the World: A Thematic Encyclopedia.* London: Kyle Cathie, 1995.
Leeming, David Adams. *The World of Myth: An Anthology.* New York and Oxford: Oxford University Press, 1990.

JOHN BARLEYCORN
A Mythic Song from Britain

Between the years of 1900 and 1910, Cecil Sharp collected a number of folk songs, and among them was "John Barleycorn." When he first heard it, he notes that he was truly astonished. This was almost certainly a survival, or at least an echo, of an ancient ritual of an agricultural deity who is sacrificed and then reborn.

Since the days of Sharp's collecting, many versions of this song have been found across Great Britain, from Oxfordshire, Sussex, Hampshire,

Surrey, and Somerset. The earliest known written copy dates to the seventeenth century. In recent years, several versions of the song have been recorded, for instance on Steeleye Span's *Below the Salt*, on Martin Carthy's *Byker Hill*, and on the Watersons' *Frost and Fire*.

There were three men came out of the west
Their fortunes for to try,
And these three men made a solemn vow
John Barleycorn must die.
They've plowed, they've sown, they've harrowed him in
Threw clods upon his head,
And these three men made a solemn vow
John Barleycorn was dead.
They let him lie for a very long time
Till the rains from heaven did fall,
And little Sir John sprang up his head
And so amazed them all.
They've let him stand till Midsummer's Day,
Till he looked both pale and wan.
And little Sir John's grown a long, long beard
And so become a man.
They've hired men with the scythes so sharp,
To cut him off at the knee,
They've rolled him and tied him by the waist,
Serving him most barb'rously.
They've hired men with the sharp pitchforks,
Who pricked him through the heart
And the loader, he has served him worse than that,
For he's bound him to the cart.
They've wheeled him around and around a field,
Till they came unto a barn,
And there they made a solemn oath
On poor John Barleycorn.
They've hired men with the crab-tree sticks,
To cut him skin from bone,

And the miller, he has served him worse than that,

For he's ground him between two stones.

And little Sir John and the nut-brown bowl

And his brandy in the glass

And little Sir John and the nut-brown bowl

Proved the strongest man at last.

The huntsman, he can't hunt the fox

Nor so loudly to blow his horn,

And the tinker, he can't mend kettle nor pots

without a little barley corn.

Sources

Carthy, Martin. *Byker Hill*. Topic Records, 1967. Compact disc.
Steeleye Span. *Below the Salt*. Shanachie Records, 1972. Compact disc.
Watersons. *Frost and Fire*. Topic Records, 1995. Compact disc.

3

MYTHS OF ORIGINS

Myths of origins are not to be confused with myths of creation. Origin tales still tend to be about important issues, such as the birth of sexual desire or the coming of cattle to humanity. But they fall just short of the major themes of the creation of the universe or the world.

An example of this issue can be seen in the myths of the placing of the moon, sun, and stars in the sky. In these myths, such as in the Pacific Northwest myths in which Raven is the protagonist or the Brazilian myth of the two brothers, it isn't a creation deity but a demigod or culture hero who does the work. In the few myths in which a deity is the protagonist, such as the story of Ra of ancient Egypt or that of Mantis of Namibia, there is a sense not of great power but of compassion or common sense.

Origin myths often explain heavenly phenomena, such as the Pleiades, the grouping of stars that many cultures have noted; earthly events, such as the origin of pine or coconut trees and the creation of natural formations; and social events, such as the origin of shamanism or of various cultures.

There are also, as mentioned above, origin myths about procreation. Psychoanalysts from Sigmund Freud to the present time have been fascinated by the symbolism to be found in sexual mythology. The symbols can be bawdy but relatively lightweight and even funny, such as those featured in the confusion between the tip of the male organ and a strawberry, found in several Coyote tales.

But sexual symbols can also be much more frightening, such as the vagina dentata, the toothed vagina, and the penis made of stone or stick. These are very primal matters, to be found in several North American, African, and Asian myths, as well as in nightmares chronicled by psychiatrists—but they are warily left out of most storytellers' retellings. Whether the symbols represent a genuine fear of the opposite gender or of the mysteries of sex is something better left to those who study the mind. However, the fact remains that any myths dealing with sex will ensure that mythologists and folklorists alike have their run-ins with prudish audiences!

MYTHS OF THE SUN, MOON, AND STARS

THE STEALING OF THE SUN AND MOON
A Myth from Siberia

This is the first of three related myths, all of them centered on the stealing of the sun, a golden globe, from the selfish one or ones who have it. In this Siberian myth, it is Raven who oversees the choosing of a champion but Hare who is the hero. In the North American myths, it is Raven himself who is the protagonist.

When Hare is about to be overtaken by the evil spirits, he kicks the golden globe apart into the sun, moon, and stars. This theme also turns up in the following myths of Raven stealing the sun. Are the similarities coincidental? Probably not. There has been a good deal of contact between the peoples of Siberia and the Pacific Northwest.

Once, in the long-ago days, there was no sun, no moon, nothing but endless night.

The animals grew heartily weary of this eternal darkness. So they held a great council.

It was Raven who knew the truth of what was and what must be done. He spoke up, saying, "We do not need to live in darkness. I have learned that not far from where we meet, evil spirits live deep within a great cavern. They keep a great golden globe called the sun for themselves, hiding it away in a plain stone pot. And they will not let anyone see the sun but themselves. We must send the biggest and strongest among us to steal the sun from them."

"Polar Bear!" everyone cried. "He is the biggest and strongest!"

"Oh, no!" cried Snowy Owl. "That will never do. As soon as Polar Bear finds a scrap of food, he'll forget all about his mission."

Raven said, "That is true enough. Then we shall send Wolf. He's almost as strong as the bear, and he is much faster."

"No!" snapped Owl. "That will not do, either. Wolf will stop to hunt the first deer he sees, and he'll forget all about his mission."

"True enough," said Raven. "Then whom shall we send?"

Mouse piped up, "Let us send Hare! He's the fastest runner of us all."

"That is very true," agreed Raven.

So Hare was chosen.

Off he raced across the dark land until at last he saw the faintest spark of light against the blackness of night. Hare followed the spark to the cavern that was the evil spirits' home, and crept inside. As he stole closer and closer to the light, Hare saw that the rays of light were shooting out from a great golden ball lying in a plain stone pot, lighting up the whole cave.

"That has to be the sun," Hare thought. "Yes, and those creatures over there in the corner must be the evil spirits."

He crept even more carefully to the stone pot. Carefully, carefully, he reached for the golden ball—then snatched it up and raced away. Oh, but it was heavy!

The evil spirits roared in rage and raced after him. Hare ran as fast as he could, but the evil spirits ran fast, too, and they started gaining on him.

"I can't let them have the sun! But . . . but it's too . . . heavy for me to carry."

The evil spirits were close, closer, too close! They reached out long, clawed hands to grab him.

But before those claws could close on him, Hare gave the golden ball so hard a kick with his hind legs that he broke it into two pieces, one small, one large. A second kick sent the smaller piece flying up into the sky, where it stayed and became the moon.

"Not bad!" Hare said.

He kicked the bigger part of the golden ball with even more force. It flew up into the sky, where it stayed and became the sun.

The world was suddenly flooded with daylight. The evil spirits shrieked with rage and pain, then fled underground, and there they stayed.

"A good day's work," Hare said.

Sources

Holmberg, U. *Finno-Ugric, Siberian Mythology*. New York: Cooper Square, 1964.

Riordan, James. *Sun Maiden and the Crescent Moon: Siberian Folk Tales*. New York: Interlink Books, 1991.

RAVEN STEALS THE SUN
A Myth from the Peoples of the Pacific Northwest

There's a reason why this myth hasn't been pinpointed to any particular people: Every tribal group from Alaska down to northern California has some variation of it. Raven appears in almost all those stories. He is a very powerful figure, a trickster who is also a creator.

As in the story "Gwion's Rebirth," in Chapter 2, this myth includes the concept of impregnation from swallowing a piece of grain or, here, a pine needle. But Raven isn't reborn in a new or more glamorous shape; he has control over the entire process, and the baby form is merely his deliberate illusion.

Here it is Raven who tears apart the golden globe of the sun and creates the sun, moon, and stars.

*I*n the days before the rules of things were set down, the world and sky alike were forever dark, so dark that nothing could be seen—so dark, in fact, that Raven could not see to hunt. He quickly grew weary of flying into rocks or tripping over roots.

"This will never do," he said.

So Raven listened. He heard, from where no one knows, that there was one source of light, one bright golden ball kept by a greedy old man who would not share it with anyone.

"This will never do," Raven repeated, and went in search of the old man.

At last he came to the old man's lodge and waited in hiding to see what he would learn.

So, now! The old man had a young daughter. Quick-witted Raven swiftly designed a plan.

"May I be a pine needle floating upon the water," he said.

And instantly he became a pine needle floating upon the water.

"May the old man's daughter have a great thirst," Raven whispered. "And may she drink me right down."

Instantly the old man's daughter was seized by a great thirst. Grabbing up a cedarwood drinking cup, she gulped down water—and drank down Raven with the water.

Soon after that, the belly of the old man's daughter began to swell with child.

"Who is the father?" the old man shouted. "Name him!"

Here, a Tsimshian frontlet represents a raven with its characteristic downward-turning beak. The raven is a powerful figure as both a trickster and a creator in stories from the Pacific Northwest. (*Werner Forman/Art Resource, New York*)

But his daughter wept and swore that she had never met another man nor given anyone her love.

So time passed with no solving of the mystery, and at last she gave birth to a plump, handsome baby boy. The old man was so delighted with his new grandson that he forgot to be angry at his daughter. He was so delighted that he wanted to fulfill his grandson's every wish.

He was so delighted that he never noticed that the baby had clever black eyes—the eyes of Raven reborn.

One day Raven began to wail. He began to whine. He began to shout and beat his arms and legs on the ground. "Gimmee!" he shrieked. "Gimmee!"

The sound was horrible. Hands over his ears, the old man asked, "Give you *what*? What do you want, grandson?"

"Gimmee! Gimmee!"

The old man gave Raven toy after toy, but Raven batted them all away.

"Gimmee! Gimmee!"

The old man was at his wits' end. "What do you want?" he shouted.

"Ball! Want golden ball!"

"No!"

"Want! Want! Want!"

With each shriek, Raven's voice grew more shrill. At last the old man could stand no more of it. Warily he opened the cedar chest in which he kept the golden ball. Instantly a beautiful golden glow spread throughout the darkness.

"Here," the old man said. "But be careful with it!"

"Oh, I will!" Raven cried.

Suddenly he was bird-Raven again. The golden ball firmly clutched in his talons, he flapped up and away.

"Come back!" the old man cried.

"Sorry, but no!" Raven called back.

Now, Raven had a rival, Eagle. In the days before light, Eagle hadn't been able to find Raven easily. But all at once he could see Raven clearly! He flew after his rival, his mighty wings gaining with every stroke. And Raven—oh, Raven was burdened by the weight of the golden ball. Eagle would catch him!

"No!" Raven shouted.

Angrily he broke off a piece of the golden ball and hurled it into the sky.

And that was the birth of the sun.

But Eagle still pursued Raven, and his mighty wings were gaining with every stroke. Raven was still burdened by the weight of the golden ball.

"No!" he shouted.

Angrily he broke off another piece of the golden ball and hurled it into the sky.

And that was the birth of the moon.

But Eagle still pursued Raven, and his mighty wings were gaining with every stroke. Raven was still burdened by the weight of what was left of the golden ball.

"So be it!" he shouted.

Crumbling up what was left of the golden ball, he threw the gleaming, glittering pieces into the sky. Lighter now, he quickly outflew Eagle.

And in the sky, well now, that was the birth of the stars.

Sources

Clark, Ella E. *Indian Legends of the Pacific Northwest*. Berkeley: University of California Press, 1953.

Norman, Howard. *Northern Tales, Traditional Stories of Eskimo and Indian Peoples*. New York: Pantheon Books, 1990.

RAVEN STEALS THE LIGHT
A Myth from the Inuit People of Alaska

This Inuit myth is included to show a variation. Here Raven, rather than working alone as he almost always does in this category of myth, has Squirrel as an accomplice.

*N*ow, this happened in the long-ago days. Back then, it was always dark. There was no sun in the sky, and people had to creep along the ground so they wouldn't bump into anything.

"This is boring," Raven said to Squirrel. "I can't even see to fly. I mean to do something about this!"

There was a wealthy man who lived with his daughter away from anyone else. But a strange story reached Raven's curious ears: It said that the man owned two toys, two globes, that glowed brightly in the dark. One of them was big, the other small, but they were both bright.

"I'm going to get those shining toys," Raven said.

So he stole to the rich man's well and turned himself into a bit of dirt; he could do that, change his shape, without trouble. And Raven said a wish-spell: "I wish that the rich man's daughter would grow thirsty and drink from this well."

As he said it, the rich man's daughter did, indeed, grow thirsty. She pulled up a bucket of water from the well and drank it down—and she drank down the bit of dirt that was Raven, too.

Soon enough, the rich man's daughter grew round with child. She gave birth to a baby boy-Raven. The only sign that he wasn't a normal human child was that he'd made a slight mistake; he'd been born with the tail of a raven.

His mother didn't like that. Neither did his uncles, her brothers. But whenever they started to tease the little boy about his tail, Raven outshouted them.

An Inuit mask depicts the moon, air, cosmos, and stars. Stories about the origin of the sun and moon are common among the peoples of the Arctic. (*Werner Forman/Art Resource, New York*)

"I want the gleaming globes!" he yelled. "I want the glittery, glowy, gleaming globes!"

"You'll only break them," he was told.

"I want the gleaming globes!" Raven yelled.

He made so much noise that at last the rich man, his grandfather now, gave Raven the globes, just to keep him quiet. Raven played with them a bit, just the way a child would play, rolling the gleaming toys about on the floor and laughing. But each time he rolled them, Raven rolled those gleaming globes a little closer to the door.

Squirrel, who had been patiently waiting all this while, crept up to the door. Raven saw him and suddenly gave the globes a great kick! Squirrel caught the larger globe and ran. Raven ran after him. The rich man ran after them both. Every time the man got too close to Squirrel, Squirrel tossed the globe to Raven. Every time the rich man got too close to Raven, Raven tossed the globe to Squirrel. At last Raven turned back to his bird-shape and flew up into the air with the globe.

"Give it back!" the rich man called.

"No."

"Give it back!"

"No."

"I have the other globe. See how it gleams?"

Raven laughed. "I'd rather have this one."

"But if you take this globe," the rich man said, "the nights will be nice and long, dark as your feathers."

"I'd rather have the days long and bright," Raven said, "to show off my feathers!"

And Raven threw the globe up into the sky, where it became the sun. Some people say the rich man was so angry that he threw the small globe up there, too, where it became the moon, but some people will say anything.

Source

Balikci, Asen. *The Netsilik Eskimo.* New York: Natural History Press, 1970.

THE THEFT OF SUN AND MOON
A Myth of the Zuni People of the Southwest

Here's an example of cross-cultural contact. While the Zuni people are not closely related to the peoples of the Pacific Northwest, their myth of the theft of sun and moon is clearly similar to those from that region. Here, though, the character of Raven is replaced by the southwestern trickster figure, Coyote, and the selfish old man or evil spirits are replaced by the southwestern spirit folk, the Kachinas. But the animosity between the protagonist and Eagle remains.

At the very beginning of things, there was neither a sun nor a moon in the sky. The Kachinas, the powerful spirit folk, kept the sun and moon safe and secret in a box that they opened whenever they wished some light.

Without a sun in the sky, the world was always dark. Without a moon in the sky, there were no seasons. The world was never cold or warm, never white with snow or green with leaves.

Coyote thought that this was a sorry state of affairs. He liked change, did sly Coyote—most certainly since he was a clumsy hunter there in the darkness that shrouded the world.

"Ho, Eagle Chief," he called, "let us form a hunting partnership. Two hunters should do better than one."

Eagle Chief looked down at Coyote from the air and laughed. What, he, the keen of eye and mighty of wing, make a pact with a flightless ground crawler?

But then Eagle remembered that Coyote, the sly one, could steal an eagle's meal, even in the darkness. Better to keep Coyote in the open light, where he could play no pranks! So Eagle Chief agreed to the partnership.

But even so, Coyote caught nothing but bugs.

"Bah! How can anyone do any decent hunting in all this darkness? Tell me, Eagle, you who fly so high, have you ever seen any light in your travelings?"

"Why, yes, from time to time I have seen a flickering of light in the west, where the Kachinas live."

"Then west we shall go."

They journeyed on and on. Eagle soared lightly on the winds, but Coyote, wingless, had to struggle through desert and mountain, river and mud.

At last the camp of the Kachinas lay before them. Coyote and Eagle hid and watched. Eagle watched the Kachinas' sacred dances. But Coyote watched only a strange, dark box. When one of the Kachinas opened it a crack, golden light poured out. When one of the Kachinas opened it halfway, silver light poured out.

"That's what we want," Coyote whispered. "We must steal that box!"

"All you think about is theft!" whispered Eagle. "I will ask the Kachinas if they will let us borrow their box of light."

Coyote said nothing. He watched as Eagle approached the Kachinas and demanded the box of light. And he watched as the angry Kachinas threw stones at Eagle, chasing him, bruised and squawking, back into the sky!

But while all the Kachinas were chasing Eagle, Coyote slid silently into their camp, caught up the box of light in his jaws, and scurried just as silently away.

The box was heavy, though. Coyote's jaws were getting tired, and his tongue lolled out of the side of his mouth. Eagle swooped down to join him. "Here, give me the box. I can carry it more easily in my talons."

He snatched it up and flew away. Coyote ran after him, panting. "Hey, Eagle Chief! Let *me* carry the box again."

"No, no, you will spoil everything."

"I won't. Let me have the box."

"You only want to see what's inside."

Coyote yelled up at Eagle, "Whose sides ache from the Kachinas' blows? Not mine! Who stole away the box with never a bruise? Not you! Now, let me carry the box."

Eagle was beginning to get tired. "Take it. But don't open it!"

"Of course I won't!" But as Eagle soared up into the sky once more, Coyote studied the box. Curiosity began to burn and burn within him. Could the sun and moon really be inside so small a thing? Surely there could be no harm if he opened the box just a bit.

Warily, Coyote raised the lid. A ray of golden light shot out and hit him right in the eyes! Coyote yelped in surprise—and the lid flew open. In a blaze of gold, the sun swooped out and up into the heavens.

The first day had begun.

"Well, now," said Coyote, admiring his fine gray coat in the new sunlight. "That's not bad, not bad at all."

He watched the sun move across the sky, till it was out of sight and darkness came again.

The first night had begun.

Eagle came flapping hurriedly back. "What have you done? You opened the box! You've let the sun escape!"

"It will return tomorrow," Coyote said.

"It will not! You've spoiled everything!"

Eagle lunged at Coyote and knocked over the box. It flew open again, and the moon came shooting out and up into the heavens. High rose the moon, higher yet, and the world grew chill. Leaves dropped from the trees, and a cold wind blew.

The first season had begun—and it was winter.

"What have you done?" shrieked Eagle. "You've brought coldness into the world!"

Coyote only grinned. He knew there would be more than winter.

Indeed there was. Coyote had brought day and night into the world. He'd brought winter—but after it spring, summer, and fall. Coyote had given the world enough changes to please even that wily gray trickster himself.

Sources

Benedict, Ruth. *Zuni Mythology*. New York: Columbia University Press, 1935.

Erdoes, Richard, and Alfonso Ortiz. *American Indian Myths and Legends*. New York: Pantheon Books, 1984.

AH-HA-LE SEEKS THE SUN
A Myth of the Miwok of California

Raven's range ends in northern California, so this Miwok story of the theft of the sun features Coyote instead.

There's an element of humor throughout the story, such as when Coyote, impersonating a branch, gets a good deal closer to the fire than he would have liked, or when, after all his hard work, the humans can't decide whether or not they actually like the sun. But that is typical of a great many Coyote myths. In addition to stories where he tricks others, he is also often involved in stories that make him look like a clown or turn him into the victim, not the victor. For an image of Coyote as loser, think of the Warner Brothers Road Runner and Wile E. Coyote cartoons. This aspect is typical of tricksters, who don't always win, but can be either winners or losers.

*I*n the long-ago days, the world was forever dark and heavy with fog. Ah-ha-le, who could be either coyote or man as the mood struck him, was living with the valley tribe at that time. And Ah-ha-le was not at all happy about the state of things.

"The people can't live in this endless darkness. And neither can I! I can't even see to hunt! And the dampness makes me sneeze. I must see about finding a better place for the people—and for me."

He left the valley and went on to the foothill country. How interesting! There was light up here, and the land was nice and dry, not like the wetness of the fog-shrouded valley.

"This looks promising," Ah-ha-le said. "But I must learn more."

So he turned himself into someone of the foothills tribe to see how they lived. And, being a creature of magic, he added, "Let no one notice I am not of the foothills tribe."

And no one noticed.

Ah, look! They kept a bright, blazing light there in a hearth, a big, golden ball. They had the sun!

Ah-ha-le ate with the foothills tribe, and none of them guessed who he really was. He spoke with them about the sun. But no! They would not give it up! Nor would they share it.

"It is ours!" they cried.

Belly full, Ah-ha-le returned to the valley tribe.

"Listen to me," he told them. "I have found a fine place where there is light and warmth and plenty of food."

"What of it?" asked their chief. "We don't need those things."

"You live here in the cold, damp darkness!" Ah-ha-le protested. "How can you say that you don't want those things?"

"Well . . . ," the chief began slowly, "maybe we do. Go and find out what that light, that sun, would cost."

But just as the foothills tribe would not give the sun away or share it, they would not sell it, either.

"The sun is ours, and ours alone!"

"This will not do," Ah-ha-le said to himself. "If they will not share or sell the sun, then I must steal it."

It would not be easy, since Ah-wahn-dah, the turtle-man, was its guardian. The turtle-man was very good with a bow and arrow, and very quick to use that bow.

"If I steal the sun," Ah-ha-le thought, "I may have to steal the turtle-man as well!"

Ah-ha-le turned himself back into a man of the foothills tribe and pretended to go hunting with their warriors. But when no one was watching, he turned himself into a big oak branch lying across the path.

"Now, let Ah-wahn-dah be the first one to come along," he chanted.

His magic worked. Along came the turtle-man and saw what he thought was nothing but a fallen branch. "Perfect for the fire," he said.

Slinging the branch, Ah-ha-le, over his shoulder, the turtle-man went back to the village. He put the branch down, but it was too crooked to lie flat. The turtle-man turned it this way and that, but it would not lie flat.

"Enough of this!" he cried, and threw the branch right into the fire.

This wasn't what Ah-hah-le had been expecting! It took a good deal of his magic to keep himself from burning up. But there he lay unharmed in the middle of the fire, trying not to sneeze from all the ash, waiting for the turtle-man to fall asleep.

At last Ah-wahn-dah yawned, lay down beside the fire, and slept. Ah-hah-le gladly leaped out of the fire, shaking embers from himself. Snatching up the great golden ball of the sun, he raced away with it, all the way back to the valley tribe.

"Look what I have brought you!" he cried.

But the people of the valley tribe weren't happy with the sun! "It's too bright," they complained.

"It's too hot."

"It hurts our eyes."

Ah-hah-le sighed. "I went through all that trouble for you. I nearly got myself burned up stealing the sun for you—and now you say you don't want it!"

"It's not that we don't want it," the chief said cautiously. "It's just that we don't understand it."

"What is there to understand?" Ah-hah-le shouted. "It gives off heat, it gives off light!"

"That's just it. We don't understand how it works."

Aiiee, these foolish, stubborn folk were driving him mad! Ah-hah-le shouted, "Then I will show you!"

He snatched up the sun and traveled far and far again to a place where there was a hole in the sky. Yes, this would do, this would do nicely! Ah-hah-le tossed the sun up into that hole and commanded it, "Come down from there every day. Cross the sky from east to west so that first the foothills tribe and then the valley tribe have light and warmth. Then go under the earth so that everyone has some darkness in which to sleep. Yes, and then circle back up into the sky and do the same thing again!"

The sun obeyed the magical command. And that, much to Ah-hah-le's satisfaction and the ordering of the world, was the beginning of day and night.

Were the foothills tribe and the valley tribe happy with this arrangement? Maybe they were. Maybe they were not. But that much the story does not say. All that is known for sure is this: At least they never did complain about such things again!

Sources

Merriam, C. Hart. *The Dawn of the World*. Lincoln: University of Nebraska Press, 1993.
Thompson, Stith. *Tales of the North American Indians*. Bloomington: Indiana University Press, 1966.

KUAT
A Myth of the Mamaiuran People of Brazil

In this myth, the lack of light is due not so much to the lack of a sun or moon but to the wings of birds forever blocking the sky. There is a slight similarity to the North American myths of the stealing of the sun in that light isn't freely given but must be taken, but once the brothers Kuat and Iae achieve their goal of getting the vulture god to agree, the myth takes a novel turn. The brothers are the ones who decide that day will alternate with night, and become the sun and moon.

There at the very beginning of time it was always night. People lived in fear, for no light could reach them. The wings of all the birds that ever were forever blocked the sky.

So it was that Kuat and his brother Iae decided that the time had come for change. They would steal some light from Urubutsin, the vulture god who was the king of all the birds.

The two brothers hid near an animal's corpse and waited. Sure enough, here came Urubutsin to feast, his great black wings outspread. Down he circled, down and down. At last he landed—and Kuat grabbed him by the legs.

The other birds took flight in fear. Urubutsin fought to get free, flapping his great wings and nearly lifting Kuat from the ground. But a vulture cannot lift a man, and at last, unable to free himself and alone, Urubutsin cawed at the brothers, "What do you want?"

"We want you to share the light with us," Kuat said.

"No!"

"Then you shall not fly free."

"Let me go!"

"Share the light."

At last, gasping, Urubutsin agreed. He would share daylight with the two brothers.

But if he had his way, the light would last only for a very short while. To make the light last for a longer time, Kuat and Iae vowed that day would alternate with night. And Kuat became the sun and Iae the moon.

Sources

Bierhorst, John. *The Mythology of South America*. New York: William Morrow, 1988.

Cavendish, Richard, ed. *Legends of the World: A Cyclopedia of the Enduring Myths, Legends and Sagas of Mankind*. New York: Schocken Books, 1982.

THE OLD MAN AND THE SUN
A Myth of the San of the Kalahari

Once again, a myth follows the theme of the sun being hidden away by a selfish man—or rather, of the selfish man actually being the sun and refusing to share his light with anyone. It's the children of the first San who throw the sun up into the sky. An explanation for the stars is given as well, as being the light shining through holes in the sun's old blanket.

*I*t is said that the sun was once a man who shone with rays of light. But he was a selfish fellow, or else a hermit, for he lived alone in a little hut and kept his light only for himself.

This could not be. The world was far too dark. The children of the first San stole up to the sun while he slept, and hurled him up into the sky where he belongs.

Now, of course, he shines upon us all. In the evening he curls up to sleep and draws his blanket of darkness over himself to keep warm. But since the blanket is old, it has many little holes in it. And the sun's light shines through those holes as the stars.

Sources

Abrahams, Roger D. *African Folktales*. New York: Random House, 1983.
Biesele, Megan. *Women Like Meat*. Bloomington: Indiana University Press, 1993.

WHY THERE IS DAY AND NIGHT
A Myth of the Cambodian Hmong

This myth begins with the problem of multiple suns and moons. For two other such, see the Chinese tales "The Orphans and the Flood," in Chapter 2, and "Hou Yi and Chang'er," in Chapter 5. Here, too, an attempt is made to shoot down the suns and moons—but the myth differs from the other two in that the suns and moons promptly go into hiding, and the right animal messenger must be found to coax them out. The crowing of the rooster, the successful messenger, brings out one sun and moon, and the others simply disappear from the myth.

*I*n the long, long ago time, there were no fewer than nine suns and nine moons. When it was day, it was a very bright day, and daytime for a very long time. When it was night, it was light and dark, dark and light, and night-time for a very long time. The people could not work during the long night, so they never had enough to eat. The suns were so bright during the long day that they could not see. And they grew angry.

"We will shoot the suns!" the people cried. "Then at least it will not be so terribly bright!"

They made a great crossbow, one that was nine *dah* long and eight *dah* wide, and went to shoot the suns.

But both the suns and the moons heard what the people planned. They were afraid, and so they all hid. For seven long years the earth was dark. The people suffered from cold and hunger.

At last they met and asked, "What can we do?"

And they decided, "We must find an animal that can go to where the suns and the moons are hiding and coax them to come out."

First they sent the powerful bull to coax the suns and the moons to come out. But the suns and the moons refused to come out.

Next the people sent the fierce tiger to coax the suns and the moons to come out. But the suns and the moons refused to come out.

Then the people sent a swift bird to coax the suns and the moons to come out. But the suns and the moons refused to come out.

At last there was only one choice left. The rooster wasn't powerful, fierce, or swift. But the rooster crowed and crowed.

One sun liked the sound. It came out for a little while, and that was the first true day. Then one moon decided that it would come out, too. It came out for a little while, and that was the first true night.

No one can say where the other suns and moons fled. But it doesn't matter. Since that time there has been daylight and nighttime, so the people can work and have enough to eat. And so they can live, even to this day.

Source

Hackin, J., et al. *Asiatic Mythology*. New York: Crowell Publishing, 1932.

THE TWO SHINING DAUGHTERS
A Myth from the Minyong People of India

This myth begins with the necessary separation of earth and sky, such as appears in the Maori myth "Rangi and Papa," then continues to the story of the two shining girls who mourn the death of their nurse so much that they, too, die and the world is left dark. What happens next is truly something out of the world of myth: the strange reincarnation of the two girls as Bomong and Bong from their buried nurse's eyes.

Then the myth changes to the theme of too many suns, when the people decide one of the girls must be shot. But once Bong is slain, Bomong goes into hiding, like the frightened suns in the preceding Hmong myth. And, like the sun and moon in the Hmong myth, Bomong is coaxed out of hiding by the rooster's crowing.

But now the myth adds a new resurrection theme: Bomong will not shine unless her sister is restored. Once Bong is returned to life, the sun shines. The myth does not specify whether Bong became the moon, but that is implied.

The myth ends with an explanation of why roosters crow at dawn.

*J*n the beginning there was darkness, and within it two forces. One was Sedi, the earth woman, and the other was Melo, the sky man. When they came together in love, their union created people and animals. But because they could not bear to be apart, their children were cramped in between them.

Then one child, Sedi-Diyor, had enough of being squashed. He kicked Melo so hard that the sky flew up into the heavens, where it remains today.

Just as Melo was fleeing, Sedi gave birth to two daughters. But because she was grieving over Melo leaving her, Sedi refused to look at them. Sedi-Diyor rescued them and got them a nurse. As they began to grow, the two girls began to glow, and soon the world was no longer dark.

But then the nurse died. The two girls mourned so deeply that they, too, died. And their light was extinguished.

Where had it gone? Was it buried with the nurse? The people dug up her body, but only her eyes were left. They glowed in the darkness so brightly that a carpenter was called. He carefully cut out the shining light—which turned into two living girls. One was Bomong and the other was Bong.

But Bomong and Bong gave off too much light and heat. When they walked, rivers dried up and leaves fell from the trees. There was no darkness now at all.

The people knew that one of the girls must be killed, so that there would be some coolness and darkness in the world. But they were afraid.

At last a frog agreed to do the deed. As Bong passed him, he shot an arrow at her, and killed her. Now it wasn't too hot or too bright. But now the people were afraid of what Bomong would do. So the rat dragged Bong's body to the river. But the body was heavy and bowed his legs. That is why rats have bowed legs today.

Bomong found her sister's body. She was afraid that the people would kill her, too, so she ran to a clearing and hid under a rock.

Now the world was dark again.

The people sent a rat, a wild bird, and a rooster to find Bomong. The light must return! They traveled and hunted, and at last the rooster found where Bomong hid. She refused to return unless the people brought Bong back to life.

What could the people do? They got the carpenter to carve Bong a new body out of wood, and brought it back to life.

When Bomong saw her sister alive again, she let her light shine. Now there was day again.

And since it was the rooster who found her, it is the rooster with his crowing who brings the coming of each new day.

Sources

Elwin, Verrier. *Myths of Middle India*. Oxford: Oxford University Press, 1949.
Nivedita, Sister, and Ananda K. Coomaraswamy. *Myths of the Hindus and Buddhists*. New York: Farrar and Rinehart, n.d.

RA'S JOURNEY
A Myth from Ancient Egypt

This is perhaps the only myth featuring an aging god who accepts his limitations and corrects his mistakes. It also gives the origin of Ra's solar boat, which is often portrayed on ancient Egyptian walls.

Ra, the sun god, travels across the sky and through the underworld in his solar boat, ensuring the balance of light and darkness. Detail from coffin of Nespawershepi, chief scribe of the Temple of Amun, c. 984 B.C.E. (*Werner Forman/Art Resource, New York*)

*I*n the days of the beginning, Ra, the sun god who was the light itself, let his brilliance shine all the time. But years go by even for the gods. As Ra grew old and older, he began to tire. He had to admit to himself that he no longer had the strength for this never-ending brilliance. And as he grew old and older, he grew wise and wiser. Ra came to think about mortal folk. He realized what harm he had done. People could not flourish under constant light.

So Ra, remorseful and weary, came up with a solution. He had a boat built for him, curved up at prow and stern, a lovely thing, and named it his solar boat.

And so it was, and so it is that Ra rides his solar boat every day. He spends half his time in the sky as a living god and half in the world of darkness as the ruler of the dead. So a balance has been created, and so mortal folk can flourish.

Source

Simpson, William Kelly, ed. *The Literature of Ancient Egypt*. New Haven: Yale University Press, 1972.

THE HIDDEN SUN
A Myth from Japan

As in the Indian myth "The Two Shining Daughters," also in this chapter, this myth deals with a sun who has hidden herself. The reason is Susanoh, brother of the sun goddess, Amateras-Ohmikami. The other gods have to trick the sun out of hiding, not with a rooster's crowing, as in the Hmong tale "Why There Is Day and Night" and the Indian tale "The Two Shining Daughters," but with the promise of a party.

Susanoh, who is more thoughtless and boisterous than evil, turns up in Chapter 5 as the hero of the myth "The Eight-Headed Serpent."

*A*materas-Ohmikami, whose name means "the goddess who shines in the heavens," is the sun, she who shines her warm golden light on the earth and all who live upon it.

But she and her brother god, Susanoh, were never happy with each other. In fact, Susanoh, who was a boisterous god who loved to fight, did everything he could to make his sweet and pretty sister's life unpleasant.

One day, trying to frighten her, Susanoh hurled a horsehide into her temple. At the time, her temple maidens were peacefully sewing. When the hide came flying into the temple, the maidens all started, their sewing falling from their hands. A sharp pair of shears slipped, and one of the maidens was stabbed.

Furious at her brother for what he'd caused, Amateras hid herself within a vast rock. Instantly the world turned pitch black.

This could not be. All the beings who lived upon the earth would die without sunlight.

But Amateras refused to come forth. So the other gods made a plan to get her out from the rock. They had a big party in front of the rock, and Amateras was so curious that she asked them what was going on. One of the gods answered, "Another great goddess appeared and we're having a party for her."

When Amateras moved the rock slightly to see outside, one of the gods pulled her out from behind it and the daylight shone on the world again.

Sources

Kawai, Hayao. *The Japanese Psyche: Major Motifs in the Fairy Tales of Japan*. Dallas: Spring Publications, 1988.

Piggott, Juliet. *Japanese Mythology*. London: Hamlyn, 1969.

THE ORIGIN OF THE MOON
A Myth of the San of the Kalahari

Here is a most unusual creation: the moon created from an old shoe tossed into the sky by a god so that he can see to travel at night; the wear and tear on the shoe explains the shadows on the moon. There is also an explanation included for the moon's waxing and waning, namely, the sun's jealousy.

*I*n the long-ago days, there was a sun, but no moon. Anyone who had to travel at night was in trouble. There was no light, no way to see where a traveler was going. He might fall in a hole or get so lost in the waterless desert he would die of thirst. Yet anyone traveling by day faced a long walk in the hot, hot sun.

One night the god Mantis decided he needed to travel. Why he decided this, where he was going, and where he was coming from—those are questions we cannot answer. But Mantis, even though he had his more-than-human powers, still couldn't see where he was going. He stubbed his toe on a rock and stumbled over a branch. Finally he said, "Enough of this! I need a light to guide me."

But Mantis had no torch or way to make one. What could he use?

Finally, with a sigh of exasperation, he took off one of his shoes. It was old and worn, but it would have to do.

With a great heave, Mantis tossed the shoe up into the sky and commanded, "Light!"

Instantly the shoe glowed with silver light.

Mantis had just created the moon. And every time it rises, we can all see that it is sometimes red with the dust of the desert, and cold as old leather, with the stains of Mantis' travels upon it.

But why should a moon-shoe change shape? Some stories add that the sun soon grew jealous of the full moon's brightness. So whenever the moon is full, the sun uses its rays to cut off slivers of the moon every night, till there is just a little left. But every month, the moon starts growing back until it has its full roundness again.

Sources

Biesele, Megan. *Women Like Meat*. Bloomington: Indiana University Press, 1993.
Van Over, Raymond. *Sun Songs: Creation Myths from Around the World*. New York: New American Library, 1980.

EATING THE SUN AND MOON
A Myth from Ancient India

There is a familiar note at the start of this myth: The gods of ancient India keep the drink of immortality in the primal oceans for their own use. So do the Norse gods keep the apples of immortality for themselves alone. The difference here is an understanding that power is dangerous in the wrong hands. But there also seems to have been a need for humanity in at least two places and times to be assured that the gods had a means for keeping themselves immortal.

The theme of the forbidden food is here, but in this myth, the *asura*, the demigod, who tastes the water gains not wisdom but punishment.

The myth ends with the explanation of solar and lunar eclipses.

*I*t happened in the most ancient of days that the gods kept *amrita*, the drink of immortality, in the primal ocean. It was for the divine ones alone. The *devas* and the *asuras*, the gods and demons, worked together, doing their best to churn the celestial ocean in quest of *amrita*, using a mountain as the churning stick and the snake Vasuki as the rope.

According to ancient Indian mythology, Vishnu, pictured here at the center of his ten avatars, took the form of an enchantress and charmed the *asuras* so the *devas* could drink *amrita*, the immortal potion. (*Victoria & Albert Museum, London/Art Resource, New York*)

What rose up first out of the waters was no *amrita*, but Lakshmi, goddess of good fortune, and after her, Chandra, god of the moon.

The *devas* and *asuras* churned on and on. But then poison fumes rose up from the waters. The *devas* and *asuras* pleaded with the god Shiva to save them. Shiva never hesitated, but drew in the poison, which turned his throat forever blue.

Now that they were safe, the *asuras* fought with the *devas* over the immortal potion. The god Vishnu took the form of an enchantress and charmed the *asuras* so that the *devas* could have all the potion. Thus was the universe protected from the wrong beings gaining immortality.

But one *asura* noted the trick and, disguised as a *deva*, won himself a drink of the water of immortality. The sun and moon gods were furious. How dare he defy the gods? They attacked the *asura* and beheaded him.

But his head couldn't die. They had left it in a terrible state, neither whole nor able to rejoin the body. So the head of the *asura* sued for justice from the gods. Surely this was far too horrible a state! Surely the sun and moon gods had known what would happen!

The gods agreed. The *asura* was given the strangest of justices: He was allowed to devour first the sun, then the moon, in a regular cycle. By this act, they would be forever reminded of their injustice to him.

And by this act, humanity became witness to solar and lunar eclipses.

Sources

Elwin, Verrier. *Myths of Middle India*. Oxford: Oxford University Press, 1949.
Nivedita, Sister, and Ananda K. Coomaraswamy. *Myths of the Hindus and Buddhists*. New York: Farrar and Rinehart, n.d.

THE CREATION OF THE PLEIADES
A Myth of the Wyandot People

This myth is one that shows how essential it is to understand the ways of a people before retelling their mythology. Why should the old woman's refusal to give the boys food result in their dancing into the sky? Outsiders can't answer that. That there are seven of the boys shouldn't automatically be taken for a magic sign; although seven is, indeed, considered a magic number in many cultures, the answer here is simply that there are seven visible Pleiades. (Nowadays, thanks to light pollution from cities, we can barely make out six; there are actually hundreds.)

Another version, collected from Mary Kelley of Wyandotte Reservation, Oklahoma, in 1911 (collector unknown but probably Marius Barbeau), adds the detail that the leader of the boys asked his friends not to look back. When one of them did, he fell from the sky and became a cedar tree. See the following Cherokee myth for the origin of the pine tree.

Once, long before now, there were seven young boys who danced and played together in the shade of a tree.

After a time, the boys became hungry. One of the seven went to an old woman's house and politely asked for some food for himself and the others.

But the old woman refused to give him even a crust of bread. "Be off with you!" she cried. "Go back to your play!"

There was nothing he could do but go back again, as she had ordered.

Another boy said, "I will try."

He went to the house and politely asked for some food.

"Be off with you!" the old woman cried. "Go back to your play!"

He went back to the others. They went on with their playing, as she had ordered. Soon they began to dance around the tree.

And as soon as they began this circle dance, their feet left the ground. They began to rise, circling higher and higher around the tree, higher and higher into the sky. Looking around for the boys, puzzled by the sudden silence, the old woman saw them dancing high up above the tree. She ran to the tree.

"Come back! Come back! I will get you something to eat!"

But they did not even notice her. They were lost in the trance of their dancing, spiraling up and ever up into the sky. At last they had risen up so high that the old woman could no longer see them. She gave up hope of seeing them again, and wept.

But they can be seen every clear night, seven boys who have become seven bright stars, the Hutiwatsija, "the cluster," which we call the Pleiades.

Sources

Barbeau, Marius. *Huron and Wyandot Mythology*. Ottawa: Government Printing Bureau, 1915.

Erdoes, Richard, and Alfonso Ortiz. *American Indian Myths and Legends*. New York: Pantheon Books, 1984.

THE ORIGIN OF THE PLEIADES AND THE PINE TREE
A Myth from the Cherokee People

While the Cherokee myth is closely related to that from the Wyandot, new details are introduced. Here the boys are so addicted to their game of *gatayusti* that their mothers refuse to feed them. The angry boys then dance up into the sky.

There's the tragic addition of one mother trying to save her son-and accidentally killing him instead. The origin of the pine tree is said to have come from her tears watering the site of his death. For a very different myth concerning the origin of the pine tree, see the Mongolian myth, "The First Evergreen Tree," later in this chapter.

*I*n the days when the world was still new, seven boys spent all their time playing *gatayusti*, a game played with a rolling stone wheel and a curved stick. They ignored their mothers, they ignored their fathers, and they refused to work in the cornfields with everyone else.

At last their mothers, angry at their sons, gave them nothing but stones for dinner. After all, it was clear that the boys liked *gatayusti* stones better than corn!

The boys were angry, too. They went down to the people's central house, muttering, "If our mothers are going to treat us this way, we'll go where we won't trouble them ever again."

So the boys began a dance, going round and round the house, round and round, praying as they danced. Soon everyone came running to see what was happening. The boys were still circling the house—but their feet were no longer touching the ground. As they danced, they rose higher and higher into the air with every circle.

One mother leaped and caught her son by the foot with his *gatayusti* pole and pulled him back down—but he hit the ground with such force that he sank into it and the earth closed over him.

The other six boys kept dancing, circling higher and higher until they had all but vanished into the sky. There they stayed and became the Anitsutsa, "the boys," which we now call the Pleiades.

As for the mother whose son had crashed into the ground, she wept over the spot day and night, watering the ground with her tears. Then one day she saw a little green plant spring up. It grew rapidly, taller and taller with every day, and at last became the first pine tree, towering over the people and sheltering them under its branches.

Sources

Bell, Corydon. *John Rattling-Gourd of Big Cove: A Collection of Cherokee Legends*. New York: Macmillan, 1955

Mooney, James. *Myths of the Cherokee*. Mineola: Dover Publications, 1995.

THE CREATION OF THE PLEIADES
A Myth from Ancient Greece

Here the seven daughters of Atlas escape the hunter Orion by fleeing up into the heavens, where they become the Pleiades, also known as the Seven Sisters. The constellation known as Orion commemorates him and his hopeless love as well. Or at least so one myth claims. Just to show how contradictory mythology can be within even one culture, see "Artemis and Apollo," the other Greek myth concerning Orion, in Chapter 4.

The giant Atlas had seven lovely daughters. They were named Electra, Maia, Taygete, Alcyone, Merope, Celaeno, and Sterope.

The hero Orion saw them and knew he must have them. Unfortunately for the hero, none of the daughters of Atlas wanted anything to do with Orion. Orion refused to accept this. Every time he saw any of the young women, he chased after them. Every time he pursued them, they managed to escape.

But their lives were becoming very unhappy. They didn't want to hurt Orion, but they also didn't want him trying to catch them. So the seven daughters of Atlas pleaded with Zeus, king of the gods, for help.

And so Zeus took pity on them. He placed the seven sisters up in the heavens as stars, forever out of Orion's reach. He can be seen up there, too, forever unable to reach the Pleiades.

Sources

Howe, George, and G. A. Harrer. *A Handbook of Classical Mythology*. Hertfordshire: Oracle, 1996.

Kerenyi, Karl. *The Gods of the Greeks*. London: Thames and Hudson, 1985.

MYTHS OF EARTH AND EARTHLY THINGS

WHY THUNDER AND LIGHTNING LIVE IN THE SKY
A Myth from Nigeria

This tale shows how a storyteller can read between the lines to learn more about a culture: Not only does this myth portray Thunder and Lightning as a loud-mouthed ewe and her hot-tempered and dangerous son, it also shows that the king is so powerful a figure that even those two perilous beings obey his commands without question.

See the following Wyandot tale, "Henqn the Thunder," for another view of the origin of thunder and lightning.

*I*n the beginning days, Thunder and Lightning lived among the people on earth. In those far-off days, Thunder took the shape of a great white ewe, and Lightning, her son, was a ram.

But they were not true animals, nor were they liked by anyone. In fact, the people feared them. For Lightning had a fierce, fierce temper. Whenever someone offended him, which was often, he would flame up in a terrible rage and burn everything in sight. Sometimes he burned down trees, sometimes huts or harvests—and sometimes Lightning even slew people.

Meanwhile, when Thunder realized what her son was doing, she would begin to shout at him. Her voice was terrible, so heavy and loud that it was unbearable to the people.

What could the people do? Lightning was burning everything, and Thunder's terrible voice was deafening them. The people went to their king and begged him to help. The king summoned Thunder and Lightning to him and ordered them to live at the farthest end of the village. He warned them not to come near the people anymore.

However, this did no good, since Lightning could still see people as they walked about the village streets and so found it only too easy to continue picking quarrels with them.

At last the king sent for them again. "I have given you many chances to live a better life," he said, "but I can see that it is useless. From now on, you must go away from our village and live in the wild bush. We do not want to see your faces here again!"

Thunder and Lightning had to obey the king and agreed to leave the village. But this wasn't the end of it. Lightning was furious about being banished, so furious that his rage set fire to the surrounding forest. The flames spread to the farms of the people and to some of their homes as well, and even as they fought the flames, they could still hear the booming voice of Thunder shouting at her son.

The king called all his counselors to him. They thought and talked, debated and thought. And after a long while of this, they found an answer to the problem. It wasn't enough to banish Thunder and Lightning to the forest. They must be banished away from the entire earth. They must be commanded to live in the sky.

So it was proclaimed. By royal decree, Thunder and Lightning were sent to live in the sky. The people rejoiced. Now the two creatures wouldn't be able to do any more harm!

But of course it didn't work out quite that way. Even to this day, Lightning still loses his temper from time to time. When he does, fire blazes down to the earth. And as for Thunder, everyone has heard the booming roar of her shouting at her son to behave.

Sources

Radin, Paul. *African Folktales*. New York: Schocken Books, 1983.

Walker, Barbara K., and S. Warren Walker, eds., as told by Olawale Idewu and Omotayo Adu. *Nigerian Folk Tales*. New Brunswick: Rutgers University Press, 1961.

HENQN THE THUNDER
A Myth from the Wyandot People

Here, by contrast with the preceding Nigerian myth, "Why Thunder and Lightning Live in the Sky," Thunder is portrayed not as a hot-tempered and deadly menace but as a rather pathetic figure, a big, powerful fellow who just doesn't know his own strength and must live in exile because of it.

*T*his was in the ancient days. Henqn was one of seven brothers who lived together. He was the strongest of the seven and was always playing and wrestling and making noise. Unfortunately, Henqn had no idea of his own strength. All he had to do was put his hand on the lodgepole, and down would come the whole lodge. He also had no idea of how his pranks were starting to bother his brothers.

They finally decided that they had to get rid of him. "His strength is dangerous enough when he is playing," they said to each other. "He would be terrible if he ever grew angry."

So the brothers decided to abandon Henqn on a far-off, lonely island where he could do no harm.

"Come with us on a hunting trip," they said to him.

He agreed. Off they all paddled in their canoes, to that far-off island. One brother tricked Henqn into following him into the dense forest, while the others hurried back to the canoes. As soon as Henqn was deep into the forest, his brother slipped away and raced back to the canoes. They all paddled hastily away.

Henqn, however, realized what was happening and came running back to the shore, shouting to his brothers. So powerful was his voice that the waves rose up and nearly swamped the canoes.

"Stop shouting!" Henqn's brothers cried. "You will drown us if you don't deafen us first!"

"Won't you take me back with you?" he asked.

"No! You have to stay on the island."

Henqn hung his head. "I almost drowned you. I will stay here, where I won't do any harm to anyone. But I won't let you forget me! You'll be reminded of me, because I mean to shout at you from time to time."

So Henqn stayed on the island to this day, wandering about during the summer and sleeping in the winter. That is why thunder is so rare in the winter. When there is a peal of thunder in the winter, why, that is simply Henqn turning over in his sleep.

Source

Barbeau, Marius. *Huron and Wyandot Mythology*. Ottawa: Government Printing Bureau, 1915.

HOW PROCREATION BEGAN
A Myth of the Ashanti People

Not every myth of a first man and woman and a serpent portrays the serpent as an evil being. Here, in contrast to the snake in the biblical Garden of Eden, Python is doing the Lord of Heaven's bidding. And here procreation is seen not as something taboo or shameful, but

A symbol of life, the python is revered as a sacred creature throughout Africa. In the Ashanti tale, it is the python that teaches the first men and women about procreation. (*Werner Forman/Art Resource, New York*)

something necessary if humanity is to survive. Is there any cross-cultural influence with the Judeo-Christian story? That can't be proved or disproved. But just to show how difficult it is to trace possible influences in mythology and folklore, there are also beneficent snake images from unrelated cultures in ancient Mesopotamia.

*I*n the very first days, there were four people, a man and a woman who had come down from heaven, and another man and woman who had come up out of the ground. The Lord of Heaven also sent Python to the world, and the snake made its home in a river.

There was a good reason for Python to be there. For in those very first days, men and women had no children. In fact, they didn't know about desire or procreation, either.

It was Python who had been sent there to teach them. He started by asking the men and women, "Do you have any children?"

They stared at him. "What are children?"

Python realized there was a good deal of work ahead of him. He explained what children were, and saw the humans' eyes widen in wonder.

"No," they told him, "we have none."

"So be it. Now I will help you."

Python told the couples to stand facing each other. He slithered into the river and came out with his mouth full of water. This he sprayed on the couples' bellies, saying ritual words: "Kus, kus." These are words that are still used in rituals even to this day.

Then Python told the couples he had worked powerful magic on them. All they needed to do now was go home, cuddle each other, and the magic would see that everything worked.

Sure enough, whether it was magic or awakened human nature, there were children born by the next year. As they grew up, they took the spirit of the river where Python lived as their clan spirit. To this day, their descendants will never kill a python. And if they find one dead, they cover it with white clay and bury it properly. They have not forgotten the service Python rendered to their ancestors.

Sources

Feldmann, Susan. *African Myths and Tales*. New York: Dell, 1963.
Radin, Paul. *African Folktales*. New York: Schocken Books, 1983.

THE BEGINNING OF MARRIAGE
A Myth of the Tswana of the Southern Kalahari

Here is a charming myth of how men and women were created in separate places and were led to each other. But there are echoes of the myths of the origin of death, as well: Here, too, as in the Khoikhoin myth "Death Comes to Humanity," there is a chameleon messenger who moves too slowly. But this myth ends happily. Note that the Mother of Gods has to make a special potion to give men the gift of human speech, which women already possess!

This was back in the very beginning of time. The gods created Tauetona, who was the first man, then created the rest of humanity, and all the animals. This time and peaceful land was called Thaya Banna, which means "the beginning of men."

But soon the peace was gone. All wasn't well in the land, because while the animals had their hes and shes, their happy couples, the men had no wives. There were no women where they lived. Yes, the gods had also created women in a far-away valley called Motlhaba Basetsana, which means "the plain of women," but the men didn't know this.

So the gods decided to clear up this problem. First they sent a message to the men that said, "Men will have to die but may return." They gave this message to Tread Carefully the chameleon. Tread Carefully did tread carefully and took a very long time to deliver the puzzling message.

In the meantime, the gods had also agreed that their first message had been too puzzling. So they sent a second message with the fast lizard that said, "You will die like the animals, but your spirits will live forever." It also said, "You will have children."

"But we have no women!" the men protested.

Later, while hunting, Tauetona discovered some strange footprints that looked very much like his own but were smaller.

"Whose tracks are these?" he asked Hyena.

Hyena yawned. He wasn't interested, because whatever had made the tracks was too big for him to catch. "I do not recognize this animal."

Tauetona went to Giraffe. "From your height, can you see who left these tracks?"

Giraffe stared off into the distance. There was the other valley, and there were figures moving about in it. Those were women! "I can see them. And I shall go and return with them."

Meanwhile, where the women lived, they, too, were lonely. All the other animals had their mates, but they had no men. They, too, had received the gods' message, but they, too, wondered how they could have children when there were no men.

Then Giraffe arrived. "I will take you to the men who long to meet you."

The women joyfully followed Giraffe, singing as they went.

In the meantime, the Mother of Gods made a potion from mimosa seeds. This she placed on the tongue of each man. This gave the men the gift of human speech, which the women already had. Now the men could propose to the women and marry them.

And so it was.

Sources

Jordan, Michael. *Myths of the World: A Thematic Encyclopedia.* London: Kyle Cathie, 1995.

Partridge, A. C., ed. *Folklore of Southern Africa.* Vol. 2 of ELISA Series. Cape Town, South Africa: Purnell, 1973.

THE ORIGIN OF THE TIBETAN PEOPLE
A Myth from Tibet

Once again, here's proof that a storyteller has to be careful to understand the story when myth is involved. To Westerners, the thought of a race claiming descent from a monkey and a rock-ogress might seem odd, to put it mildly. But this is the Monkey King, an enlightened being who agonizes over his decision. Not only is their marriage given as the explanation for the Tibetan people, it is also given as the explanation for the different natures and types of people as well.

*T*he Monkey King, who had taken a layperson's religious vows, had been sent by divine will to meditate in the mountains of Tibet.

There he sat and quietly contemplated kindness, compassion, and enlightenment. A sad and lonely rock-ogress saw him and felt a sudden blaze of love. She did her best to express her love and passion, but the mon-

The Monkey King, pictured here with Brahma (right), is regarded as an enlightened being throughout Tibet. In the legendary tale, the Monkey King marries the rock-ogress, and together they produce hundreds of monkey-children. Many Tibetans believe that their people descended from these first monkey-children. (*Borromeo/Art Resource, New York*)

key ignored her. The rock-ogress changed her shape to that of a woman and tried again, saying, "I do not speak of crude affairs. Let us be married!"

The monkey replied gently, "I cannot. It would go against my vows were I to become your husband."

The rock-ogress, almost in tears, slid back into her rightful form. "If you reject me, I will kill myself!" But then she caught her breath and said, "O great Monkey King, think of me a little. Hear my plea.

"By the weight of my karma, I was born into the ogre race. Now my loneliness drives me to fall in love with you.

"But if you will not marry me, then I must take a rock-ogre husband. Every day, in ogre ways, we will slay ten thousand living beings, and every night we will devour a thousand more. I will bear cruel ogre children and fill this land with ogre realms. Everything that lives will be an ogre's prey."

The rock-ogress burst into tears. "Is it not better to show me your compassion?" she sobbed.

The Monkey King didn't know what to do. Instead of answering her, he flew instantly to the sacred Mount Potala and begged the Sublime One for advice. "Compassionate Protector of Beings, I have protected my vows as I would my life. Compassionate Protector of Loving-Kindness, hear my plea."

When the Monkey King had finished, the answer resounded from the sky: "Marry the rock-ogress. Great goodness shall come of it for the future."

So it was that the Monkey King and the rock-ogress were wed. With time, the rock-ogress bore six monkey children, each one with a different temperament, each one reborn from one of the six classes of beings. The monkey child reborn from the hell realms had a stern countenance and could withstand great hardships. The child from the realm of hungry ghosts was hideous, with an appetite that was never satisfied. The one reborn from the animal realm was stupid. The monkey child from the human realm was born with wisdom. The child from the realm of the demigods was aggressive and jealous of everyone. And the monkey child from the realm of the gods was patient and virtuous.

The Monkey King and his family spent three years in the Forest of Assembled Birds. When they returned, the Monkey King was shocked to see that his children now numbered no fewer than five hundred. Five hundred children, who had eaten everything in sight and were now starving.

"Father, what can we eat? Mother, what can we eat?"

The Monkey King flew to Mount Potala. "Alas, alas, Compassionate Protector of Loving-Kindness, how can I help my children? I am in this predicament at the Sublime One's behest, yet we now are like a city of hungry ghosts. I beseech you, protect us with your compassion."

The Supreme Being assured him, "I shall protect your progeny," and cast down to the earth below barley, wheat, peas, buckwheat, and rice. Wherever they landed, crops sprang up that needed no cultivation. The Monkey King led his monkey children there, showed them the food, and said, "Zotang, eat!" That place is still known as Zotang Gongpori.

Once they had eaten these crops, the monkey children's hair and tails grew shorter. They became human.

And from these children, it is said, descend the people of Tibet. Those who are of the Monkey King's lineage are patient, faithful, compassionate, and diligent. Those who are of the rock-ogress mother's lineage are lusty, angry, greedy, strong, foolish, and profit-seeking.

Sources

Hackin, J., et al. *Asiatic Mythology*. New York: Crowell Publishing, 1932.
Leeming, David Adams. *The World of Myth: An Anthology*. New York and Oxford: Oxford University Press, 1990.

THE ORIGIN OF THE INCA PEOPLE, VERSION ONE
A Myth from Peru

The following three origin myths of the Inca are included to show how one people can have more than one concept of their beginning. The mountainous nature of their Andean terrain probably had something to do with this, though once the Incans had completed their sophisticated system of roads and their network of trained runners, their entire empire and its culture became more homogeneous.

It's worth noting, incidentally, that Incan buildings, made without mortar but with beautifully fitted stones, have lasted even through recent earthquakes in Peru, while more modern structures (including, ironically, those built by the Spanish invaders) have not.

The three myths begin the same way, with the motif of the great flood. But in the first version, it is a llama that warns a farmer to take shelter on a hill that miraculously grows tall enough to rise above the floodwaters, thanks to divine help. It's the farmer and his children who are said to be the ancestors of those in the region. The incest question isn't raised, though everyone who as a child asked, "Where did Cain get his wife?" knows there are questions that can't be answered logically.

*I*n the long-ago days, a farmer happened to notice that his llamas were looking very unhappy. This was in the days when humans and animals still understood each other, so the man asked one of the llamas, "What's wrong?"

The llama answered, "We have overheard the stars talking. They say that there will be a great flood that will destroy the earth."

The farmer took the llama's warning seriously. He gathered up his six children and all the food and llamas that they could collect, and climbed to the top of a big hill called Ancasmarca.

Sure enough, the flood swept down over the land. But when the floodwaters started rising, the great god Viracocha made the hill rise as well, so the farmer and his family were safe.

After the flood, the hill returned to its original height. The farmer and his family were saved, and it was his children who lived on to repopulate the province.

Sources

Bierhorst, John. *The Mythology of South America*. New York: William Morrow, 1988.
Urton, Gary. *Inca Myths*. Austin: University of Texas Press, 1999.

THE ORIGIN OF THE INCA PEOPLE, VERSION TWO
A Myth from Peru

In the second myth, it is two brothers who survive the flood by taking refuge in a cave. Then the theme of the mysterious helper appears. For another use of the theme, see the Huichol myth "The Man and the Dog," in Chapter 2. In this case, the helpers are two young bird-women sent by the divine Viracocha to aid them. It is from the wedding of the brothers and the women that the land is repopulated.

*W*hen the great flood came, two brothers managed to survive by taking refuge in a cave. After the floodwaters subsided, the brothers found themselves alone. They built themselves a shelter and lived off what they could gather from the countryside.

One day, after spending it looking for food, the brothers returned to their shelter to find that it was already full of food to sustain them.

This happened several times. Every time they would run out of food and look for more, there would be provisions waiting for them when they returned.

At last the brothers decided to pretend to leave, then hide so they could solve the mystery of who was leaving them food.

Before too long, two guacamayas flew in to the hut. These bright-colored birds then turned into two beautiful young women and began setting out food for the brothers. The two men sprang out of hiding and caught the women. The women were frightened at first and wanted to escape. But the brothers managed to calm them and asked where they were from. The young women answered that they had been sent by Viracocha to take care of them.

Soon the brothers married the two women, and their children went on to populate the land.

Sources

Bierhorst, John. *The Mythology of South America*. New York: William Morrow, 1988.
Urton, Gary. *Inca Myths*. Austin: University of Texas Press, 1999.

THE ORIGIN OF THE INCA PEOPLE, VERSION THREE
A Myth from Peru

The third myth is the more "official" one. In this one, there is a cave called Pacaritampu, though the myth is unclear as to whether the people who come out of it after the flood have taken refuge in it or have come up from the underworld, as in the Apache and Hopi myths of origin. It is these people, specially created or re-created by the god Viracocha, who are the direct ancestors of the Incas.

*T*his was in the long-ago days, so long ago that no one now is sure of what happened. All agree that there was a great flood that destroyed the land, and a great cave, Pacaritampu.

After the flood was gone, people came out of the cave. Who were they? These were new people, those who had been created by the great god Viracocha. And they stepped out in wonder to a new world. They were the ancestors of the Incas, and went on to populate all the world.

Sources

Bierhorst, John. *The Mythology of South America*. New York: William Morrow, 1988.
Urton, Gary. *Inca Myths*. Austin: University of Texas Press, 1999.

Sculpted stele representing the god Viracocha, a creator deity originally worshiped by pre-Inca inhabitants of Peru. In many variations of the Inca creation myth, Viracocha saves his people from the great flood by either shielding them in a cave or placing them on top of a hill. (*Werner Forman/Art Resource, New York*)

THE ORIGIN OF THE BEAR
A Myth of the Cherokee People

This myth does more than explain the origin of a species. It shows the origin of a mythic kinship between the bear and the people, as well as the origin of the chants used by the Cherokee bear hunters.

*O*nce, in the long ago time, there lived a family within the Ani-Tsa-gu-hi clan that had a son who used to spend almost all his days in the mountains. He would not return till night, no matter how his parents scolded him and worried about him. They worried all the more when they noticed that he was starting to grow hairy all over.

"Why do you like to be in the woods so much?" they asked him. "What do you find to eat?"

"There is plenty to eat," the boy replied. "I like it far better than our corn and beans. Soon I will live in the woods all the time."

"You can't do that!" his parents cried. "You must stay with us!"

"Don't worry about me," the boy said. "It is a far better life there than here. Don't you see this hair of mine? I am starting to be different from people here, so I *must* live in the woods. Why don't you come with me? There is plenty for us all in the woods, and you won't have to work hard to get it. But if you want to come," their son warned, "you first must fast for seven days."

He went back into the woods. His father and mother talked it over for a long time. What should they do? At last they went to the headmen of their clan. They all held a council and discussed the matter.

And at last it was decided. "Here we must work and work, yet never have enough. In the woods, the boy says there is plenty for all, and no hard work. We will go with him."

So the clan fasted for seven days. At the end of the fast, the Ani-Tsa-gu-hi followed the boy into the woods.

The people of other clans sent messengers to persuade the Ani-Tsa-gu-hi not to live in the woods. But when the messengers caught up with them, the messengers saw that the people were already covered with hair. For seven days they had not tasted human food, and the change had already begun.

The Ani-Tsa-gu-hi told the messengers, "We are going where there is always plenty to eat. From now on, we shall be known as bears. When you are hungry, come into the woods and call us and we will give you our flesh. You need not be afraid to kill us, for we shall live always."

They taught the messengers the songs with which to call them, and bear hunters today still know these songs. When they had finished the songs, the Ani-Tsa-gu-hi went on into the woods and were bears.

Sources

Bell, Corydon. *John Rattling-Gourd of Big Cove: A Collection of Cherokee Legends*. New York: Macmillan, 1955

Mooney, James. *Myths of the Cherokee*. Mineola: Dover, 1995.

THE ORIGIN OF SHAMANS
A Myth of Mongolia

The Mongolian myth shows us brother deities of good and evil, the same pair that appear in "The Two Sons of Heaven," in Chapter 1. See the Micmac myth "Glooscap and His People," in the same chapter, for another pair of good and bad brother deities.

It's the evil brother here, Erleg Khan, chief of the spirits of the east, who creates disease, and the good brother, Ulgen Tenger, who creates the first shaman from the mating of an eagle and a human woman. But a very human problem results: arrogance and the misuse of too much power. The myth also shows a deity who is angry not because the shaman Hara-Gyrgen is evil but because he is too powerful. The implication here is that Hara-Gyrgen might dare challenge the gods themselves. And Hara-Gyrgen's growing weariness is given as the reason why shamans today are not godlike magicians.

*I*n the ancient days, when Ulgen Tenger created humanity, the people were all happy since they lived without trouble or disease.

But Ulgen Tenger's crueler brother, Erleg Khan, chief of the spirits of the east, created disease and sorrow for humanity. Now people fell ill and died.

Ulgen Tenger and the spirits of the west gathered in the Pleiades to see what could be done to help humanity. They sent Eagle down to earth to be the first shaman.

But when Eagle came down from the upper world, he found a problem. He tried to tell the humans that he was there to be a shaman for them—but he didn't know the human language. Discouraged, Eagle returned to the upper world and told Ulgen Tenger and the spirits that he could not help humanity.

"Return," Ulgen Tenger told him. "Find a human woman for your mate. Your child will become the first shaman."

So Eagle flew back to earth and found a human woman for his mate. Sure enough, their child was born full of wisdom, and became humanity's first shaman. Even today shamans remember the flight of the eagle in their dances.

But now there was a new problem. Although shamans were wise and could heal the sick, those earliest of shamans were very powerful and grew very arrogant.

One of the most famous, and most arrogant, of shamans was Hara-Gyrgen. Looking down from the sky, Ulgen Tenger decided to test him. So he took away the soul of a girl from Hara-Gyrgen's clan, and the girl lay as though she were dead.

When Hara-Gyrgen arrived, he knew at once that the girl's soul had been taken, so he flew up to the upper world, straight to Ulgen Tenger. The girl's soul was in a bottle, and Ulgen Tenger was holding it closed with his thumb.

Hara-Gyrgen turned himself into a bee and stung Ulgen Tenger on the cheek. When Ulgen Tenger dropped the bottle to slap the bee, the shaman grabbed the girl's soul and flew back to the earth.

Ulgen Tenger was angry and decided that the shaman must be punished for being too powerful. Hara-Gyrgen's punishment was to jump up and down on a mountain forever. When the mountain has been worn down, shamans will no longer have their powers. By now, Hara-Gyrgen is growing weary, which is why shamans are not as strong as they used to be, and why people no longer understand many of the shaman songs.

Sources

Hackin, J., et al. *Asiatic Mythology*. New York: Crowell, 1932.
Metternich, Hilary Roe. *Mongolian Folktales*. Boulder, CO: Avery, 1996.

ANGARA, DAUGHTER OF LAKE BAIKAL
A Myth from the Lake Baikal Region

This tale is included as an example of a mythic explanation for a natural phenomenon: Lake Baikal in Siberia, the largest freshwater lake in the world. It is true that over three hundred rivers feed it, and only one, the Angara, flows out of it. This is an unusual geological situation, and it didn't go unnoticed by the people who lived near the lake, who came up with a rather romantic myth to explain it.

The lake today, by the way, is a battleground for local environmentalists, who are trying to preserve both its relative lack of pollution and the lake sturgeon that live in it.

*B*aikal, the *ezen* or master spirit of the great lake, had 337 daughters. The loveliest of all of them was Angara. She had many suitors, but none of them yet had pleased her.

One day, however, young Yenisey the Brave came as a guest to their home—and he and Angara fell in love. They promised each other that they would wed. But they must keep this promise a secret until there could be a formal agreement with Baikal.

Before he left, Yenisey gave Angara a gift of a white bird.

Soon after that, powerful Prince Irkut came to visit and asked for Angara's hand. Baikal, impressed by the proud prince, agreed at once, and refused to listen to Angara's pleas.

Angara was miserable. As soon as she could, she gave the white bird a message and sent it to Yenisey.

Days passed. There was no word from Yenisey. Angara ran away in the direction of his far-off land. In his fury, Baikal grabbed a huge boulder and threw it after her. The rock missed Angara and crashed down onto the shore of Lake Baikal. It can still be seen there: Shaman's Rock.

Meanwhile, Prince Irkut and his brother, Akha, heard what had happened, and went racing off after Angara. But she had too great a lead. Irkhut collapsed at one point, and Akha at another.

Angara never returned. She met up with Yenisey, and they wed.

And today that is why the Angara River is the only river flowing out of Lake Baikal, while the 336 rivers of her unwed sisters flow into Lake Baikal. Where Irkut collapsed, the Irkut River flows into the Angara. Where Akha collapsed, the Akha River flows into the Angara. And further west, where Angara and Yenisey were reunited, near the border of Tuva, the Angara and Yenisey Rivers merge to form one of the greatest rivers of Siberia.

Source

Personal communication, Siberia, 1980.

THE MOUNTAIN OF FIRE
A Myth of the Klamath People

About seven thousand years ago, in what is now Oregon, Mount Mazama, one of the many volcanoes running up the Pacific Northwest's side of the Ring of Fire, exploded with such force that most of the mountain blew itself out of existence. The top of what had been Mount Mazama collapsed in on itself, and what was left of it, the caldera, or crater, gradually became filled with snow melt until it was a lake: Crater Lake.

Since artifacts show that the Klamath people were in the area at the time of the eruption (at, one hopes, a safe distance), it's not at all surprising that so awe-inspiring and terrifying an event should have its own mythology—in this case a war between the essences of volcanoes, the second being nearby Mount Shasta.

*I*n the ancient days, the spirits of earth and sky often spoke with humankind. One was Llao, the spirit of the below-world. Llao lived beneath Lao-Yaina, which is now known as Mount Mazama. Another was Skell, the spirit of the above-world. And the two were sworn enemies.

Llao often rose up through Lao-Yaina and stood on top of it. When he did so, he stood tall enough for his head to touch the stars near the home of Skell. There was no lake then, not as there is today, just a hole in the mountain through which Llao passed to see the outside world.

One day, while standing atop his mountain, Llao saw Loha, who was the daughter of the chief of the Klamath people. He saw her, yes, and fell in love with her beauty. He paid her visits, but each time Loha rejected him, both because he was ugly and because he was from the below-world.

At last Llao's love turned to hate. Raging, he swore he would have his revenge on Loha and all her people. He would, Llao swore, destroy them all with the curse of fire from the below-world.

What could humans do against spirit folk? The Klamath chief asked Skell for help.

Skell soared down from the sky to the top of what we now call Mount Shasta and shouted at Llao to leave the humans alone and fight him.

And fight they did, Skell and Llao. Their combat made the earth tremble and roar as they hurled red-hot rocks at each other. The whole sky turned black with the force of their battle, and soon all the spirits of earth and sky were involved. Hoping that their sacrifice would quell the fury, two Klamath shamans jumped into the heart of the below-world.

Skell was so impressed by their desperate courage that he fought even harder, defeating Llao, driving him deep down into the below-world. Skell threw down Lao-Yaina on top of him so that Llao would stay forever underground.

But where the mountain had been was now a dark, gaping pit. Skell wanted beauty to return now that the battle was won, so he filled up the pit with clear blue water.

We now can see exactly where Lao-Yaina, Mount Mazama, stood, because Crater Lake is still where Skell wanted it, marking the site of the mountain's collapse.

Sources

Clark, Ella E. *Indian Legends of the Pacific Northwest*. Berkeley: University of California Press, 1953.

Thompson, Stith. *Tales of the North American Indians*. Bloomington: Indiana University Press, 1966.

THE BIRTH OF THE COCONUT TREE
A Myth from the Chamorro of Guam

This is a bittersweet myth that sounds almost like a fantasy story, about a young girl who dies for want of something that cannot exist save after her death and from her grave. It includes the motif of self-sacrifice for the good of the people.

*L*ong ago among the Chamorro people, there lived a family with a lovely and kindhearted young daughter. She was loved by the entire tribe.

One day the girl became strangely thirsty, with a thirst that could only be quenched by juice from a certain special fruit. But when she was asked what she wanted, she could not name it. Everyone in the tribe tried to find the fruit she described, but no one could succeed.

And not long after, the girl became very ill and died.

Her father buried his daughter, and the people covered her grave with flowers.

One day, not long after, the tribe noticed that a strange plant like none they'd ever seen before was growing on the girl's grave. Was it magic? No one knew. So just in case, they built a shelter about it to protect it.

In five years, the plant had grown into a tall tree, and strange-looking fruits appeared amid its branches.

One of the fruits dropped to the ground, and its hard brown shell cracked open. The mother of the dead girl tasted the fruit and found it sweet and nicely chewy.

This was the first coconut from the first coconut tree—a gift after death from the girl who had died for want of it.

Source

Knappert, Jan. *Pacific Mythology*. London: Aquarian Press, 1992.

THE FIRST EVERGREEN TREE
A Myth from Mongolia

The evil Erleg Khan is in the background of this myth, though he doesn't appear as he did in the two other Mongolian myths, "The Two Sons of Heaven" and "The Origin of Shamans." But the actual myth is one of immortality lost and gained, just as the snake winds up with the gift of immortality in "The Epic of Gilgamesh," in Chapter 5.

*I*n the early days of the earth, there were no pine trees that retained their needles all year, no evergreens at all. Every tree lost its leaves in the fall. But of course it regained its leaves in the spring.

Humans were not like the trees, with rebirth coming every spring. Thanks to the hatred of the dark supernatural being Erleg Khan, disease was in the world, and humans sickened and died where once they had been immortal.

Raven alone felt pity for humanity. He wanted to restore that lost immortality. Now, in those beginning days, there was a great mountain, Humber Ula, at the center of the world. At its peak grew a golden aspen with silver leaves, and beside it was the spring of the water of life. Whoever drank from the waters of this spring would be restored to health and would live in health forever.

So Raven flew to that spring of the water of life and scooped up as much water as his beak could hold. His plan was to sprinkle the water of life over the humans and hope that those drops would be enough to restore them to immortality.

But as he flew back to the humans, Raven passed over a stand of pines. His shadow startled an owl, which let out a loud hoot. That startled Raven in turn, and the water of life spilled from his opened beak down onto the pine trees. Why did Raven not return for more of the water of life? No one knows. Perhaps the magic could only be worked once.

But that mishap created the evergreen tree. Thanks to the drops of the water of life, pine trees stay green throughout the year, while the leaves of other trees, like humans, grow old, fall down, and die.

Sources

Hackin, J., et al. *Asiatic Mythology*. New York: Crowell, 1932.
Metternich, Hilary Roe. *Mongolian Folktales*. Boulder, CO: Avery, 1996.

PROMETHEUS STEALS FIRE
A Myth of the Ancient Greeks

One of the oddest themes in mythology is that of the theft of fire. It crosses cultures and eras, and turns up almost everywhere. The story of Prometheus is perhaps the best known of these theft of fire myths to Westerners, though not that many are likely to know the background story, or that Prometheus is as much or more a trickster who takes on Zeus himself as he is a symbol of heroic defiance.

Even as the Greek Prometheus is bound to a rock in punishment, with that eagle tearing out his liver every day, so the Norse Loki was bound to a rock in punishment—in his case because he'd deliberately caused a death—with a serpent dripping venom in his face. Mythology has some very unpleasant recurring themes!

For those interested in seeing an interpretation of Prometheus as hero, there is a statue of him in New York City's Rockefeller Center.

A seventeenth-century painting depicts the myth of Prometheus. A Titan, master craftsman, and ultimate trickster, Prometheus is credited with stealing fire from the gods and giving it to the human race. (*Art Resource, New York*)

*P*rometheus was not truly one of the gods of Mount Olympus. He was a Titan, born from the union of the Titan Iapetus and the nymph Asia. It was Iapetus who had led an unsuccessful revolt against the gods, and one of Prometheus' brothers, Atlas, wound up carrying the weight of the world as a punishment after that.

But Prometheus had not revolted. And so when Zeus, king of the gods, was smitten by a terrible headache, it was Prometheus who was trusted to help him. The help took the form of striking Zeus on the head so that the goddess Athena could be born, fully grown, from his forehead.

Not long after this strange event Prometheus and his brother Epimetheus traveled down from Olympus to the Greek province of Boitia. There they looked around at the lovely landscape. But it needed something. So the two Titans made a series of clay figures and showed them to Athena. She breathed life into the figures that Prometheus had created, and they became human beings who honored him. The figures that his brother Epimetheus had created became animals, which attacked him.

Zeus was furious. How dare these upstarts interfere with his divine rights? He forbade Prometheus from teaching humanity any of the ways of civilization.

Athena didn't approve. She ignored what Zeus was ordering, and taught Prometheus so that he might teach humanity.

Fuming, Zeus demanded that humanity make sacrifices to the gods to show that they were properly obedient and worshipful. The humans went to Prometheus to ask what belonged to them and what belonged to the gods.

Prometheus told them to sacrifice an ox, then divide the sacrifice into two bags. In the first bag they were to put the bones, and place the fat from the ox on top to hide them. In the second bag, they were to put the meat, and place the ox's intestines on top to hide that as well.

Prometheus called to Zeus so that he might choose which portion of the sacrifice would be his. Zeus, seeing the fat in the first bag, assumed that it must also contain the meat, so he chose that one—ending up with the bones of the ox as the sacrifice.

Now Zeus was truly furious. He would not let humanity thrive! So he forbade any of the gods to let humanity have the gift of fire.

Prometheus was angry as well. If fire was denied to humanity, the humans could never be more than animals. Zeus had set guards at the entrance to Olympus, but Athena secretly told Prometheus about an unguarded back entrance into Olympus.

So Prometheus sneaked into Olympus that night through the back entrance and stole his way to the chariot of the sun. Fires forever burned there, and Prometheus quickly lit a torch, then extinguished it and hid the hot coals in a fennel stalk so no flames would be seen. He hurried down Mount Olympus to the humans and gave them the gift of fire.

Now all of Zeus' fury was centered on Prometheus. He created the lovely Pandora and gave her a box into which Zeus had placed all the evil of the world, then sent Pandora and her box to Prometheus as a gift from Zeus himself.

Prometheus instantly saw the curse that Pandora and her box carried. He refused the gift, giving it instead to his brother Epimetheus. It was Epimetheus who opened the box and released the evils upon the world—although he also released hope as well.

Zeus no longer tried stealth. Prometheus was captured and chained to a rock in the Caucasus Mountains, where a great eagle would eat his liver every day, leaving only at nightfall. Then the liver would grow back, in time for the eagle's return the next day.

Zeus offered to free Prometheus if he would tell Zeus the details of the prophecy that told of Zeus' dethroning. But Prometheus refused.

At last the half-god hero Heracles freed Prometheus from the rock. Zeus' order had stated that Prometheus be bound to the rock for the rest of eternity, but Prometheus and Heracles solved that problem. Heracles simply broke off a link of the chains, set it with a chip of the rock, and gave it to Prometheus to wear.

From that day on, men began wore rings with stones and gems set into them to honor Prometheus for what he had undergone on their behalf. And even to this day, the name of Prometheus has come to stand for the strength that withstands all oppression.

Source

Frazer, Sir James G. *Myths of the Origin of Fire.* Barnes and Noble Books, 1996.

THE THEFT OF FIRE
A Myth of the Ojibway People

There is a definite parallel between this myth of the theft of fire and the stories of the theft of the sun, such as those about Raven. Here, too, there is a selfish old man who will not share what he has. Here, too, there is a culture hero, in this case Manabozho, who also performs a transformation trick. Though he doesn't go as far as Raven, who was reborn in baby shape, he takes on the form of a rabbit to trick the old man's daughters.

*O*nce, in the very long ago, in the cold northern lands, Manabozho asked his grandmother, Nokomis, "Why do the people have to freeze all winter? These winters are long and very cold. Is there no way that they can stay warm?"

Nokomis answered, "There is a rumor that in some faraway land there lives an old man who has the gift of fire. But he is selfish, that old man, and keeps it hidden away. He will not share it with anyone but his daughters."

"I will travel to that land," Manabozho told Nokomis. "I will get some fire from the old man."

Nokomis didn't like the idea of Manabozho traveling so far away. But she knew that once his mind was made up to do something, he would do it. So she wished him well as he left. Manabozho called back over his shoulder to her, "Be ready with kindling for the fire I'll bring back!"

He traveled far and far again till he had reached the camp of the old man. Now Manabozho needed a plan for getting inside. He disguised himself as a small, shivering rabbit.

Sure enough, the old man's younger daughter saw this sad, shivering little rabbit.

"Oh, you poor thing!" she cried. "You must be freezing out here."

Tucking him under her shawl, she took him inside, where the fire was burning merrily and the lodge was cozy with warmth.

There sat the old man. "What is this?" he shouted when he saw the rabbit. "I do not let any strangers into this lodge!"

"But this is only a rabbit!" his daughters said. "Please let the poor thing stay."

The old man was growing drowsy from the fire's warmth. Soon he fell asleep and didn't speak of the rabbit again.

The girls put the rabbit near the fire so that he could get warm, and went to prepare their father's dinner.

As soon as the girls looked away, Manabozho caught a spark of fire on his back and ran off. Behind him, he could hear the old man and the girls shouting at each other, realizing that they'd been fooled, but there was nothing they could do about it. But the fire was hot, so Manabozho ran as fast as he could run. As he reached his grandmother's camp, he shouted, as well as a rabbit could shout, "Have that kindling ready!"

"It is," Nokomis replied.

She snatched the fire from the rabbit's back, and Manabozho turned back into himself with a sigh of relief, brushing off cinders. As Nokomis coaxed the fire to burn steadily in their fire pit, Manabozho went outside and called to the people.

"Come and get a spark from the fire! From now on, you will be able to keep yourselves and your families warm through all the winter."

So it was.

That is all.

Source

"The Theft of Fire." *Canku Ota—A Newsletter Celebrating Native America*. Issue 03 (www.turtletrack.org/Issues00/Co02122000/CO_02122000_Theftfire.htm), February 12, 2000.

THE BIRTH OF WENEBOJO AND HIS THEFT OF FIRE
A Myth of the Chippewa-Speaking People

This myth also parallels the theft of the sun stories of Raven. But it begins with a different motif: the birth of the culture hero in an unusual fashion. In this case, Wenebojo is created fully grown and with all his powers from clotted blood stored in an old woman's mitten.

Now the myth parallels the Ojibway story above, not surprising since Chippewa is basically a linguistic separation, not an ethnic or cultural one. The main differences here are the details of the sliding across the ice and the old man's knowledge of Wenebojo's existence.

One time there was an old woman who was alone in the world. One winter she was, very hungry and very cold, without so much as a flint to spark a fire into life.

Then word came to her that somebody had killed a moose. By the time she rushed there, the poor woman found that there was nothing left but the skeleton and a few clots of blood. So hungry was she that she thought this was better than nothing; at least she might be able to make some kind of soup. So she scooped up the frozen blood in one of her mittens.

On her way back to her home, the woman suddenly heard a voice—one that was coming from her mitten!

It was Wenebojo. That is the strange way that he was born.

And what he said was, "Noko, Grandmother, we're both freezing. Don't worry! I'll go across the ocean to get us some fire."

Leaping out of the mitten, Wenebojo turned in a flash into a rabbit. Crossing the ocean was no problem for him. He had the power to make the ice on the ocean freeze smooth and dry as glass. Then all Wenebojo did was make the wind blow his way so that he could just slide across the ocean.

On the other side of the ocean there lived an old man and his two daughters. One of the daughters happened to have gone down to the ice to get some water just as Wenebojo arrived. He instantly stopped sliding and pretended to be nothing but an ordinary little rabbit. The girl thought he looked cute and petted him. When Wenebojo pretended to be enjoying the attention, the girl picked him up and took him to show her father her new pet.

The old man snapped, "Why did you bring that rabbit in?"

"But Father—"

"Haven't you heard about what happened on the other side of the ocean? I told you about that old lady who had a pair of mittens, and how Wenebojo was born in one of them!"

"But Father, this is only a rabbit!"

"Is it? Don't you know how Wenebojo plays tricks, how he'll do or be any-thing? How do you know that's not Wenebojo turned into a rabbit?"

"It is!" Wenebojo said.

Leaping out of the girl's arms, he grabbed some of their fire and slid back across the ocean to his grandmother.

Sources

Barnouw, Victor. *Wisconsin Chippewa Myths and Tales*. Madison: University of Wisconsin Press, 1977.
Johnston, Basil H. *Tales the Elders Told*. Toronto: Royal Ontario Museum, 1981.

THE ORIGIN OF CATTLE
A Myth of the Maasai

The Maasai of Kenya live by their cattle, around whom their existence is built. Therefore, it's not surprising that they should have a myth surrounding the origin of something so important to their culture.

Here is another variation on the land in the sky. In this case, it's the cattle that descend to the world below.

In a myth or folktale, a broken taboo is often disastrous. In this case, the breaking of the command against making noise results in the cutting off of any chance of more cattle descending from heaven, which makes the existing cattle more precious. It is explained that the reason the Maasai love their cattle is that they recognize that the cattle are a gift from heaven.

*I*n the earliest of days, the Maasai did not have any cattle. Then it hap-pened that the creator summoned Maasinta, who was the first Maasai, and told him, "You must make a large enclosure. When it is done, come back and tell me."

So Maasinta went and did as he was instructed, and came back to report on what he had done.

Then the creator told him, "Early tomorrow morning, you are to stand against the outside wall of your house and wait. You will be given some-

The Maasai of Kenya believe cattle are a gift from the creator. Maasai cattle are known for their large size and superior condition, particularly in comparison to the cattle of surrounding tribes. (*Drew Conroy, Ph.D., University of New Hampshire*)

thing called cattle. Whatever you hear or see, do not say a word. You must keep very still." Very early the next morning Maasinta went to wait for what was to be given him. Maybe his heart was pounding, maybe he was burning with curiosity, but he stood against the outside wall of his house and refused to move.

Soon he heard a rumble of thunder. A long leather thong unrolled itself from the sky down to the earth. And down this thong descended four-legged animals. These must be cattle!

As more and more of them descended, the earth shook under the force of their hooves. Maasinta was gripped with fear, wondering if the shaking would grow greater and bring down his house. But he did not move or make any sound.

Unfortunately, there were other people living in his house. The shaking and thunder brought them outside. At the sight of the cattle, one of them cried out in astonishment, "Aiiee!"

With that, the cattle stopped descending, and the thong curled back up into the sky. So it was that Maasinta wasn't as rich as he might have been. But he did have all those cattle who were already in the enclosure. He loved them and treated them well, since they had come from the creator.

And that is why the Maasai still love cattle very much.

Sources

Abrahams, Roger D. *African Folktales*. New York: Random House, 1983.
Kipury, Naomi. *Oral Literature of the Maasai*. Nairobi: Heinemann Educational Books, 1983.

THE ORIGIN OF THE DURIAN FRUIT
A Myth from the Philippines

Durian fruit really does exist in the Philippines, and it is sometimes imported in one form or another into the United States. In its unprocessed form, it is just as prickly and smelly as the myth claims. In fact, the myth almost certainly originated with someone wondering how anyone could ever have wanted to try eating a fruit so seemingly inedible.

Calinan, once a separate kingdom, is now a district in Davao City, while the Sea Pirate Kingdom consisted of several nearby islands, Ligid, Talicud, and Samai.

Love spells are so popular in the world's mythology and folklore that it would be impossible to list here all the countries in which such spells exist. Some, such as the love potion that drew the Arthurian hero Tristan and the princess Iseult together, have tragic consequences, but others, such as the potion in this story, create happy endings.

Quests for magic ingredients are also very common in world tales, usually being imposed as tests of a lover's worth.

And anyone familiar with the tale "Sleeping Beauty" in its many forms knows that the failure to invite someone powerful to a feast can have dire consequences. How fortunate for the royal couple that the hermit chose only to make the fruit odorous!

King Barom-Mai, ruler of Calinan, had made peace with Tageb, ruler of the Sea Pirate Kingdom. And to seal the treaty, Barom-Mai wed Tageb's daughter, Madayaw-Baybo.

Madayaw-Baybo was young and beautiful. Unfortunately, she was also spoiled and inexperienced in the ways of wisdom. And even though Barom-Mai was truly a good man, it cannot be denied that he was also very ugly. The princess refused to see how her new husband had fallen in love with her. She refused to admit how kindly he treated her. All Madayaw-Baybo saw was that the king was ugly.

"I can never love such a hideous man!" she cried, stamping an angry foot.

But Madayaw-Baybo did more than merely stamp her feet. She ran away several times. Each time, of course, she was brought back to Barom-Mai before she'd gone very far. But Barom-Mai began to despair. Yes, he needed that treaty with his wife's father. But more than that, oh, how it hurt him to see Madayaw-Baybo run from him!

"You must help me," he told his wise men. "Tell me how to keep my wife at my side. Tell me how to make her love me!"

But the wise men all shook their heads. They had discovered the uses of fire, the making of metals, many useful things. "But we are not gods, O king! Even we don't know how to make Madayaw-Baybo love you."

"Then what good are you?" the king cried in anger. "I should be rid of you all!"

"Wait!" his chief minister said hastily. "There is still someone wiser than we. In the cave of Mount Abo lives a hermit. Some say he's only half mortal. All say that he possesses great powers. If any can aid you, it's surely the hermit."

So Barom-Mai traveled off to Mount Abo. Sure enough, there sat the hermit, his face so serene it was easy to believe he was only half mortal, his eyes dark with wisdom. The king gave him many fine gifts, all of which the hermit ignored.

"You wish a difficult thing," the hermit said without being asked. "Yet it shall be done. Ah, but no man can have his heart's desire unless he works a bit to gain it. You must bring me three things, Barom-Mai. The first is the black tabon's egg. The second is the white carabao's milk. And the third is the nectar from the flower of the tree of make-believe. Go. Gather these things, then return to me."

Barom-Mai went, shoulders sagging. Three things, and he wasn't even sure how to obtain the first! The tabon was a bird, but since she laid her eggs only at night, he'd never even seen a tabon's egg. His sad sigh roused the interest of another king: Pawikan, king of the sea turtles. "What is wrong, human king?"

"Alas, I love my wife, but she hates me. I would win her back, but first I must find the black tabon's egg."

"Is that all? I saw her lay her eggs on the beach last night, right there!"

Happily thanking Pawikan, the king dug up a black tabon egg, carefully leaving the rest of the clutch of eggs untouched. He hurried back to his palace, where the milk of a white carabao was easily found.

But now he must find the nectar from the flower of the tree of make-believe. And how could any man find that? Again Barom-Mai sighed, more sadly than before. His sad sigh roused the fairy of the air, Hangin-Bai. "What is wrong, human king?"

"Alas, I love my wife, but she hates me. To win her love, I must first find the nectar from the flower of the tree of make-believe. I have no magic! How can a mere man find something like that?"

"You have no magic," said the fairy, "but I do. The tree of make-believe stands in my sister's garden, the garden of the fairy of the woods—but I'm angry at my sister for stealing a flower from me, so I'll take you there! Hold fast to my hair."

Barom-Mai took a firm grip on the fairy's long, flowing hair. She flew through the air as lightly as a breeze, taking the king, grimly clinging to her hair, with her.

The fairy of the air landed lightly. The king landed not so lightly. "There is the tree of make-believe, and that beautiful golden glow comes from its flower," Hangin-Bai whispered.

"But your sister's sitting right under the tree," Barom-Mai whispered back. "Ah, wait. I know." The king hummed a lullaby while Hangin-Bai fanned her sister with her hair, softly as a summer breeze.

Sure enough, the fairy of the woods fell asleep. The king tiptoed past her and plucked the flower. He thanked Hangin-Bai for her help and returned to Mount Abo.

The hermit glanced up from his studies. "You had help. Never mind. You did the task assigned to you even so."

He cracked open the black tabon's egg, pouring it into a bowl. "The tabon's egg is to soften the heart of the princess."

The hermit added the white carabao's milk. "The milk is to make her heart kind." He then let the drops of nectar from the flower fall into the mixture and stirred it with his magic stick. "The nectar will make the princess see you as handsome."

Barom-Mai began to thank him, but the hermit stared at the king so steadily that Barom-Mai had to struggle not to look away. "You must under-stand," the hermit said sternly, "that this spell is only a temporary thing. It will soften the heart of the princess, yes, but keeping her love is up to you. Do you understand?"

"I do. And I will do my best."

"So be it. Promise only to invite me to the feast you will give to share your happiness."

"Of course."

"So be it. Take this mixture and plant it in your royal garden. A fruit tree will grow from it. Eat one fruit and see that your wife eats the other."

Barom-Mai went home and planted the mixture in the royal garden. But he was sad at heart. It took years for a tree to grow and bear fruit. Madayaw-Baybo would never stay with him that long!

But in the morning the king found that a great tree had grown overnight. Two fruits hung from it, so deliciously fragrant that Barom-Mai and Madayaw-Baybo both devoured them. Barom-Mai could not love his wife any more than he already did, but as for Madayaw-Baybo, it was as though a curtain had been removed from her eyes. She saw the love in her husband's eyes and not his ugliness, and in that moment fell madly in love with him.

Even when the spell of the fruit wore off, Madayaw-Baybo still loved him, for now that she had a chance to think, she came to see the true handsomeness within her husband's heart and soul.

"The treaty is saved!" the wise men crowed.

"Our love is saved," the king and queen corrected.

In their joy, they gave a great feast. But so lost in love for each other were Barom-Mai and Madayaw-Baybo that, alas, the king totally forgot to invite the hermit.

"Ingrate," the hermit muttered in his cave in Mount Abo. "I'm glad there's peace between husband and wife, and I won't change that. But Barom-Mai isn't going to forget me again!"

From his cave, he cast a powerful spell. The next fruits to grow on that wondrous tree were covered with thorns and gave off a foul aroma.

And so it is with the durian fruit even today: smooth as an egg, creamy as milk, tangy as nectar—but smelly as a hermit's toe and thorny as his ire.

Sources

Eugenio, Damiana L. *Philippine Folk Literature: The Myths.* Diliman, Quezon City: University of the Philippines Press, 1993.
Torrente, J. M. "The Durian Legend," *Sunday Times Magazine* (Manila), May 17, 1959, p. 23.

WHY THE CROW IS BLACK
A Myth from Ancient Greece

This brief myth is included to show how closely the worlds of mythology and folklore can overlap. Stories of "how and why" like this can be, and often are, considered as either. Since the gods are involved, this tale of color changing as punishment seems to fit more comfortably into the world of mythology. But elsewhere, the blue jay gets its beautiful coloring in a folktale from India.

*T*he god Apollo was known for his many loves. But when he fell in love with the nymph Larissa, he told himself she was the one true wife for him. So Apollo and Larissa wed, and for a while Apollo was very happy indeed, sure that Larissa loved him as he loved her.

But alas, one day the crow, who was Apollo's favorite bird, whispered in his ear that his wife was not faithful to him. Apollo went wild with jealousy and threw a dart at Larissa—and slew her.

Why, oh why had he acted so hastily? Why had he not listened to her story? Horrified at himself, Apollo ached to bring Larissa back to life. But not even a god could do that.

But he could avenge her in one way. The crow who had brought the fatal message was, in those days, purest white, but in his rage, Apollo turned the crow's feathers black.

"From now on," he proclaimed, "you shall not fly with the other birds. When they see you, they shall fly from you, or attack."

And so it is with crows, even to this day.

Sources

Kerenyi, Karl. *The Gods of the Greeks*. London: Thames and Hudson, 1985.
Ovid. *The Metamorphoses*. Translated by Horace Gregory. New York: Viking Press, 1958.

THE FIRST STORY OF KAMA PUA'A
A Myth of Hawaii

Kama Pua'a, the hog-man and shape-shifter, is a strange being, indeed, one of earthly power. But in this myth, the goddess Pele is too strong for him, and he becomes the *ama'u* fern forever surrounding Kilauea's caldera. However, for a conflicting myth giving a different interpretation of the fern, see "Pele," in Chapter 4.

*K*ama Pua'a was a strange being, neither god nor human, both hog and man. To add to his strangeness, he also held fish and fern shapes when he wished it.

Now, Kama Pua'a had heard of Pele, lovely and perilous goddess of volcanic fires, and came to her home, the volcanic mountain Kilauea, seeking to woo her.

But Pele was disgusted by him and by his hoggish manners. She refused him, shouting in anger, "*A'ohe 'oe kanaka he pua'a*—you are not a man, you are a pig!"

That sparked a furious battle between them. Pele hurled fire and molten lava. Kama Pua'a fought back with storms of rain. Steam boiled up where lava and water met.

But Pele's fires were too strong for Kama Pua'a. Cornered, unable to escape in any other way, Kama Pua'a became the *ama'u* fern, forever surrounding Kilauea's caldera.

Sources

Beckwith, Martha. *Hawaiian Mythology.* Honolulu: University of Hawaii Press, 1970.
Kalakaua, David. *The Legends and Myths of Hawaii.* Rutland, VT: Charles E. Tuttle, 1972.

THE SECOND STORY OF KAMA PUA'A
A Myth of Hawaii

In this second version of the myth, the hog-man is first seen as the wild, savage son of a king who gets so infuriated with the hog-boy that he threatens him with death. When Kama Pua'a angers Pele, she chases him to the sea, where he leaps into the ocean and becomes the *humuhumunukunukuapua'a* fish—which is now the state fish of Hawaii.

*I*n the ancient days, there lived a king on the island of Oahu who had a son named Kama Pua'a, whose nature seemed more wild pig than boy. He would do wild-animal things like destroying taro patches or chasing livestock. In fact, some tales say that he wore hog form more often than boy shape.

At last his father lost all patience with his strange son and swore that if he caught him, Kama Pua'a would be put to death.

By now Kama Pua'a was no longer a child. The young man fled Oahu and moved to Maui. There he caught the eye of Pele, goddess of volcanic fire. For a time they were happy. But Pele is changeable in nature and quick to anger. And maybe she grew weary of Kama Pua'a's wild nature.

Whatever the reason, Pele's rage sent her chasing Kama Pua'a with a scalding stream of lava. Kama Pua'a turned into a wild hog for greater speed and fled down the slopes of Haleakala, toward the sea. But the lava flow was swifter yet, and he could feel its heat at his back. The sea was before him,

Pele's wrath behind him, and Kama Pua'a desperately called to his grandmother back on Oahu, "Grandma, Grandma, what should I do?"

His grandmother answered, "Leap into the ocean and you shall save yourself."

Kama Pua'a leaped into the ocean and changed into a fish with a pig's snout. And there he remained forever.

Today, Kama Pua'a is remembered in the fish's name: *humuhumunukunukuapua'a*. He has found fame as the state fish of Hawaii.

Sources

Beckwith, Martha. *Hawaiian Mythology*. Honolulu: University of Hawaii Press, 1970.
Kalakaua, David. *The Legends and Myths of Hawaii*. Rutland, VT: Charles E. Tuttle, 1972.

4

MYTHS OF THE GODS

Deities in the world's mythology are remote and unknowable except as abstractions, such as the Egyptian Ptah. These primal beings, as a result, have few myths centered about them.

Other deities are more clearly codified. They have specific appearances and attributes, such as the Greek goddess of wisdom, Athena, who is usually portrayed with a spear and her sacred bird, the owl, or the Hindu deity, Krishna, who is usually pictured with his flute and blue skin and is often portrayed as a lover of women. Such deities tend to be the center of a cycle of myths, or are at least a main character in such a cycle. There are gods who are clearly personifications of human emotions, such as the closely linked ones of love and lust, from Inanna of Sumer to Ishtar of Babylon to Aphrodite of the Greeks. Inanna and Ishtar were actually goddesses of both love and war. Aphrodite, having lost that link in her own persona, is described in Greek myths as being the lover of Ares, god of war.

Other gods are the essence of the natural world, like Pan, who is half human, half goat in appearance. He is the Greek god of the forest, whose panpipe made humans run wild with panic. Another such deity is the man-shaped but stag-horned Cernunos of the Celts, who was lord of the animals. Still other demideities may be harmless nature spirits like the Greek dryads, who are women-shaped souls of the trees, or vengeful like the *rusalky*, the Slavic water women who are the spirits of drowned human women.

Some cultures, though not all, go so far as to almost completely humanize their deities, downplaying the deities' omnipotence in favor of giving them familiar human motives and failings. While the Norse chief god, Odin, can be terrifying and dark in and of himself, the Norse showed him with his wife, Freya, as an old married couple. The Greeks went further with that idea, showing their chief god, Zeus, and his wife, Hera, as an unfaithful husband and his bitterly jealous wife.

There are even myths of hero-gods. The Babylonian hero-god Ninurta undertakes many great deeds, such as defeating Anzu, the monstrous lion-bird who had stolen the Tablets of Destiny. Another hero-god, Horus, the son of the Egyptian deities Osiris and Isis, takes on the familiar role in mythology and fiction of avenger. When Osiris is murdered by Set, his brother, Horus hunts down his treacherous uncle and avenges Osiris. This is a mythic theme that should be familiar to anyone who has

219

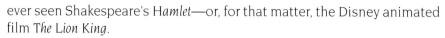

ever seen Shakespeare's *Hamlet*—or, for that matter, the Disney animated film *The Lion King*.

There is a related category of myths of humans who become deified after their deaths. All Egyptian pharaohs and many Roman emperors were considered divine, joining their fellow gods when they died. But the myth applies to some nonroyal figures as well, such as the brilliant Egyptian vizier-physician Imhotep, who lived in the third millennium B.C.E. After his death, he became worshiped as a physicians' deity.

Yet another related category of myths involves humans who become divine prophets. In Indian mythology, for example, Buddha, born a mortal prince, conquers time itself. In Islamic popular culture, after the death of the prophet Mohammed, not a divine figure himself, a cycle of stories sprang up. In Britain, the figure of Merlin, the magician of Arthurian myth, became confused with another Merlin, a Celtic prophet, and the myths of the two men became entwined. That Merlin's Welsh name is, according to tradition, Emrys, which is probably the name of a minor Celtic deity, only adds elements to the mythology. And that Merlin is said to be the son of a human mother and a demon father adds another connection, this to the afterworld of the deities.

ISIS GAINS HER MAGIC POWERS
A Myth of Ancient Egypt

As noted before, Egypt was a compilation of provinces, each with its own religious system. And when Egypt became a country, the different systems were merged into one pantheon. This meant rationalizing what didn't easily fit.

The Egyptians seem to have been perfectly willing to accept that the older gods had literally grown old. See, for instance, the myth "Ra's Journey" in Chapter 3.

Isis bore the title of mistress of magic—yet the earlier tales of Ra gave him supreme magical powers, in this case the knowledge of how to speak true names. Therefore, this myth explains how Isis could become the primary magic wielder through a trick and some fierce determination.

*I*n the beginning of days, Ra, the sun god, was a force of immense power. He it was who created all the things that live upon the earth. And he created these things with the power of their names. Simply by speaking

The goddess Isis gained the title "mistress of magic" by devising a venomous plan to learn the sun god Ra's secret name. Only by learning Ra's secret name was Isis able to secure the key to his magic. This sculpture of Isis is located at the Museo Gregoriano Egizio, Vatican Museums. (*Timothy McCarthy/Art Resource, New York*)

the proper name of something, Ra created it. As soon as he named each bird, each animal, each living thing, it appeared.

Because Ra had made all things, he also controlled them, ruling heaven and earth.

But there were strong younger gods. Isis, wife of Osiris, was a powerful deity in her own right. She already knew many of the ways of magic but envied Ra's power. It wasn't a desire to rule, but a desire to become truly what one of her divine titles claimed: mistress of magic.

What Isis needed most to know was Ra's secret great name. That, she knew, was the key to his magic, and knowing it would transfer magical power to her. But he would never share that name with her, or indeed with anyone.

But even as Osiris and Isis were the younger gods, so was Ra an old god. And as he grew older and feeble, Isis devised a plot. The mouth of the old god twitched with age, so that he sometimes dropped his spittle on the ground. When one day the old god drooled, Isis gathered up his spit. Kneading the spit with soil, she modeled a serpent in the shape of a spear and gave it magical life, then threw it in a coil down upon Ra's daily path across the sky. The ancient, noble god stepped forth in his radiance, and as he walked as he did each day, the serpent reared up and stung him.

Ra opened his mouth, and the voice of his majesty and pain rang out through the heavens. But when the other gods cried out and asked what had befallen him, he could not answer them. The poison flooded through him as the Nile floods the land.

Soon Ra began to burn from the serpent's venom. He was confused by the serpent's behavior and dismayed to discover that he had no power over it since he had not created it. He could not cure his body of the terrible pain, no matter what he tried. Ra called to his children for help, but they could not end his suffering, either.

Then Isis stepped forward, she who is full of wisdom, whose words are full of the breath of life, stating that her magic would cure Ra and end his pain.

"Behold, a snake has done you this wrong. Tell me your name, divine Father, the secret great name. For he whose name is spoken shall live."

Ra offered up to her a list of names. "I am he who created heaven and earth," he told her.

But Isis shook her head.

"I am he who made the water and caused the flood."

Still she shook her head.

"I am he who made all living things."

But the poison did not fade. It continued to burn. And Isis said, "Those are not your names." He was merely offering her a list of his attributes and titles. "Tell me your name that the poison may be conquered. He whose name is spoken shall live."

At last, fearing for his life and desperate to be healed, Ra surrendered. He transmitted the secret great name from his heart to that of Isis. She healed Ra—and from then on, having his magical power, truly became mistress of magic.

Sources

Hart, George. *Egyptian Myths*. Austin: University of Texas Press, 1990.

Quirke, Stephen. *Ancient Egyptian Religion*. New York: Dover Publications, 1995.

Simpson, William Kelly, ed. *The Literature of Ancient Egypt*. New Haven: Yale University Press, 1972.

THE WAR OF HORUS AND SET
A Myth from Ancient Egypt

This is one of the most complex myths in the Egyptian system, showing the battle between Horus and his treacherous uncle Set both as a legal fight, in which we get to see the older gods and younger ones at council, and as a literal war. The argument isn't so much that Set is a murderer, since Osiris is alive in the afterworld (and sending irate letters), but that he is a usurper. Horus is suing for his rightful inheritance. But Horus is also the avenger, so the legal battle spills out onto the battlefield. As befits his nature, Set doesn't play fair, but Horus can always manage to turn the tables on his uncle and win his case.

Isis takes on the role of devoted mother in this myth, fighting for her son's rights with a ferocity that crosses over into obsession. When she finally goes too far, interfering with Horus' fight—and accidentally spearing him in the process—he cuts off her head. Once she's restored, Isis stays out of the rest of the battle, almost like a human mother who is offended that her child doesn't want her help after all she's done for him.

The Western mind, trained by stories of villains being punished and good triumphing, might want a final reckoning with Set—but that doesn't come. After all, he's not a demon but a god, one who has a function in the balance of existence. So the myth reveals that he loses the court battle but not his life.

*H*orus, the divine son of the god Osiris, came before the assembled gods. With the goddess Isis, his mother, beside him, the young falcon-god spoke of the cruel murder of Osiris at the hands of Set, his own brother. Horus spoke, too, of the usurpation of the throne of Egypt by Set.

The gods were impressed by how well and how clearly the young falcon-god spoke, and indeed they pitied him. But they were not decided on what course they should take.

First spoke Shu. "Right should rule over might. Mighty Set does have force on his side, but none can deny that Horus has justice on his. We should, therefore, do justice to Horus by proclaiming, 'Yes! You will have the throne of your father!'"

Then spoke ibis-god Thoth, lord of wisdom. "This is right a million times!"

Hearing that, Isis gave a great cry of joy. She told the winds to blow westward to tell the news to Osiris, who waited in the afterworld.

So the god Shu declared, "Giving the throne to Horus seems right to us all. Thoth shall give the royal signet ring to Horus, and we shall crown him king."

Set strode into their meeting. "It is I, no other, who daily slays the enemy of Ra. It is I, no other, who stands in the prow of the bark of millions of years, and no other god can do it. It is I, no other, who should receive the kingship!"

The gods murmured among themselves about the forces of chaos. They murmured that Set was right.

Hearing them, Horus exclaimed, "Should you give kingship to the uncle when the son is present?"

And Isis raged at the gods for their indecision. So fierce were her words that at last they gave way to her will and promised that justice should be given to Horus.

Now Set roared, "How dare you cowards speak so softly? I will strike one of you down each day till you see my cause! And I will not argue any case of mine when Isis is present!"

Ra proclaimed, "We shall cross the river to the island in the midst and try the case there."

He gave secret orders that the divine ferryman not ferry Isis across. But Isis, mistress of magic, overheard his plan. She easily changed herself into the likeness of a bent old woman carrying an offering of flour and honey cakes, and offered the ferryman a gold ring for her passage. Soon they were across, and Isis moved silently to where the gods met. Set stood apart from the rest, so Isis changed her shape again into that of a lovely young widow and approached him.

"Who are you, lovely one?" Set asked. "Why are you here?"

The disguised Isis pretended to weep. "O great lord, I was the wife of a herdsman, and I bore him a son. My dear husband died, and the boy began to tend his father's cattle. But then a stranger came and told my son that he would take our cattle and turn us out. When my son tried to argue, the stranger threatened to beat him. Great lord, help us! Be my son's champion!"

"Do not cry, lovely one. I shall destroy the villain. How dare a stranger take the father's property while the son is still alive!"

Isis gave a fierce laugh of triumph, turned into a hawk, and flew up into an acacia tree. "You are the one to weep, Set!" she called down. "You have just condemned yourself! You have judged your own case!"

Rea had heard everything. "It is true, Set. You have judged yourself."

And so the gods made plans for the coronation of Horus.

But Set would not admit defeat. He challenged Horus to a duel, and turned himself into a hippopotamus in the Nile. Horus dove into the Nile as a second hippopotamus, and the two fought there, great jaws biting and great muscles thrashing.

Isis waited on the shore, terrified that Set would slay her son. The battle raged on, sending the Nile waters up in torrents, and seemed never to end. Quickly Isis created a magical spear and a line by which to haul it back, and hurled it into the turbulent Nile.

Suddenly Horus surfaced with a roar. "Mother! You just stabbed me! Let me go!"

With a hasty spell, Isis brought the spear back to her hand. She threw it again, and this time it was Set who rose with a bellow of pain and rage. "What have I done to you? Let this be a fair fight. Let me go!"

She did, but she had already broken the balance of the fight. Set fled, and Horus rose with a leopard's rage, leaped out of the river, and cut off his mother's head.

This, of course, was no serious matter for a goddess. She calmly strode away and waited for her head to be restored. But from then on, Isis stayed out of the battle.

Meanwhile, after a long, exhausting chase through the desert, the weary Horus found an oasis. Throwing himself down in the shade of a palm tree, he fell asleep.

It was a terrible mistake. Set caught him there and gouged out his eyes. Then Set calmly returned to the other gods and said, "I have found no trace of my poor nephew."

It was the goddess Hathor, Isis' gentle sister, the lady of the southern sycamore, who finally found Horus in his agony. She caught and milked a gazelle, then gently dripped the milk onto his wounds. At once the pain vanished. When Horus opened his eyes, he found that he could see again.

Hathor hurried to the other gods. "Set lied to you! He blinded Horus, then left him to die. I have healed Horus, and he is here!"

Ra called Horus and Set before him and told them that this battling had continued long enough. They must end their quarrel.

But Set demanded one more contest with Horus. "Let each of us build a ship of stone. We shall race them down the Nile. He who wins the race shall wear the crown of Osiris."

Horus agreed at once.

Mighty Set took up a club and struck the top off a mountain. He built a huge ship of that solid stone and dragged it to the river, to the sacred Nile.

There was Horus' ship already afloat. The falcon-god had secretly made a boat of pine and plastered it to make it seem all stone.

Set tried to launch his boat. But without magic to buoy it up, it sank to the bottom of the Nile. All the gods laughed. Raging, Set leaped into the water, once more a hippopotamus, and attacked the boat of Horus. It splintered and sank under Set's fury. Horus grabbed his spear and thrust at Set—and here some tales claim the story ends, with Horus living and Set dead. But other tales continue thus:

The gods all shouted at Horus to stop. And he had to obey. Instead, he made his furious complaint against Set:

"We have now been in the court for eighty years, yet they do not know how to judge among us.

"I have contended with Set in the Hall of the Way of Truth. I was found right against him.

"I have contended with Set in the Hall of the Horned Horus. I was found right against him.

"I have contended with Set in the Hall of the Field of Rushes. I was found right against him.

"I have contended with Set in the Hall of the Field Pool. I was found right against him."

Wearily Ra asked the others, "What shall we do about this eighty-year-old case?"

At last they made a ruling. Set would be king of southern Egypt, up to the place where he was born, which was called Su. Horus would be king of northern Egypt, up to the place in which his father died, which is the division of the two lands.

But Horus was unhappy with the thought of this division. "It is not good to defraud me of my father's office."

The gods Shu and Thoth sent a letter to Osiris in the afterworld. Soon their messenger returned with an angry letter from the god, wanting to know why his son had been robbed of the throne. Further, he demanded to know if the other gods had forgotten that it was he, Osiris, who had given the world the precious gifts of barley and wheat.

Ra was offended at Osiris' words and sent back a letter chiding the god.

After some time, a messenger returned with a new letter from Osiris:

"Has justice sunk into the underworld? Listen to me: The land of the dead is full of demons who fear no god or goddess. If I send them out into the world of the living, they will bring back evildoers to the place of punishment. Who among you is more powerful than me? Even the gods must come, at last, to the beautiful west."

That meant the afterworld. And at that thought, even Ra was afraid.

Then it seemed wrong to the gods that the portion of Horus should be like the portion of Set. So at last they gave Horus his rightful inheritance.

Then Horus stood at last over a united Egypt.

Sources

Hart, George. *Egyptian Myths*. Austin: University of Texas Press, 1990.
Quirke, Stephen. *Ancient Egyptian Religion*. New York: Dover Publications, 1995.
Simpson, William Kelly, ed. *The Literature of Ancient Egypt*. New Haven: Yale University Press, 1972.

THE DEEDS OF NINURTA
A Myth from Ancient Sumer

This myth, like all the others from Sumer, dates from at least the second millennium B.C.E., so information about the gods' adventures is limited at best, particularly since what was written down was written on clay tablets, which have chipped or broken over the millennia.

However, what myths have come down to us indicate that Ninurta was, indeed, a heroic figure as well as king of the gods. His sentient mace, Sharur, may make the reader think of modern superheroes—or of the Norse god Thor and Mjolnir, his mighty hammer. See as well the Irish myth "Lugh," in this chapter, where the hero's enchanted spear was so blood-hungry it needed to be drugged when not in use.

Asaq, the warrior of living stone, may make modern readers think of horror movies, or science fiction films. Clearly the image of a monstrous being made out of stone or clay, like the —Golem of Jewish folklore, or machinery, like the killer robots of movies, is one that has been in the human psyche, for whatever reasons, for a long time indeed.

But once the rains have washed away Asaq, the myth turns into a tale of origins, as Ninurta invents irrigation and gives the rocks their proper uses.

*T*his happened in the beginning days, when the laws of nature were not yet fixed and certain. Ninurta, who was both a hero-god and the king of the gods, was happily feasting with the other gods in their palace when Sharur came rushing in. Sharur was not a being, not exactly. It was Ninurta's magical, sentient mace, a loyal weapon whose name meant "smasher of thousands." Sharur was able to move about under its own power and often scouted the land for Ninurta.

Just now, Sharur brought alarming news. Up in the mountains, the spirits of rocks and plants were rising up to make war against the spirits of the plains. Their leader in this disturbing uprising was named Asaq. More alarming still, he was no human or god, but a fierce warrior made of living stone. He was immune to blows from spear and axe, and ignorant of pity or mercy. Thanks to his actions, there were constant rock slides and earthquakes that were crushing the cities on the plains and imperiling the people who lived there. Sharur warned Ninurta that what Asaq meant to do with his revolution was take control of the entire eastern border, clearly with an eye to usurping Ninurta's kingship.

Ninurta hastily prepared for war, even though Sharur warned that although the warrior-god had defeated monsters in the past, stony Asaq was like none of his previous opponents.

Ninurta ignored Sharur and pressed on to attack Asaq. But Asaq sent avalanches crashing down at him, and shook the earth under him until Ninurta was forced to retreat.

The god Enlil counseled Ninurta to wait for the appropriate time. With the power of the rains, Asaq would be defeated.

Indeed, this was exactly what took place: The rains came in such torrents that Asaq lost his footing. Washed down from the mountains, he shattered into pieces.

And then good came from attempted evil. For in the process, Ninurta learned to direct the mountain streams to flow down into the plains so that none of their waters were wasted. This further inspired him to puzzle out how mountain waters could be used to sustain the barley in the fields and the fruits and vegetables in the orchards and gardens.

Now Ninurta decided how to use the rocks that had caused all the trouble. Some rocks were made vulnerable to erosion, while others became grinding powders used to break down other rocks. Ninurta punished lava and basalt by making them into molds for goldsmiths. Limestone was destined to crumble rapidly in water. Flint was punished by flaking easily.

But some rocks had sided with Ninurta during the battle. These became precious stones cherished by all.

Sources

Dalley, Stephanie. *Myths from Mesopotamia*. Oxford: Oxford University Press, 1989.

Jacobsen, Thorkild. *The Harps That Once . . . : Sumerian Poetry in Translation*. New Haven: Yale University Press, 1987.

THE BUILDING OF ASGARD'S WALL
A Myth from the Ancient Norse

Here is another myth featuring new gods and old, but unlike the Egyptian peaceful absorption of deities, the Norse old and new gods battled for dominance. In this myth, we see the war continuing through the rebuilding of Asgard: The giant Hrimthurs is of the old pantheon, while Odhinn represents the new. Odhinn is a dubious figure, one who does some dark deeds, especially considering his rank as head of the gods. In this myth, there is the barest hint of the beginning of the trouble, namely, Odhinn's willingness to agree to a false business deal, that will eventually lead to Ragnarok, the final battle.

But the major figure in this myth is not Odhinn but Loki, he who is of neither the old nor the new pantheon. He is the essence of fire, and some scholars think that his parents' names mean "lightning" and "pine tree." Loki is also a trickster, one whose role grew darker and closer to the demonic with the growing influence of Christianity. But here he is all trickster.

*I*n the most ancient of times, there had been a terrible war between the Aesir, the new gods, and the Vanir, the old ones. When it was done, the Aesir had won. Now they knew that they must rebuild the shattered wall that had once surrounded their magnificent home, Asgard. Or rather, they needed to have the wall rebuilt by someone capable of doing the job correctly.

One day a tall man came across Bifrost, the rainbow bridge that was the only path to Asgard, and told Heimdall, the god who was its guardian, that he had a plan for the wall's rebuilding to bring before the gods.

Odhinn, leader of the Aesir, gathered all the gods and goddesses to hear what the stranger had to tell them.

RAGNARÖK, THE LAST BATTLE.

Norse mythology tells of Ragnarok, the final battle in which even the gods die. Originating through a false deal in which Odhinn agrees to surrender Aesir's immortality as well as the sun and the moon, Ragnarok is known as the "Twilight of the Gods." (*Mary Evans Picture Library*)

The stranger—who was actually the perilous giant Hrimthurs in disguise—told them all, "I can rebuild the wall surrounding Asgard, and complete it in less than two mortal years."

Warily Odhinn asked him, "What payment do you ask for such a job?"

"For payment," the stranger said smoothly, "I would take the sun and moon, plus the goddess Freya for my wife."

The gods cried out in protest. Bad enough to lose the sun and moon, but Freya was the one who grew the magical golden apples that kept the Aesir immortal!

Furious, Odhinn snapped, "We will never give up Freya, nor will we surrender the sun and moon. Leave us at once!"

One figure alone had shown no anger. This was Loki, who ruled over fire. Tricky and sly was Loki, wise in his own convoluted way. He begged the gods, "Do not be so hasty." And to the mason he said, "Pray give us some time to consider your offer."

"So be it," the mason replied, and left.

The gods and goddesses gathered around Loki. Smiling narrowly, he suggested that they force the mason to agree to build the wall in six mortal months, and that if he would so agree, he would win the prize he'd named.

The gods started to complain, but Loki held up a hand for silence. He explained, "There is no way that any mason can finish such a job in so short a time. He will finish enough of the wall, though, that you will be able to complete it without him. And you won't have to pay the mason at all."

It seemed like an excellent idea to them all. So Odhinn called the mason back into the hall and put Loki's plan before him. The mason hesitated, then said he would agree to the terms if he was allowed to use his horse, Svadilfari, to help him.

The gods agreed and the bargain was struck.

The mason set to work almost immediately. In an alarmingly short amount of time he began making amazing progress on the construction. While he and his men cut huge blocks of stone and set them in place, his mighty horse hauled loads heavier than anything the gods had ever imagined. Throughout all the winter the wall began to take shape. As winter began to melt into spring, the gods grew increasingly uncomfortable. It was beginning to look all too possible that the wall was going to be completed on schedule. If so, they really would have to give up Freya along with her golden apples of immortality, as well as the sun and moon.

"Loki, you trickster!" they shouted angrily. "It was your plan that led us into this trap!" They demanded he use his cunning to ensure that the wall would not be completed on time.

Loki grinned. "Have no fear. You won't grow old and wrinkled. I've noticed that the mason's marvel of a horse, Svadilfari, is a stallion."

More than that, Loki wouldn't say. But three nights before the wall was to be completed, a lovely filly sauntered along past Svadilfari. The stallion whinnied a greeting, but she continued sauntering along, twitching her fox-red tail at him. Svadilfari whinnied again, then broke free of his harness and began chasing the filly. She broke into a trot, then a canter, then a full gallop, and Svadilfari lumbered after her. Roaring, the mason chased after Svadilfari but could not catch him. In fact, the mason ended up chasing his stallion all night, in vain.

The next day, without Svadilfari to help, not as much work was done as had been done before. And at last the mason had to admit that he would not be able to complete his work on time. He stormed into Asgard, shouting that he'd been cheated. He flew into such a rage, in fact, that he threatened to destroy everything in Asgard. Thor struck him a single blow with his hammer, Mjolnir, and that ended that.

Several months later, Loki returned to Asgard leading a colt with eight legs, and gave him to Odhinn, who named the young horse Sleipnir. But who were the colt's parents?

Loki shrugged. "His sire is Svadilfari."

And his dam? Why, none other than Loki, who had disguised himself as that sauntering filly.

Source

Crossley-Holland, Kevin. *The Norse Myths*. New York: Pantheon Books, 1980.

THOR AND THE MIDGARD SERPENT
A Myth from the Ancient Norse

The previous Norse myth contains many powerful themes, from the war of the gods to the building of the gods' home to the birth of the eight-legged horse, Sleipnir. By contrast, this myth is typical of those about Thor. He was almost always portrayed as the god of the common people, a powerful fellow forever willing to fight, wench, or drink. There's nothing devious about him, and nothing of the darkness. And here he goes after the Midgard Serpent not in any sort of hero's quest, but merely because he likes fishing, and the serpent poses the greatest test for any fisherman. Notice that Thor, like Maui in Chapter 5, might actually have achieved his goal if it hadn't been for the line being cut.

One day Thor, god of thunder, took it into his head to go fishing. He disguised himself as a young man, left the gods' palace of Asgard, and wandered until night, when he met up with a giant named Hymir and spent that night in Hymir's home.

When the day came, Hymir made ready to go fishing in the sea. Thor said, "Let me go rowing with you."

Hymir laughed. "What, such a scrap of a youngster go out on the open ocean? The cold and wet will make you catch cold if we row out as far as I usually do."

Thor promptly forgot all about his disguise. "I am well able to row a long way out, and it won't be me who first demands to be rowed back! Now, what are we going to use for bait?"

"Get your own," Hymir muttered.

So Thor went to a herd of oxen owned by Hymir, selected the largest ox, and struck off its head with his powerful hammer, Mjolnir. Taking the ox head with him, Thor climbed into Hymir's boat and rowed them both out with amazing speed.

"This is far enough," Hymir said.

"Not yet," Thor replied, and kept rowing.

Thor (center), the Viking god of thunder, stands with his father, Odin (left), the god of the warriors and battle, and Frey (right), the god of fertility and marriage. They carry an axe, a hammer, and an ear of corn. From a Viking tapestry, twelfth century. (*Werner Forman/Art Resource, New York*)

"This is far enough!" Hymir repeated a few minutes later. "We're so far out that we are in danger. The Midgard Serpent might surface under us! We're too far out!"

The Midgard Serpent was the enormous snake that encircled the globe underwater, and little did Hymir suspect that it was Thor's goal.

"No, we're not," Thor replied, and kept rowing.

Hymir wasn't at all pleased with this. He went right on complaining until at last Thor said, "This is far enough."

He shipped his oars and prepared a strong fishing line and a stronger hook. Baiting the hook with the ox head, he cast the line and waited.

Sure enough, it wasn't long at all before the Midgard Serpent itself snapped at the ox head bait—and got caught by the hook. It gave so powerful a jerk, trying to get free, that it nearly dragged Thor overboard. He dug in his heels so hard that his legs went right through the boat and his feet were braced on the bottom of the ocean itself. Hand over hand, he drew up the serpent till he was staring right at it. The Midgard Serpent stared right back, spitting poison.

"Have you gone mad?" Hymir cried in terror.

Thor merely raised his hammer, reading to strike the serpent over the head and finish it. But Hymir was too frightened to think. Before Thor could strike, Hymir grabbed his bait knife and sliced the fishing line.

The Midgard Serpent dove back into the sea. Thor flung his hammer after it but missed. The Midgard Serpent is still down there, encircling the earth.

"I had to do it!" Hymir began.

He got no further. The furious Thor struck him a blow that hurled him overboard. By the time Hymir had floundered back aboard, Thor, god of thunder and frustrated fisherman, had waded ashore.

Sources

Crossley-Holland, Kevin. *The Norse Myths*. New York: Pantheon Books, 1980.
Sturluson, Snorri. *The Prose Edda*. Translated by Jean I. Young. Berkeley: University of California Press, 1954.

LUGH
A Myth from Ancient Ireland

Lugh, the Irish Celtic sun god, has been compared to the Greek god Apollo. Like Apollo, Lugh is radiantly handsome, and loves all the arts—and mortal women. Unlike Apollo, though, there is no nasty streak to Lugh: Mortals don't have to fear him so much as respect him. Lugh's enchanted blood-hungry spear is not the only sentient weapon. Remember Sharur, the sentient mace in "The Deeds of Ninurta," earlier in this chapter. And in fantasy and science fiction, sentient weapons abound, from the evil sword Stormbringer in Michael Moorcock's Elric stories to the living ships of television's science fiction series *Farscape*.

In Irish myth, there are three great invasions. The first is the coming of Lugh's people, the Tuatha de Danaan, or children of Danaa, the mother goddess. These are the golden, elegant people who later in Irish lore became the Sidhe, the high folk of Faerie. That their capital city should be believed to be Tara, which later became the ritual capital of the high kings of Ireland, is hardly a coincidence.

Then came the more violent invasion of the Fomor, the ugly, warlike beings led by Lugh's grandsire, Balor of the One Eye. Balor, with that eye that could shoot out deadly rays, seems to modern readers to be an ancestor of some science fiction monster! And the blinding of Balor by the magical stone cast by Lugh's sling has echoes both of the biblical David bringing down Goliath with a stone and of Odysseus blinding the one-eyed Cyclops.

The third invasion of Ireland brought in the Milesians, the humans, and with them came iron, which the Tuatha de Danaan, like the Faerie folk, could not stand. This marked the end of their dominance in Ireland.

Is there any truth to these invasions? Possibly. But though scholars have argued over the matter, there's as yet no firm archaeological proof one way or the other.

*L*ike all of his godly kin, the Tuatha de Danaan, the sun god Lugh was strikingly handsome, a golden-haired lover of music, the arts, and women, as well as a skilled warrior. He possessed an enchanted spear that had such a lust for blood that he had to keep it drugged with poppy juice between battles. And so deadly a shot was the god with the sling that humans came to call the Milky Way "Lugh's Sling."

But Lugh did have one touch of darkness to him: While he was truly of the Tuatha de Danaan, his mother's father was none other than Balor the One-Eyed, leader of their bitterest foe, the Fomors. Balor's one eye was a weapon in itself, since he could send a deadly force from it by simply looking at whomever he wished to slay.

Lugh, however, had never had any desire to ally himself with the Fomors. Instead, he went boldly up to the Tuatha de Danaan in their capital of Tara. This was at a time when everyone was preparing for what would surely be war against the Fomors, and Lugh wanted it clear that he was no friend of his dark grandsire.

Approaching the palace's great bronze door, Lugh proclaimed his lineage, as was proper, nor did he hide his relationship to Balor.

But the porter wouldn't let him pass. "First," the fellow stated, " you must name your skill. No one is admitted to Tara without skill in a craft. Which do you claim?"

Lugh smiled. "Do you want the whole list?"

He began tallying them off on his fingers: smithing, war, woodcraft, music, healing, poetry, magic.

"Ha. Tara already has plenty of those."

Lugh's smile widened. "Ah, but ask the king if he has any one man who is master of all these crafts."

Sure enough, that got Lugh into Tara, where he presented himself before King Nuada and his court. Lugh then played the harp so well all wept and laughed for joy, worked bronze into so intricate a knot none could untangle it, and in fact proved to them all that he was just as he'd claimed: master of all his crafts.

King Nuada decided that while the Tuatha de Danaan prepared for battle with the Fomors, Lugh should serve as their war king while he took the role of sage.

Then the Fomorian tax collectors made the mistake of attempting to collect the annual tribute from Lugh and the Tuatha de Danaan. Lugh made short work of them and sent a clear message to the Fomors.

Battle after fierce battle followed, and Lugh proved his worth as a strategic genius. In fact, the rest of the Tuatha de Danaan decided that he was far too valuable to risk his life in what was to be the final battle. Over Lugh's protests, they set a troop of warriors to guard him and keep him safe.

But Lugh had no intention of being left behind. He eluded his determined guards and drove his chariot at full speed to the battlefield. And there Lugh proved his true skill as a warrior. With a magical stone, a *tathlum*, flung from his well-aimed sling, Lugh blinded his grandfather, Balor, ending the deadly blaze from that one eye.

With the blinding of Balor and the loss of their chief weapon, the Fomor fled the land completely.

Sources

MacCana, Proinsias. *Celtic Mythology*. London: Hamlyn, 1970.
Rolleston, T. W. *Myths and Legends of the Celtic Race*. London: George Harrap, 1949.

SRI KRISHNA
A Myth from Hindu India

The first thing that has to be understood about the story of Krishna is that the god Vishnu was concerned with the good of humanity and would take on an avatar, a new form and birth, whenever it was needed for the help of humanity. And so Krishna was born as one of the avatars of Vishnu.

Two familiar motifs turns up at the start of the myth. There is the usurping, evil king, familiar to so many folktales and fiction as well. And there is the prophecy that a child yet unborn will be the king's death. See "Perseus," in Chapter 5, for another example of that prophesy.

Of the eight incarnations of Vishnu, Krishna is the most honored of Hindu gods. Here, Krishna appears with his brother, Balarama, in the forest with the cowherds. (*Werner Forman/Art Resource, New York*)

While the switching of babies who are both divine avatars is unique, the idea of a boy raised in the country or wilderness for his own safety can be found both in mythology and in actual history: William the Conquerer, for a historical example, really was sent to live with his commoner relatives to keep him safe.

Krishna very early on reveals his amazing powers, saving his own life while still a baby. Like the Greek demigod Hercules, who strangled serpents while still in the cradle, Krishna strangles two demons in a row. He also reveals a trickster nature, playing constant pranks on everyone but escaping real punishment through his charm.

The two brothers, Krishna and Balarama—even if they aren't, strictly speaking, related—resemble the hero twins in Chapter 5 in that they work as a team to defeat evil and are never at odds with each other

The tournament scene and the slaying of Kamsa follows the mythic pattern familiar to Western readers of the tales of Robin Hood or viewers of many a Hollywood historical epic. So does the romantic episode with Rukmini, rescued in the nick of time from an unwanted marriage.

But there are more serious elements to the myth. Krishna becomes part of one of the earliest epics, the massive *Mahabharata*, and is said to have been the creator of the wisdom code, the B*hagavad Gita*.

*I*n the ancient days, there was the Yadava dynasty, with its capital city in Mathura, on the banks of the Yamuna River. Their king was Ugrasena—but he was deposed and imprisoned by his own son, Kamsa.

Now, Kamsa became a truly wicked king. Heedless of his people's welfare, he plundered the wealth of his land and turned a blind eye to the lawlessness that was everywhere. But as of yet he had not bothered thinking of Devaki, his cousin, as a threat to him, not even when she married a kinsman, Vasudeva. No, only when he was driving their wedding chariot to the new husband's house did matters change. For suddenly Kamsa heard a voice roar down from heaven, "Oh, you fool of a king! The eighth son of this lady will one day slay you!"

Kamsa brought the chariot to a halt so swiftly that the horses tried to rear, and drew his sword. He was about to slay Devaki, but Vasudeva hastily moved between them.

"We will give you all our children as soon as they are born. Only spare my wife."

"So be it," Kamsa said.

He ordered that Devaki and Vasudeva be thrown into prison under close guard, and waited. Each time the unhappy wife bore a child, Kamsa snatched it away and slew it. He killed seven children this way.

Now Devaki became pregnant for the eighth time. Her eighth child was born at the stroke of midnight. And as he was born, the prison cell was filled with a blaze of light, and Devaki and Vasudeva saw a glimpse of the divine Vishnu. They realized with awe that this eighth child, this son, was not a true human, but an avatar, a divine incarnation.

And in the village of Gokul, on the other side of the Yamuna River, at the very moment that Krishna was born in the prison cell, Yasoda, wife of Nanda, bore a girl child who was also a divine incarnation.

As Devaki and Vasudeva cradled their child, Vasudeva heard a heavenly voice saying to him, "Take your male child across the Yamuna to Gokul and exchange him for Yasoda's daughter, born this very night. Then you can return to prison before anyone learns of the birth of Devaki's eighth child."

Since it would save his newborn son, Vasudeva put the child in a basket and, trusting in Vishnu, went forward. Sure enough, the doors of the prison parted silently for him. All the guards were asleep. Vasudeva reached the bank of the Yamuna River, but it was in flood. Staring at the roaring waters, he wondered how he would cross. But the river smoothly parted in two, making way for the baby Krishna, and Vasudeva was able to walk on dry land over to Gokul. There he found all the people asleep as well. Wondering, he entered Nanda's house, gently placed the baby Krishna beside the slumbering Yasoda, put her baby girl in the basket, and returned to Mathura. Behind him, the river waters roared back together.

Vasudeva returned to the prison and placed the girl baby at Devaki's side. Behind him, the prison doors shut themselves. As the baby woke, it began to cry, and the guards, too, woke, startled by the sound. They rushed to Kamsa.

"Devaki's eighth child has been born!"

This was the child that was to kill him! Kamsa rushed to the prison to slay the baby.

Devaki screamed. "Kamsa, please! This is only a female child. How can this baby do you any harm?"

Ignoring her, he snatched up the baby and tried to hurl it down on the stone floor. But the baby didn't fall. It rose up out of his reach in the form of a goddess. She had eight arms, and every arm bore a weapon.

"O fool of a king!" she cried. "You will gain nothing by killing me. The one who will destroy you is elsewhere!"

With these words, the goddess disappeared. Kamsa felt a twinge of penitence and set free Vasudeva and Devaki from the prison.

Meanwhile, in Gokul, the villagers rejoiced over the birth of a son to Nanda's household. On the eleventh day after the happy event, priests performed the rites to bless the child and named the child Krishna.

One day Nanda crossed the river to Mathura to pay his standard tribute to Kamsa. And in the process, Kamsa learned of the new baby, Krishna, and saw Vasudeva's start. He heard Vasudeva warn Nanda to be wary. And Kamsa knew now what had happened.

Ah yes, but Kamsa had already contacted demonkind and invoked a she-demon called Putana. He had ordered her to kill all the newborn boys in cities and towns, villages and lonely huts. Putana knew that there was a newborn boy in the village of Gokul, in the home of Nanda, and so off she flew to find and slay the baby.

When Putana reached the village, she took on the shape of a beautiful woman and went to where Krishna lay smiling in his bed. Pretending to be nothing more than human, she lifted the baby into her arms and began to breast-feed him. Her milk was demon's milk, deadly poison to a human child. And that, she was sure, would destroy this child.

But Krishna was more than mere baby. He knew what was wrong, and he knew who held him—and the divine force in him sucked not milk but the life force from the demon. She fought him, struggling to free herself, but her strength was useless. Soon it was the end of Putana, and the end of the first threat against Krishna.

But it was not the last. A whirlwind swept down upon Gokul soon after that, and while people ran about in terror, the wind swept Krishna up into the sky—it was no true whirlwind, but a second demon, one called Trinavrita. But the demon quickly found what he'd thought to be a mere baby was a great deal more. Krishna's baby hands closed about the demon's throat and clung, strangling Trinavrita in midair. The demon crashed to the ground, but Krishna was unhurt.

Now Nanda and Yasoda knew why Vasudeva had warned Nanda to be wary. This was hardly an ordinary baby!

Yasoda admitted to her husband that she had already experienced something truly extraordinary about Krishna, something so strange that she'd thought she'd imagined it. Krishna had been playing with some other children when one of them ran up to Yasoda, crying, "Krishna just put a whole handful of earth into his mouth!"

Yasoda had run to Krishna, crying, "You mischievous little boy! Open your mouth, let me see what you have in your mouth."

At first Krishna had refused and had tried to squirm away from Yasoda. But after repeated coaxing, she managed to make Krishna open his mouth. And what she had seen . . . In Krishna's open mouth, Yasoda had seen a miraculous vision of the entire universe: the earth with its mountains, oceans, and continents, the sun, the moon, the stars, and all the planets, as well as her own village and herself surrounded by the children and Krishna opening his mouth to her.

"Am I dreaming?" Yasoda had cried.

But now she realized with a shock that all changing things are rooted in a changeless spirit.

Now, Nanda and Yasoda had another son, Balarama. He and Krishna were utterly unalike to the eye. Balarama's complexion was fair, while Krishna's was dark. Balarama was strongly built while Krishna was slim as a sprite. But the two were dearest friends and played pranks on everyone. Krishna was the leader. He would steal butter from the kitchen pots or milk out of the milk pots.

The milkmaids would come to complain to Yasoda. "Mother Yasoda, your boy Krishna is a very naughty child! He untethers our calves just before milking time so that the cows won't let down their milk. When we try to catch him, the rascal just laughs and runs away. He steals milk from our kitchen and shares the curds with his friends. When he finds the milk pots empty, he breaks them and runs away. We tried to keep the pots away from his reach by hanging them from the roof. What does that naughty boy do? He reaches these pots by standing upon a bench or throws a stone to break a hole in the milk pot, then catches the dripping milk for himself and his friends. Tsk, look at him, Yasoda. He acts like the most innocent of boys. What a mischievous child you have brought into Gokul, Yasoda!"

Krishna knew they weren't really angry. They loved him for that very mischief. He darted off, calling over his shoulder, "I'm going. You can tell everything to my mother while I'm gone!"

And the milkmaids, sure he couldn't hear them, said, "What a darling you have brought into Gokul, Yasoda!"

Sometimes Krishna did more than mischief. One day, after he'd stolen butter from her kitchen, Yasoda lost her temper and tied him to the heavy wooden mortar with a strong rope. Maybe that would keep him away from his childish pranks for a while! Krishna went down on all fours and started crawling, dragging the heavy mortar after him, out into the garden. The mortar got caught between two trees, and as Krishna tried to pull it through, the two trees fell. Two *siddhas* emerged from the fallen trees and threw themselves down at Krishna's feet. "O Krishna! We were the sons of Kubera, god of wealth, but were turned to trees to punish us for our pride in wealth and power. Now you have freed us!"

But Kamsa was still hunting for his enemy. The evil king made a contract with a demon known as Bakasura to kill Krishna.

Bakasura took the form of a gigantic bird and soared over Gokul, terrorizing everyone. But when he opened his beak, Krishna sprang up into the great bird's mouth, then squirmed about inside Bakasura until the demon vomited Krishna out with such force that Bakasura fell down dead.

Now Bakasura's brother, Aghasura, came after Krishna in the form of a gigantic serpent—but this *asura* had not learned by his brother's mistake. Krishna sprang into the serpent's mouth and slew Aghasura, too.

Such strange occurrences could hardly go unnoticed by the people of Gokul. Now they were beginning to wonder if their village hadn't become the target for all manner of evil spirits. Was Gokul in danger?

Upananda, an old cowherd, said to the others, "Let us get out of Gokul before some other strangeness hits us."

The others agreed, and the cattle herders, male and female, moved up into Brindavan forest. Krishna and Balarama went with them and had a good time in the quiet green forest. While the boys tended the cows and calves, Krishna would entertain them both by playing on his flute. Krishna flirted with and played tricks on the shepherdesses, who were all in love with him. His favorite was Radha, and they spent many joyous hours together.

One hot day the cowherds and Krishna were playing together on the banks of the Yamuna. Two of the boys drank from the river—and collapsed, unconscious. Krishna revived them and realized what had happened. There was a great serpent called Kaliya that had taken up residence in the river and was poisoning the river and the forest on either side. Even the birds that tried to fly over the river fell down dead because of the poison in the air.

Krishna dove into the river to fight Kaliya. The huge serpent loomed up out of the water, a monstrous creature with a hundred black hoods and a hundred purple tongues, then dropped with a mighty splash, coiling about Krishna's body and dragging him down. The cowherds rushed to the river-bank—and saw a strange thing happen. Krishna grew larger and larger yet, and the serpent could no longer hold him. As it lost its grip and uncoiled, Krishna caught Kaliya by the tail and started dancing on one of the serpent's hoods to kill Kaliya.

But the many wives of Kaliya surfaced and pleaded with Krishna to spare their husband. So sweetly did they plead that he agreed to spare Kaliya—if they would all leave the river Yamuna and go on to the ocean. They agreed and left for the ocean, and soon the Yamuna River and its banks were restored.

Word of Krishna's deeds reached Kamsa's ears. He sent a messenger, Akrura, to Brindavan to announce that a tournament would be held in the capital city. Kamsa's plan was to station a mighty elephant at the entrance to the tournament grounds. The animal would be driven toward Balarama and Krishna as soon as they entered and crush them to death. If that strategy failed, Kamsa hired two wrestlers, Chamura and Mushtika, to challenge Krishna and Balarama to a wrestling match and kill the latter in the contest.

Now, Akrura hated Kamsa, as did all the other righteous subjects of the kingdom, and knew that all the strange deeds of Krishna proved that this was a deity incarnate. Akrura extended the official invitation from Kamsa to Nanda and the others, but secretly told Krishna of Kamsa's wicked plans.

When Krishna and Balarama heard of the king's plans, they laughed. "Accept the invitation!" they urged Nanda and the others. "Go to the tourney!"

The shepherdesses were all in tears as they watched their lovely Krishna ride off.

As the party rode on, the day grew warm, and they stopped on the banks of the Yamuna river for a rest. Akrura dove into the river for a brief, cooling swim. There in the waters, he saw Krishna's form. Akrura swam to the surface—and there was Krishna sitting on one of the chariots. Akrura, puzzled, dove again, only to find Krishna in the waters. As he climbed out of the river, there was Krishna seated on the chariot. As Akrura wondered what was going on, he glimpsed Krishna in divine form and understood. He had, indeed, known the truth about Krishna before he'd had any proof.

As they rode, villagers stood along the road to catch a glimpse of Balarama and Krishna and to be touched by the beautiful Krishna.

Finally, Krishna's party reached the outskirts of Mathura. People crowded into the streets or peeked out of their windows to see the two brothers.

They, too, had heard that heavenly voice announcing the eighth child of Devaki. Now they could see the divine being in human form, vivacious and joyous.

Once they had reached the tournament arena, Krishna and Balarama found guards trying to take them prisoners, but the brothers easily defeated the guards and went on toward the wrestling grounds.

There, as Kamsa had planned, at the gates of the wrestling stadium, stood the mighty elephant, Kuvalayapida. He was set upon Krishna and Balarama and seized Krishna with its trunk. But Krishna easily slipped out of the hold, raced under the elephant, and caught it by the tail. The elephant whirled in fury, trying to crush Krishna under its feet. But Krishna clung to the tail, and the elephant couldn't reach him. It tried to gore him to death with its tusks, but hit the ground instead, breaking its tusks. Krishna let go of the tail, raced about to catch the elephant's trunk, pulled its head down to him, and stabbed it with one of the broken pieces of tusk.

Armed with the broken tusks of the elephant, Krishna and Balarama entered the wrestling arena. With a blare of trumpets and a pounding of drums, the wrestlers entered.

Chamura, the head wrestler, said to Krishna and Balarama, "O sons of Nanda, you are welcome to Mathura's wrestling match. Come, show your skills to please King Kamsa."

Krishna said, "Balarama and I are happy to be here. But we are only boys, not professional wrestlers. Do you think it will be a fair match?"

Chamura laughed. "You two are not mere boys. We've all heard of your exploits. Come, I will wrestle you. Mushtika here will fight with Balarama."

"We accept," Krishna said.

The spectators shouted "Unfair! These are two professional wrestlers, and those are just boys! You can't do this!"

Kamsa ignored the protests and signaled for the matches to begin.

It was not the massacre he'd been expecting. The wrestlers tried every trick they knew to pin Krishna and Balarama—and failed. The boys were smaller than the men, but they were more agile and clever, and tired out the professionals. At last the wrestlers were gasping helplessly. Krishna caught Chamura by the neck and brought him crashing to the ground. Balarama punched Mushtika once on his face, once on his chest, and the exhausted Mushtika fell.

The crowd cheered. Kamsa was furious. "Seize the boys!" he shouted. "Seize all of the visitors from Brindavan!"

As Kamsa drew his sword, Krishna leaped up to where the king stood, caught him by the hair, and dragged him down onto the sands of the wrestling arena. There Krishna strangled the evil king and fulfilled the prophesy.

Kamsa had indeed been killed by the eighth child of Devaki.

After Kamsa's death, Ugrasena was brought back to the throne and pro-claimed as king. All those who had fled from Mathura to escape Kamsa's regime returned. And peace and harmony were restored to Mathura.

Time passed. Balarama and Krishna learned the arts and sciences, as well as the arts of war, and grew to be young men.

Now, Rukmi was prince of Vidarbha, and had a sister named Rukmini. Rukmini had longed for Krishna ever since she had first heard of his beauty and charm. But her brother, who was coldhearted and cared nothing for his sister's wishes, told her she was to marry Sisupala, the king of Chedi.

Rukmini sent a frantic, secret message to Krishna. "O my love, I have dreamed of you as my lord. Come to me soon and claim me as your wife. I am being married to the Chedi king against my wish. Save me! We will be going to the temple of Parvati, just outside the city, the day before the mar-riage day. You can rescue me then. If you do not come, I swear that I will cast off my body and quit this world!"

Krishna received the message, and soon he and his charioteer were racing to save Rukmini. When Balarama heard that Krishna had gone alone to Kundina, he assembled a large army and set out after him, just in case.

Meanwhile, preparations for the wedding of Sisupala and Rukmini con-tinued unchecked. Rukmini was busy tormenting herself. Had the message reached Krishna? Had Krishna listened? Would he come?

It didn't comfort her to know that the people were on her side. All the citi-zens of Kundina were murmuring, "How sad that that Rukmini will not be marrying Krishna; it would have been an ideal match. Rukmini should have a swan and is getting a swarthy crow instead. But who can overcome destiny?"

The bridal procession began. Women moved gracefully forward, carrying gold and silver bowls filled with flowers and fruits, spices and incense. Musicians followed, playing joyous melodies. The royal guards marched with them, and people threw flowers and rice in blessing.

The bridal party reached the temple, and Rukmini went into the shrine, where she prayed to the goddess Gauri and the great god Shiva. "O Mother! O Divine! I pray to you that Krishna will be my husband."

As Rukmini left the temple, she found herself facing Krishna, who stood in a chariot pulled by four white horses. Their eyes met, and a thrill passed through Rukmini. Krishna pulled her into the chariot, and they were away before anyone realized what had happened. Balarama turned back the enemy army with the force and skill of his own men. Krishna joined the fight and captured Rukmi. But he spared the prince's life for Rukmini's sake.

Krishna married Rukmini with all rejoicing, and they were a happy couple. He played his part in the great war between Kauravas and Pandavas, but that is another story. But best of all, Krishna gave humanity the wisdom of the B*hagavad Gita.*

Sources

Nivedita, Sister, and Ananda K. Coomaraswamy. *Myths of the Hindus and Buddhists.* New York: Farrar and Rinehart, n.d.

Dharma, Krishna, trans. *Mahabharata: The Greatest Spiritual Epic of All Time.* Los Angeles: Torchlight Publications, 1999.

Mitchell, Stephen. *The Bhagavad Gita: A New Translation.* New York: Harmony Books, 2000.

GANESH
A Myth from India

In the myths of Lord Shiva and the lovely Parvathi, they are portrayed as a loving couple—but a couple who are often quarreling. It's not at all surprising that a god who's been away fighting and is coming home to a lovely wife does not want to be stopped by a mere door guard. That he goes so far as to behead the guard is something else again, and understandably it leads to another fight with Parvathi.

Now a motif appears that can be found in the world's mythology and folklore. Lord Shiva vows to replace Ganesh's head with that of the first living creature that was sleeping with its head to the north. In stories from Europe and Asia, a father promises to sacrifice the first creature he sees, which usually turns out to be his own child, or a demon agrees to take the first creature over a bridge and winds up with nothing more than a dog, or a hero agrees to wed the first woman he meets and winds up with an enchanted creature who turns into a lovely maiden. The main element in these stories is the force of chance versus the force of destiny.

Images of Lord Ganesh can be seen today in the United States in many Indian-run enterprises.

In the long-past days, the time when Lord Shiva was away from his home, fighting for the gods, his wife, the lovely goddess Parvathi, was left alone at home.

Now it happened that she needed someone to guard the house when she was going down to the river for a bath. But there was no one. So at last, since there seemed to be no other choice, Parvathi used her powers to create a son for herself, and named him Ganesh. She told Ganesh that he was

An Indian sculpture depicts Ganesh with a human body and the head of an elephant. Ganesh, son and protector of the goddess Parvathi, was beheaded by Lord Shiva. Realizing his mistake, Lord Shiva replaced Ganesh's head with the first living creature he found sleeping with its head to the north. (*Nimatallah/Art Resource, New York*)

to keep a strict watch over the entrance to the house and that he was not to allow anyone into the house.

Ganesh agreed and went on guard, keeping the strictest of vigils.

In the meantime, there had been a glorious victory for the gods. Lord Shiva returned happy, looking forward to seeing his lovely wife—but was stopped short at the entrance to his house by Ganesh. Ganesh, of course, had no way of knowing who this angry stranger might be, and no reason to believe the stranger when he claimed to live there. No, Ganesh continued to act on Parvathi's orders, and hers alone, and flatly refused to allow Shiva to enter the house.

Lord Shiva, tired and in no mood for this foolishness, lost his temper beyond all managing and slashed out with his sword, taking off poor Ganesh's head.

Parvathi, meanwhile, had just finished a leisurely bath and was aghast to be met with her stunned husband and the headless body of Ganesh. She was furious at her lordship for slaying her newly created son, the son who was just trying his best to protect her.

Now Lord Shiva was sorry for his hasty action. More than anything else, he wanted to make it up to Parvathi. The head of Ganesh was gone, vanished into nothingness. So Lord Shiva vowed to return life to Ganesh by replacing it with the head of the first living creature to be found that was sleeping with its head to the north.

He sent his soldiers off in search of such a being. The first creature that came into the soldiers' sight happened to be an elephant. It was asleep with its head to the north. And so Lord Shiva re-created his son with the head of the elephant. That is why Lord Ganesh bears a human body but an elephant's head.

Parvathi was not completely satisfied with the way things had turned out. She wanted more in recompense for what Ganesh had endured. After some thought, Lord Shiva granted Ganesh this reward: Before people began any sort of undertaking or task, they would worship Lord Ganesh. With this, Parvathi was content.

And so it continues to this day: Before starting any work, people worship Lord Ganesh.

Sources

Brown, Robert L., ed. *Ganesh: Studies of an Asian God*. Delhi: Sri Satguru Publications, 1997.

Danielou, Alain. *The Myths and Gods of India*. Rutland, VT: Inner Traditions International, 1991.

THE BAAL EPIC
A Myth from Canaan in Ancient Palestine

This is another ancient myth, one that was first written down over three thousand years ago. The name Baal may sound familiar, as Baal also appears in Judeo-Christian tradition, but as a false god at the least and a demonic figure at worst. It's a classic case of one man's god being another man's demon.

In this myth, as in the Egyptian myth "The War of Horus and Set," earlier in this chapter, the issue is a battle for the kingship of the Canaanite pantheon. As Horus was nearly cheated out of his patrimony, so Baal actually is cheated, in a divine case of nepotism: the

A Canaanite gold and silver foil-covered bronze figure of Baal, 1900 B.C.E. In the epic tale, Baal sought kingship of the gods and won the role after destroying the tyrant Yam-Nahar. (*Werner Forman/Art Resource, New York*)

judge is the father of the winner. When the new king god turns out to be a tyrant, Baal and he first engage in a ritual exchange of insults—including a warning not to blame the messenger—and then in a swift, deadly battle that ends, of course, with the winner being Baal.

*N*ow, it happened in the ancient days that Baal, son of mighty Dagon, wanted the kingship of the gods. Also wanting the kingship was Yam-Nahar, the double son of kindly El. The two young gods Baal and Yam contended. But El decided the case in favor of his son and gave the kingship to Yam and the power to the judge Nahar.

But Yam was not a kindly god like his sire. No, fearsome Yam ruled the gods with a harsh hand, and they were forced to labor under the force of his reign. At last the gods called aloud to their mother, Asherah, begging her to intercede with Yam on their behalf.

So the mother, kindly Asherah, went into the presence of royal Yam. She came before the judge Nahar. She begged that he release that powerful grip upon the gods. But fearsome Yam refused to hear her request. Powerful Nahar refused to soften his heart for all her pleas.

Finally, kindly Asherah, who loved her children, offered her own body up to him for the sake of the gods. Yam-Nahar agreed to this, and Asherah went before her children, the gods, and told them of her plan.

Baal was infuriated by the idea, and furious, too, at the gods who would allow it. He would not consent to surrendering great Asherah to the tyrant Yam-Nahar. And in that moment of rage Baal swore to the gods that he would destroy Yam. He would lay to rest the tyranny of Nahar.

Yam-Nahar learned of Baal's vow. So he sent two messengers to El's court. Their message was this, "Hear the message of Yam, your lord. Surrender the one you harbor, O gods. Give up Baal so that I may inherit his wealth!"

And Yam's father, El, replied, "Baal is your slave, O Yam! He will bring you tribute!"

But Baal was enraged. He snatched up a dagger, but the goddesses Anath and Astarte seized his hands. "You cannot smite the messengers! They have merely brought the words of Yam, their lord and master."

Baal agreed and spared the messengers' lives, sending them back to their master with a message: "Baal will not bow to Yam. He will not be the slave of Nahar. And he states once more that he will slay the tyrant!"

And he followed close after, in his one hand the great cudgel Yagrush, in the other the strong cudgel Aymur. Yagrush sprang from Baal's hand like an eagle and struck Yam in the chest. Before the tyrant could recover, Aymur also sprang from Baal's hand and struck Yam true between the eyes. Yam collapsed dead upon the ground.

So it was ended, and so did Baal come to reign as king of the gods.

Sources

Dalley, Stephanie. *Myths from Mesopotamia*. Oxford: Oxford University Press, 1989.
Gaster, Theodor H. *The Oldest Stories in the World*. Boston: Beacon, 1952.

ARTEMIS AND APOLLO
A Myth of Ancient Greece

Although these two deities may seem typically Greek, there has been some scholarly debate about whether or not they may originally be from the Near East or even Asia. The evidence does seem to point to a foreign origin, especially when one considers the strange statue of Artemis that was found at Ephesus, in what is now Turkey. Although Artemis is said to be a virgin goddess, the statue portrays her instead as a fertility goddess, one who is either many-breasted or wearing a garland of severed male organs. Since priests of the Near Eastern fertility goddess Cybele gelded themselves in her honor, the later interpretation isn't too outlandish!

There is also some circumstantial evidence for a foreign origin in the fact that Apollo's famous oracle at Delphi had to be established by him by force: He first slew Python, the dragon guarding the site, then installed his oracle, possibly even superceding an earlier cult to Gaea, the earth mother.

Foreign or local, Artemis is one of the stranger gods of the Greek pantheon: She is determined to be forever a maiden and is a devoted hunter, yet she also has those aspects of being a fertility deity. She is the goddess of the moon, which can be seen as a symbol of cold purity, yet it waxes and wanes in a way that has been linked by many cultures to a woman's natural cycle. And there is that odd statue of her.

Artemis and Apollo can hardly be described as beneficent. They can be kind, but their gifts usually have a sting, and for a human to insult them means sure death.

As for the death of Orion, given here as the result of Apollo's jealousy, note the contradictory version in the Greek tale of the Pleiades in Chapter 3. There are also contradictory myths as to who sent that scorpion to sting him. Some say it was Artemis, whom he had challenged, while others say that it came from Gaea, angry over his boasting about how many animals he would slay.

Zeus, king of the gods who dwell on Mount Olympus had a love for mortal women. Indeed, he had sired a good many half-mortal children from his various affairs. Most of these offspring remained on mortal soil among humankind. But the twins, brother and sister, that he'd sired from a love affair with charming Leto on the Greek island of Delos were beautiful enough to be noteworthy to the god. Indeed, he thought, seeing their shining faces, they were clearly divine, not human.

The divine twin children of Zeus and Leto, Artemis (right) and Apollo (center) grew up to become unexpectedly powerful, according to Greek mythology. Relief from the Parthenon in Athens, Greece, 440–432 B.C.E. (*Erich Lessing/Art Resource, New York*)

And so Zeus had them taken from the mortal lands and brought up to Olympus, where they were named Apollo and Artemis. Time passed, and the two lost all hint of mortal birth. Indeed, they became unexpectedly powerful.

First there was Apollo, who grew to love the arts—but owned a fiery temper as well, suitable for someone as golden as the sun. Zeus gifted him with a golden bow and a quiver of gleaming arrows, a quiver that could never be emptied.

Then there was his sister Artemis, a wild young thing unwilling to be tame. When Zeus asked Artemis what she wished, she answered: "I wish to be forever your maiden, never a woman, with many names by which mortals may call me. I wish fifty nymphs to sing for me, and twenty nymphs to hunt with me. I wish the freedom of mountain and forest for my realm."

"So it shall be," Zeus said.

Soon after, mortals saw her riding to the hunt over the mountains, wielding a silver bow, followed by her maidens and their torches. Some who saw her called her Goddess of the Moon or Goddess of the Night. Some who saw her called her Maiden of the Silver Bow. Others feared her as the Huntress or the Lady of the Beasts, or warily named her simply the Maiden or the Woodland Goddess. So indeed she had her many names.

Meanwhile, Apollo became the deity of divine distance. It was he who made mortals aware of their guilt, he who punished or purified them from afar. It was through his oracle at Delphi that he communicated with humanity, telling them in cryptic messages the will of Zeus. He grew to be quicksilver in mood, and only the lyre, which he played with elegant skill, showed his gentler side.

Indeed, even the gods walked warily near Apollo when that golden bow was slung over his shoulder. And like his sister, he bore several names. As protector of herds, he was Noimos, the Herdsman, and Lyceius, guarding them against wolves. Because he was so bright and shining in appearance, he was also known as Phoebus, and some even confused him with Helios the sun god.

But even Apollo could know grief and run into trouble. When a half-mortal son of his was slain by the Cyclopes, Zeus' armorers, Apollo slew them in turn and willingly endured the penance placed upon him: He served King Admetus of Pherae not as a divine being nor as a hero, but in the lowly role of groom and herdsman.

True to her fiercely independent nature, Artemis let no man approach her, and took quick revenge on those who tried. Once a young man named Actaeon glimpsed her bathing in a stream. The sight he witnessed was so beautiful he could not bear to go away but hid there, watching, heedless of his peril. But Artemis spied him watching and cried out in rage. Immediately Actaeon was turned into a stag. Artemis hunted him down, and her hounds tore him to pieces.

Apollo, meanwhile, had many a love affair, though most ended unhappily. One of them began because of his self-confidence in his skill as an archer. Eros, son of Aphrodite, goddess of love, was also well known as an archer. In fact, Eros, who is also known as Cupid, was the one responsible to send arrows of love into mortal—and sometimes divine—hearts.

When Apollo mockingly belittled Eros' skill, Eros promptly snatched up two arrows. The first was dipped in gold and inspired fierce love in whatever heart it struck. The second arrow was dipped in lead and inspired utter loathing of love in whatever heart it struck. Before Apollo knew what was happening, the golden arrow struck him—just as he was looking at lovely Daphne, daughter of the river god, Peneus. Unfortunately, Eros' second arrow, the lead-dipped one, struck Daphne. As Apollo, fierce with love, raced for her, she looked at him with loathing, then turned and fled.

Now desperate for her, Apollo chased after her, and she fled away from him. Exhausted and terrified that Apollo would catch her, Daphne cried to her father for help and was instantly transformed from a maiden into the lovely laurel tree.

Apollo still loved Daphne, but now he knew his love was hopeless. In memory of what could not be, he made the laurel his sacred tree.

Nor did matters run much more smoothly with his other loves. He loved Cassandra, daughter of King Priam of Troy, but she tricked him, gaining from him the gift of prophecy but then refusing to become his lover. The gift turned to a curse when no one would believe her prophecies and Troy fell to the Greeks.

Apollo trusted the mortal woman Coronis, with whom he had a son, Asclepius the healer. But Coronis proved untrue to him. It was Artemis who avenged her brother's honor, shooting the treacherous Coronis.

But even when Artemis might choose to like a mortal man, that fact didn't make him safe. Orion was the mortal son of Poseidon, god of the sea, and was a strong and handsome hunter. He was chosen by the goddess to go hunting with her.

Was there something more than hunting on her mind? Apollo clearly thought there was. He was determined that his twin sister should not fall in love with a mere mortal—or perhaps he was seeking a devious revenge for the slaying of Coronis. At any rate, Apollo sent a monstrous scorpion to slay Orion. Orion fought the scorpion with sword and arrows, but it would not die. To escape the creature, he dove into the sea and swam away, since scorpions cannot swim.

Just then Artemis arrived, searching for the mortal hunter. Apollo told her that the man who swam so far out from land had just attacked one of her maidens and was trying to escape. Furious, Artemis sent a fatal arrow winging toward Orion and slew him.

Then she learned whom she had slain. Furious now at her brother instead, Artemis turned Orion into a constellation, where he can still be seen today, forever pursued by the scorpion that will never catch him.

But Artemis forgave her brother with time. They sometimes worked together as a deadly team. In the mortal realm, the unwise Niobe compared his own children to the twins and mocked Leto, claiming that his children were far more beautiful. When Artemis and Apollo heard this slight and saw their mother's tears, they took revenge. Apollo slew the sons of Niobe, and Artemis the daughters.

Mortals knew from then on to be truly wary. And Artemis and Apollo, perilous twins, were worshiped—from afar.

Sources

Howe, George, and G. A. Harrer. *A Handbook of Classical Mythology*. Hertfordshire: Oracle, 1996.

Kerenyi, Karl. *The Gods of the Greeks*. London: Thames and Hudson, 1985.

CREATING GODS AND LIFE
A Myth of Samoa

This is a continuation of the Samoan tale of creation begun in Chapter 1. Here the methodical placement of the right beings in the right sites continues, and humanity is set into existence.

After he had created the heavens and the earth, Tagaloa sat still for a time. Then he began his work anew. He created the other gods from himself.

Tagaloa the creator said to Tagaloa-le-fuli, Stable Tagaloa, "Be chief in the heavens." And Stable Tagaloa was chief in the heavens.

Then Tagaloa the creator said to Tagaloa-savali, Messenger Tagaloa, "Be ambassador in all the heavens, from the Eighth Heavens down to the First Heavens, to tell them all to gather together in the Ninth Heavens, where Stable Tagaloa is chief."

And so it was done, and order was made among the heavens, nine in one.

Then Tagaloa the messenger went to Night and Day and asked them if they had any children who had not yet been appointed to their proper roles. Night and Day answered, "We have four boys who have not yet been appointed: Manu'a, Samoa, Sun, and Moon."

Tagaloa the creator said to Night and Day: "Let Manu'a and Samoa go down below to be chiefs over the offspring of Fatu and 'Ele-'ele. Let Sun and Moon go and follow you two, Sun when Day comes and Moon when Night comes."

Then Messenger Tagaloa went down to visit the mortal land, and wherever he stood, wherever he prayed to Tagaloa the creator, new land sprang up. Messenger Tagaloa returned to the heavens and said, "We have countries."

Tagaloa the creator went down in a black cloud to look at the countries and said, "They are good."

And he sent humans into being to people the lands.

Sources

Grey, Sir George. *Polynesian Mythology*. London: Whitcombe and Tombs, 1956.

Mead, Margaret. *Coming of Age in Samoa: A Psychological Study of Primitive Youth for Western Civilization*. New York: William Morrow, 1961.

Sproul, Barbara C. *Primal Myths: Creating the World*. New York and San Francisco: Harper and Row, 1979.

PELE
A Myth of Hawaii

Pele is one of the few deities in whom even those who aren't worshipers still believe—ask anyone living in Hawaii about that! In fact, stories about her continue to spring up. One such modern belief that seems to date to after 1930 states that no lava rocks may be removed from Pele's mountain, Kilauea. Literally hundreds of rocks have been returned to the islands by tourists and other visitors who claim that taking the rocks brought them ill fortune.

How Pele should have arisen from water spirits is one of the mysteries of mythology. How it is that her path should have accurately followed the actual track of Polynesian volcanism is another, since no Polynesian, even the earliest to reach the region, could have seen so long-lived a phenomenon.

The fire goddess Pele, depicted here in a statue made of wood and hair, is said to rule over Hawaii and all of its volcanoes. (*Werner Forman/Art Resource, New York*)

*P*ele was the only fiery one, hot of temper and nature in her divine family of cool-natured water gods. And understandably, a fire goddess could have no happy home in the ocean.

So Pele left, sailing over the open ocean. For many months she followed a star from the northeast that seemed brighter than the rest, and navigated in its direction.

At last she saw land, a mountain with haze at its peak, a living volcano. This, she knew, would be her new home. Stepping ashore, she named the land Hawai'i. With her enchanted staff, Pa'oa, she climbed the mountain to where it had collapsed in on itself. Here she planted the staff and named the mountain Kilauea. The crater looked down into the earth's fires, Pele's fires, and she named this, her chosen abode, Halema'uma'u.

As it happened, there was already a fire god living on Kilauea. His name was 'Ailaau, which means "forest eater," and he was not the sort to wish to share. Neither was hot-tempered Pele willing to retreat. They fought, throwing fire at each other, forests blazing about them. But Pele had never yet surrendered in a fight, and 'Ailaau had never had to fight. He suddenly gave up and fled to a safe hiding place deep under the surface of the earth, where he remains yet. Pele alone would be the deity to rule Hawai'i.

Now, before Pele had left her first home, her mother had given her an egg. Out of that egg hatched Pele's new sister, the beautiful Hi'iaka'i-ka-poli-o-Pele. That this sister—who grew to young womanhood with the swiftness of the gods—was loved by Pele shows in the meaning of her name, Hi'iaka of the bosom of Pele. Others loved her, too. Kamohoali'i, the shark god, taught Hi'iaka the art of surfing.

But with her fiery nature, Pele could be harsh even with her sister. For Pele fell in love with a man she saw in a dream. His name was Lohi'au, and he was a chief of the island of Kaua'i. Pele sent her sister Hi'iaka to fetch Lohi'au to Hawai'i. She gave Hi'iaka forty days to bring Lohi'au back. If she failed, Pele warned, Hi'iaka's friend Hopoe would suffer.

When she reached Kaua'i, Hi'iaka was dismayed to find that Lohi'au had died. She quickly rubbed his body with magical herbs and chanted to the gods for help. And to her relief, she brought the young chief back to life. Grateful to Hi'iaka, as well he might be, Lohi'au agreed to return with her to Hawai'i.

Meanwhile, the forty days were almost up. Pele, not waiting for the end of the fortieth day, suspected that Hi'iaka and Lohi'au had fallen in love and were not coming back. Her sudden blaze of fury caused an eruption that turned poor Hopoe into stone.

On her return to Hawai'i with Lohi'au, Hi'iaka found Hopoe turned to stone. She took her revenge by throwing her arms around Lohi'au and kissing him passionately—where Pele could not miss seeing them. White-hot with fury, Pele cast out a wave of lava that engulfed Lohi'au.

The two sisters fought, fire against water. Now Pele triumphed, now Hi'iaka drowned the fire. But at last the two grew weary. Their anger subsided. And at last the sisters were remorseful. One had just lost a friend, the other had just lost a lover.

At last Pele decided that the only way to solve this struggle was to bring Lohi'au back to life to let him choose which sister he would love. Pele, of course, was sure that Lohi'au would choose her. Hi'iaka hoped that Lohi'au would chose her.

Lohi'au, revived for the second time in his short life, did choose Hi'iaka. Pele, no matter what she thought or felt about the issue, gave the two lovers her blessing, and Hi'iaka and Lohi'au sailed back to Kaua'i.

But Pele remained as she still remains: goddess of Hawai'i and its volcanoes.

Sources

Beckwith, Martha. *Hawaiian Mythology.* Honolulu: University of Hawaii Press, 1970.
Westervelt, W.D. *Hawaiian Legends of Volcanoes.* Rutland, VT: Charles E. Tuttle, 1963.
———. *Myths and Legends of Hawaii.* Honolulu: Mutual, 1987.

SEDNA
A Myth of the Inuit

This is one of the most important myths of the many related Inuit peoples, as well as one that may seem alien to some storytellers. It should not be remolded too far from its roots if it is to remain true.

The opening segment shows Sedna as a vain young woman reluctant to marry anyone but the best. This theme appears in myths and folktales from around the world, including several from North America and, in specific, "King Thrushbeard" in the collections of the Brothers Grimm. It does not appear, not surprisingly, in matrilineal cultures.

Sedna's severed fingers become seals and whales, a similar theme to the building of the world from the body of a god or monster, as occurs in the Norse myth "Ymir and the Creation" or the Indian myth "The Cosmic Egg," both in Chapter 1.

*O*nce, Sedna was mortal, human, a lovely girl of the Inuit people who lived with her father. She was proud of her beauty and too vain to marry anyone but the most perfect of men.

At last her father told her, "We have no food, and soon we will starve. You must accept the next strong hunter who asks for your hand so that he may bring us meat."

Sedna refused to listen.

Just then her father saw a strange hunter, a man dressed in thick, elegant furs, proving his success and wealth. Sedna's father hastily told the stranger, "I have a beautiful daughter. She can cook and sew and will make you a good wife."

Neither he nor the hunter listened to Sedna's protests. Furious, she found herself in the hunter's kayak, traveling to his camp. But her new home was nothing but bare, cold rocks, and her only food was raw fish. And her husband—he was no human, no handsome hunter, but a seabird spirit.

Miserably unhappy, Sedna cried for her father. So strongly did she cry that he heard her even through the howling of the cold winds. And he felt sorrow for what he had done. So he paddled his kayak through wind and wave to where Sedna waited. She hastily scrambled into the kayak, and they paddled away. But the bird spirit flew after them, shrieking in fury—and with each shriek, a storm boiled up, darkening the sky. The waves roiled up, terrible gray walls of water, and the kayak was tossed about as though it were nothing but a twig.

Terrified, Sedna's father cried, "If you want your wife, here, take her!"

He caught Sedna in his arms and hurled her over the side. Sedna struggled in the icy water and clung to the edge of the kayak with frantic fingers. But now her father was too terrified to think. He was sure she would sink them both, so he slashed off her fingers with his knife. Some of them turned to seals, others to whales.

And Sedna, no longer able to fight, sank under the waves. But her anger kept her alive. She did not drown, but changed. Now she has become the goddess of the northern sea. Her friends are the sea creatures, and it is her anger against men that creates the savage northern storms. To placate her, shamans travel to her realm and comb the tangles from her long black hair. And hunters forever treat her with the greatest of respect, so that the people may eat and thrive.

Sources

Balikci, Asen. *The Netsilik Eskimo.* New York: Natural History Press, 1970.

Norman, Howard. *Northern Tales: Traditional Stories of Eskimo and Indian Peoples.* New York: Pantheon Books, 1990.

Turner, Patricia, and Charles Russell Coulter. *Dictionary of Ancient Deities.* Oxford and New York: Oxford University Press, 2000.

5

MYTHS OF THE HEROES

Every culture has its heroes, both living and mythic. Hero myths can be divided into two main categories. First are the myths of the purely human hero. A prime example of this category is King Arthur of Britain. Arthur is certainly surrounded by a great deal of magic and mythic symbols, from Merlin to Excalibur, but he is himself of completely human birth. Another human hero is Moses, who is divinely inspired but of purely mortal origins.

Then there are the hero myths of the divine or semidivine heroes, such as Hercules of Greece, whose father was Zeus, or Raven of the American Pacific Northwest. Interestingly enough, Hercules has had a modern rebirth in a more traditionally heroic form as the star of an animated feature film and a television series. This reshaping of the hero is hardly unique to Hercules. Thanks to the pervasiveness of the modern media, the basic hero's adventures filter down to us through fairy tales, motion pictures, television, and fantasy and science fiction.

Why are tales of heroes so popular? Hero myths give us hope that we are not powerless in a hostile universe. The hero is the living symbol of a people and their well-being.

Related to the hero myths are the myths of great kings, such as Alexander, about whom a mythic cycle was forming even during his brief life. He is generally not portrayed as a true hero, but rather as a mighty king who learns humility. Other myth cycles have formed about King Arthur of Britain, Charlemagne of the Frankish lands, and Prince Vladimir of Kiev; these myths deal with the adventures of the knights and, in the case of Arthur, the quest for the Holy Grail, with its Christian elements and pagan roots. There are also myth cycles from Egypt and England, among others, about great sages or magicians (who are the same to many peoples) such as Vol'ka of Russia or Merlin of Britain.

LONE HEROES

THE EPIC OF GILGAMESH
A Myth from Ancient Mesopotamia

This is the earliest complete epic that we possess. It must have been considered highly important—or highly worthy of scribal test copying—since there are several versions that have come down to us from Sumer and Akkad, dating to about the second millennium B.C.E.

The first motif that appears is the old theme of "all power corrupts, absolute power corrupts absolutely," in which the young King Gilgamesh, with no checks on his power, begins turning into a tyrant. This in turn leads to the second motif, the wild man. Enkidu has his echoes in modern ideas like the wolf children of India and elsewhere, and also in modern pop icons like Rudyard Kipling's Mowgli and Edgar Rice Burroughs' Tarzan.

Now the epic turns into what seems to us today like a "buddy movie," with the two heroes going after monsters and facing off against the gods. But when Enkidu dies, the mood darkens. Gilgamesh sets out on a heroic quest to find the antidote to death.

When he reaches mythic Dilmun, he meets Utnapishtim, who relates to him the story "The First Great Flood" (which here appears in Chapter 2) and tells him of the magical plant at the bottom of the sea.

Now there is an ironic touch: Gilgamesh loses the precious plant to a snake. This brings in the "how and why" motif of why the snake sheds its skin.

And of course the final motif: Humanity remains mortal.

Gilgamesh was king of Uruk, with a youthful strength and lust that left him with no rivals. He was not an evil man. But with no checks on his power, he was rapidly growing to be a tyrant. The gods knew that he must have a friend of equal strength to keep him under control. So they asked the goddess Aruru to make him a brother. This she did, and thus was Enkidu created.

Enkidu was a wild creature, human but knowing nothing of being human, living in the wilderness with the beasts and eating grass in the hills. He was

Gilgamesh, the king of Uruk, appears in an Assyrian relief from the palace of Sargon II, Khorsabad. According to the legend, Gilgamesh was both a god and a man, while his brother, Enkidu, was both an animal and a man. Together the heroic brothers take on many adventures as they face off against the gods and battle monsters. (*Giraudon/Art Resource, New York*)

strong, perhaps even the strongest man in the world, and when a trapper chanced to see him, the man was so terrified of the shaggy, tangle-haired Enkidu that he was sure he'd seen a monster. He went straight to Gilgamesh in the royal city of Uruk to tell him this.

Gilgamesh suspected from the trapper's description that this was no monster but a wild man. He had already experienced dreams that had told him a friend who would be a brother to him was to arrive in Uruk. Was this the man? Gilgamesh had a woman sent to Enkidu to tame him. And indeed, Enkidu was led by her into the ways of being human. The wild beasts fled from him, and he followed her to the city of Uruk.

Their friendship did not start smoothly. Gilgamesh was about to steal a man's new bridge, but Enkidu stopped him. The two men fought, and Gilgamesh prevailed—but by so narrow a margin that they never tried to fight again. Enkidu was alarmed that he was no longer as strong as he'd been in the wild. And Gilgamesh knew, underneath the bluster, that Enkidu would be the one to keep him from abusing his power. After that, the two did become the truest of friends.

Their first adventure together happened when Gilgamesh decided to raise a temple of cedars to the gods. Unfortunately, the best of the cedar trees were guarded by a fearsome giant called Humbaba. Gilgamesh stated boldly that he was not afraid of Humbaba. Enkidu in his wanderings in the wilderness had seen Humbaba, though, and was worried. However, he willingly fought at his friend's side against the giant. And this time Gilgamesh was right: Humbaba was vanquished by the double power of Gilgamesh and Enkidu.

But one thing Gilgamesh had not expected. This was that the god of the earth, Enlil, was not happy about the humans' victory, and threatened vengeance on them both.

Ignoring all warnings, Gilgamesh and Enkidu returned to Uruk. There, as Gilgamesh put on his glittering royal robes, the goddess Ishtar saw and desired him. She came to him, promising marriage and every wonder he wished.

Gilgamesh had no intention of getting trapped into a marriage with an immortal. Instead of agreeing, he reminded Ishtar of how unfaithful she had been to all her previous lovers. Insulted and furious, Ishtar flew up to the heavens to ask her father, Anu, lord of the heavens, for the Bull of Heaven so that she could have her revenge on Gilgamesh.

The Bull of Heaven appeared on earth, roaring and snorting with rage. Its first snort cracked the earth and slew a hundred men. Gilgamesh and Enkidu rushed to the attack. A sweep of the bull's mighty horns sent Enkidu flying, but Gilgamesh took advantage of the moment to get in under the horns and slay the bull.

Together, the heroic friends cut out the bull's heart and made an offering to the god Shamash. This hardly gentled Ishtar's rage. She appeared on the city walls and cursed Gilgamesh for slaying the bull. Enkidu cut short the curse by flinging the bull's thigh at her.

Ishtar vanished. But that night Enkidu dreamed of a council of the gods in which it was ruled that, because of his involvement with the deaths of Humbaba and the Bull of Heaven, Enkidu must die.

It was a prophetic dream. Enkidu fell ill that very day, and despite all of Gilgamesh's prayers, the hero died.

Gilgamesh wept bitterly for his brother—and for himself, since his greatest fear was death. He determined to find Utnapishtim, who lived in the land of Dilmun, in the Garden of the Sun. To him alone had the gods granted eternal life.

It was a long and difficult quest. Gilgamesh at last reached the Mountains of Mashu, the gate of which was guarded by two man-scorpions. They warned him that no mortal man had ever done what he meant to do, but they opened the gate for him.

After walking for twelve leagues in utter darkness, Gilgamesh reached the Garden of the Gods, which glittered with riches. There he met the god Shamash, who warned him that he would never find what he sought. But Gilgamesh refused to turn back.

Reaching the sea, he met Siduri, goddess of wine, who warned him that no mortal man could ever find eternal life. But when Gilgamesh still refused to turn back, she told him that Utnapishtim lived across the ocean, in the land of Dilmun. Gilgamesh was carried across by the boatman Urshanabi.

And at last Gilgamesh met Utnapishtim, who was a tranquil old man. Utnapishtim warned Gilgamesh that nothing on earth is permanent—but Gilgamesh countered that Utnapishtim himself was immortal.

With a sigh, Utnapishtim told Gilgamesh his story, which was the story of the great flood and the great boat he'd built. It was thanks to Utnapishtim's obedience to the will of the gods, and his saving of the animals in his boat, that he and his wife had been granted the gift of immortality and life here in the peaceful land of Dilmun.

Gilgamesh refused to give in. Surely there was another way to become immortal. Utnapishtim told Gilgamesh to prevail against sleep for six days and seven nights if he wished to gain eternal life.

Alas, Gilgamesh, being only mortal, could not stay awake. He slept, and woke despairing. But Utnapishtim offered him one last scrap of hope—there was a magical plant that could be found only at the bottom of the sea. This plant could restore lost youth.

Instantly Gilgamesh dove into the sea. Down and down he swam, down to the very bottom of the sea, where he plucked the plant.

But on his way back to Uruk, Gilgamesh lost the plant to a snake, which devoured it. And so it is the snake that retains eternal youth by shedding its skin, and man who must grow old and die. Saddened, but finally accepting of the way it must be, Gilgamesh returned to Uruk, where he ruled well for the rest of his life.

Sources

Gardner, John, and John Maier. *Gilgamesh*. New York: Alfred Knopf, 1984.

Heidel, Alexander. *The Gilgamesh Epic and Old Testament Parallels*. Chicago: University of Chicago Press, 1949.

Sandars, N. K., trans. *The Epic of Gilgamesh*. Harmondsworth, England: Penguin Books, 1972.

LITUOLONE
A Myth of the Sesuto People of Africa

Here is a myth that contains three ancient motifs. The first is the destruction of the world, with only one (or more often two) survivor. For more examples of this, see Chapter 2. The second is the hero born without a father, or with an unknown father. These figures range from the ancient Persian god Mithra to the modern Luke Skywalker in the original *Star Wars*. And the third is the miraculous birth of a culture hero, who grows to manhood in a day. These heroes turn up in myths and stories from around the world.

Then there is the familiar theme of the hero who deliberately lets himself be swallowed by the monster, then cuts his way out, killing it in the process. See also the myth of Geser later in this chapter. This theme was even used in the movie *Men in Black*!

The story of Geser also shares with this myth the image of all the swallowed people, unharmed, pouring out of the slain monster.

Once, in the long-ago world, there was a monster named Kammapa, a terrible creature that devoured humans. So savage and deadly was Kammapa that at last there was only one human left in all the world. This was an old woman who had fearfully gone into hiding when she saw what was happening.

But there may have been another reason for Kammapa not finding her. There was a touch of magic to her. And one day, without the aid of a man, the woman gave birth to a boy-child. He, too, bore that touch of magic, for he was born adorned with amulets. The woman named her magical son Lituolone in honor of her god.

By nightfall the baby was a fully grown young man. He asked his mother where the other people were. She told him of Kammapa and the savage devouring of the human race.

Without another word, Lituolone snatched up a knife and raced off to fight the monster.

He didn't have far to go before Kammapa confronted him, looming up like a great mountain with deadly fangs. How could he possibly slay it? Lituolone, suddenly inspired, charged Kammapa. The monster opened its enormous mouth and swallowed him down in one gulp.

Finding himself unharmed in the beast's stomach, as he'd planned, Lituolone used his knife to cut his way out. Kammapa roared and bucked, but it was already too late. In another moment the monster fell dead.

Not only had Lituolone slain Kammapa, but in tearing apart the monster he freed the thousands of human beings who had been trapped inside. They escaped with Lituolone, and the world was repopulated again.

Sources

Parrinder, Geoffrey. *African Mythology*. New York: Peter Bedrick Books, 1982.

Partridge, A. C., ed. *Folklore of Southern Africa*. Vol. 2 of ELISA Series. Cape Town, South Africa: Purnell, 1973.

HOU YI AND CHANG'ER
A Myth from China

This myth begins with the Asian theme of the multiple suns, such as also appears in the Chinese myth "The Orphans and the Flood" and the Hmong myth "Why There Is Day and Night," both in Chapter 2. But here the focus is on the hero figure of Hou Yi, the miraculous archer who not only shoots down nine of the ten suns but goes on to slay monsters as well. Heroic archers turn up in almost every culture's tales, including the two most famous to Westerners, the British Robin Hood and the Swiss William Tell.

Tales of falsely accused heroes turn up around the world, too, although in Western stories we expect the hero to fight to clear his name. In this Chinese myth, there seems to be no recourse for Hou Yi save to accept banishment for himself and his wife, a fact that leads to the end of their marriage. The concept of a potion of immortality appears, but it is here used to add to the tragedy in that only Chang'er takes it, and creates a "how and why" motif as she becomes the woman in the moon.

Hou Yi meets the end of many a mythic hero: Like Robin Hood, he is betrayed and murdered.

The story of Chang'er's flight to the moon is very familiar in China, and has been known at least since the Warring States period (475-221 B.C.E.). It has been frequently used as a subject by poets and playwrights since the eighth century C.E.

*I*n the reign of the Emperor Yao, in the days of myth, ten suns came to fill the sky. Their blazing heat wilted crops and parched fields, killed animals and birds, and left people lying breathless and unconscious on the ground. Fierce beasts, frantic for food, fled boiling rivers and fiery forests to attack whatever humans they could catch.

Up in the heavens, the immortals were moved to pity by the world's suffering. The emperor of heaven sent the marvelous archer Hou Yi, a prince, to help restore order.

So Hou Yi, together with his lovely and beloved wife Chang'er, descended to earth. Hou Yi carried with him the vermilion bow and white arrows that had been given to him by the emperor of heaven.

The people greeted the archer with joy. At last, here was a hero come to save them from their torment.

Without a word of boasting, Hou Yi strode to an open space, drew his mighty bow, and took aim at the first of the terrible suns.

His aim was perfect. In a blur of time, nine suns were shot from the sky. Emperor Yao stopped Hou Yi just in time from shooting down the last sun. There must be one, and only one, if life was to thrive on earth.

Now Hou Yi went after the monsters that were plaguing the people. His peerless archery slew the chisel-tusked beast in the wilderness of Ch'ou Hua, the beast with nine gullets near the Hsiung River, the giant gale at Ch'ing-ch'u Marsh, and all the other monsters, and at last there was order on the earth.

But now there was jealousy among the immortals. They slandered Hou Yi to the emperor of heaven. And at last Hou Yi and his wife were banished to the earth, to live as mortals among the mortals.

There are several versions of what happened next. All agree that Chang'er was saddened and resentful about her harsh new life. Hou Yi, feeling guilty that his wife had to suffer for his sake, or perhaps fearful of losing her love, went to Xiwangmu, queen mother of the west, and begged her for an elixir of immortality. Then, even though he and Chang'er were doomed to life on earth, they would be able to escape mortality.

But some say that Xiwangmu had only enough for one and that Hou Yi gave it to his wife. Others say that Chang'er was so bitter over what her husband had cost her that she swallowed the entire potion and left him. Whichever it was, Chang'er flew from him to the moon, where she still can be seen. Did she ever regret leaving Hou Yi behind? No one can say.

And what of Hou Yi? Saddened over the loss of his wife, he may have turned from heroism to corruption. Or he may have not seen the envy of another archer, Pang Meng. All the tales agree, though, that Hou Yi, the hero archer who'd saved the world, met a mortal fate and was murdered.

Sources

Christie, Anthony. *Chinese Mythology*. New York: Barnes and Noble Books, 1983.
Werner, E. T. C. *Myths and Legends of China*. Singapore: Singapore National Printers, 1922.

LI BING FIGHTS THE RIVER DEITY
A Myth from China

This myth is also from China, but it is as different as could be from the previous one. Here is an honorable governor who also happens to be a shape-shifter, and who takes on a menace with both trickery and courage. He is, in short, one of the most unlikely of characters: a bureaucrat-hero.

*W*hen King Zhao of Qin conquered the region of Shu, he appointed Li Bing to be the area's governor. It was a wise choice, because Li Bing was a good, wise governor who refused to oppress the people. He was also, though no one knew it, able to shift his shape when need be.

But when Li Bing was just settling into his new office, he didn't know that the people had a worse problem than a new ruler. A river flowed through Shu, and in that river lived a cruel river deity. Each year he demanded two virgins as his wives. Of course, they could not live for long underwater, not even with the river deity's magic, and that was why he needed two new wives every year.

When Li Bing heard of this, he was shocked. But not by the slightest twitch of an eyebrow did he reveal that he was planning to put an end to this tyranny. He waited. Sure enough, one day the official who was responsible for keeping the river deity happy came to report to Li, "We must collect a million copper coins so that we may buy two more women for the river deity."

"Don't bother," Li Bing said him. "I already have two nice, well-mannered virgins for him. Just tell me when the event takes place."

When the day came, Li had his two daughters nicely dressed, as if they were quite ready to be thrown into the river to meet a watery bridegroom. Li stepped onto the terrace of his manor, which overlooked the river, and poured a proper libation, as though for a highly respected son-in-law. With a bow, he said, "Mighty river god, I am greatly honored, humble human that I am, to become a relation of yours. Please, my river god, come out of your realm. Come, honor the occasion with your respected presence, and allow me to propose a toast to you."

When he'd finished, Li emptied his cup, then waited as though he really did expect the river deity to leave his watery home. But of course nothing happened. The wine in the cup set aside for the deity remained full to the brim.

This was what Li was expecting. "Since you hold me in such contempt, there is no choice for me but to fight you!"

Drawing his sword, Li leaped off the terrace and disappeared into the river.

Everyone raced down to the river's edge, terrified and amazed. With a great splashing, two huge gray water buffaloes surfaced, ignoring the humans, fighting fiercely in the shallows. Suddenly, Li reappeared, breathless and bleeding, and gasped to his aides, "The buffalo with a white stripe is me. The white is the ribbon for my seal."

Then he disappeared again to go back to his fight. His chief secretary raced for a bow and shot arrow after arrow into the solid gray buffalo. With a final lunge of his horns, the white-striped buffalo slew his foe.

The buffalos disappeared. In their place stood Li Bing, straightening his now tattered robes as best he could. That was the end of the river deity and all the trouble he had caused.

Sources

Birrell, Anne. *Chinese Mythology: An Introduction*. Baltimore: Johns Hopkins University Press, 1993.

Walls, Jan, and Yvonne Walls. *Classical Chinese Myths*. Hong Kong: Joint Publishing, 1984.

GESER
A Myth of Tibet

Geser is the major culture hero of Tibet, and his adventures have been published in many forms. As is not uncommon with such heroes, he is of divine birth, in this case reincarnated deliberately as a human to protect humanity from monsters. His adventures are so episodic it seems clear that they were originally in oral tradition, with each teller in turn adding on a new adventure or, for that matter, a new wife for Geser.

Like the Sesuto hero Lituolone, Geser follows the motif of the culture hero who grows up with supernatural speed. Like the baby Hercules, he kills the creatures sent to kill him while he's still an infant.

Another familiar motif appears when Geser kills the monster deer Orgoli, and out from the deer's body crawl the forty people Orgoli had swallowed. A similar image also appears in the story of Lituolone.

Since this is an open-ended epic, there's no firm ending to Geser's story, which makes it unique among epics.

*I*n the very earliest of times, there in the upper world were the fifty-five *tenger*, the divine spirits, of the western direction and the forty-four *tenger* of the eastern direction.

The leader of the western *tenger* was Han Hormasta, the leader of the eastern *tenger* was Atai Ulaan, and there was such anger between them that at last they fought. Han Hormasta won, tearing Atai Ulaan to bits. But when the pieces drifted down to earth, they turned into evil spirits and disease.

Soon the people were in despair. There was a powerful female shaman, Sharnaihan Shara, who threw her drumstick to the sky with such magical force that it landed on the table of Manzan Gurme Toodei, mother of all the sky spirits. Manzan Gurme Toodei took out her shaman mirror and saw the perils from evil and disease facing humanity. She called a meeting of the *tenger* to decide how to save humanity.

Han Hormasta had three sons. He decided to send the middle one, Bukhe Beligte, down to earth. Reborn as a human, he would become the protector of the people.

Meanwhile, on earth, there lived a poor husband and wife named Sengelen Noyon and Naran Goohon. They had no dog, no livestock, and practically no possessions, and survived by gathering wild onions and garlic, netting small fish and catching rabbits with snares. But despite their poverty, they were overjoyed when Naran Goohon found that she would have a child.

Soon after the baby was born, he lifted his right hand as though about to strike someone, bent his left leg, then looked at his parents with his right eye wide open and his left eye squinted. And to his parents' amazement, the baby spoke.

"I hold up my right hand to show that I will always strike my enemies. I bend my left leg to show that I will always kick my enemies. My open right eye shows that I will always see the right path. My squinted left eye shows that I will always see through deceit."

Thus was Bukhe Beligte reborn as a human being.

Meanwhile, the evil spirits had discovered this fact. Meeting in their barren, sunless home, they plotted to kill the newborn child. They sent a giant rat with a bronze muzzle to kill him. But the baby struck the rat so hard that it shattered into ninety mice.

Then the evil spirits sent a raven with an iron beak and claws to kill the baby. The baby smashed the raven into bits and threw the bits all the way back to where the evil spirits were meeting.

Last, the evil spirits sent a mosquito as large as a horse to kill the baby. The baby cried, "Be forever hungry and fly among the grass!" and struck it so hard that the giant mosquito shattered into a cloud of gnats.

The evil spirits were stunned. Their enemy had destroyed three monsters—and he was still just a baby!

So they went to their foul leader and cried, "O most powerful evil one, a magical boy has been born. We need to kill him, smash him, crush him!"

"I shall do this," their leader snapped.

He took on the guise of a human shaman and appeared before Sengelen Noyon and his wife. "I am a shaman who has come to help and protect your new son."

But as soon as the baby saw who had entered, he started screaming.

The shaman said, "Why is the boy making so much noise? Is he ill?"

He approached the cradle, ready to snatch up the baby. But as soon as he grew near, his disguise vanished. The hideous creature gnashed his iron fangs and roared, "I shall cut off your life and eat your soul!"

The baby simply grabbed the iron muzzle of the monster and kicked out so hard that the evil thing's head flew off.

The evil spirits left him alone after that.

The young hero grew so rapidly that he grew as much in a day as ordinary children grew in a year. He was never ill, never tired, and played happily every day.

One day Sengelen Noyon's older brother came to visit. When he saw that they had a child he was very happy. "But the boy needs playmates," he said. "Let me take this child with me so that he can grow up and play with my own two sons."

The boy's parents agreed.

When Sargal Noyon got home, he held a feast to celebrate the boy's arrival. He told his guests, "Up to this time this boy has no name. To whoever gives him a name, I will give meat and fat in exchange."

An old man leaning on a walking stick said, "The boy is sweaty and muddy. Why not call him Nuhata Nurgai, 'slimy face'?"

Everybody laughed. It was a silly name, a perfect name for a boy who had not yet earned an adult name. And so it was the newly named Nuhata Nurgai who watched Sargal Noyon's animals and played with Sargal Noyon's own sons, Altan Shagai and Mungun Shagai. They were older than the boy and were forever trying his strength and the quickness of his mind. But Nuhata Nurgai never failed. He grew and thrived.

Now, the ruler of the northwestern lands, Temeen Ulaan, had a beautiful daughter, Tumen Jargalan. He announced that he would give his daughter in marriage to any man who was able to win three contests of strength. Warriors came from far and wide for the contest. Nuhata Nurgai also was there, wearing old clothes and riding a mouse-brown colt.

Then the contests began. For the first, Nuhata Nurgai picked up a boulder and threw it so hard that it shattered into flints. For the second, he uprooted a pine tree and threw it so hard that it shattered into splinters. For the third, he pulled up an ephedra bush and threw it so far that no one could see it land. No one else could match him, and so Nuhata Nurgai took Tumen Jargalan home as his wife.

But he left behind a jealous rival, his uncle, Hara Zutan, who hated him from that moment on.

Soon after returning home, Nuhata Nurgai set out again, riding his mouse-brown colt. He reached a country where its ruler, Shaazgai Bayan, was promising to give his daughter in marriage to any man who could defeat a giant warrior.

The giant had a powerful body, with a chest as wide as the sea. His armor was of black forged iron, his bow was the trunk of a tree, and his quiver was made of planks. But Nuhata Nurgai dodged his arrows, caught him up, and threw him out of sight. He took Shaazgai Bayan's daughter, Urmai Goohon, back to his home, and as the custom was for their people, she became his second wife.

Tumen Jargalan and Urmai Goohon got along well together. But they couldn't understand why Nuhata Nurgai seemed to want the three of them to have a very dull life together.

They didn't know that their husband was only waiting for the right time.

And then one night Nuhata Nurgai climbed to the summit of Mount Sumber and did a ritual to honor the *tenger*. Then and there he changed into his true form as Bukhe Beligte, with a warrior's strong face and body, blazing eyes, and long black hair.

Looking down from the upper world, Han Hormasta saw his son and nodded. He was ready. So Han Hormasta sent down a warrior's horse and equipment. The horse was a bay, with hooves like iron and legs that would never tire. Lightning glittered in its eyes, and its name was Beligen, "gift."

The warrior who had now become Geser grabbed the red reins of the horse, put his feet into the silver stirrups, sat upon the silver saddle, and rode down into the world.

Sengelen Noyon and Naran Goohon rejoiced to know they had borne such a heroic son, and Tumen Jargalan and Urmai Goohon rejoiced to realize they were married to such a handsome warrior.

One day Geser went hunting in the Altai Mountains. After three days of hunting he had not found a single deer. On the fourth day he saw a spotted deer running in the forest and followed it. Just as he was about to shoot, a young man on a chestnut horse dashed out of the forest and shot the deer, swung it up on his horse, and galloped away.

Geser rode after him, angry at losing the deer. They came to the shores of Lake Baikal, but the young man never stopped. He rode his horse right into the water and disappeared.

Geser left his horse and warily followed, down into the land of Uha Loson, chief of the water spirits. The rider of the chestnut horse was none other than his daughter, Alma Mergen, who had disguised herself as a young man while hunting. Uha Loson was delighted to see Geser, because he had known Geser's father, Han Hormasta, quite well. Furthermore, they had once agreed that his daughter and Han Hormasta's son would be married. According to this custom, Alma Mergen became Geser's third wife.

Geser and she rode to his home, where he built three houses for his three wives. All was happiness for a time. Geser would say to his family, "Is the sun in the sky beautiful, or is Tumen Jargalan beautiful? Is the sun in the heavens beautiful, or is Urmai Goohon beautiful? Is the golden sun beautiful, or is Alma Mergen beautiful?"

But life could not stay peaceful for Geser for long. The head of Atai Ulaan, the *tenger* who had been slain and dismembered by Han Hormasta, had turned into the monster Arhan Chotgor. Now the monster was near Geser's home, hiding in wait.

Arhan Chotgor grabbed the first man who came by. It wasn't Geser, but his uncle Hara Zutan, who still hated Geser. Terrified, Hara Zutan told the monster, "I will help you hurt him. I will break Geser's bow and arrows. I will steal his wife Urmai Goohon and you can have Tumen Jargalan."

The monster agreed. Late that night Hara Zutan stole into Geser's house, broke the antler arrowheads off Geser's arrows, cut his bowstring, broke his sword, and smashed the tip of his spear.

When Geser came home and found himself weaponless, he dared not wait, not with the lives of two wives at stake. He caught up with Arhan Chotgor and fought with all his skill, without weapons. At last he managed to break the monster's neck and slay him.

Then he went after Hara Zutan, who fell to his knees before Geser, promising, "I won't do anything like this again!"

Since this was Geser's uncle, the hero reluctantly forgave Hara Zutan and sent him home.

But his trouble with Atai Ulaan hadn't ended just yet. Another demonic creature, Gal Nurman Khan, had sprung from the first vertebra of Atai Ulaan's severed neck. This monster sprang up from the dry, desolate home of the evil spirits and attacked the human world, setting things on fire wherever he went.

Geser tracked Gal Nurman Khan to his wilderness home, and they fought. The fiery demon was stronger than Geser, and this time things looked bleak for the hero. But during their fight, the force of it sent a large chunk of rock crashing down from a cliff onto the evil being and crushed him.

Geser knew that Gal Nurman Khan wasn't living alone. He went on to fight and slay the evil demon wife and demon child as well.

As time passed, Geser's fame grew. He tracked down the monster deer Orgoli, who had swallowed forty people whole. Orgoli tried to swallow Geser as well, but as Orgoli tried to suck him in, Geser wedged his spear crosswise in the deer's mouth and held on. Drawing his sword, he chopped off Orgoli's head. Out from the deer's vast body crawled the forty people Orgoli had swallowed, saved now by Geser.

Many other adventures followed in the following years. Geser was not too proud to seek help when it was needed. Once, when he knew he could not defeat a monster, the powerful Sherem Minaata Khan, Geser listened to the advice of his wives and went to the upper world. There he asked his immortal grandmother for aid. She gave him a stick that she used to beat fleece for felt making. Sure enough, that simple little stick was the one thing that could slay Sherem Minaata Khan. One blow over the monster's head, and he lay dead.

Returning home, Geser said to his wives, "Now that it is a peaceful time, I will fill my quiver with arrows."

But there can never be rest for a hero. Geser's life was forever full of adventures, far too many to be recounted here. He defeated monsters, demons, and enemies of the realm, and with his efforts continually kept peace and happiness for the people.

And he and his wives lived happily for three days and three years—which was to be the space between the hero's never-ending adventures.

Sources

David-Neel, Alexandra, and the Lama Yongden. *Superhuman Life of Gesar of Ling.* Boston: Shambhala Books, 1987.

Wallace, Zara, and Elizabeth Cook, eds. *Gesar! The Wondrous Adventures of King Gesar.* Berkeley: Dharma, 1991.

THE EIGHT-HEADED SERPENT
A Myth from Japan

Susanoh is the brother of Amateras, the goddess of the sun, who causes trouble for her in Chapter 3. That he's exiled to earth doesn't bother him, and he instantly switches from deity to warrior hero. He is faced with the same mission that many a mythic or folkloric hero has faced: the many-headed serpent that eats young women. Many-headed snakes or dragons turn up around the world, from the Greek Hydra to monsters in African tales. It is impossible to list the number of tales in which a hero is promised the hand of the princess if he slays the dragon.

But Susanoh is no fool. He gets the monster drunk first, then slays it. The same motif turns up in a tale from China in which a lone girl does the same to a dragon, then cuts off its head. And the hero Odysseus gets out of the Cyclops' cave by first getting the giant drunk, then blinding him.

And as in any good tale of the hero slaying the monster to gain the hand of the princess, there's a proper ending of "happily ever after."

*S*usanoh was the brother of Amateras, the goddess of the sun. But whereas she was a lady goddess, he very soon won a reputation for himself of being a boisterous fellow, even a brawler—very much, the other gods decided, like a human.

So the gods got together and exiled the wild Susanoh from heaven. He landed on mortal soil, near the town of Izumo, and after the first shock found that he wasn't really displeased about that at all.

Then Susanoh heard that every year a serpent with eight heads ate one of the town's young women. This year the chosen victim was supposed to be Princess Kusinada. Susanoh took one look at her and made an offer to her parents: He would marry Princess Kusinada if he could save her life.

Her parents accepted his offer with great relief.

Following Susanoh's instructions, the townspeople built a great fence with eight gates, and placed a jar filled with sake at each gate.

Then the eight-headed serpent slithered up to the fence. He stopped, eight heads flickering their tongues. Then each of his heads went to one of the gates and started to drink the sake.

Of course, with eight heads and only one stomach, the monster quickly got drunk and collapsed, snoring from eight mouths. Susanoh took up a sword and calmly cut him into eight neat pieces while he was sleeping.

That was the end of the peril. Susanoh married Princess Kusinada, as had been promised, and he built a big palace in Izumo, where they lived happily ever after.

Source

Davis, F. Hadland. *Myths and Legends of Japan*. London: George G. Harrap, 1913.
Piggott, Juliet. *Japanese Mythology*. London: Hamlyn, 1969.

KABAI AND KUBIL
A Myth from Dauan Island, the Torres Strait

Can any of this myth have a basis in fact? On Dauan Island there was said to be, at least up to the 1960s, a piece of pumice trapped in a mango tree—the pumice left by Kabai. The nearby coconut tree was said to be the descendant of the one he planted. The islands of the Torres Straits belong to Australia, although the people are not the same racial stock as those of Australia; they are mostly Polynesian rather than Melanesian.

As for the structure of the tale, Kabai's journey to the spirit world has its connections to the otherworld journeyings of shamans around the world, though those are often much more difficult, involving drumming rituals or even the shaman's temporary death. See the myth of Inanna in Chapter 2 for a journey to the underworld.

Kabai's casual slipping from this world to that is also reminiscent of the many Celtic tales of travel from this world to that of Faerie. Also similar to motifs in those tales of Faerie is the altered sense of time, in which what seems only a day is actually several years.

*K*abai lived in the days before everyone had quite figured out the natural laws. And even though he had magical gifts, that didn't stop the rest of the folk in his village from arguing with him. What they argued about was this: *kubil*, darkness.

"Sun and moon are two separate things," Kabai stated. "And *kubil* has little to do with either."

"Not so, not so," everyone else cried. "There is only the one thing, *kubil*, and darkness changes its shape and nature into light now and then so that it looks like sun or moon to us. Darkness is night, and darkness is day—it's all the same."

"I don't believe that," Kabai said. "And I'll go and find out."

Kabai took up his *topi lani*, the bag that held his magical tools, and went down to the beach. There he took out a feather from the bag and murmured over it. He tossed the feather into the sea, and it became a fine canoe.

"Zei, southwest wind, take me to the next island."

He came ashore on Daudai, spent the night there, then cried again, "Zei, southwest wind, take me to the next island."

And so Kabai traveled on and on. At last there were no more islands, but still he sailed. And finally Kabai reached Kibukut, island of the spirits, there at the very edge of the world. The moment he stepped onto land, his hair turned white, for no mortal man enters that realm untouched. Kabai murmured over his canoe, turning it back to a feather. Placing the feather back into his magic bag, he set out to see what he could learn.

For a long while he saw nothing much, no signs that anyone had ever lived here on Kibukut. But then Kabai reached a house. Odd, odd—not a footprint showed anywhere in the dirt around, yet the house did not look abandoned. He entered and found several skeletons lying peacefully on the floor. Nothing else was to be seen, and Kabai sighed and sat down outside to wait. The spirits were clearly those who could appear only after dark.

Sure enough, with the setting of the sun came a stirring within the house. Kabai got to his feet and reentered. He found the skeletons replaced by spirits, ghosts who looked very much like ordinary humans—yet, of course, were far from that.

"Who are you?" they asked. "Where are you from? And what do you want?"

"I am Kabai. I come from the island of Dauan. And I have come to settle an argument and learn the truth about the basic laws of things."

"Speak."

"The people of Dauan say that sun and moon are one and the same and that day and night are only different forms of *kubil*. This does not sound possible to me. I say that sun and moon are separate things, as are light and darkness, day and night." He paused. "Who is right?"

"You are right," the spirits told him. "Sun and moon are separate things, and *kubil*, darkness in all its forms, is still not the same as light."

"I thank you, but what proof is there to offer the people?"

"In our gardens grow three types of plant. One belongs to the sun, one to the moon, and one to *kubil*, to darkness. We will give you some of each to take back with you to your people."

Kabai turned his magic feather back into a canoe. The spirits placed three types of plant in the canoe. "This is coconut, light-colored as sunlight. It belongs to the sun. This is taro, not light, not dark. It belongs to the moon. And this is sugarcane, dark as the night. It belongs to *kubil*, to darkness."

Kabai got into his canoe. "Naiger, northeast wind, take me home. Spirits," he added, "shorten my journey to Dauan so these plants may live on that island."

The spirits agreed. The canoe was caught by Naiger, the northwest wind, and sped over the ocean so swiftly that a big, round chunk of pumice, that lava stone so filled with air it floats, came washing into the canoe. Kabai used it to prop the coconut plant in place, then sat back and wondered at his speed.

Ha, here was Dauan! His journey to Kibukut had taken many long days, yet here he was home again in only a day.

But how long had he stayed on Kibukut? How long had he been away? When Kabai had set out from Dauan, his wife had been newly pregnant, yet here she was now with a near-grown girl at her side, their daughter.

"I have named her Kadau, as we agreed so long ago," Kabai's wife told him. "I always knew you would return to meet her. I knew your magic was strong enough for that."

Kabai hugged his family to him joyfully. Then he went to settle his argument with the people. "I have come from Kibukut, island of the spirits," he told them. "And here is coconut, plant of the sun, taro, plant of the moon, and sugarcane, plant of *kubil*."

He needed to say nothing more. Here was proof that sun and day were separate things and that *kubil* was not the same as daylight. For what man would argue with spirits?

Kabai went home to his wife and daughter. Since the pumice had come from the sea, he placed it in a tidal pool. He had given the people the taro and sugarcane plants, but he planted the coconut near him.

And then Kabai, his wife and daughter, walked to a large, flat rock that was just the right size for sitting, and sat. For they had years to discuss and many tales to tell. And now, with Kabai's journey ended, there was time to tell them.

Source

Lawrie, Margaret, coll. and trans. *Myths and Legends of Torres Straits*. New York: Taplinger, 1971.

MAUI
A Myth of Hawaii

Maui is usually considered a demigod, a hero, and a trickster. Notice the way he overcomes his poor fishing skills in this myth by tricking his brothers out of their catch. But then he uses a magical fishhook to prove himself truly a hero by fishing up the islands of Hawaii. In fact, the implication here is that if his brothers hadn't panicked, there might have been even more land than the islands.

Another example of a panic-stricken fisherman turns up in the tale of "Thor and the Midgard Serpent" in Chapter 4.

*U*ntold ages ago, Maui was born, more than human, less than truly divine. His father, some say, was the guardian of the path to the heavens, and his mother, some say, was the guardian of the path to the netherworld.

Maui was the smallest of his family, but he had the quickest of minds and a bold sense of humor.

Now, Maui wasn't a particularly good fisherman. His brothers were much more skilled, and laughed at him for his lack of luck.

They should have known better than to mock him. In revenge, Maui positioned his boat very carefully. Now, whenever one of his brothers began to pull in a fish, he would distract them all, giving him the chance to pull his line across theirs, stealing their fish.

Soon enough, Maui's brothers began to marvel at their younger brother's sudden turn of luck. However, they eventually caught on to his trickery.

"You fish thief!" they cried. "We will not let you come fishing with us again."

Needless to say, Maui's fishing luck dropped off after that, or rather, fell back to normal. At last his mother sent him to his father.

"He has many special fishhooks. One of them is sure to help improve your luck."

But Maui decided to get more than even the most special of fishhooks. When he went to his father, he instead said, "I have come to borrow the magical hook that's known as Manaiakalani, the hook fastened to the heavens."

His father might have been surprised by the request, but he gave Maui that hook.

A woodcut depicts Maui in the hands of his mother, Taranga, who later cast him into the sea. In a myth from Hawaii, Maui uses a magical fishhook to successfully fish up the islands of Hawaii.

Maui returned with his hook and joined his brothers in another fishing expedition. But they didn't want him with them. Laughing at Maui, they threw him out of the boat, so he had to swim back to land. But when they returned from their expedition, they were empty-handed.

"Instead of throwing me overboard," Maui scolded, "if you had only let me join you, you would have had far better luck."

The brothers looked at each other and shrugged. One of them said, "Any catch is better than no catch at all." So they allowed him to join them for one more chance. They paddled far into the deep ocean and threw their lines overboard.

But to the brothers' dismay, they caught nothing worth eating, only the occasional shark. Turning to Maui, they snapped, "Where are the fish you promised us?"

"Watch and learn," Maui said.

He threw the magical hook Manaiakalani into the ocean. Chanting a spell of power, Maui commanded the hook to catch the Great Fish.

All at once, wild waves surged up.

"Paddle with all your strength!" Maui commanded his brothers. "Do not look back!"

For two days Maui held the magic line and hook taut while his brothers kept paddling furiously. Then from under the sea rose the tops of great mountains, a series of sharp peaks breaking the ocean's surface.

"Keep paddling!" Maui cried.

He pulled with all his might, and dragged the peaks even farther out of the water.

But the suspense was too much for one of his brothers. He gazed back and gasped at the sight of the rising land. In his astonishment, he stopped paddling. The magic line slackened in Maui's hands, then snapped. The magic hook Manaiakalani was lost forever beneath the sea.

Maui was furious at his brothers. "Here I was trying to raise a vast land. But thanks to your weakness, all I have to show for my efforts are these few islands."

But they were very special islands. For that is how the islands of Hawaii came to be.

Sources

Andersen, Johannes C. *Myths and Legends of the Polynesians*. Rutland, VT: Charles E. Tuttle, 1969.

Westervelt, W. D. *Hawaiian Legends of Volcanoes*. Rutland, VT, and Tokyo, Japan: Charles E. Tuttle, 1963.

CUCHULAIN OF ULSTER
A Myth from Ancient Ireland

Cuchulain may or may not have existed somewhere in the first few centuries B.C.E. But as he is portrayed, he has become a traditional hero, born of a human mother but with the sun god, Lugh, as his father. For more about Lugh, see his story in Chapter 4.

Cuchulain is at the center of the great Irish epic, *The Tain*, which centers on a disastrous cattle raid. His story contains many heroic adventures, too many to be detailed here, as well as a prophecy: He will perform great deeds but die young.

Bricriu of the Bitter Tongue is a gadfly who always seems to be behind any story of trouble at King Conor's court. Here he's happy to cause trouble over who should have the "champion's portion," a specific and favored cut of whatever roast was being served. At Celtic feasts in ancient Ireland, it was the custom for men to leave their swords outside, but since they kept their knives, there was still a chance for the sort of fighting that the king here wisely refuses to allow.

Where King Conor may be based on an actual ruler of Ulster, King Ailill of Connaught and, even more so, Curoi of Kerry have clearly become people out of myth. Their tests are all magical ordeals, from the monster cats to the ritual and eerie beheadings. The latter part of the Celtic myth, with Curoi disguised as a giant, was later reinterpreted in Arthurian lore as the story of Sir Gawain and the Green Knight, in which the magician-king is replaced by an even more mythic figure who may well represent a medieval version of the Lord of the Forest, the fertility deity of the woods.

*N*ow, no one ever denied that Cuchulain was the nephew of King Conor of Ulster, since he was the son of the king's sister, Dechtire. But it was said—and, for all anyone knew, said truly, since Dechtire was dead and had never spoken of the boy's sire—that his father was no mortal man, but the great god Lugh of the sun's splendor.

Whether or not he was half divine, Cuchulain was raised by his uncle, and even as a young boy he showed signs that he would grow into a true hero. Indeed, by the time Cuchulain was seventeen, he had no equal among the warriors of Ulster. And since he was a handsome youngster, Conor's men were glad that he was a modest sort who never looked for trouble with other men's wives. Still, they were also glad when he won the hand of Emer, daughter of Forgall the Wily.

The warrior Cuchulain rides his chariot into battle. In the myth from ancient Ireland, Cuchulain proves himself through a series of magical ordeals and earns the title "champion of heroes of all Ireland." (*Mary Evans Picture Library*)

But not everyone appreciates peace and tranquility. One of King Conor's men was known as Bricriu of the Bitter Tongue, since he forever liked making barbed remarks and delighted in making mischief. Inviting the members of King Conor's court to dinner, Bricriu arranged that a contest should arise over who should have the "champion's portion," knowing that there were three hot-blooded young men who could claim that honor. They were Laegire, Conall Cearnach, and Cuchulain.

So successful was Bricriu in playing to their pride and to the secret insecurity of young men that there was nearly a fight there and then. King Conor, furious at this breaking of the laws of hospitality, ordered the three hot-bloods to take their argument elsewhere. And to avoid a bloody fight, the three heroes went off to submit their claims to the championship of Ireland to King Ailill of Connaught.

Ailill put the heroes to a strange test. Their dinner was served them in a separate room. Suddenly three monstrous cats, black as night and blazing red of eyes, burst into the room. The startled Laegire and Conall leaped up among the rafters, but Cuchulain stood his ground. He waited till a cat attacked, then struck it a sharp blow with his sword. With that, the three monstrous cats disappeared.

Cuchulain claimed that he had won the championship. But Laegire and Conall protested fiercely that they had been too startled to have a chance to properly react and that this test had been an unfair one.

King Ailill must have sighed with frustration, or perhaps shaken his head wryly, remembering his own youth. But without any argument, he sent the three rivals off to Curoi of Kerry, who was a just and wise man—and one who was wise in the ways of magic. Curoi ordered that the three stand watch in turn outside his castle that night.

First it was Laegire's turn. Suddenly he was confronted by a huge giant, a great boulder of a being who hurled spears that were the trunks of trees at him. The young man dodged and tried to attack, but the giant reached down, caught him up like an unwanted kitten, and hurled him over the castle wall. Laegire landed with a thump, too winded and bruised to go back outside.

"You are no champion!" Conall sneered, and went to take his turn on guard.

But he, too, was confronted by the huge giant, who hurled those terrible spears at him. Conall, too, dodged and tried to attack. But he met with the same fate as Laegire, being caught up and hurled over the castle wall. He, too, landed too winded and bruised to go back outside.

Cuchulain didn't sneer or boast. He simply went outside to stand watch. The giant loomed out of the darkness and began hurling his terrible tree-trunk spears. Cuchulain dodged but waited to attack, biding his time. Only when the giant moved in to seize him did Cuchulain cast his own spear. He pierced the giant to the heart—and the giant vanished.

But that was not the end of his trials. The young man was beset by monsters on every side, and fought fiercely with sword and spear to survive. Then a great winged creature came lunging down at him. Cuchulain sprang up with a great hero leap, thrust his hand down the thing's throat, and tore out its heart. As the monsters disappeared as the giant had done, Cuchulain made another great hero leap over the castle wall in triumph.

"Not fair!" was the cry of his rivals. "He used magic to win, where we had none."

"So be it," Curoi said. "Return to King Conor's court at Armagh and await my judgment."

Off they went. And there were all the Ulster heroes in King Conor's great hall one night. Suddenly a stranger entered, hideous and gigantic, eyes of blazing yellow. One mighty hand clasped a great, gleaming axe.

"What business have you here?" King Conor asked as calmly as though this were just an ordinary man.

The stranger replied in a voice that boomed like thunder, "Behold my axe! Whoever grasps it today may behead me—if I may, in the same way, cut off his head tomorrow. Come, who will take up the challenge? If there is none who dare face me, I will state that Ulster has lost her courage and her honor!"

Laegire sprang to his feet, shouting, "Ulster has not lost her courage! I accept your challenge."

With a shrug the giant laid his head on a block. Laegire swung the axe with all his force and with one blow severed the giant's head from his body. But to the horror of everyone in the hall, the giant got to his feet, took his axe in one and his head in the other, and strode from the hall.

The following night the giant returned, head on his shoulders, as sound as ever. But Laegire's courage failed him, and he sneaked off into the night.

"So *this* is the courage of Ulster!" the giant sneered.

Conall Cearnach sprang to his feet. "I will not fail you!" he shouted.

Once again the giant knelt, and once again he was beheaded. Once again he stalked off, head in hand—and once again, when he returned, there was no Conall Cearnach to be found.

"Is there no true warrior in all Ulster?" the giant jeered.

"There is," Cuchulain said quietly.

As the other two had done, he cut off the giant's head at one stroke. As before, the giant strode away with head in hand.

The next night Conor and his men waited to see what Cuchulain would do. He did nothing, save sit quietly. To Conor he murmured, "This night will surely see my death. But I would rather die than break my sworn word."

The giant strode into the hall, swinging his axe. "Where is Cuchulain?" he cried.

Cuchulain got to his feet. "Here I am."

"Ah, poor boy!" the giant said. "The fear of death lies heavy on you. At least you have kept your word and have not failed me."

As the giant stood with the great axe ready, Cuchulain knelt to receive the blow, and laid his head on the block.

But the giant wasn't satisfied. "Don't cringe. Stretch out your neck."

"Slay me quickly," Cuchulain retorted. "I did not keep you waiting last night."

The giant raised his axe till it crashed through the rafters of the hall, then swept it down with a crash like thunder. The men of Ulster closed their eyes in horror. But when they looked for Cuchulain, they cried out in surprise. The axe hadn't so much as scratched him. It had struck the ground instead, and the young man knelt where he was, unharmed.

The giant was no longer the giant. Smiling and leaning on his axe was none other than Curoi of Kerry.

"Rise," he told Cuchulain. "I proclaim that the championship of the heroes of Ireland is yours from this day forth, and the champion's portion at all feasts; and to your wife I adjudge the first place among all the women of Ulster. Woe to any who dares dispute this decision!"

With that, Curoi vanished. The warriors with one voice proclaimed Cuchulain champion of the heroes of all Ireland, and he kept that title for all his days.

Sources

Gregory, Lady. *Cuchulain of Muirthemne*. Gerrards Cross, England: Colin Smythe, 1970.
MacCana, Proinsias. *Celtic Mythology*. London: Hamlyn, 1970.

PERSEUS
A Myth from Ancient Greece

This myth begins with a primal theme: the father who is warned that his son, or grandson, will slay him. It appears in the Greek myth of Cronos and Zeus, in the story of Jason (of the Argonauts), and in many folktales from around the world. Psychiatrists may think that this theme represents a father's basic fear that he will be replaced by his son, the younger, stronger man, but such interpretations are outside the scope of this book.

The next familiar motif is Danae locked up in a bronze tower with no door and only one small tower: the princess in the glass tower. For another use of the motif, see the Polynesian myth "Pare and Huto," in Chapter 2.

Of course, the tower prison proves ineffectual, as it always does with this motif. So another familiar motif is added, when Danae and Perseus are shut into the chest and cast into the sea. Here is yet another variation of the baby in the basket in the water, like the story of Gwion in Chapter 2 and, as mentioned earlier, those of Moses, Superman, and others.

Next comes a classic quest, in this case for the head of Medusa. As in many a quest, the hero has helpers along the way—in this case, divine ones, none other than the goddess of wisdom and the god of messengers and trickery. Whether or not the original tellers realized it, these are a perfect combination for a story that depends on both aspects.

Medusa, by the way, was turned into a snake-headed Gorgon for the crime of desecrating Athena's temple by sleeping with Poseidon in it. She has, ironically, become something of a designer's darling. Her image can be found on everything from furniture from the 1800s to the modern scarves of the late Gianni Versace. She shares with the medieval monster the basilisk, the ability to turn people to stone.

The Graeae are a strange lot, the three sisters born with gray hair and with one eye (and in some versions, one tooth as well) that they share. They are said to be the daughters of Ceto and Phorcus, and are the sisters of the Gorgons. They are also supposed to be the protectors of the Gorgons, though they don't seem to serve that function in this myth. Are they, perhaps, odd versions of the three Fates that turn up in Greek and Norse mythology? Or do they represent a weird personification of old age?

The gifts that the Stygian nymphs give Perseus have their parallels elsewhere. In particular, the cap of darkness that will make him invisible also turns up as the tarncap in Norse mythology, and cloaks and caps of invisibility turn up frequently in the world's folklore as well.

Next comes the rescue of Andromeda, although with the use of Medusa's head, it seems almost too easy! The theme of the damsel in distress, of course, has been used so many times in so many ways that they can't be listed here.

The fulfillment of the prophecy made to Perseus' father, rather than being the crux of the story, comes true in an almost offhanded way when Perseus accidentally kills the old man during a discus-throwing contest.

There once lived a king named Acrisius whose daughter was named Danae. But an oracle warned Acrisius that a son of Danae would be the one to kill him. Loving life more than his daughter, Acrisius locked Danae in a bronze tower with no door and only one small tower. Now, the king thought, his daughter would never marry or have children. He would be safe from the prophecy.

Acrisius had not reckoned with the gods. A bright shower of gold blazed in through the window in Danae's tower and turned into the splendid Zeus, chief of the gods. God and mortal woman loved each other, and with time Danae bore a son, whom she named Perseus.

When Acrisius found Danae with her son, he was terrified and furious. He would not let the prophecy come true! So he had Danae and Perseus shut into a large chest and cast out to sea.

But the chest did not sink. It floated safely over the waves to the island of Seriphos, where they were rescued by King Polydectes. Perseus grew up to become a fine, clever young man. But King Polydectes grew obsessed with Danae's beauty. He asked for her hand, but she refused him. Polydectes would have wed her by force—but Perseus stood between them.

What could the furious Polydectes do? He couldn't simply have Perseus slain. That would not be a kingly act. Instead, he secretly plotted to be rid of the inconvenient young man. The king announced that he would be marrying another royal woman and that everyone who was loyal to him must bring a suitably noble present. Perseus alone could bring nothing, because, as Polydectes knew very well, Perseus owned nothing. But this was the king's chance. He pretended to be offended, claiming that the young man to whom he'd given hospitality was useless and disloyal—knowing perfectly well what would happen.

Sure enough, the insulted Perseus cried that he could bring Polydectes anything the king might wish.

"Then bring me the head of the Gorgon Medusa!" King Polydectes stated.

"Done!" Perseus retorted.

Only as he set out on his quest did he discover what he was hunting. There were three Gorgons, Eryale, Stheno, and Medusa. They had once been human sisters, but they had offended the gods, and now they laired together, three monsters. Medusa was the most terrible of the three—but also the only one of the three who was still mortal. She had writhing serpents for hair, and her stare could turn a man instantly to stone. Perseus secretly despaired, wondering how he could ever take her head.

Fortunately for Perseus, the goddess Athena hated Medusa. She appeared before the startled Perseus, a tall, handsome, cool-eyed woman, and beside her stood a golden-haired young man wearing winged sandals. This was Hermes, the messenger of the gods.

"We have decided to help you slay Medusa," Perseus was told.

Hermes gave him the winged sandals and the deadly metal sickle that Cronos had once used to overpower his father, Uranus. Athena gave him a highly polished shield, shiny as a mirror. Perseus would be able to slay Medusa by looking only at her reflection, and not be turned to stone.

"Now you must find the Graeae," Hermes said. "You must win from them the way to the Stygian nymphs."

With that, the two gods vanished.

Perseus set out to find the Graeae. When he reached their cave, he hid, watching them. What strange beings they were! They seemed almost like ancient women, but they had only one eye among the three of them, and took turns using it—when they weren't busy fighting over whose turn it was.

As soon as one took out the eye to give to another, Perseus sprang from hiding and snatched the eye from them. "Tell me how to find the Stygian nymphs, or I won't give you back your eye," he said.

Grumbling, the Graeae gave him directions. Giving them back their eye, Perseus flew off on the winged sandals.

The Stygian nymphs provided friendlier than the Graeae. They gave Perseus the cap of darkness, to make him invisible, and a magic wallet in which he could safely place Medusa's head, then told him how to reach the Gorgons' lair.

Perseus flew on, following their directions, until he came to a mountainous island. To his horror, what he had taken to be rocks were stone figures that used to be men. He'd reached the Gorgons' lair.

Perseus raised his shield, using it as a mirror, and saw Medusa and her sisters asleep. Hastily he put on the cap of darkness and flew down. Still watching only in the shield-mirror, he swung the sickle and felt it cut through Medusa's neck. Not daring to look away from the image in the shield, he forced Medusa's head into the magic wallet. As Medusa's sisters woke to attack, Perseus flew quickly away.

Perseus did one kindness on the flight back to Seriphos. He met Atlas, the huge Titan who had been sentenced by Zeus to hold up the sky, and, at the Titan's weary request, showed Atlas Medusa's head, turning him to stone so that he could no longer feel the weight of his burden.

Perseus flew on, skimming the seacoast. Suddenly he saw what looked like a lovely statue chained to a rock—but as Perseus flew lower, he realized that it wasn't a statue, but a beautiful young woman.

"Who are you?" he cried. "Why are you chained here?"

She turned a tearful face up to him. "I am Andromeda, and I am here because my mother boasted about me. She claimed that I was more beautiful than the Nereids, the nymphs of the sea. That angered Poseidon, who proclaimed that I must be sacrificed to a sea monster."

Even as she finished, a hideous creature rose from the sea, tentacles waving and beak clashing. Andromeda screamed, but Perseus simply pulled Medusa's head out of the wallet, and the sea monster turned to stone. It fell back into the sea and crumbled to pieces.

"It, not you, was the sacrifice," Perseus said.

Cutting Andromeda's chains, he flew with her to her father, King Cepheus of Phoenicia. By this time the young people were clinging to each other happily. And when Perseus asked Andromeda's hand in marriage Cepheus gladly agreed.

So Perseus took Andromeda in his arms once more and set off for Seriphos. But he wasn't Hermes, to fly around the world without getting weary. On the way, Perseus and Andromeda stopped to rest at Larisa. There Perseus tried his hand in some athletic games. But when he threw the discus, the wind caught it. The discus hit an old man in the head and slew him.

It was none other than King Acrisius, he who had tried to prevent Danae from having a child. The prophecy had come true no matter what the king had tried to prevent it. Perseus mourned for the proper while, though it might have been difficult to mourn for a grandfather who had cast his daughter and grandson into the sea to die.

When they arrived at Seriphos, Perseus learned that King Polydectes had never married and had forced Danae to serve as his handmaiden.

Furious, Perseus strode into the palace and shouted out, "Let all who are my friends shield their eyes!"

With that, he raised Medusa's head. In an instant, Polydectes and his courtiers were changed to statues. Danae happily rushed into her son's arms.

Perseus and Andromeda lived happily for many years, and their descendants became great kings. Perhaps the greatest of these was the famous Hercules, the strongest man in the world.

Sources

Kerenyi, Karl. *The Gods of the Greeks.* London: Thames and Hudson, 1985.
Larousse World Mythology. Secaucus: Chartwell Books, 1977.

SIGURD
A Myth from Ancient Norway

A Viking believed that no man could live without luck, and so this myth begins with the old king knowing he must die because his luck is gone. The loss of his luck ties in with the breaking of his sword.

The broken sword that must be mended, the sword that only a hero may wield, is a familiar theme in mythology. There is, for instance, a broken sword in the Germanic version of this myth. This sword was originally stuck by Wotan—the Germanic Odhinn—into a tree, to be withdrawn only by a hero, Sigmund, the father of Siegfried, the Germanic Sigurd. The sword in the tree is reminiscent of the Arthurian sword in the stone, which could only be withdrawn by the rightful King of England. In his epic fantasy, *The Lord of the Rings*, J. R. R. Tolkien also made use of the motif of the broken sword, which is inherited by the hero Aragorn, who will reforge it.

The queen and her maid change clothes, pretending to be each other, but cannot fool the Danish king. The idea of figuring out who is the real queen (or princess, or noblewoman) by means of odd questions is also found in folklore, in tales such as the Norwegian "The White Bear" and the German "The Goose Girl."

The next theme in the myth is Sigurd's choosing of a horse through a swimming test. Other heroes, such as the Persian Rustram, also choose their horses through tests of stamina.

Dragons, of course, play a major role in much of the world's mythology and folklore, but how they are regarded varies from culture to culture. While dragons in Chinese lore tend to be intelligent and often beneficial, dragons in Western European lore are generally evil or at least predatory and seldom are viewed as intelligent. In Christian iconography, in fact, the dragon is often viewed as a symbol of Satan. As for the golden hoard, in Western European dragon lore dragons are often noted for their hoards of treasure.

Regin's story begins a tale within a tale: We are now deeper into Norse mythology than the tale of Sigurd. The three magical sons are Fafnir the dragon, Otter, the shape shifter, and Regin, the master smith. Some versions of the myth state that it is Loki who kills Otter, while others are less specific. It may also be Loki, acting on the instigation of Odhinn, who steals Andvari's gold and sets the curse in action.

At any rate, magic rings, and rings that have been cursed, also turn up in the world's mythology and folklore, and are full of more powers than can be easily listed here.

Forewarned by the birds, Sigurd slays the treacherous Regin with his sword. The battle is depicted in this wood carving from a twelfth-century stave-church portal in Norway. (*Werner Forman/Art Resource, New York*)

But now the myth returns to the present, to Sigurd, whose father's broken sword is reforged and who becomes Dragonslayer. He also, like the Welsh Gwion in Chapter 2, accidentally gains the power to understand what the birds are saying.

Now the myth brings in the theme of the princess in the glass tower, or in this case, the ring of flame. Brynhild, like the folkloric Sleeping Beauty, must wait for her true love to waken her. And like Sleeping Beauty, she sleeps because she pricked her hand on an enchanted thorn. Another folkloric theme appears in her vow never to marry a man who has known fear. This concept turns up in Teutonic folktales such as "The Boy Who Could Not Shudder," he who has never shivered in fear.

Now the modern reader is faced with one of the most improbable
scenes in the myth: Sigurd, after awakening the Sleeping Beauty,
doesn't spend any time with her, but merely gives her the ring—
Andvari's cursed ring—and rides away. Was something lost in the many
retellings?

At any rate, the motif of the magic potion appears, this time as a
potion of forgetfulness so that Gudrun may wed Sigurd. There is also
the theme of the disguised husband or lover, which also turns up in the
British story of Merlin's disguise of Uther Pendragon so that Arthur may
be engendered. In this myth, of course, it leads to tragedy, murder, and
the death of the hero and his beloved.

This myth fascinated the Germans as well as the Norse. It turns up in
Germany as the epic saga *The Nibelungenlied* and was the basis for
composer Richard Wagner's equally epic series of operas known as the
Ring cycle.

*O*nce there was an old king, a hero who had once won many wars but
whose strength was failing. He had a young wife who was wanted by
another prince.

A war followed. The old king fought well, but his sword shattered, and he
was sorely wounded. That night, when the battle was over, his young wife
searched for him among the slain.

At last she found him, but the old king was past the point of healing. "My
luck is gone," he told her weakly. "My sword is broken. And I must die. But
you shall live and bear a son. And he will be a great hero who will avenge
me. Keep the broken sword for him so that he may remake it."

Then he died. The young queen told her maid, "Let us change clothes. You
shall be called by my name, and I by yours, in case the enemy finds us."

But they were found not by the enemy, but by some Danish traders who
carried them off in their ship to the Danish court. The two women were
brought before the king. He studied them and thought that the maid looked
like a queen and the queen like a maid. So he asked the one dressed as a
queen, "How do you know in the dark of night whether the hours are wearing to the morning?"

She replied, "Why, when I was younger, I used to have to rise and light the
fires, and so I still waken at the same time."

"A strange queen who lights the fires," the king said. He asked the one who
was dressed like a maid, "How do you know in the dark of night whether the
hours are wearing near the dawn?"

"My father gave me a gold ring," she said. "And every night, just before the
dawn, it grows cold on my finger."

"A rich house where the maids wear gold," said the king. "You are no maid, but a king's daughter."

He gave her royal hospitality. As time went on, it was clear that she was with child. And as more time passed, she gave birth to a strong, handsome son whom she named Sigurd.

As Sigurd grew, a tutor, Regin, was assigned to him. One day the tutor told him to ask the king for a horse.

"Choose a horse for yourself," the king told Sigurd.

The boy went to the wood, where he met an old man. "Help me in choosing a horse," Sigurd said.

The old man nodded. "Drive all the horses into the river, and choose the one that swims across."

So Sigurd drove them. Only one was willing to swim across. Sigurd chose him and named him Grani. Grani was a fine horse indeed, for he came of Sleipnir's breed, and Sleipnir was the horse of the god Odhinn and was swift as the wind.

Not long after Sigurd had gained a horse Regin, his tutor, told him, "There is a great golden treasure hidden not far from here, and it would be fine for you to win it."

Sigurd shook his head. "I have heard stories about that treasure, and I know that the dragon Fafnir guards it. He is so huge and dangerous that no man dares to go near him."

"He is no bigger than any other dragon," Regin retorted. "And if you were half as brave as your father, you would not fear him."

"I am no coward!" Sigurd snapped. "But why are you insisting that I fight Fafnir?"

"Because," Regin said, "all that great hoard of gold once belonged to your own father."

Regin's father had three sons. The first was Fafnir the dragon; the next was Otter, who could take the shape of an otter; and the next was himself, Regin, and he was a great smith and maker of swords.

"Now there was, in that time, a dwarf called Andvari, who lived in a pool beneath a waterfall. He had hidden a great hoard of gold there as well. One day Otter went fishing in that pool, in otter form. He had killed and eaten a salmon and was sleeping on a stone.

"Then someone came by, perhaps one of the gods from Asgard, and threw a stone at the otter and killed it, flayed off the skin, and took it to the house of Otter's father.

"Then he knew his son was dead. To punish the person who had killed him, he said he must have Otter's skin filled with gold and covered all over with gold. Then the person who had killed Otter went down and caught Andvari and took the treasure from him, down to the very ring the dwarf wore.

"Then Andvari was so angry that he swore an oath that the gold would bring only bad luck to all the men who might own it.

"Then the otter skin was filled with gold and covered with gold. But as the dwarf had sworn, it brought good luck to nobody. Fafnir the dragon went mad for it and killed his own father. Now he wallows in the gold, and no man dares go near it."

When Regin was done, Sigurd said, "Make me a good sword so that I may kill the dragon."

Grinning, Regin made a sword. Sigurd tried it with a blow on a lump of iron, and the sword broke.

No longer grinning, Regin made another sword, and Sigurd broke that one, too.

Then Sigurd went to his mother, asked for the broken pieces of his father's blade, and gave them to Regin. Regin wrought the pieces into a new sword, sharp as the wind. Sigurd tried this blade on the lump of iron, and it split the iron in two. Then he threw a lock of wool into the air, and when it floated down against the sword it was cut into two pieces.

"The sword will do!" Sigurd exclaimed. He named it Gram.

But before he went against the dragon, Sigurd used the sword to hunt down and slay the prince who had slain his father. That vengeance was fulfilled.

When he had returned long enough to be rested, Sigurd rode out again with Regin to the heath where the dragon had been seen. The dragon's track was as clear in the earth as though a great river had rushed through and cut a deep valley.

Sigurd climbed down into that deep track and waited, sword drawn. Soon the earth began to shake as the dragon crawled to the river to drink. A thick cloud of venom flew before him like roiling fog. It would have been death to stand before him.

Sigurd waited until the dragon was directly overhead, then thrust his sword into Fafnir's heart. The dragon roared in pain, lashing his tail so fiercely that trees crashed down about him. Then, dying, he said, "Whoever has slain me, know that this gold shall be your ruin, and the ruin of all who own it."

Sigurd said, "All men die, and no brave man lets that frighten him."

And after that Sigurd was called Fafnir's Bane, and Dragonslayer.

Regin rushed to Sigurd. "Roast Fafnir's heart right away and let me taste it!"

Sigurd may have thought it a strange revenge, but he put Fafnir's heart on a stake and roasted it. But as it roasted, the meat spattered fat on his finger and burned him. With a startled gasp, Sigurd put his finger in his mouth, and so tasted the heart of Fafnir.

In that moment he knew why Regin had wanted the heart so badly, because Sigurd immediately understood the language of birds.

He heard one bird chirping, "There is Sigurd roasting Fafnir's heart for another, when he should taste it himself and learn all wisdom."

The next bird chirped, "There lurks Regin, ready to betray Sigurd, who trusts him."

The third bird chirped, "Let him cut off Regin's head and keep the gold."

The fourth bird chirped, "Then let him ride over Hindfell, to the place where Brynhild sleeps."

Sigurd whirled. Sure enough, Regin bore a knife, ready to strike. Sigurd cut off Regin's head with one blow of the sword Gram.

Then all the birds broke out singing, "We know a fair maiden sleeping. Sigurd, be not afraid. Sigurd, win the maid. High over Hindfell, fire is flaming. There is the maiden, she who will love you. There must she sleep till you wake her."

Sigurd took gold from Fafnir's hoard and took, too, the helm of invisibility, and packed it on Grani's back, and then he rode south to Hindfell.

When he reached it, the sky was dark. On the crest of the hill a fire blazed, and within the circle of the fire was a castle. Grani leaped over the fire with ease, and Sigurd dismounted and entered the castle.

Within, he saw an armor-clad figure sound asleep. Thinking that it must be uncomfortable to sleep in armor, Sigurd removed the sleeper's helmet—and found himself looking down at a beautiful woman. Her eyelids fluttered and she woke, and Sigurd was smitten with love at that moment. Smiling up at him, she said, "Ah, and are you Sigurd, come to break the curse and waken me at last?"

The curse had struck her down when she had disobeyed the god Odhinn and been pricked with a thorn from the tree of sleep. She had vowed never to marry a man who had known fear or who dared not ride through the fence of flaming fire, for she was a warrior herself.

But she and Sigurd loved each other and promised to be true to each other. He gave her a ring as a token—and it was that last ring that had been taken from the dwarf Andvari.

Then Sigurd rode away and came to the house of a king who had a fair daughter. Her name was Gudrun, and her mother was a witch. Gudrun fell in love with Sigurd from the moment she first saw him, and grew weary of hearing him speak only of his dear Brynhild. So she slipped magical drugs into Sigurd's drink. Instantly he forgot Brynhild and loved Gudrun, and they were married with great rejoicings.

Gudrun's brother, Gunnar, wanted Brynhild, so he and Sigurd, who had no memory of her at all, rode off together. Gunnar set his horse at the fire surrounding her castle, but the horse shied aside. Then Gunnar tried riding Sigurd's horse, Grani, but Grani would not move with Gunnar on his back.

But Gunnar had been taught some magic by his mother, and he used it to make Sigurd look like him and himself look like Sigurd. Sigurd, in Gunnar's shape, went and carried off Brynhild. She had no choice but to promise to wed this new man who had shown no fear. He gave her a ring, and she gave him back the only one she possessed, the one he had given her before in his own shape as Sigurd—that last ring of the dwarf Andvari.

Sigurd and Gunnar rode home and secretly regained their normal shapes. Sigurd gave Andvari's ring to his wife, Gudrun. And Brynhild, despairing, wed Gunnar.

But by the time that the wedding was over, the last of the magic drugs was gone from Sigurd, and he remembered all that he'd been forced to forget. But what could he do now that the wedding was finished and legal?

Meanwhile, Brynhild saw the ring that Sigurd had given to Gudrun, and she recognized it and turned as pale as a dead woman. She told Gunnar, her husband, that he was a coward and a liar, and added that he would never see her glad in his hall, never drinking wine, never playing chess, never embroidering with the golden thread, never speaking words of kindness. Then she rent all her needlework asunder and wept aloud, so that everyone in the house heard her.

Sigurd tried to explain and comfort her, but she would not listen. He gave up the effort and left.

And Brynhild determined to slay him. She mixed serpent's venom and wolf's flesh in one dish and gave it to her husband's younger brother. Driven mad, he raced into Sigurd's chamber while he slept and ran Sigurd through. Sigurd caught the sword Gram into his hand and threw it at the man as he fled, cutting him in half.

And then died Sigurd, Fafnir's Bane, whom no ten men could have slain in fair fight. Brynhild, hearing Gudrun mourning, collapsed, heart broken, and Grani, too, died of grief.

So the men of the castle built a great pile of wood on board Sigurd's ship. And at night they laid on it the dead Sigurd and the dead Brynhild in their full armor, the fatal ring on Brynhild's hand, and with them was placed the good horse, Grani. Then the men set fire to the ship and launched it. The wind caught the sail and sent the blazing ship out to sea, flaming into the dark.

So were Sigurd and Brynhild united in death. And so was the curse of the dwarf Andvari fulfilled.

Sources

Lettsom, William Nanson. *The Nibelungenlied*. New York and London: The Colonial, 1901.

Morris, William, trans. *Volsunga Saga*. New York and London: Collier Books, 1962.

LUGALBANDA
A Myth from Ancient Sumer

This myth begins like a traditional story of men at war, with a young officer leading his troops into battle, only to be stricken by fever, and his men being forced to go on without him. Then it seems more like a story of survival, with one man—a city man, no less—against the elements. Even the dream elements seem like a feverish man's delirium.

But then the story brings us firmly into mythic elements, with the adventure with the Anzu Bird and Lugalbanda's kindness to the chicks, then with the reward for kindness, Lugalbanda being given superhuman speed and stamina. Western readers may see a parallel here to the origins stories of comic book superheroes. But where the myth differs from modern expectations is with Lugalbanda's use of his powers not to win fame for himself but to save his troops. Perhaps that makes him even more truly a hero.

Sumerian literary tradition, incidentally, claims that Lugalbanda was a god-king of Uruk. He is generally held to be Gilgamesh´s father, and the Sumerian king list claims he ruled the city for no fewer than twelve hundred years.

At the time when his strange adventure began, Lugalbanda, who would someday be king, was but a young man, an officer in another king's army, leading a division of Uruk´s troops on the mountain road from that city-state to its rival, Aratta.

But Lugalbanda was not to reach the end of his mission. For halfway along that mountain road he was struck down by a terrible fever. So powerful was it that he lay unconscious, seemingly near to death.

What could his comrades do? They were sure he would die before any help could reach him, and they had their mission in Aratta to complete.

So they left Lugalbanda in a sheltered cave with food and drink laid out and his weapons beside him. If he died, at least he would have the dignity of proper funerary goods, and the soldiers would give him proper burial when they returned.

Sorrowing, for Lugalbanda was a popular officer, they left him and went on.

But Lugalbanda did not die. How long he lay unconscious, he could not know. At last, though, he did awake, still ill and alarmed by his surroundings. He was a city man, not someone used to this cold, barbaric mountain wilderness. Desperately he prayed to Utu, god of the sun, and Inanna, goddess of love and war:

"In this mountain cave, in this most terrible place upon the earth, let me not perish! Let me be ill no longer! Here there is no mother, there is no father, there is no acquaintance, no one whom I value. My mother is not here to say, 'Alas, my child!' My brother is not here to say, 'Alas, my brother!' In the unknown mountains, Utu, is a lost man in a terrible situation. Let me not come to an end in the mountains like a weakling!"

Worn out, he slept. That night, in the evening, Lugalbanda set off through the mountains, a wasteland in the moonlight. There was no other person to be seen. But there was a herd of the brown wild bulls of the mountains, and while they were browsing about among what plants they could find, Lugalbanda captured one and tethered it to a juniper tree of the mountains.

Then Zangara, god of dreams, appeared to Lugalbanda in the form of a bull, his voice like the bellow of a bull. "Who shall slaughter a wild bull for me? Who shall sacrifice it to the gods?"

Lugalbanda awoke—it had been a dream. He shivered and rubbed his eyes, overawed, knowing the gods had heard his plea. He took up his axe and dagger and hunted a sacrifice. Like an athlete, he caught the brown wild bull of the mountains; like a wrestler, he made it submit. Its strength left it, and Lugalbanda sacrificed it in the moment before the sun rose. And from that moment on, his health returned in full.

But he was still lost in the mountains. He wandered for a while but could find no way back to his men or to civilization. And at last Lugalbanda lay idle in the mountains, in the faraway places. No mother was with him to offer him advice, no father was with him to talk to him. No one was with him whom he knew, whom he valued—no one at all was there to talk to him. Lugalbanda said suddenly to himself, "I shall seek out the Anzu Bird."

The Anzu Bird was a strange, fearsome being with the body of a great eagle, the head of a lion, and the teeth of a shark. The bird was also known to have amazing powers.

"I shall treat the bird as befits him," Lugalbanda continued to himself. "I shall treat Anzu as befits him. I shall greet his wife affectionately. I shall seat Anzu's wife and Anzu's child at a banquet, and give him the finest of beer. When Anzu has drunk the beer and is happy, he can help me find the place to which the troops are going. Anzu can put me on the track of my brothers."

Perhaps that sounded strange even to his ears. But Lugalbanda was now determined to find the Anzu Bird. The bird nested, Lugalbanda knew, near the splendid eagle-tree of Enki on the summit of Inanna's multicolored carnelian mountain. The eagle-tree stood like a tower, its shade covering the mountain like a widespread cloak. In that shade no snake slithered, no scorpion scurried, and that was where the Anzu Bird had its nest of juniper and boxwood twigs.

But when Lugalbanda, after long and lonely traveling, found the eagle-tree and the nest near to it, there was no Anzu Bird. The great bird had flown off, hunting. But there was a fledgling in that nest, huddled piteously alone. Lugalbanda's own loneliness made him pity the small and hungry thing. He gave it food from his provisions, salt meat and sheep's fat, sweet cake with honey. The fledgling snapped up every bite.

Lugalbanda set about to tidy the nest, straightening the twigs and putting them more firmly in place, then settled the fledgling back into the nest. Finished, he withdrew, not sure yet what the Anzu Bird's reaction might be.

All that while, the Anzu Bird had been hunting the wild bulls of the mountains. Now he returned with a bull in his talons and another across his shoulders.

But when the Anzu Bird called to his nest there came no answer from the fledgling. The bird called a second and third time but heard no reply. Then the Anzu Bird uttered a cry of grief that reached up to heaven. "Who has taken my child from its nest? Who has taken the Anzu from its nest?"

But the fledgling had not been stolen. There it was, settled into the newly cleaned and straightened nest, well fed, safe, and sound asleep. The Anzu Bird rejoiced. "I am he who decides the destiny of the rivers. I keep the righteous on the path of honor. If I fix a fate, who shall alter it? If I but say the word, who shall change it? Whoever has done this goodness to chick and to nest, if you are a god, I will speak with you—indeed, I will befriend you. If you are a man, I will fix your fate. I shall not let you have any opponents in the mountains. Henceforth your name shall be Hero Strengthened by Anzu."

Lugalbanda stepped out from hiding. Partly from fright, partly from delight, he flattered the Anzu Bird. "Bird with sparkling eyes, your wingspan is like a bird net stretched out across the sky, and your talons are like a trap laid for the wild bulls and wild cows of the mountains! Yesterday I escaped safely to you, and now I have entrusted myself to your protection. I offer my greeting and leave you to decide my destiny."

The bird rejoiced over him. "I shall grant you what you put to me. I shall assign you a destiny according to your wishes."

In his wanderings in the mountains Lugalbanda had well thought out what he wished. "Let the power of running be in my thighs," he said. "Let me never grow tired! Let there be strength in my arms; let my arms never become weak! Let me go wherever I look to, set foot wherever I cast my glance, reach wherever my heart desires! In return, I shall have the wood-carvers fashion statues of you, and you will be breathtaking to look upon. Your name will be made famous in all of Sumer."

And the Anzud Bird told Lugalbanda, "The power of running be in your thighs! Never grow tired! Strength be in your arms! May your arms never become weak! Go wherever you look to, set foot wherever you cast your glance, reach wherever your heart desires!"

With his new gifts, Lugalbanda was able to race back through the mountains to the siege of Aratta and rejoin his comrades, who embraced him joyfully.

A year passed in that siege, but there was no sign of the defenders yielding. From the walls of Aratta javelins rained down as if from the clouds. Weary and dejected from the endless wait, King Enmerkar was sure that he had lost the favor of the goddess Inanna. So he asked for a volunteer to carry a message back across the mountains to the goddess in Uruk. If she would allow him and his army to return in safety, he promised to put aside his spear and allow Inanna herself to shatter his shield.

Lugalbanda, whose gifts meant that his legs would never tire, at once claimed for himself the honor of delivering the message. He had no need to listen to the warnings of his comrades, who feared it was too far for any one man to run and told him, "You will not come back from the great mountains! No one returns to humankind from there!"

But with the power granted him by the Anzu Bird, Lugalbanda reached Uruk before midnight on the same day, just as offerings were being made to the goddess. He delivered the message, and Inanna answered that she did not want King Enmerkar to give up the war. Lugalbanda took back to the king the message that victory over Aratta was assured.

So at last it was. And Lugalbanda was honored as a true hero.

Sources

Dalley, Stephanie. *Myths from Mesopotamia*. Oxford: Oxford University Press, 1989.
Foster, Benjamin R. *From Distant Days: Myths, Tales and Poetry of Ancient Mesopotamia*. Bethesda: CDL, 1995.

BEOWULF
A Myth of the Anglo-Saxons

The epic of Beowulf's adventures is believed to date to about the eighth century C.E., although parts of it were almost certainly being recited in royal halls long before the whole was written down. We are fortunate indeed to have this epic at all, since it survived to the modern age in only one copy!

The basic form of the epic should be clear to readers, even those who are reading a literal translation. Although the written epic has heavily Christianized wording, the first part of the story is basically the archetypal tale of the demon in the dark so familiar to viewers of horror movies, and that of the outsider hero, he who steps in to make things right.

But the story of Beowulf and Grendel was clearly inspired by the earlier and very similar Irish Celtic tale of the hero Finn MacCool, who comes to the court of the high king and defeats Ailill, a dark being from out of the Hollow Hills of the Faerie realms.

It's after the defeat of Grendel that the Beowulf epic takes off on its own, with the appearance of Grendel's mother. She is definitely a mythic figure, a Hag. The capitalization is deliberate. Today we use the word, if we use it at all, as an insulting term for an ugly or sharp-tongued old woman. But it originally meant a female being of great force, not necessarily always evil, but always potentially deadly. We still have the archaic term *hagridden*, which originally meant being literally possessed by a witch or witches. That Grendel's mother is seeking to avenge her son adds an element of understanding for her side—until the epic makes it clear that she and her son have been happily devouring humans for some time.

There's a certain irony to the fact that the "modern" war sword given to Beowulf is useless to him. Instead, it is the ancient broadsword, which is, intentionally or not, a link to the pagan past, that saves his life and lets him slay Grendel's mother and win free.

Incidentally, Beowulf's story doesn't end there. It continues through his maturity to old age and a fight with a dragon that ultimately slays him. It can be argued that this ending represents a Christian point of view: Beowulf won against Grendel and Grendel's mother because he was in the right, but he lost against the dragon because he was only after its gold.

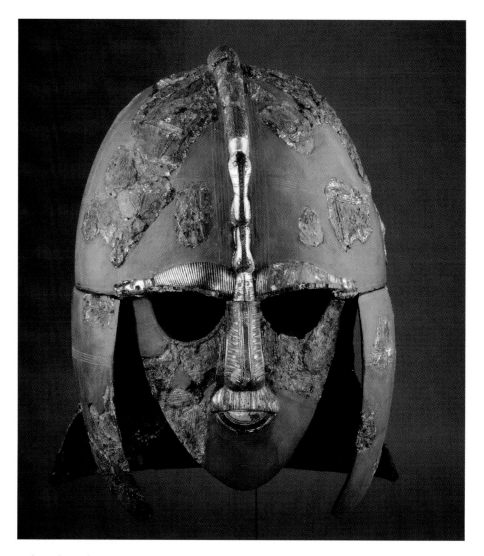

Helmet from the Sutton Hoo ship burial. The ship burial, discovered in 1939 at the burial site of Sutton Hoo, and the epic poem *Beowulf* are considered the most important surviving examples of Anglo-Saxon culture in England. Scholars believe that the ship burial provides archeological evidence of the many customs described in *Beowulf*. (© *The British Museum*)

*H*rothgar was king in Denmark and built him a mead hall, Herot. It was the finest ever known in all the world, high-towered, tall, and wide-gabled. There he shared with young and old alike all that God gave him. And in that hall echoed the words of the poets, the sounds of the harps, the joy of the people.

But evil was waiting out there in the wilderness, Grendel the demon, possessor of the moors.

One night the Danes settled in the hall for sleep, knowing no sorrows. Then the evil creature, the monstrous Grendel, grim and hungry, grabbed thirty warriors and went home laughing.

At dawn, when the Danes learned of Grendel's predation, there was great sorrow. The old king sat sadly, crying for his men. Nothing was found of the monster but bloody footprints.

The following night, and for many nights after, Grendel killed more and felt no remorse, evil that he was. No one could fight him, no one stop him. And so Grendel ruled, one against many, and the greatest hall in all the earth stood empty at night.

But a brave Geatish warrior, young Beowulf, heard of Grendel's doings. Strong and noble, Beowulf called for a ship and said he would cross the ocean and help the king who needed help.

At Heot, when Hrothgar learned of Beowulf's arrival, the old king was pleased. He'd once helped the father of the young hero. Now here was the offspring to save them from Grendel.

So Beowulf was made welcome in Hrothgar's sight and given all honor. That night the young hero lay down within Heot, pretending to sleep but waiting for Grendel.

And then in the night came that walker in darkness, Grendel stalking his way to the hall. When he just touched the door, it gave way at once, iron bands snapping and breaking apart. Quickly the monster entered the hall, moving with ease over the smooth, well-made floor. He expected to rip the life from the bodies of warriors sleeping within that great hall.

Forward came Grendel, and reached down for Beowulf.

Beowulf grasped his arm and sat up. And Grendel at once knew he never had met anyone yet with so powerful a grip. For the first time the monster's spirit was frightened, eager to flee to his dark hiding place. He strove to escape, but Beowulf held firm and would not release him. The noise of their struggle rang through all Heot. Amazing that it still stood fast in the force of that fight!

Outside, all the warriors listened in wonder. They heard lamentation, a frightening wail. Grendel was wailing, knowing his peril. But Beowulf, mightiest of warriors alive, held fast. He would not for any reason allow his murderous visitor to escape alive, to keep any longer the days of his life.

At last the bones of the monster's shoulder gave way. Mortally wounded, he fled without his arm, back to his sad home under the fen slope.

The hope of the Danes had come to pass. He who had come from afar had cleansed Hrothgar's hall and saved it from harm. The fact was made plain when Beowulf laid that arm and shoulder down, Grendel's claw, under the vaulted roof.

But soon the word spread that after that trouble, there still lived an avenger: Grendel's mother. She was a monster, a woman-thing living under the water. Grim as the gallows, she went on her journey to avenge the death of her son. At Heot she seized her son's arm, then caught up a warrior, Hrothgar's most trusted man, and took him as well.

Beowulf cried, "I promise you this: She will not escape, go where she will!"

They followed her track along the forest paths, over the murky moors, down among steep bluffs to the sea and the homes of water monsters. The Danes cried out in horror when they saw on the sea cliff the warrior's head, while below that, the sea boiled with his blood.

Beowulf put on his armor, his mail shirt and helmet. Unferth, Hrothgar's spokesman, gave him the sword called Hrunting. Hardened in blood, it had never failed a man who grasped it in hand to battle in a hostile place.

Beowulf said this: "Remember, Hrothgar, wise king: If I, in your service, lose my life, be a protector of my warriors, my comrades. Send the treasure you gave me to Hygelac, king of the Geats. I will do my glory work with Hrunting—or death will take me."

Waiting for no reply, Beowulf dove into the water.

She who had fiercely guarded that water for a hundred half-years quickly saw that some man from above was exploring her home. She seized the warrior in her horrid clutches, but the armor protected him, and she could not break his mail shirt with her claws. Instead, she bore Beowulf down to her dwelling place under the water. For all his struggles, he could not free his sword from its scabbard.

Then Beowulf found himself in a hostile hall. The sea would not harm him: The roof held it back. He saw firelight shine in a brilliant flame off treasures from all those the monster had slain.

Then the warrior saw that monster woman. He swung his battle sword quickly and did not hold back—but the sword would not bite her, the sword could not take her life. He threw down the useless sword and grappled with the monster, throwing her down. She paid him back quickly with angry claws and clutched him against her, pulling him down.

At that moment the strongest of warriors felt sick at heart as he fell and was helpless. She sat on her hall guest and drew a dagger, wide and brown-edged—she would avenge her son, her only offspring. Only the mail shirt saved Beowulf's life.

He fought his way free. Among all the treasure he saw an old sword, one forged by giants, the glory of warriors, larger than any a warrior used. Beowulf, fierce and despairing of life, caught the chain-wound hilt of the sword and angrily struck.

It cut off her head.

She fell to the floor and the battle was done.

Beowulf stood triumphant. The treasure went back with him, back to the surface. And all men praised Beowulf, hero indeed.

Sources

Chickering, Howell D., trans. *Beowulf: A Dual Language Edition*. Garden City, NY: Anchor Books, 1977.

Heaney, Seamus, trans. *Beowulf*. New York: Farrar, Straus and Giroux, 2000.

Tolkien, J. R. R. "Beowulf: The Monsters and the Critics," *The Monster and the Critics and Other Essays*, ed. Christopher Tolkien. Boston: Houghton Mifflin, 1983.

———. "On Translating Beowulf," *The Monster and the Critics and Other Essays*, ed. Christopher Tolkien. Boston: Houghton Mifflin, 1983.

SUNDIATA
A Myth from Mali

Sundiata was a real man, the ruler of Mali, circa C.E. 1200, but as usually happens to important people, his history was overlaid with mythic elements, in this case attached by the griots, the bards of Mali.

We are put firmly into the world of myth right from the opening, when we learn that Sundiata's father comes from a line of heroes able to communicate with the supernatural. We are also confronted with the odd prophecy that the king will marry an ugly woman—who also turns out to be supernatural, a shape-shifting woman who can take the form of a water buffalo. Furthermore, we next see the motif of the magic of the king's touch: As soon as he touches the wild woman, she loses her supernatural abilities. In Europe, too, until the last century, there was a belief that the touch of a king could heal illness.

Now a new theme enters the story: Sundiata, heir to his father's throne, is a crippled boy, unable to stand, let alone walk. So, too, was the Russian folk hero Illya Murametz. In Illya's story, it is three miraculous visitors—possibly saints—who heal him. In Sundiata's story, it is his own will, as well as the help from a blacksmith's iron bar, that heals him. While iron is often seen as a force against magic in mythology and folklore, here it is probably seen as a symbol of strength.

Interestingly, the king proclaimed Sundiata his heir by making him a gift of a griot, a bard, Balla Fasséké, who is the son of the king's own griot. For a basically nonliterate people, like those of Sundiata's Mali or of the Celtic lands, a griot or bard becomes highly important. This is,

One of the three Malinke towns that formed the foundation of Sundiata's great empire of Mali. It was here that he fought the famous battle with his rival Soumaoro in 1235. (*Werner Forman/Art Resource, New York*)

after all, a trained "rememberer" who knows the history and laws of the people and who can sing praise of the king and heap scorn on his enemies.

Now Sundiata has to go into exile, since his half brother, Dankaran, is on the throne. Dankaran tries to destroy Sundiata's power by sending Balla Fasséké, Sundiata's griot, off to a sorcerer-king, Soumaoro Kanté. Given the importance of a griot, Dankaran is doing more than sending away Sundiata's ally. He's also sending away Sundiata's voice. It's not surprising that Sundiata goes into exile.

Also sent to the sorcerer-king is Sundiata's half sister. She is never named; this is basically a male-oriented story.

The battles between Sundiata and Soumaoro are partly realistic, partly fantastic. Soumaoro has a secret: He has only one weakness. As in folktales from around the world, it is the half sister, the woman captive, who learns the secret and tells Sundiata that Soumaoro can be slain only by a rooster. There is a clear connection between the rooster and daybreak, but it is imposing outside ideas upon the story to say that Soumaoro is a creature of night.

After the death of the sorcerer-king the epic returns to reality and ends with the historic Sundiata as ruler of Mali.

*N*aré Fa Maghan, king of Mali, came from a long line of notable men, heroes who were known for their bravery and their ability to communicate with the jinns, those spirits that influence human lives.

But then a prophecy was made by a man from the north that startled Maghan and his griot, his bard. It said that soon two hunters would bring the king a hideous woman. And he, the prophecy stated, must wed her despite her ugliness. If he did, then she would bear him the greatest king Mali would ever know.

Indeed, it was not many days after Maghan heard the prophecy that two hunters appeared with a hideous woman as their captive. They told the king that this was Sogolon Kedju, a shape-shifter who in the form of a water buffalo had been attacking the land of Do, killing whoever crossed her path. They had managed to capture the buffalo, which had then become the woman. Since she possessed strange powers, they'd brought her to the king of Mali.

What could Maghan do? Broken prophecies led to disaster for the king and the land, so this one must be honored. As soon as he put a hand on the hideous woman, she seemed to lose her wildness, so he reluctantly married her. And sure enough, she soon did grow great with child.

Now King Maghan had a first wife, as was proper. Her name was Sassouma, and she was a jealous woman. She had borne the king a son, Dankaran Touman, and had always been certain he would be the one to claim the crown of Mali. Now here was this ugly interloper, coming to threaten her son's royal destiny.

Sassouma plotted and planned ways to kill Sogolon, but they all came to nothing. The strange buffalo woman's powers were too great. What was more, her baby was born—and it was a son. He was officially named Mari Diata. But when one has so unusual a mother, people can't ignore her. So, since he was the son of Sogolon, people began calling him Sogolon Diata. This grew into his final name: Sundiata.

Soon after the baby was born, Sassouma realized that her fears had been for nothing. How could she have ever worried that a buffalo woman would bear a normal child? The new arrival was no princely being, but an ugly, lazy glutton. Why, by three years old, when other boys walked freely and talked freely, Sundiata could not walk and rarely spoke.

The years passed, and still Sassouma had no worries. Even at seven, the buffalo woman's boy still crawled, spent all his time eating, and had no friends.

King Maghan was deeply troubled. How could this pathetic excuse for a child become a great king? Still, a prophecy must be honored. And as

Maghan grew ill and fell dying, he gave the apparently useless son a gift that said Sundiata was the royal heir—a gift of a griot named Balla Fasséké, the son of the king's own griot.

But of course once the king was dead, no one wanted a useless cripple on the throne. Sassouma saw to it that her own son, Dankaran, claimed the throne.

Sundiata, still crawling, unable to walk, could do nothing to stop her.

One day Sundiata's mother needed some leaves from a baobab tree for her cooking, and she asked Sassouma if she could borrow some. Sassouma agreed but took the opportunity to add some truly cruel, truly nasty insults about Sogolon's "useless son."

It was finally too much for Sogolon to bear. She returned home weeping with rage and sorrow. But to her astonishment, her "useless son" looked up at her with a smile and said, "Don't cry, Mother. Today I am going to walk."

Sundiata had her call for the blacksmith, then told him, "Forge for me the heaviest iron rod you can design."

The blacksmith did just that.

Then, struggling and grim with will, Sundiata pulled himself up. So much strength did he use that the heavy iron rod was bent into the shape of a bow. As a crowd gathered to stare, Sundiata stood upright and straight-backed at last. His overjoyed griot composed and sang "The Hymn to the Bow" then and there, and that hymn is still being sung by griots today.

But of course now that Sundiata was clearly able to claim the throne, as his father had wished, he represented a great threat to the false king Dankaran and to Dankaran's plotting mother, Sassouma. Dankaran's first move was to send Balla Fasséké, Sundiata's griot, together with Sundiata's half sister, on a mission to Soumaoro Kanté, the sorcerer-king of the Sosso.

Sundiata was furious about losing his griot, but his mother convinced him that this was not the time to set things right. That would come later. For now, she said, they must flee into exile for their safety.

Promising he would return to claim his crown, Sundiata went into exile. He reached manhood in the years of travel, learning wisdom and the arts of hunting and fighting. He developed all the skills needed by a warrior and a king. But, sadly, his mother died during their exile.

One day, in the far-off kingdom of Mema, Sundiata came across merchants from Mali. They told him that the evil sorcerer-king Soumaoro had conquered Mali. Dankaran had been too terrified to fight and had fled.

At once Sundiata set out to gather willing fighters, the core of an army. The time had come for him to reclaim his kingdom!

Meanwhile, Balla Fasséké, Sundiata's griot, and Sundiata's half sister remained captives at Soumaoro's court at Sosso. The young woman and the griot managed to whisper plots to each other. She was secretly learning some of Soumaoro's spells, but the griot must learn what else he could find out about the sorcerer-king. So one day, while Soumaoro was away, Balla Fasséké managed to steal into the evil king's secret chamber.

To the griot's shock, he found urns containing writhing masses of poisonous snakes, and huge owls standing watch over the severed heads of the nine kings Soumaoro had already defeated. Any ordinary mortal would have died instantly in this chamber, but Balla Fasséké, being a true griot despite his youth, had protective sorcery of his own.

Then the griot forgot his shock. Amid the horror was the most wondrous harp that Balla Fasséké had ever seen. He began to play it, and its magnificent sound charmed even the snakes and owls.

Just then Soumaoro burst into the chamber, furious to find the griot there. But the quick-thinking Balla Fasséké improvised so clever a praise song to Soumaoro that it disarmed the evil king. Soumaoro promptly declared Balla Fasséké his own griot, which made war between Soumaoro and Sundiata inevitable.

Meanwhile, Sundiata was making his way homeward. As he passed through all the kingdoms he had seen during his exile, he gathered his army.

At Tabon, near the Malian city of Kita, Sundiata's army launched a surprise attack on Soumaoro's forces and sent the Sosso forces into retreat.

At the next battle, Sundiata and Soumaoro came face-to-face, but Soumaoro escaped through magic. One moment the sorcerer-king in his horned helmet stood before Sundiata, but in the next moment Soumaoro appeared on a distant ridge. Sundiata despaired, sure that his enemy's magic made him invincible.

Now that Sundiata knew he would need more than might to defeat Soumaoro, he summoned soothsayers to counsel him on supernatural powers. Following their advice, Sundiata sacrificed one hundred white oxen, one hundred white rams, and one hundred white roosters.

Just then Balla Fasséké and Sundiata's half sister arrived. While Soumaoro had been occupied in warfare, they had managed to escape. Sundiata's half sister told him that while she had been forced to be Soumaoro's wife, she had learned the secret of his magic. Soumaoro's sacred animal, the source of his amazing power, was the rooster. This bird alone had the power to destroy Soumaoro. Armed with this knowledge, Sundiata fashioned a wooden arrow with a white cock's spur as its tip.

The confrontation between Soumaoro and Sundiata came at the battle of Kirina. On the eve of the battle, the two men observed the ritual of declaring war. Each sent an owl to the other's encampment, and the owls delivered messages of bravado.

"I am the wild yam of the rocks," Soumaoro boasted. "Nothing will make me leave Mali."

Sundiata replied, "I have seven master smiths in my camp. They will shatter the rocks. Then, yam, I will eat you."

Soumaoro's next message said, "I am the mushroom that poisons even the fearless."

Sundiata replied, "I am the rooster. Poison does not matter to me."

Soumaoro retorted, "Behave yourself, little boy, or you will be burned. I am the red-hot cinder."

Sundiata replied, "I am the rain that extinguishes the cinder. I am the flood that will carry you off."

And the war began. While the warriors battled, Sundiata hunted only for Soumaoro. Time and again he caught glimpses of the sorcerer-king, only to lose sight of him once more.

And then at last Sundiata got a clear view of his foe. He aimed his special arrow with its cock's spur tip and fired. The cock's spur grazed Soumaoro's shoulder, and he cried out as though mortally wounded.

In that moment all was lost for the evil king. And when Sundiata's victorious forces entered Soumaoro's city and opened his secret chamber, the snakes were lifeless, the owls lay flopping on the ground—and the sorcerer-king lay dead.

Now the victorious Sundiata invited the leaders of all the twelve kingdoms of the savanna to come to him. He said that they could keep their kingdoms but that all would now join in a great new empire. They agreed. And from that day forth, Sundiata's word became the law, and the great Empire of Mali was born.

Sources

Bertol, Roland. *Sundiata: The Epic of the Lion King.* New York: Thomas Y. Crowell, 1970.

Niane, D. T. *Sundiata: An Epic of Old Mali.* London: Longmans, 1965.

HERO TWINS

THE HERO TWINS OF THE MAYA
A Myth from the Quiche Maya

Mayan ball games were something like a cross between soccer and basketball. They were played with a hard rubber ball and were important enough to the Maya people, with ritual underpinnings, for every city to have had a ball court. This myth makes it clear that it could be a noisy sport as well.

The Mayans shared with other peoples the concept of an underworld, a subterranean world of the dead. Their lords of death seem allied to demons, and their underworld torments echo those seen in both Christian and Chinese mythology.

The quest to reach the underworld can never be easy. Here the twins must get past ritual obstacles to reach the lords of death, just as shamans must do the same to reach the worlds of the spirit. Just as with the Greek river Styx, the Mayan underworld has its perilous rivers.

What is interesting here is what is omitted. There are no indications that there are to be tests, yet once the twins fail to recognize that they're greeting wooden statues, they accept that they've failed a test. They fail the second test, too, mostly by being too cocky, and are sacrificed.

But the myth presents us with a miraculous resurrection, as the twins are reborn out of the body of their first mother's daughter. Only after their rebirth are they worthy of taking the names of true Hero Twins, Hunahpu and Xbalanque.

Sure enough, they once again return to the underworld, but they are wise enough to trick the lords of death into revealing their names and into avoiding the trap of the fiery bench. They are confronted with a series of ritual ordeals, which is typical of a shamanistic journey to the spirit world as well. But where we might expect the winning of the ball game to be the end of the myth, here there is a difference. The Hero Twins must die ritualistically if they are to ultimately triumph.

So there is a second sacrifice and a second rebirth. It is by trickery that the Hero Twins finally triumph over the lords of death, fooling them into killing two of their own. A similar theme of pretended suicide or sacrifice and rebirth appears in European folktales as well, in which a hero or a trickster animal fools a giant or other animal into dying.

The myth ends with an origin theme. Since there is no more work for the Hero Twins, they become the sun and the moon.

*I*n their first life, One and Seven Hunahpu were superb ballplayers. In fact, so good were they—as well as being a noisy pair of players—that the lords of death grew interested in them and invited them to play in Xibalba, land of the underworld. Since one did not wisely say no to the lords of death, the Hero Twins hid their rubber ball and ball-playing gear up under the rafters of their mother's house, then set out on their dangerous journey.

They climbed down a steep cliff and managed to get across a river of knives and a river of blood. There was the dark throne room of the lords of death— and on those thrones sat the fearsome lords of death themselves. The Hero Twins greeted them—and then found that they'd greeted wooden statues instead.

It was a test, and they had failed it. Now the real lords of death appeared and commanded the Hero Twins to sit. They tried—but the only seat turned into a burning fire, and that they could not manage.

This, too, had been a test, and this test, too, they had failed. The lords of death sacrificed them and buried their bodies under the ball court in Xibalba.

But that was not the end of them. They were miraculously reborn out of the body of Blood Woman, the daughter of their first mother, and were now the true Hero Twins, named Hunahpu and Xbalanque.

At first the Hero Twins didn't know their true role, or that they were wondrous ballplayers. Instead they were doing their best to tend a patch of garden, and not doing too well at that, because every time they tried to clear away some underbrush, one or another animal would replace it.

At last a rat told the Hero Twins who they were and where to find the ball-playing gear they had hidden in that earlier life. They didn't want to try explaining who they were to their grandmother, who had been their mother, so they tricked her into going out to the well for water, and while she was gone they stole the ball-playing gear out of the rafters.

Sure enough, the Hero Twins instantly regained their skills as ballplayers, and their happy noise as they played was heard down in Xibalba. The lords of death were insulted: How dare these Hero Twins return?

Not long after, the Hero Twins received a message summoning them to a ball game in Xibalba.

But now the Hero Twins were wiser than they'd been the first time around. They knew that the first test was to greet the lords of death by their names. So before they entered the throne room, one of the Hero Twins plucked a hair and turned it into a mosquito. He sent that into the throne room to bite one of the lords of death. When there was no reaction from the figure, the Hero Twins knew that this was one of the wooden statues. They said nothing.

Then the mosquito bit another lord of the dead. He let out a startled yelp. The one beside him called him by name, asking what was wrong.

The Hero Twins could greet that one by his right name.

The mosquito bit each of the other lords of the dead in turn, and each in turn cried out and was asked what was wrong.

Soon the Hero Twins had all the right names. They entered the throne room, greeted the real lords of the dead properly, and said that they weren't about to waste words on the wooden images.

The lords of the dead told them to sit down. The Hero Twins replied that they saw no chair, no bench, only a fire.

Now the lords of the dead told the Hero Twins that they must face a special series of tests.

First they were taken to the Dark House, where they were given each a torch and a burning cigar. These, the lords of the dead told the Hero Twins, must be returned in the morning exactly as they had been received. How could burning objects not change? The Hero Twins quickly solved the puzzle. They changed the torches' flames to a scarlet macaw's tail feathers, and the burning embers of the cigars to fireflies. These stayed all night and never changed.

Next the Hero Twins were sent to the Razor House. There sharp blades attacked, meaning to cut them up. But the Hero Twins quickly told the blades their proper name and use: These were tools intended to work for men to cut up animals. The blades agreed and did not harm the Hero Twins.

Next the Hero Twins were sent to the Jaguar House, where they were to be eaten. But the Hero Twins befriended the hungry jaguars, feeding them bones till they no longer wanted to eat the Hero Twins.

Next the Hero Twins were sent to the Cold House. They dove inside and locked out the cold and were quite comfortable.

Next the Hero Twins were sent to the Fire House. But they took a little bit of the cold with them. The fire didn't burn them, but only made them pleasantly warm.

Next the Hero Twins were sent to the Bat House. And here they made their first mistake. One twin, Hunahpu, peeked outside the house to see if it was morning yet. When he did so, a bat sliced off his head, which went rolling out onto the ball court of Xibalba.

The other twin, Xbalanque, hastily called all the animals to him, each with its favorite food. The coati brought a squash, and this became Hunahpu's new head. The Hero Twins told a rabbit to hide outside the ball court.

When the lords of the dead started the game, it was Hunahpu's head that they used for the ball. But when they kicked the ball, Xbalanque deflected Hunahpu's head toward where the rabbit hid. As planned, the rabbit hopped off, and the lords of death thought it was the bouncing ball and raced off in pursuit.

This gave Xbalanque a chance to put Hunahpu's rightful head back on his shoulders. The Hero Twins put the squash in its place. When the game began again and Xbalanque gave the ball a particularly energetic boot, it split open and all its seeds came spilling out. The Hero Twins had won the game.

But there was only one way out of Xibalba, and the Hero Twins knew it. And when the lords of the dead challenged the Hero Twins to jump over a blazing fire, the Hero Twins jumped into it instead.

The lords of the dead rejoiced. At last they had slain the Hero Twins! They ground the Hero Twins' bones into powder and threw the powder into the river.

This, though the lords of the dead didn't know it, was exactly the magic that could bring the Hero Twins back to life. At first the Hero Twins came back in the form of fish, but then they came back as their true selves.

Disguised as a pair of ragged wandering magicians, the sort who perform tricks for a living, they began showing off their skills. They could burn down a house, then have it spring up again, unharmed. They could even slay each other and then spring up again unharmed as well.

Word of these amazing skills reached the ears of the lords of the dead, who summoned the Hero Twins to perform for them. They commanded the Hero Twins to sacrifice a dog, and then bring it back to life.

The twins did this.

Now the lords of the dead commanded that a man be sacrificed and then brought back to life.

The Hero Twins did this, too.

Now the lords of the dead asked the Hero Twins to sacrifice each other.

So Xbalanque sacrificed Hunahpu, cutting out his heart, then danced about his dead brother, commanding Hunahpu to join him. And the dead twin sprang up, alive and whole again, and danced with him.

What a wonder! This was too amazing for the lords of the dead to resist. Now *they* wanted to be sacrificed and brought back to life!

This was exactly what the Hero Twins had awaited. They sacrificed the two foremost of the lords of the dead—but they did not bring them back to life.

With that, the remaining lords of the dead knew that they had been defeated. From that day forth, Xibalba lost its glory. And though death could not be destroyed, it became merely part of a whole.

Then the Hero Twins, Xbalanque and Hunahpu, their work on earth completed, flew up into the sky and became the sun and the moon.

Sources

Taube, Karl. *Aztec and Maya Myths*. Austin: University of Texas Press, 1994.

Tedlock, Dennis, trans. *Popol Vuh*. New York: Simon and Schuster, 1985.

ROMULUS AND REMUS
A Myth from Ancient Rome

This is an example of a deliberately created myth, created by the ancient Romans to give their city a dramatic origin, in the same way that rulers in the past might create an ancestry linking them with their gods.

And so this myth of Rome's founding begins in a traditional fashion, with the babies put in a basket and thrown into the river. The same motif, of course, can be found in the biblical story of Moses, as well as in the story of King Sargon of Akkad and, in this chapter, in the story of Perseus.

The wolf-boy or girl, the child raised by wild animals, is part of world lore, from folklore to Mowgli of Rudyard Kipling's *Jungle Book* and Edgar Rice Burroughs' Tarzan to the real-life examples of Kamala the Wolf-girl and the Wild Boy of Avignon. Did a wolf ever actually suckle a human baby? Possibly, although the likelihood is remote.

As for Romulus and Remus, they aren't true wolf-boys, since they are quickly saved from the wilderness and raised by the king's shepherd. Their wild natures are clear, though, not surprisingly for sons of Mars, and soon they fall into the role of warring twins, though neither can be described as truly good or truly evil.

Once Remus has been slain, the myth seems to edge closer to reality, though there's no evidence for there ever having been a Romulus or a Remus. There's no evidence of a mass stealing of the Sabine women, either, though it can't be ruled out, at least not in part, since the theft of women has occurred all through history.

The legendary twin founders of Rome, Romulus and Remus, are suckled by their wolf foster mother. It is believed ancient Romans created the sensational myth of Romulus and Remus to link their ancestry with the gods. (*Scala/Art Resource, New York*)

Romulus, in true founding hero fashion, doesn't grow old and die but is carried off by his father, Mars, in a chariot of fire. Other heroes or religious figures share the same theme of being carried up into heaven without dying, including the Jewish prophet Elijah and the Moslem prophet Mohammed. Unlike them, Romulus was considered to have thus become a god.

*I*n days long past, Numitor, rightful king of Alba Longa, was deposed by his brother, Amulius. Amulius was merciful enough not to kill Numitor's only child, his daughter, Rhea Silvia. Instead he forced her to become a vestal virgin. This meant that she could never wed and thus, Amulius thought, would never give birth to a son who might be trouble to him.

But men can never plan on how the gods may intervene. So it happened in this case. Rhea Silvia was a beautiful woman, and Mars, god of war, saw her and fell in love with her. In due course Rhea Silvia gave birth to twin sons.

Now Amulius was doubly worried. Fearing that one or both of the boys would grow up and attempt to overthrow him, he tore the babies from Rhea Silvia's arms. But that merciful touch in his nature kept him from slaying them. Instead Amulius had them put into a wooden basket and thrown into the turbulent, flooding river Tiber. The gods would take care of things, he thought.

But again, the plans of men are often overturned by the gods' will. The basket bounced and rocked over the waves but neither sank nor overturned. And at last, as the floodwaters fell, the basket, with the two babies still safe inside, washed ashore.

This jarring shock woke the babies, who started crying from hunger. A she-wolf who had lost her cubs heard the sound and recognized it as a hunger cry. She sniffed the babies, then carried them, one by one, from the basket into the wilderness, where she licked them dry and let them nurse as though they were her own cubs returned in this strange shape. Now, it was no coincidence that had brought her to that area: The wolf is sacred to Mars. A woodpecker also brought the two boys food, for the woodpecker, like the wolf, is also sacred to Mars.

The boys' fate, though, was not to grow up as wild things. They were found one day not long after by Faustulus, who was the king's shepherd. Delighted to find two healthy babies, since he and his wife had none of their own, he took them home to his wife, who was overjoyed. They adopted their foundlings and named the twins Romulus and Remus. The twins grew up bold and strong, leaders of a band of shepherds that were as much warriors and even bandits as herders of sheep.

One day Remus' wild deeds went too far. He was captured and brought before the deposed king, Numitor, for punishment. Numitor, noticing how unlike a shepherd's son he was and how strangely familiar the young man looked, questioned him—and realized from putting together what little Remus remembered with that teasing resemblance to Rhea Silvia that he'd just found a grandson—two grandsons, in fact!

Numitor was too weary from exile for a fight for the throne. It was the young, strong Romulus and Remus who rose up against Amulius, gathering Numitor's men behind them. The twins killed Amulius and restored the kingdom to their grandfather.

But what was there for two hot-blooded and active young men to do now? They were both ambitious, but neither wanted to depose Numitor, nor did they want to be harsh enough to hope for his death.

So they decided to found their own town. For a site, the twins chose the spot where the she-wolf had suckled them. After studying the omens to be read in the flights of birds, they determined that the omens meant that Romulus and Remus would each be in charge of part of the new city. But Romulus read the signs to mean that his portion would be twice the size of that of Remus. In fact, he used a plow pulled by a white cow and a white bull to cut a furrow marking the boundary of his portion.

Remus had read the signs another way. He was angry at his brother for getting the larger part and for being so quick to claim it. He jumped over the furrow into his brother's portion, and the twins fought.

Romulus won the fight. But in the process, as a true son of Mars the war god, he slew his brother.

Whether or not Romulus mourned for Remus, whether or not he felt guilt, no one can say. But whatever he felt or failed to feel, Romulus went on building the new city and named it Roma, Rome, in his own honor.

At first Rome's only citizens were fugitives, outlaws, and outcasts from outlying communities whom Romulus invited to settle upon the Capitoline Hill, where he had built a sanctuary. But men need wives if a city is to thrive, so Romulus decided to steal some. He announced that games were to be celebrated in honor of the god Consus, and invited the tribes of the Latins and the Sabines to his celebration. While the Sabine men were distracted by the games, Romulus' men rushed in and carried off the women.

The Sabine men were understandably furious. With their king, Titus Tatius, they attacked Romulus. The war dragged on for some time, while the Sabine women prayed for peace. At last, when the fighting seemed likely to slay both sides, the women, who by now were growing fond of their new husbands, rushed between the ranks and insisted that there be an end to war. They begged the two tribes to unite and form one people, one nation.

Unfortunately, the peace was short-lived, and Titus Tatius, who was co-reigning with Romulus, was killed in a new battle.

Romulus continued his reign alone not only over the Latins but also over the Sabines. He never died, but was carried off by his father, Mars, in a chariot of fire. From then on, he was worshiped as Quirinus, guardian god of Rome.

Sources

Gesell, Arnold. *Wolf Child and Human Child*. London: Scientific Book Club, 1942.

Howe, George, and G. A. Harrer. A *Handbook of Classical Mythology*. Hertfordshire: Oracle, 1996.

Plutarch. *The Lives of the Noble Greeks and Romans*. Franklin Center, PA: Franklin Library, 1979.

THE TWIN BROTHERS
A Myth of the Dine, the Navajo People

This is one of the most sacred myths of the southwestern peoples and, as such, must be treated with respect by storytellers.

The adventures of the Hero Twins are different from any others in that they all take place in a time that is mythic but places that are within the real world. The most basic reason for the Hero Twins' adventures is to free the earth from monsters so that order can be created out of chaos.

Within the adventures are many mythic themes. One is the rainbow over which the Hero Twins travel; like in the Wyandot and ancient Norse myths, the rainbow is seen as a bridge. Another is the need to hide within the house of the deity or, for that matter, the giant; the theme, of course, turns up in folklore as well, as in "Jack and the Beanstalk." The animal-people, so much a part of the Southwest's mythology, are well represented in this myth, in their fluid shaping, now beast, now human-seeming.

Grandmother and *grandchildren* are terms of respect rather than indications of literal kinship.

The last four ills are the only ones left unslain, because of the necessity for their survival: There can be no wealth without poverty, no wisdom of the old without old age, no compassion without the survival of the smaller ills, and no new life without death.

The myth ends, as it must, with the monsters slain and order returned. And now it is proper for the Dine, the Navajo, to be created.

*T*he twin brothers, who are also to be called little war gods, were the sons of White Bead Woman, though they didn't know their father's name. They were well treated as babies, surely, but not much can be said of them until the fifteenth day, when they had both grown into young men.

One day the Hero Twins were exploring when they saw a coyote watching them. They were about to shoot their arrows, but the animal raced out of sight. They hurried home and were told by the elders that they had seen the spy of the giant elk, Anaye'tee'leget.

Shortly thereafter the Hero Twins were exploring when they saw a great bird with a red bead flying toward them, but it flew away before they could shoot. They hurried home again and told the elders, who were alarmed this time. The elders said, "That was the turkey buzzard, the spy of Tse na'hale, the giant birds who devour people. You must no longer go so far from home."

But the Hero Twins were young and full of curiosity and simply couldn't stop from exploring. One day they returned to tell the elders they had seen a black bird with shining eyes. Just as they had taken aim it flew away. The elders said that the bird was the spy of the monsters, and scolded the Hero Twins again for wandering so far.

Now the boys were afraid to go toward the south, west, and north, the directions from which the spies had come. The only safe direction, they thought, would be the east, so they ran eastward, playing and chasing chickadees.

Then Dotso, the all-wise fly, said to them, "My grandchildren, your father is the sun. Ask your mother to name him. She will tell you that your father is a cactus or a rock. Then you must reply that those could not sire human beings. You must reply that you know that the sun is your father."

Sure enough, when the Hero Twins asked the question and received the answer, they said that they knew the sun was their father. The elders were stunned when the Hero Twins added that they intended to go to the home of their father.

When the boys left the hogan, they stepped onto the rainbow and were immediately on top of the mountain Chol'i'I, where their mother had first been found. The next few steps took them far to the east, to a country they did not know, a land of nothing but desert sand.

There sat an old man who asked if they were on the way to see their father. They told him this was so, and he warned, "My grandchildren, your father is a fierce one who will kill you if you are not wary." He vomited and said: "My grandchildren, take this. You must use it when your father tries you with his tobacco." They took what the old man had given them and continued their journey.

At last the Hero Twins reached the door of a huge house all of turquoise. An old woman stood in the doorway and asked what they wished. When she heard that they had come to see their father, she exclaimed, "Then you are my grandchildren! I am the sun's mother. Come with me."

She took them inside and wrapped them in the sky's four coverings: dawn, daylight, twilight, and night.

There came the sound of galloping hoofs. The sun was coming home, riding his turquoise horse. He entered and frowned. "Who is here?"

His mother replied, "Who would be here but us?"

"At noon I saw two small things headed here. What are they?"

His wife entered, and she was a jealous woman. She snapped, "They are your offspring, not mine!"

With that, their grandmother brought the Hero Twins out to their father. He took down his turquoise pipe, filled it, and handed it to the boys. They smoked the pipe until all the tobacco was burned, then shook out the ashes. This they repeated four times. Then the sun asked, "How do you feel?"

The Hero Twins answered, "We feel well."

"Then you are my sons."

But the sun wasn't quite certain about it. So he prepared a sweathouse for the two boys and placed powerfully heated stones inside it. Their grandmother gave the Hero Twins four feathers and whispered, "Keep these feathers under your arms when you enter."

They stripped and entered the sweathouse. Soon they heard a call: "Are you warm yet?"

They answered: "No, we are not warm yet."

The question was asked a second, third, and fourth time. After the fourth time the boys said, "Yes, we are warm now."

With that, the sun poured cold water in on the powerfully heated stones, and the entire sweathouse exploded. But the feathers carried the boys safely to one side.

Now the sun was certain that these were his sons. He asked the Hero Twins to choose whatever they wished of his possessions. The Hero Twins told him, "Father, we do not want anything in your house."

So the sun led them outside and showed the Hero Twins the horses he owned. But the Hero Twins did not want any of them. He showed them his domestic animals. But the Hero Twins did not want any of them. He showed them precious stones. But the Hero Twins did not want any of them. They told their father, "It is not for these that we are here."

Instead, they pointed at a bow and arrows hanging on the wall. This was the lightning.

"What would you do with such a weapon?" the sun asked.

"We would put an end to the monsters that are destroying human beings every day," the Hero Twins answered. They named the monsters one by one, then added, "Father, if they eat everyone on earth, including themselves, for whom will you travel?"

The sun was silent for a long while. He knew that one of the monsters the Hero Twins had named was his son, their own half brother, though no one but the sun knew it.

And yet the Hero Twins' goal was honorable. His monster-son was not.

"You may use this weapon for a short time," the sun said at last. "But you must give it back to me. Human beings would use it to destroy themselves."

Now the sun took the Hero Twins for a final test before he would let them have so potent a weapon. He pointed to the directions in turn, asking veiled questions. But the Hero Twins guessed right each time that he was testing their knowledge of the location of all the sacred mountains. When they had answered all his questions, the sun gave over the weapon into their keeping.

Now the Hero Twins began their quest. First on their list of monsters was Yeitso the giant. This, though they did not know it, was the monster-son of the sun. They went to where he lived at Tqo'sedo, the hot springs, and waited for him. At last they saw him coming over the hill from the south.

The giant drank four times from the spring, drinking up all the water. Then he spat it back four times, and the spring was just as it had been before.

Now he said to the Hero Twins, "What are these two beautiful things that I see? And how shall I kill them?"

The Hero Twins called back, "What beautiful big thing is walking about? And how shall we kill it?"

They called this challenge to each other for a ritual four times. Then the little breeze, who had followed the Hero Twins, warned, "Jump high in the air."

They jumped as one, and the black knife, which was the giant's powerful weapon, whirred harmlessly under their feet. They caught it as it passed.

The little breeze warned, "Low!"

The blue knife, the giant's next weapon, whirred over their heads. They caught it as it passed.

The little breeze warned, "To the side!"

The Hero Twins jumped as one to the side, and the yellow knife, the giant's next weapon, whirred by them. They caught it as it passed.

The little breeze warned, "Leap high!"

They leaped as one, and the white knife with many points whirred under them. They caught it as it passed.

"He has no more weapons," the little breeze said.

The Hero Twins shot at the giant. There was a blinding flash of lightning, but he remained standing. They hurled the black knife at him, but he was unharmed. They hurled the blue knife at him, but he was unharmed. They hurled the yellow knife at him, but he was unharmed. They threw the last knife, the white knife, at him—and he fell so hard that the ground rumbled under him.

Blood began to flow from the giant's mouth. The little breeze warned, "Stop the blood before it runs into the water."

The Hero Twins quickly placed a stone knife and an arrow point between the blood and the water. The knife remains to this day, as does the flow of the giant's blood, which turned to stone.

The Hero Twins cut off the giant's scalp. When they saw that his clothing was made of stone knives—which was why it had been so difficult to slay him—they gathered some of the knives and threw them to the east, the south, the west, and the north; they covered the whole country. The Hero Twins proclaimed, "The giant's spirit has departed from you. From now on the people of the earth shall use you."

The Hero Twins, carrying the giant's scalp, went home and hung the scalp on a pole to the east of the hogan. When they entered the hogan, they found First Man, First Woman, and White Bead Woman huddled back against a wall in fright. They did not recognize the Hero Twins. The two had been reshaped in the house of the sun and were now not boys but tall, handsome young men.

"Mother, do not be afraid," they said. "We are your sons. We have been to our father's house, and killed the giant Yeitso. His scalp hangs on the pole outside."

Then there was rejoicing.

But the Hero Twins' quest had not ended. Since they knew they were to work together, they decided that the wisest way to do it would be for the younger brother, the twin who had been born second, to stay at home with a magical collection of sticks and hailstones. He would keep watch over the medicine sticks while the elder brother, who had been born first, would go out against the monsters.

The elder brother said, "When you see one of the medicine sticks start to burn you will know that the enemy is getting the better of me."

Then the younger brother would help him by drawing the smoke from the burning medicine stick into his mouth and blowing the smoke onto the sticks and the hailstones one by one. Then he would complete the protective ritual by drawing in some more smoke from the burning medicine stick and blowing the smoke in the four directions.

After the Hero Twins had arranged this, elder brother asked the elders where he could find the giant elk. First Woman told him that the giant elk could be found on Bikehalzi'n, the Red Plain.

"But no one can get near him," she warned. "When he sees anyone in the distance he charges them, catches them, and eats them alive. That is a dangerous place."

The elder brother was not afraid. All the monsters the Hero Twins meant to slay had supernatural strength from the rainbow and the lightning, and all of them were very powerful. "In all the world there is no such thing as a dangerous place," he said.

While the younger brother remained, watching the medicine sticks, the elder brother set out to find the giant elk.

When the elder brother reached the Red Plain, he gathered up a tall bunch of grass, held it in front of him, and crept forward. Peering through the grass, he saw the giant elk. It was a huge monster, dark against the sky, with two enormous horns that rose up from its head. The elder brother crept around the giant elk in a wide circle, trying to get closer, but could find no way.

Just as he was beginning to lose hope, a tiny old woman, the mother gopher, rose up out of the ground. "What do you want, my grandchild?"

The elder brother said, "Grandmother, I am trying to get near enough to the giant elk so that I can kill him."

"Grandchild, it is impossible for you. But when my children are cold I burrow up to him and chew off some of his hair for my nest."

"Grandmother, if you can help me, you shall have a precious gift."

"Wait here," she said, and hurried off.

At last the mother gopher returned. "I have chewed away the hair right over the giant elk's heart. Now, follow me."

But the elder brother was too big to follow her down the gopher hole. The mother gopher blew four times into the entrance, and suddenly it was large enough for the elder brother. He hurried down the tunnel until he was directly under the giant elk and could hear the monster's heart beating. The elder brother took aim from that sound and fired the sun's bow.

The giant elk leaped up, then fell, horns first, tearing up the tunnel. The elder brother ran back down the tunnel with all his might, the horns tearing it up behind him. He was almost back to the tunnel's mouth before he heard the elk crash down, dead.

The elder brother climbed out of the tunnel and found the mother gopher clutching her hands at her heart. "Oh, I am still sick with fear! If those horns had dug any further, the giant elk would have eaten us up!"

A tiny man raced up. He was the chipmunk, and he wanted to be sure the giant elk really was dead.

"If he is really quite dead, I'll wave to you from the top of one of his horns."

Sure enough, the chipmunk soon waved from the top of one of the horns. The chipmunk raced down and wiped some of the giant elk's blood down his back. And that is why chipmunks have a dark stripe down their backs. The mother gopher wiped some of the blood on her palms and face, and that is why gophers today have dark faces.

The elder brother skinned the giant elk and made a coat from the hide. He took two of the blood vessels and made a pouch of them, in which he kept some of the giant elk's blood. And he took the giant elk's horns.

"Grandmother, this is all I wish. You and your family may have all the rest of the giant elk."

As the mother gopher rejoiced, the elder brother returned home.

Now two of the monsters had been killed.

The morning after the elder brother had returned from killing the giant elk, he asked, "Mother, Grandmother, where do the giant birds live?"

"The giant birds live at a place called Tse an' iska', which means 'a tall rock standing,'" First Woman said.

"It is a dangerous place," White Bead Woman added. "No one can go there."

The elder brother said, "In all the world there is no such thing as a dangerous place."

So the Hero Twins made their plan. The elder brother put on his elkskin coat and the pouch containing the giant elk's blood. He took the two sacred feathers given to him by the sun's mother, the black knife of the giant, a horn of the giant elk, and the sun's lightning bow and arrow. With these he started out.

When he neared the mountain where the giant birds lived, the elder brother suddenly began to wonder if they had seen him. A portion of the sacred chant he sang went like this:

"I wonder if the lone eyes are watching me.

I wonder if the lone eyes are watching me.

I wonder if the lone eyes are watching me.

I am he who has killed the monsters.

The lightning is before me.

All is beautiful behind me."

As he was singing his chants, the elder brother saw a black speck over the mountains. It was one of the giant birds, circling high overhead. Then the enormous thing swooped down like a hawk after a chicken. The elder brother lay facedown, flat on the ground. The giant bird scratched at the back of his coat with its great talons but could not get a hold. The elder brother chanted:

"The big bird has missed me.

The big bird has missed me.

I alone have been missed.

I alone have been missed."

But the bird had not given up. It circled around and dove again. It dove and missed three times, while the elder brother continued his sacred chant. The fourth time, though, the elder brother turned onto his back. When the giant bird swooped down again, its great talons caught the lacings of his coat. Then the elder brother changed his chant:

"The big bird got hold of me.

The big bird got hold of me.

I alone shall be saved.

I alone shall be saved."

Eight times he repeated this chant, and eight times he blew on the bird. The giant bird carried him over a high peak and over a great smooth rock, and there it dropped him. But the elder brother landed lightly thanks to the power of the two sacred feathers. He cut open the pouch around his neck. The giant elk's blood poured out, and the giant bird was sure its prey was dead. It called its two chicks to eat.

The two fledglings hurried to the elder brother, but he hissed at them, and they backed away. The young birds hurried to the giant bird and said, "He's alive, Father."

The giant bird told them to hush and go eat.

But when the fledglings approached, the elder brother hissed at them again, and they backed away. "He's still alive, Father!"

At last the giant bird grew impatient with the chicks and flew away, calling back over his wing that if they were hungry, they should go ahead and eat.

The fledglings didn't know what to do. They began to cry. But the elder brother told them, "Hush. I will not harm you. Take me to your nest."

So the young birds took him to their nest, and the three camped there that night, covered by all the white flowers that grow on the mountains, soft as a feather quilt.

In the morning the elder brother asked the fledglings when their father would return.

"Our father will return when you see the male rain begin to fall," they told him.

So when the male rain began falling the young birds began looking up. "Look! Our father is coming with a burden."

The elder brother looked into the sky but could see nothing.

"Where will your father land?" he asked.

The fledglings showed him the spot, and the elder brother hid there, waiting, bow ready.

As the giant bird flew over the peak he threw a young man down on the rock where he had thrown the elder brother the day before. Then the great bird circled and landed just where the young birds had said he would. Before the giant bird's wings were closed the elder brother shot his arrow. The giant bird tumbled dead off the mountain and landed far below with a crash like thunder.

The two fledglings began to cry.

"Hush," the elder brother told them. "I will not harm you. I will save you."

He asked them when their mother would return.

"When the female rain falls," they told him, "then our mother will return."

He waited, and the next day the female rain began to fall. The young birds looked up and said, "Look! Our mother is coming with a burden."

The elder brother asked them where the mother bird would land when she came home, and they told him the place. He went to that ledge and sat under it, waiting.

When the mother bird flew over the rock she threw down a young woman. As soon as the giant bird landed, the elder brother shot her. The giant bird tumbled off the mountain and landed with a crash like thunder.

The two young birds began to cry again, but the elder brother told them, "I shall not harm you. You will be saved."

To the older of the two birds he said, "From this day on you will not think as your father thought. You will not think as your mother thought. You will forget all that has happened to you, and the spirits of your father and mother will not enter you again. Now, fly."

The young bird flew up into the sky and out of sight. He was now the eagle.

Then the elder brother said to the younger bird, "From this day on you will not think as your father thought. You will not think as your mother thought. You will forget all that has happened to you, and the spirits of your father and mother will not enter you again. Now, fly."

The young bird did not fly as high as the eagle, but flapped just over the rocks. He was now the owl.

But now that the elder brother was alone on top of the great rock, he was with a new problem: There was no way to descend.

As he circled the cliff again and again, hunting a way down, he saw old Bat Woman carrying a basket below him, and called down to her, "Grandmother, help me. Take me down from here in your basket."

She hurried behind a rock in fright. No one had ever called down from the giant birds' home.

The elder brother realized why she was so afraid. "Grandmother, there is no longer any danger up here. I have slain the giant birds." He coaxed her, "If you take me down, all the feathers from the giant birds are yours."

"Not so fast, not so fast. First you go over to the edge and dig a hole in the ground and put your head into it and wait until I come up."

He knew she wanted him to do this so that he couldn't attack her. So he did as she said. He stayed there with his head in the ground, listening to her singing to herself as she came up. It took a long time until she reached the top of the rock.

"Get up, my child," she said to the elder brother when she was finally there. "What are you doing here?"

"I am trying to get down from this tall peak."

"Very well," the grandmother bat said. "Get into my basket."

It was made of tiny bits of twigs woven together. "Grandmother, those twigs will never hold me."

"Huh," she said. Filling her basket with heavy stones, the grandmother bat danced around with it.

When she dumped out the stones the elder brother said not another word but got into the basket.

"You must close your eyes," the grandmother bat warned.

To make sure of this she wrapped his head in a baby buffalo hide.

They started the climb down the cliff. It seemed a very long time to the elder brother, too long a time. He wondered, "Where is she taking me?" And he opened his eyes a crack.

In that moment Bat Woman started to fall. She reached back over her shoulder with her walking stick and whacked him with it. "Foolish-headed boy. You will wander where you do not belong."

And she continued to whack him with the stick until they had reached solid ground. As the elder brother climbed out of the basket, he asked, "What happened, Grandmother?"

But she refused to answer. The elder brother found where the giant birds had fallen, and filled her basket with their feathers. "Do not go through the grove of sunflowers," he warned her. For himself, he took only some wing and tail feathers, and started for home.

The grandmother bat told herself that if the elder brother had disobeyed her, she would disobey him. And she headed straight for the sunflowers.

A jackrabbit hopped up and asked, "Grandmother, what have you in your basket?" Before she could tell him, he pulled out two tail feathers, stuck them through his headband, and cried, "Now I am quite fine!"

And that is why jackrabbits have long ears.

When Bat Woman arrived in the sunflower grove, the feathers became thousands of little birds that flew out of her basket. She tried to pull them back, but she lost them all.

And that is how all the little birds in the world were created.

When the elder brother reached home, he found the younger brother waiting for him. "I was watching the medicine sticks," the younger brother said, "and I saw the black stick start to smoke—but then the smoke went out, and I knew that you had won."

"I have indeed," said the elder brother, and the Hero Twins entered the hogan. "Mother, Grandmother, Grandfather, I have killed the two giant birds."

He showed them the feathers as proof, and they rejoiced.

The next morning the elder brother asked his mother and grandmother where the big rolling rock could be found. They told him, "It can be found at a place called Betchil gai, the shining rock. But the rolling rock is dangerous. It chases down a person and rolls over him."

But the elder brother replied, "In all the world there is no such thing as a dangerous place."

Taking all his knives, the elder brother started off for the shining rock. When he was near it, he took out his black knives, crossed them, and planted them, blades up. He went a little farther on and planted the two blue knives, crossed, blades up. He went a little farther, and planted the two yellow knives, crossed, blades up. Last were the serrated knives. These, too, he crossed and planted blades up.

Now the elder brother moved forward so that the rolling rock could sense him. The rock started forward, rumbling over the ground with terrifying speed. The elder brother ran and jumped over the serrated knives. The rock struck them, and a huge piece of it broke off. The elder brother jumped over the yellow knives. The rock struck them, and another huge piece of it broke off. The elder brother jumped over the blue knives. The rock struck them, and another piece broke off. The elder brother jumped over the black knives. The rock struck them, and by now there was only a little piece of it left. The elder brother chased this last little piece of the rock into a river, where it sank.

The elder brother tracked down a broken-off piece of the rolling rock. He told it that the thoughts of the rolling rock had left it and would never again be in it. It would become flint, from which people would strike fire.

With that, he went home and told the people the good news.

The morning after the elder brother had returned with the fragment of the rolling rock he asked, "Mother, Grandmother, where can I find the twelve antelope who devour people?"

This time the women didn't even try to argue him out of his mission. They simply told him, "They are to be found at a place called Hale gai' e dinla'."

This was not the elder brother's most difficult mission at all. He started out for the plain with a torch of bark. When the twelve antelope who devoured people saw him heading toward them, they burst into a run toward him, seeing him as easy prey. But he lit the torch and touched off the dry grass. As the antelope dodged aside to avoid the fire, he was easily able to kill eleven of them.

He caught the twelfth antelope and said to it, "All the thoughts and spirits of your comrades have departed from you. Those thoughts will never enter you again." With that, he let it go. "Your home will be on the plains," he told it.

And that was the first pronghorn antelope.

The morning after the elder brother returned from killing the antelope, he asked, "Mother, Grandmother, where do I find Tse'tahotsilta'li, the Kicker?"

This was a monster in human form who lay in wait near the edge of a cliff. Anyone who passed by he kicked over the edge, down to where his cannibal children could reach and eat him. This being, the women told the elder brother, lived on Wild Horse Mesa.

The elder brother journeyed to the top of Wild Horse Mesa. All of a sudden he saw a man lying on his back, his arm doubled under his head, and knew he'd found the one he'd sought.

"Grandfather," the elder brother asked, as though in all innocence, "is it all right to pass through here?"

The person answered, "Yes, Grandson, people pass back and forth through here."

The elder brother pretended to take a quick step forward, then stepped back instead. Sure enough, the being had kicked.

"What does this mean, Grandfather?" the elder brother, asked as though puzzled.

The being replied, "Oh, I simply had a bad cramp in my leg."

The elder brother pretended to take another step forward, then stepped back. Sure enough, the being tried another kick. Before the being could recover, the elder brother drew his long knife and killed him, then threw the body down over the cliff to where the cannibal children waited.

He heard shouting.

"Mine is the head!"

"I want the heart!"

But then they all shouted, "This is our father's body!"

To the elder brother's shock, he heard their mother say, "It is meat now. Eat it."

When the elder brother reached them, he saw that they were ugly and dirty, and he had not the will to slay them. First he told them to eat if they wanted the head and the heart of the monster. Then he talked to the wife and the children.

"You will travel west. The thoughts and the spirit of your father, your husband, have departed from you. But because you did not fight against the evil he did, you will always be a poor people."

They went on their way and became the poorer tribes.

Once they were gone, the elder brother took the Kicker's scalp and went home.

The next morning the elder brother asked the women, "Where are the slashing reeds to be found?"

The women told him that they were to be found at a place called Tse'nee'tlene. White Bead Woman added that they were dangerous reeds, that they waved with or without the wind and cut people to pieces.

The elder brother made armor for himself out of pieces of flint, picked up a bark torch, and started out. When he arrived near them the reeds began to slash about in a savage frenzy, struggling to cut him to pieces. But they could not harm him because of his flint armor. The elder brother lit his torch and burned all the reeds but one. He spoke to this one.

"You will forget all the evil actions of the slashing reeds. You will become the reed used in the medicine stick, and do good from now on."

He waved the reed in all the directions, then planted it. Instantly medicine reeds sprang into being.

The elder twin took one for his people and went home.

Now, the swallows back then were not harmless birds. They were killers. So the elder brother asked, "Mother, Grandmother, Grandfather, where are the swallow people to be found?"

They told him that the swallow people were to be found at Tqo tzosko, which means "water in the narrow canyon." So he traveled there—and found to his dismay not a few, not a hundred, but thousands and thousands of swallow people.

He killed them left and right. The elder brother killed and killed, but there were always more. He killed and killed until he had worked his way to the mouth of the canyon.

Then the elder brother began running. He was tired, and there were still thousands of swallow people to be killed. By the time he had reached the second rock near the canyon's river, he was very tired.

At home, in the hogan, the younger brother cried out in alarm. All the medicine sticks were burning!

Hastily he took the smoke from the first stick and blew it on the hailstone next to it, and continued on like that for all four. Then he blew the smoke in the four directions.

Suddenly a great black cloud shot out of the sky over the place where the elder brother was resting. A great storm broke, with roars of thunder, blinding lightning, fierce spears of rain, and hail hard as rock. The elder brother took shelter and watched. The hail destroyed all but one of the remaining swallow people. That one the elder brother caught.

"You will be harmless from now on," he told it, and let the sparrow go.

Then the elder brother took the scalp of one of the dead swallow people and started for his home.

Now, although the elder brother knew that the swallow people had been the last of the great ills, he also knew that there were other monstrous things that destroyed humans. There was a place called Tse'a haildehe', where the rocks deliberately moved. It was a narrow space between two cliffs. If anyone tried to step across, it would suddenly widen, then just as suddenly crash together, crushing the person who had fallen into the crevice. As the elder brother was on his way home, he came to Tse'a haildehe'. He knew it was so because when he reached it there was only a narrow space between the cliffs. He raised a foot as though about to step across—and the space instantly widened. When he stepped back, the cliffs snapped together with a terrible grinding roar of rocks.

This was easily solved. The elder brother waited until the cliffs had moved apart. Then he placed the giant elk's horn over the gap and commanded the cliffs never to move again.

He took a chip from the cliffs to bring home.

Now the elder brother asked his mother and grandmother about the evil eyes. They told him that these evil beings lived at Tse' ahalizi'ni, the rock with a black hole.

So the elder brother slung a bag of salt over his shoulder and traveled there. When he reached the rock with a black hole, he built a fire and got it burning brightly.

Sure enough, here were the whole family of beings, come to stare with their many, many eyes. These were the creatures that brought sore eyes and blindness to humans.

But before they could do anything to him, the elder brother threw the bag of salt onto the fire. A great cloud of smoke billowed up, hurting the beings' many eyes, making tears flow so that they could not see.

So the elder brother slew them. This time he did not spare one. This time he could see no good coming from such beings.

Now there were only four ills left in the world. When the elder brother asked where to find them, White Bead Woman and First Woman said that the four last ills could be found south of their home.

He traveled southward and found a ragged old man. This was Tie en, Poverty. The elder brother was about to kill him when the old man said, "No, my grandson, you must not kill me. In six months people will have good clothing, and at the end of that time, in autumn, they will use it for the winter, in order to keep themselves warm. Without Poverty, there would be no joy in gaining good clothing or in being warm."

The elder brother, knowing that the virtue accompanying poverty is appreciation, let Poverty live.

He walked on and found an old, old woman. He was about to kill her, for she was San, Old Age, but she stopped him and said, "No, no, my grandson, do not kill me. People must grow old along with every other growing thing. It will be the old people who tell the young people what happened in years past. It would not be well if there were only young people on the earth."

The elder brother knew that wisdom walked with old age, and he let her live.

Then he found the two E ya a', the lice, and he was about to kill them when they said, "No, don't kill us. We shall be seen on animals at different times. When we get on people they will say, 'Sister, there is something on me. Look for it,' and be friendly. Let us live."

The elder brother let them live, for although they were evils they brought with them compassion.

The fourth ill that the elder brother met was a strange bluish being. The elder brother was about to kill him, for this was Death. But Death said, "Do not kill me, Grandson. Spare me, for if every creature lived there would be no place on earth for youth and laughter."

The elder brother thought deeply of the earth and the waters and the sky. It was true: If there was no death, there could be no new life.

So he left Death unharmed.

The elder brother went to the east and returned. All was well in the east.

"There are no more monsters there," he said.

He went to the south and returned. All was well in the south.

"There are no more monsters there."

He went to the west and returned. All was well in the west.

"There are no more monsters there."

Last, he went to the north and returned. All was well in the north.

"Mother, Grandmother, Grandfather, all is well to the ends of the earth. All the monsters have been slain. Our work is finished."

So the elder brother took off his armor and laid down his knives and the lightning weapon that the sun had given him.

The sun appeared and said, "My son, it is all well now. I shall take my weapons back with me. I want White Bead Woman, your mother, to live in a beautiful white shell house in the west. A house like the turquoise house in the east."

So White Bead Woman went to the top of Chol'i'I, where she had been found as a baby. She lived in her beautiful white shell house. And with her power she made her people, the tribe called Dine. So it is partly through the power of White Bead Woman that the monsters were destroyed and that the tribe called Dine came to this country and multiplied.

Sources

Link, Margaret Schevill. *The Pollen Path: A Collection of Navajo Myths*. Stanford, CA: Stanford University Press, 1978.

Zolbrod, P. G. *Dine Bahane: The Navajo Creation Myth*. Albuquerque: University of New Mexico Press, 1992.

BIBLIOGRAPHY

Abrahams, Roger D. *African Folktales*. New York: Random House, 1983.

Alpers, Antony. *Maori Myths and Tribal Legends*. London: John Murray, 1964.

Andersen, Johannes C. *Myths and Legends of the Polynesians*. Rutland, VT: Charles E. Tuttle, 1969.

Apollodorus. *The Library*. Translated by Sir James G. Frazer. Cambridge: Harvard University Press, 1921.

Balikci, Asen. *The Netsilik Eskimo*. New York: Natural History Press, 1970.

Barbeau, Marius. *Huron and Wyandot Mythology*. Ottawa: Government Printing Bureau, 1915.

Barnouw, Victor. *Wisconsin Chippewa Myths and Tales*. Madison: University of Wisconsin Press, 1977.

Barrère, Dorothy B. "The Kumuhonua Legends: A Study of Late 19th Century Hawaiian Stories of Creation and Origins." *Pacific Anthropological Records* 3 (1969), Bishop Museum, Honolulu, HI.

Bartlett, Sarah. *The World of Myths and Mythology: A Source Book*. London: Blanford, 1998.

Beckwith, Martha. *Hawaiian Mythology*. Honolulu: University of Hawaii Press, 1970.

Bell, Corydon. *John Rattling-Gourd of Big Cove: A Collection of Cherokee Legends*. New York: Macmillan, 1955.

Bell, Rosemary. *Yurok Tales*. Etna, CA: Bell Books, 1992.

Benedict, Ruth. *Zuni Mythology*. New York: Columbia University Press, 1935.

Berndt, Ronald M., and Catherine Berndt. *The Speaking Land*. Rutland, VT: Inner Traditions International, 1994.

Bertol, Roland. *Sundiata: The Epic of the Lion King*. New York: Thomas Y. Crowell, 1970.

Bierhorst, John. *Mythology of the Lenape*. Tucson: University of Arizona Press, 1995.

———. *The Mythology of Mexico and Central America*. New York: William Morrow, 1990.

———. *The Mythology of South America*. New York: William Morrow, 1988.

Biesele, Megan. *Women Like Meat*. Bloomington: Indiana University Press, 1993.

Birrell, Anne. *Chinese Mythology: An Introduction*. Baltimore: Johns Hopkins University Press, 1993.

Brinton, Daniel G. *The Myths of the New World*. 1876. Reprint, New York: Greenwood, 1969.

Brown, Robert L., ed. *Ganesh: Studies of an Asian God*. Delhi: Sri Satguru Publications English, 1997.

Budge, E. A. Wallis, trans. *The Book of the Dead*. London: Arkana, 1923.

Carthy, Martin. *Byker Hill*. Topic Records, 1967. Compact disc.

Cavendish, Richard, ed. *Legends of the World: A Cyclopedia of the Enduring Myths, Legends and Sagas of Mankind*. New York: Schocken Books, 1982.

——. *Mythology: An Illustrated Encyclopedia*. New York: Little, Brown, 1992.

Chagnon, Napoleon A. *Yanomamö, the Fierce People*. Holt, Rinehart and Winston, 1977.

Chickering, Howell D., trans. *Beowulf: A Dual Language Edition*. Garden City, NY: Anchor Books, 1977.

Christie, Anthony. *Chinese Mythology*. New York: Barnes and Noble Books, 1983.

Clark, Ella E. *Indian Legends of the Pacific Northwest*. Berkeley: University of California Press, 1953.

Codrington, R. H. *The Melanesian: Studies in Their Anthropology and Folklore*. Oxford: Oxford University Press, 1891.

Cole, Mabel Cook. *Philippine Folk Tales*. Chicago: A. C. McClurg, 1916.

Contributions to Anthropology 21 (1935), Columbia University Press, New York.

Courlander, Harold. *Tales of Yoruba Gods and Heroes*. Greenwich, CT: Fawcett Publications, 1973.

——. *A Treasure of African Folklore*. New York: Marlowe, 1996.

Crossley-Holland, Kevin. *The Norse Myths*. New York: Pantheon Books, 1980.

Dalley, Stephanie. *Myths from Mesopotamia*. Oxford: Oxford University Press, 1989.

Danielou, Alain. *The Myths and Gods of India*. Rutland, VT: Inner Traditions International, 1991.

David-Neel, Alexandra, and the Lama Yongden. *Superhuman Life of Gesar of Ling*. Boston: Shambala Books, 1987.

Davis, E. Adams. *Of the Night Wind's Telling: Legends from the Valley of Mexico*. Norman: University of Oklahoma Press, 1946.

Davis, F. Hadland. *Myths and Legends of Japan*. London: George G. Harrap, 1913.

de Civrieux, Jean-Marc. *Watunna, an Orinoco Creation Cycle*. Translated by David M. Guss. San Francisco: North Point Press, 1980.

Degh, Linda. *Folktales of Hungary*. Chicago: University of Chicago Press, 1965.

——. *Hungarian Folktales: The Art of Zsuzsanna Palkó*. Jackson: University Press of Mississippi, 1995.

Dharma, Krishna, trans. *Mahabharata: The Greatest Spiritual Epic of All Time*. Los Angeles: Torchlight Publications, 1999.

Dorsey, George A., ed. *Traditions of the Caddo*. Washington: Carnegie Institute, 1905.

Dundes, Alan, ed. *The Flood Myth*. Berkeley: University of California Press, 1988.

Edmonds, Margot, and Ella E. Clark. *Voices of the Winds*. New York: Facts on File, 1989.

Eliot, Alexander. *The Universal Myths*. New York: Truman Talley Books/Meridian, 1976.

Elm, Demus, and Harvey Antone. *The Oneida Creation Story*. Lincoln and London: University of Nebraska Press, 2000.

Elwin, Verrier. *Myths of Middle India*. Oxford: Oxford University Press, 1949.

Erdoes, Richard, and Alfonso Ortiz. *American Indian Myths and Legends*. New York: Pantheon Books, 1984.

Eugenio, Damiana L. *Philippine Folk Literature: The Myths*. Diliman, Quezon City: University of the Philippines Press, 1993.

Farmer, Penelope. Beginnings: *Creation Myths of the World*. New York: Atheneum, 1979.

Faulkner, Raymond, trans. *The Egyptian Book of the Dead, the Book of Going Forth by Day*. San Francisco: Chronicle Books, 1994.

Feldmann, Susan. *African Myths and Tales*. New York: Dell, 1963.

Flood, Josephine. *Archaeology of the Dreamtime*. Honolulu: University of Hawaii Press, 1983.

Foster, Benjamin R. *From Distant Days: Myths, Tales and Poetry of Ancient Mesopotamia*. Bethesda: CDL, 1995.

Frazer, Sir James G. *The Belief in Immortality and the Worship of the Dead.* London: Macmillan, 1913–1924.

———. *Folklore in the Old Testament.* London: Macmillan, 1918.

———. *Myths of the Origin of Fire.* Barnes and Noble Books, 1996.

Furness, William H. *Folk-lore in Borneo: A Sketch.* Wallingford, PA: n.p., 1899.

Gardner, John, and John Maier. *Gilgamesh.* New York: Alfred Knopf, 1984.

Gaster, Theodor H. *Myth, Legend, and Custom in the Old Testament.* New York: Harper and Row, 1969.

———. *The Oldest Stories in the World.* Boston: Beacon, 1952.

Gbadamosi, Bakare A. *Not Even God Is Ripe Enough: Yoruba Stories.* London: Heinemann, 1968.

Gesell, Arnold. *Wolf Child and Human Child.* London: Scientific Book Club, 1942.

Giddings, Ruth Warner. *Yaqui Myths and Legends.* Tucson: University of Arizona Press, 1959.

Gifford, Douglas. *Warriors, Gods and Spirits from Central and South American Mythology.* Glasgow: William Collins, 1983.

Gregory, Lady. *Cuchulain of Muirthemne.* Gerrards Cross, England: Colin Smythe, 1970.

Greimas, Algirdas J. *Of Gods and Men: Studies in Lithuanian Mythology.* Translated by Milda Newman. Bloomington: Indiana University Press, 1992.

Grey, Sir George. *Polynesian Mythology.* London: Whitcombe and Tombs, 1956.

Hackin, J., et al. *Asiatic Mythology.* New York: Crowell, 1932.

Hart, George. *Egyptian Myths.* London: University of Texas Press, 1990.

Heaney, Seamus, trans. *Beowulf.* New York: Farrar, Straus and Giroux, 2000.

Heidel, Alexander. *The Gilgamesh Epic and Old Testament Parallels.* Chicago: University of Chicago Press, 1949.

Heissig, Walther. *The Religions of Mongolia.* London: Routledge and Kegan Paul, 1980.

Henderson, Joseph L., and Maud Oakes. *The Wisdom of the Serpent: The Myths of Death, Rebirth, and Resurrection.* Princeton: Princeton University Press, 1963.

Hesiod. *Theogony.* Indianapolis: Library of Liberal Arts, 1953.

Hinnells, John R. *Persian Mythology*. London: Paul Hamlyn, 1973.

Holmberg, U. *Finno-Ugric, Siberian Mythology*. New York: Cooper Square, 1964.

Hoppin, Frederick C. *Great Adventures in History and Legend*. Philadelphia: David McKay, 1940.

Howe, George, and G. A. Harrer. *A Handbook of Classical Mythology*. Hertfordshire: Oracle, 1996.

Howey, M. Oldfield. *The Encircled Serpent*. New York: Arthur Richmond, 1955.

Howitt, A. W. *The Native Tribes of South-East Australia*. London and New York: Macmillan, 1904.

Jacobsen, Thorkild. *The Harps That Once . . . : Sumerian Poetry in Translation*. New Haven: Yale University Press, 1987.

Johnston, Basil H. *Tales the Elders Told*. Toronto: Royal Ontario Museum, 1981.

Jordan, Michael. *Myths of the World: A Thematic Encyclopedia*. London: Kyle Cathie, 1995.

Judson, Katharine B. *Myths and Legends of the Mississippi Valley and the Great Lakes*. Chicago: A. C. McClurg, 1914.

Jung, Carl G. *Four Archetypes: Mother/Rebirth/Spirit/Trickster*. Vol. 9, Part I, *The Collected Works of C. G. Jung*. Princeton: Princeton University Press, 1973.

Kalakaua, David. *The Legends and Myths of Hawaii*. Rutland, VT: Charles E. Tuttle, 1972.

Kawai, Hayao. *The Japanese Psyche: Major Motifs in the Fairy Tales of Japan*. Dallas: Spring Publications, 1988.

Kerenyi, Karl. *The Gods of the Greeks*. London: Thames and Hudson, 1985.

Kinsella, Thomas. *The Táin*. London and New York: Oxford University Press, 1970.

Kipury, Naomi. *Oral Literature of the Maasai*. Nairobi: East African Educational, 1983.

Knappert, Jan. *Pacific Mythology*. London: Aquarian Press, 1992.

Kramer, Samuel Noah. *Sumerian Mythology*. New York: Harper and Brothers, 1961.

Kramer, Samuel Noah, ed. *Mythologies of the Ancient World*. Garden City, NY: Anchor Books, 1961.

Kroeber, A. L. *Indian Myths of South Central California*. Vol. IV of *American Archaeology and Ethnology*. Berkeley: University of California Press, 1907.

Larousse World Mythology. Secaucus, NJ: Chartwell Books, 1977.

Lawrie, Margaret, coll. and trans. *Myths and Legends of Torres Straits*. New York: Taplinger, 1971.

Leach, Maria. *The Beginning*. New York: Funk and Wagnalls, 1956.

Leeming, David. *A Dictionary of Asian Mythology*. New York and Oxford: Oxford University Press, 2001.

Leeming, David Adams. *The World of Myth: An Anthology*. New York and Oxford: Oxford University Press, 1990.

Leeming, David Adams, and Margaret Adams Leeming. *A Dictionary of Creation Myths*. New York and Oxford: Oxford University Press, 1995.

Leland, Charles G. *Algonquin Legends*. Mineola, NY: Dover Publications, 1992.

LeRoy, John, ed. *Kewa Tales*. Vancouver: University of British Columbia, 1985.

Lettsom, William Nanson. *The Nibelungenlied*. New York and London: The Colonial, 1901.

Link, Margaret Schevill. *The Pollen Path: A Collection of Navajo Myths*. Stanford, CA: Stanford University Press, 1978.

Long, Charles H. *Alpha: The Myths of Creation*. Toronto: Collier Books, 1963.

Lonnrot, Elias. *The Kalevala*. Translated by Francis Peabody Magoun Jr. Cambridge: Harvard University Press, 1963.

——. *The Kalevala*. Translated by W. F. Kirby. London: Athlone, 1983.

MacCana, Proinsias. *Celtic Mythology*. London: Hamlyn, 1970.

MacKenzie, Donald A. *Myths of Pre-Columbian America*. Mineola, NY: Dover Publications, 1996.

Marriott, Alice, and Carol K. Rachlin. *Plains Indian Mythology*. New York: New American Library, 1975.

McAllister, J. Gilbert, ed. *Kiowa Apache Tales*. College Station, TX: Papers of the Texas Folk Lore Society, 1949.

McCall, Henrietta. *Mesopotamian Myths*. Austin: University of Texas Press, 1990.

Mead, Margaret. *Coming of Age in Samoa: A Psychological Study of Primitive Youth for Western Civilization*. New York: William Morrow, 1961.

Merriam, C. Hart. *The Dawn of the World*. Lincoln: University of Nebraska Press, 1993.

Metternich, Hilary Roe. *Mongolian Folktales*. Boulder, CO: Avery, 1996.

Miller, Lucien, ed. *South of the Clouds: Tales from Yunnan*. Seattle: University of Washington Press, 1994.

Mitchell, Stephen. *The Bhagavad Gita: A New Translation*. New York: Harmony Books, 2000.

Mooney, James. "The Jicarilla Genesis." *American Anthropologist* 11 (1898).

——. *Myths of the Cherokee*. Mineola, NY: Dover Publications, 1995.

Morris, William, trans. *Volsunga Saga*. New York and London: Collier Books, 1962.

New Larousse Encyclopedia of Mythology. Translated by Richard Aldington and Delano Ames. London, New York: Hamlyn, 1968.

Niane, D. T. *Sundiata: An Epic of Old Mali*. London: Longmans, 1965.

Nivedita, Sister, and Ananda K. Coomaraswamy. *Myths of the Hindus and Buddhists*. New York: Farrar and Rinehart, n.d.

Norman, Howard. *Northern Tales, Traditional Stories of Eskimo and Indian Peoples*. New York: Pantheon Books, 1990.

Opler, Morris Edward. *Myths and Tales of the Chiricahua Apache Indians*. New York: Dover Publications, 1994. Reprint of *Memoirs of the American Folk-Lore Society*, Volume XXXVII, New York, 1942.

——. *Myths and Tales of the Jicarilla Apache Indians*. New York: Dover Publications, 1994. Reprint of *Memoirs of the American Folk-lore Society*, Volume XXXI, New York, 1938.

Ovid. *The Metamorphoses*. Translated by Horace Gregory. New York: Viking Press, 1958.

Palmer, Martin, and Zhao Xiaomin. *Essential Chinese Mythology*. London: Thorsons, 1997.

Parrinder, Geoffrey. *African Mythology*. New York: Peter Bedrick Books, 1982.

Parsons, Robert T. *Religion in an African Society*. Leiden, Netherlands: E. J. Brill, 1964.

Partridge, A. C., ed. *Folklore of Southern Africa*. Vol. 2 of ELISA Series. Cape Town, South Africa: Purnell, 1973.

Partridge, Emelyn Newcomb. *Glooscap the Great Chief and Other Stories*. New York: Sturgis and Walton, 1913.

Piggott, Juliet. *Japanese Mythology*. London: Hamlyn, 1969.

Plutarch. *The Lives of the Noble Greeks and Romans*. Franklin Center, PA: Franklin Library, 1979.

Poignant, Roslyn. *Oceanic Mythology*. London: Hamlyn, 1967.

Portilla, Miguel Leon. *Pre-Columbian Literatures of Mexico*. Norman: University of Oklahoma Press, 1969.

Quirke, Stephen. *Ancient Egyptian Religion*. New York: Dover Publications, 1995.

Radin, Paul. *African Folktales*. New York: Schocken Books, 1983.

——. "The Winnebago Indians." *The Thirty-Seventh Annual Report of the Bureau of American Ethnology*, Washington, DC, 1923, pp. 212–213.

Reed, A. W. *Myths and Legends of Maoriland*. Sydney: Angus and Robertson, 1950.

Riordan, James. *Sun Maiden and the Crescent Moon: Siberian Folk Tales*. New York: Interlink Books, 1991.

Rolleston, T. W. *Myths and Legends of the Celtic Race*. London: George Harrap, 1949.

Rosenberg, James L., trans. *Sir Gawain and the Green Knight*. New York: Holt, Rinehart and Winston, 1962.

Russell, Frank. "Myths of the Jicarilla Apache." *Journal of American Folklore* 11, 43 (1898).

Salomon, Frank, and George Urioste. *The Huarochiri Manuscript*. Austin: University of Texas Press, 1991.

Sandars, N. K., trans. *The Epic of Gilgamesh*. Harmondsworth, England: Penguin Books, 1972.

Shafer, Byron E., ed. *Religion in Ancient Egypt: Gods, Myths, and Personal Practice*. Ithaca, NY: Cornell University Press, 1991.

Simpson, William Kelly, ed. *The Literature of Ancient Egypt*. New Haven: Yale University Press, 1972.

Smith, William Ramsay. *Aborigine Myths and Legends*. London: Senate Books, 1996.

Spicer, Stanley T. *Glooscap Legends*. Hantsport, Nova Scotia: Lancelot, 1997.

Sproul, Barbara C. *Primal Myths: Creating the World*. New York and San Francisco: Harper and Row, 1979.

Steeleye Span. *Below the Salt*. Shanachie Records, 1972. Compact disc.

Storm, Rachel. *The Encyclopedia of Eastern Mythology*. London: Lorenz Books, 1999.

Streblow, T. G. H. *Aranda Tradition*. Melbourne: Melbourne University Press, 1947.

Sturluson, Snorri. *The Prose Edda*. Translated by Jean I. Young. Berkeley: University of California Press, 1954.

Taube, Karl. *Aztec and Maya Myths*. Austin: University of Texas Press, 1994.

Tedlock, Dennis, trans. *Popol Vuh*. New York: Simon and Schuster, 1985.

Teit, James A. *Mythology of the Thompson Indians*. New York: Brill and Stechert, 1912.

Te Kanawa, Kiri. *Land of the Long White Cloud*. Auckland: Viking Press, 1990.

Thompson, Stith. *The Folktale*. Berkeley: University of California Press, 1977.

———. *Tales of the North American Indians*. Bloomington: Indiana University Press, 1966.

Tolkien, J. R. R. "Beowulf: The Monsters and the Critics." *The Monster and the Critics and Other Essays*, ed. Christopher Tolkien. Boston: Houghton Mifflin, 1983.

———. "On Translating Beowulf." *The Monster and the Critics and Other Essays*, ed. Christopher Tolkien. Boston: Houghton Mifflin, 1983.

Torrente, J. M. "The Durian Legend." *Sunday Times Magazine* (Manila), May 17, 1959, p. 23.

Turner, Patricia, and Charles Russell Coulter. *Dictionary of Ancient Deities*. Oxford and New York: Oxford University Press, 2000.

Urton, Gary. *Inca Myths*. Austin: University of Texas Press, 1999.

Van Over, Raymond. *Sun Songs: Creation Myths from Around the World*. New York: New American Library, 1980.

Vitaliano, Dorothy B. *Legends of the Earth*. Bloomington: Indiana University Press, 1973.

von Franz, Marie-Louise. *Patterns of Creativity Mirrored in Creation Myths*. Dallas: Spring Publications, 1986.

Walker, Barbara K., and S. Warren Walker, eds., as told by Olawale Idewu and Omotayo Adu. *Nigerian Folk Tales*. New Brunswick: Rutgers University Press, 1961.

Wallace, Zara, and Elizabeth Cook, eds. *Gesar! The Wonderous Adventures of King Gesar*. Berkeley, CA: Dharma, 1991.

Walls, Jan, and Yvonne Walls. *Classical Chinese Myths*. Hong Kong: Joint Publishing, 1984.

Waters, Frank. *Book of the Hopi*. New York: Ballantine Books, 1963.

Watersons. *Frost and Fire*. Topic Records, 1995. Compact disc.

Werner, E. T. C. *Myths and Legends of China*. Singapore: Singapore National Printers, 1922.

Westervelt, W. D. *Hawaiian Legends of Volcanoes*. Rutland, VT, and Tokyo, Japan: Charles E. Tuttle, 1963.

——. *Myths and Legends of Hawaii*. Honolulu: Mutual, 1987.

Whitten, Norman E. Jr. *Sacha Runa*. Urbana: University of Illinois Press, 1976.

Wilbert, Johannes. *Folk Literature of the Yamana Indians*. Berkeley and Los Angeles: University of California Press, 1977.

——. *Yupa Folktales*. Los Angeles: University of California, 1974.

Wyndham, John. *Myths of Ife*. London: Erskin MacDonald, 1921.

Zampleni, Arpid. *Turanian Songs: Legendary and Historical Hero-Songs*. Translated by Gregory A. Page. Budapest and New York: Franklin Society, 1916.

Zolbrod, P. G. *Dine Bahane: The Navajo Creation Myth*. Albuquerque: University of New Mexico, 1992.

Zong In-Sob. *Folk Tales from Korea*. London: Routledge and Kegan Paul, 1952.

GENERAL INDEX

CHARACTER NAME INDEX

CULTURE INDEX